P9-CNB-470

"Reb Mordechai Gafni's Torah on love and eros is *l'ayla u'l'ayla*—the highest of the high. Everyone needs to hear it."

— Reb Zalman Schachter-Shalomi, Wisdom Chair, Naropa Institute

"Into a world filled with hate and boredom comes a tour de force on love and passion. Gafni has written a remarkable book, inviting the reader to understand and to feel the energy at the heart of all of life. Erudite and simple, wise and personal, mystical and pragmatic, this book can change your life!"

— Irwin Kula, President, CLAL (Center for Learning and Leadership)

"Gafni has written an important book which unpacks with depth, power and clarity an important strain of Kabbalistic thought. His original readings will engage and provoke both the scholar and lay-person alike."

— Dr. Daniel Abrams, Kabbalah Scholar, Bar-Ilan University; Editor, Cherubim Press

"As a woman and a feminist, this was the most important book I've read in a long time. I can only hope that all of our daughters, sisters, and mothers will read this book and internalize its healing messages. Gafni does what great spiritual teachers rarely do: shares with us his imperfection and vulnerability, which makes his wisdom so much more true."

— Erica Fox, Faculty, Program on Negotiation at Harvard Law School

"There is great power in breaking down divisions, in celebrating the unity of all we know and all we intuit. Gafni brings us back to the sacred stories and liberates their hidden sparks. In *The Mystery of Love*, he shares both his strength and his joy—a wonderful, provocative, and enchanting book! After encountering its warmth and wisdom, we dance away enriched by his insight, his depth, and his courage."

— Rabbi Bradley Shavit Artson, Dean and Vice President, University of Judaism

"Rabbi Marc Gafni offers us a fascinating gift: a kaleidoscope of endless color and vision. As we turn the pages, Gafni's brilliance, creativity, and love take us into a deep journey of the soul."

— Rabbi J. Rolando Matalon, Congregation B'nai Jeshurun, New York City

"Rabbi Marc Gafni is a uniquely creative and exciting philosopher on the Israeli scene. Like Martin Buber, the philosopher of dialogue, he has built a bridge from the insights of original Hasidic and mystical texts to the most contemporary needs of tens of thousands of seekers. In sophisticated lectures, on television, in Woodstock-like spiritual festivals, in books both popular and academic, Gafni is redefining what it means to be a Rebbe in the modern world."

— Noam Zion, Shalom Hartman Institute in Jerusalem, author of *A Different Night: The Family Participation Haggadah* and *A Different Light: The Hanukkah Book of Celebration*

"Marc Gafni offers a radical, profound and important guide to enable each reader to find out why he is on this earth—and what he can do to make sure that he actualizes the person he or she is meant to be."

— Rabbi Joseph Telushkin, author of *The Book of Jewish Values*

Also by Marc Gafni

Soul Prints

IN HEBREW

Reclaiming Uncertainty

Redefining Certainty

Lilith, Luria and Sacred Feminism (with Ohad Ezrahi)

The
MYSTERY
of LOVE

Marc Gafni

ATRIA BOOKS

New York   London   Toronto   Sydney   Singapore

ATRIA BOOKS

1230 Avenue of the Americas
New York, NY 10020

Copyright © 2003 by Marc Gafni

All rights reserved, including the right to reproduce
this book or portions thereof in any form whatsoever.
For information address Atria Books, 1230 Avenue
of the Americas, New York, NY 10020

ISBN: 0-7434-4220-2

First Atria Books hardcover printing March 2003

10 9 8 7 6 5 4 3 2 1

ATRIA BOOKS is a trademark of Simon & Schuster, Inc.

For information regarding special discounts for bulk purchases,
please contact Simon & Schuster Special Sales at 1-800-456-6798
or business@simonandschuster.com

Printed in the U.S.A.

To my wife and partner Cary (Chaya'le),

a poetess,

a prophetess,

and a priestess.

The picture on the cover is an imaginative rendering of the Ashera tree, divine symbol of feminine eros in ancient Canaan. It is now time for the contemporary prophets of biblical myth to reclaim the legacy of the sacred Ashera and reinstall her within the precincts of the temple.

Zohar—Magnum Opus of Hebrew Myth:
"The Altar [in the temple] *is* Ashera."

Renaissance Mystic Moshe Cordevero:
"Shechina [the feminine Divine] is Ashera."

Twentieth-century mystic Abraham Kook:
"It is time to reclaim the sacred sparks of paganism."

※

Even as the trees that whisper round a Temple
become soon as dear as the Temple's self.
—JOHN KEATS

※

Jerusalem's Temple, the place where heaven and earth kiss.
—THE ZOHAR

※

Leshem yichud Kudsha Brich-hu u'Shechinteh.
May this be for the sake of uniting the masculine God with the feminine Goddess.
—KABBALISTIC MEDITATION

CONTENTS

The Dance of Eros

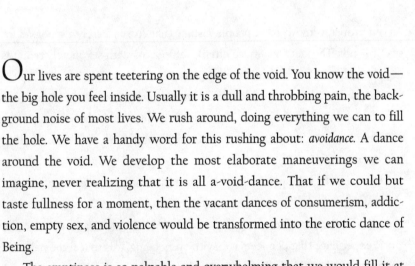

Our lives are spent teetering on the edge of the void. You know the void—the big hole you feel inside. Usually it is a dull and throbbing pain, the background noise of most lives. We rush around, doing everything we can to fill the hole. We have a handy word for this rushing about: *avoidance*. A dance around the void. We develop the most elaborate maneuverings we can imagine, never realizing that it is all a-void-dance. That if we could but taste fullness for a moment, then the vacant dances of consumerism, addiction, empty sex, and violence would be transformed into the erotic dance of Being.

The emptiness is so palpable and overwhelming that we would fill it at virtually any price. We seek immediate gratification—a quick fix—a book, a drug, a relationship, a job—anything to fill the gaping hole in our wholeness. We run desperately looking for the next watering hole that might fill up the yawning chasm we feel so deeply and try so hard to hide.

On the outside our mad dashing about may look like a dance, but we are really gasping for air. Picture the image of a bee in a bottle. Seen from the outside the bee darts from side to side in an ecstatic dance. On the inside, however, there is neither dance nor ecstasy. The bee is slowly dying, suffocating. It was not meant to be this way. Life should not be a pathos-filled scramble for some snatches of authenticity in between empty charades.

The ancient wisdom of the great Hebrew mystics makes one essential promise: *There is a better way to live.* In the midst of uncertainty and anxiety, joy and meaning remain genuine options. We can choose life and love, or death and fear. To experience the fullness of every moment, to move from isolation to deep connection, is our birthright if we but claim it.

The great invitation of the spirit is to heal our pain, opening us up to the possibility of joy, ecstasy, and love. There is another way to dance: the dance of eros. The dance in which we all have a place. This book is about sharing the dance of eros with you.

As you probably know, most people assume that eros is merely a synonym for sex. It is not. The fact that we so often confuse eros with sex merely reminds us of how distant we are from true erotic engagement.

To dance with eros is to live and love erotically in all the arenas of our lives, beyond the merely sexual. That is what it means to be holy. Just as holiness should not be limited to our houses of worship, eros should not be limited to our bedrooms.

Eros is to be fully present to what is. It is to open your eyes and see for the first time the full beauty and gorgeousness of a friend. To smell the richness of an aroma, to feel the fullness of throbbing desire, and to taste the erotic experience that connects you with every being. It is to feel the palpable love that dissolves the walls of ego, anger, and anxiety.

Eros is the feeling you have when you stop trying to get someplace because you realize with great joy that you are already there. To be erotically engaged is to feel the radical interconnectivity of being as a living reality in your life. For the mystics, eros is the key that provides deep meaning to everything— satisfying work, joyful relationships, effective parenting. Starvation, fundamentalism, greed, war, and the rape of the earth are all the result of lack of eros.

It is the mystery of eros that was at the core of the teachings of the Temple in ancient Jerusalem. I will call these teachings the path of Hebrew tantra.* One of the meanings of the Sanskrit word *tantra* is "to expand." Hebrew tantra is about expanding eros beyond the sexual to include all the nonsexual areas of our lives. Hebrew tantra is a means of utilizing erotic energy to become one with the divinity that courses through us at every moment.

These ancient teachings about eros have never been taught publicly—and for good reason. Read superficially, they could be misunderstood as merely sexual license or an abandonment of interpersonal ethics. As we shall see, however, they are neither. Rather, the Temple mysteries are a profound and powerful path of love and eros. For the Temple mystics the goal of life was erotic living. The essence of their teachings is to transform sexuality into a loving guide to fullness, eros, and joy.

As we shall see in chapter 1, at the epicenter of holiness in the ancient Hebrew Temple in Jerusalem was the Ark of the Covenant. You may remember it from the cinema—it is the very same ark that Indiana Jones sought to retrieve in the classic movie *Raiders of the Lost Ark*. Atop this ark was carved a pair of figures called cherubs. Surprisingly the cherubs were locked in a sexual embrace. These entwined cherubs were not only atop the ark but were also the major decorative motif all over the temple walls, doors, and sacred vessels. Even if you absolutely affirm the sexual as a wonderful part of your life, sexually entwined cherubs at the *axis mundi* of holiness in the Jerusalem Temple creates a totally wild and provocative image. What might this mean?!

The ancient Temple in Jerusalem was the center of a society where the Hebrew mysteries were practiced and taught. At the core of the Temple mysteries lies an ancient set of radical understandings about sex, love, and eros. *In the esoteric Temple mystery, it is sex that models for us what it might be like to live erotically in all dimensions of our lives.*

---

*For a more detailed explanation of the genesis of the term *Hebrew tantra* and the way I am drawing from the ancient sources, see Scholar's Page, page 361.

* * *

In the Hebrew tradition mysteries are meant to remain esoteric, secret. Therefore allow me to share with you why in our generation it is both permit- ted and even a sacred obligation to share these mysteries—why I wrote this book! We live in an age when ancient wisdoms long relegated to the base- ments of the spirit are being reclaimed. The Zohar, the magnum opus of Hebrew mysticism, teaches that our era is the one in which the "gates of wis- dom will be opened." For the first time, after several eons of intense spiritual evolution, we have the vessels to hold the light of the ancient secrets. The mystics suggest we may well be able to hold the light more deeply today than even the ancients for whom the wisdom was initially intended. It is only now, after the vessels of law, science, and ethics have been integrated into our psyches, that we can go back and fully reclaim eros and enchantment. It is in the service of the great Hebrew Goddess of Eros (Shechina) that I wrote this book.

* * *

I am, or at least strive to be, a biblical mystic. I study, teach, and try to live the sacred texts at my spiritual community, Bayit Chadash, nestled in the hills of the Galilee in Israel, as well as at Oxford University in England. The Hebrew mystery texts have been my guides and friends for many years. Of course, like every mystic who engages sacred text, I hear the text in accordance with the inner melody of my soul. I now share this song with you in the form of this book. You are invited to find the place in your soul where you can receive and integrate this ancient wisdom into your own song.

You need not have studied mysticism or biblical myth in order to under- stand the concepts we will explore on our journey together. This book is for you if you seek a passionate, joyful, yet deeply grounded and serious explo- ration of the ancient mysteries as your guide to transformation.

* * *

Here is the briefest outline of the journey we will undertake together. The mystery begins with the cherubs in the inner precincts of Solomon's sacred Temple in Jerusalem, unraveling the deep, wondrous, and provocative rela- tionships between sex, eros, love, and the sacred. I devote the first two chap- ters to explaining the inner nature of eros.

After we understand the eros that lies at the heart of the Temple mysteries, we can then turn to answering our core question. If, as we shall show, the essence of the Temple—and of every journey of the spirit—is eros not sex, then why is sex such a prominent feature of the Temple? In response to this question we will explore the essence of the mystical secret of the cherubs in chapter 3.

After this discussion of the Hebrew mystery tradition, each of the remaining ten chapters lays out a unique path of Hebrew tantra modeled by the sexual. Each path will offer you a compelling spirit map for living erotically in every facet of your being. Those paths form the essence of the ancient Hebrew tantric mysteries of love.

The invitation and the challenge of the spirit in our generation is to create a politics of eros and love. That can only begin to happen when each person in the polis takes responsibility for the erotic quality of his or her life. We need to, and we can, realign our souls with the vital currents of loving energy that course though our universe. We can decide to enter the flow, and from that place on the inside we can transform first our lives and, ultimately, our planet.

> *May we be escorted through these pages by the spirit of eros.*
> *May word meld with word merge with heart move to hand*
> *that we should hold the world a little lighter,*
> *with a little more love than before.*

Let this be not a monologue but a sacred conversation. Share with me your words, your thoughts, the poetry of your soul, and I will be honored to receive: rmgafni@netvision.net.il.

With all the love and blessings in the world and beyond,

Marc Gafni
September 1, 2002
Jerusalem, Israel

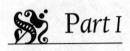

Part I

ONE

Sex in the Temple

I magine the scene: You walk into your local place of worship—church, synagogue, mosque, or meditation center. The pastor or rabbi has apparently
decided to redecorate while you were away on vacation. You find that he has
installed atop the ark or altar a statue of sexually intertwined golden figures.
In addition he positions among the pews another freestanding set of sexually
embracing figures. And just in case you missed the point, vivid pictures of
these effigies adorn most of the sanctuary walls.

I daresay that as open as we are, and as much as we affirm sexuality as
a wonder and central good in our lives, the pastor's contract would not be
renewed. However, in the pastor's defense, let me share with you a secret.
These precise images were the central display in the archetype of all holy
places—the ancient Temple of Jerusalem.

The figures were called cherubs. The primary set was positioned in the
center of the Temple, atop the Ark of the Covenant. According to Hebrew myth
this spot is the earth's epicenter, the *axis mundi*, the place where heaven and
earth kiss. A second set of golden cherubs was freestanding and the rest were

in pictographic form on the walls and even on some of the Temple vessels. These provocatively entwined cherubs were for the mystics the very key to the mystery of love, a mystery that lay at the heart of the Jerusalem Temple, a mystery that lies at the heart of all our lives.

Unraveling this mystery is the purpose of our journey together.

Let the mysteries begin!

Raiders of the Lost Ark—*The Seat of the Secret*

Remember the movie *Raiders of the Lost Ark*, featuring Indiana Jones adventuring through the dusty Middle East in search of the Ark of the Covenant? Lives are lost, blood is let. One was tempted to ask why he didn't just let the ark stay lost!

The answer: The ark, perhaps more than any other earthly object, is of overwhelming mystical significance. The ark was an elegant container that held the original tablets on which were inscribed the Ten Commandments. Described in the sources as something akin to a spiritually creative, life-giving nuclear reactor, it was lost when the Temple of Jerusalem was destroyed some twenty-five hundred years ago. It has been sought after—physically and metaphysically—ever since. The search for the ark is the original grail quest of biblical myth.

Jerusalem holds the secret. It is the cradle of three faiths, each today in its own way in desperate need of renewal and resouling. At the center of Jerusalem stood the Temple built by Solomon and destroyed by the Greeks, then rebuilt by Ezra and destroyed by the Romans. It is a Temple that awaits rebuilding in our own inner lives, for the Temple in the Hebrew mystery tradition of the Kabbalah is not so much a place on earth as a powerful idea of the spirit. The essence of Hebrew mysticism lies hidden in the grain of the Temple's wood and the folds of her curtains.

The loss of the Temple is considered by the biblical mystery tradition to be the greatest spiritual disaster in history. The rebuilding of the Temple through the reclaiming of Temple energy in our lives is the overarching goal of the entire biblical project. This desire is expressed time and again in a thousand different ways in Hebrew ritual and liturgy. It is the idea that shaped all of the spiritual offsprings of the Hebrew religion—that is to say, much of civilization as we know it.

The Temple myth is so powerful, so fertile and teeming with life, that it has given birth to most of the great systems of the spirit created by humanity. Hebrew mysticism, beginning with Abraham, gave birth to Judaism, Christianity, and Islam. All three religions in their pure forms are rooted in the Temple of Jerusalem. Hence the mythic power of the Christian Templars, the Islamic Dome of the Rock, and the Hebrew Temple mount.

Further, Kabbalistic tradition tells of the sons of Abraham who in the book of Genesis are sent eastward, to the land of the Buddha. The Kabbalists teach that Abraham's heirs are the progenitors of Buddhism. There is even an old oral Kabbalistic tradition claiming that the builder of the Temple, King Solomon, and the Buddha are, if not the same person, then at least masters in the same sacred tradition. While historically inaccurate, it points to the deep spiritual affinity between Solomon's teachings and those of the Buddha hundreds of years later.

So the Hebrew Temple with her eternal flame is the source of the fire that sparked, and continues to light, so many of the pure wicks of the spirit that illuminate our world. Those who have lost touch with the mystery kill one another today in order to control the Temple's geographical site, a sad betrayal of the spirit that the Temple incarnated.

But what is the great wisdom hidden in the Temple myth? What perennial message of the spirit does she yearn to share with us?

The simple answer is Love. The Temple plans were drawn up by David and manifested by his son Yedidya, better known as Solomon. Both names, David and Yedidya, mean "loved by the spirit." These kings are the great lovers of biblical myth. They love greatly and are greatly loved, Solomon by God, the queen of Sheba, and a thousand wives; David by God, the people,

Jonathan, and biblical myth readers throughout history. The Temple mystery was thus born and sired by men whose name was love.

What is the secret of this ancient love hidden in the Temple's origins? What is the mystery of the Lost Ark, crowned by her sexually intertwined cherubic lovers? Why is the mythic ark's metaphorical recovery so absolutely crucial for our lives? Could this ancient and esoteric wisdom have something radically new and important to say about the love lost in our lives and the road to its recovery? Can the cherubs lead us back to love?

The Approach

To understand the mystery of the Temple and what it has to teach us, we need to approach her more carefully. Indeed gradually approaching the center is always the essential formula in the quest of the spirit. The Temple itself was built somewhat like an exquisite mandala. The mandala invites the gazer to pass through layer after layer of imagery before beholding its wondrous core. Similarly, we find that the Temple was a layered structure. The high priest would ascend the great staircase to the outer Courtyard of Song, pass through the courtyard and into the chamber called the Holy, and from there into the innermost sanctum—the Holy of Holies. In this sanctum sanctorum of the Temple, behind fine brocaded curtains, stood the golden Ark of the Covenant. The ark contained within it the two tablets of stone upon which were carved the Ten Commandments. They were magical lapidary tablets, sculpted by the God-gripped hand of Moses himself.

Most essential, though, is that which rests atop the ark. Sitting perched aloft the ark are our two winged figures—the celebrated cherubs. Indeed, their cherubic faces have graced everything from the greatest works of art to countless covers of Hallmark cards. Yet here, according to the esoteric tradition, these images were not of the Hallmark variety. As we mentioned at the outset, these two cherubs were male and female, face-to-face, *meurim zeh b'zeh*— intertwined in sexual embrace. In the language of the biblical source text the cherubs were: "As one embraced with his lover." These carved creatures are the focal point, the epicenter, of the mandalalike Temple space. They sit, like the guarded pupil of the eye, at the source of the sacred.

That such provocatively sexual figurines would have such prominence in the Holy of Holies is a mystery indeed. It is called by the Kabbalistic initiates the *sod hakeruvim*—the secret of the cherubs. And though full initiation into this secret cannot be wholly transmitted in the pages of a book, together we can at least hint at its wonder and strive to scrutinize the inscrutable.

The Lion of Fire

The best way to behold such mysteries is through the gleaming prism of story. Thus we begin with a spellbinding ancient text that sits at the core of the mystery tradition. This esoteric tale describes an extraordinary scene that takes place in Jerusalem in roughly 500 B.C.E., almost two centuries before Plato and Aristotle.

The masters of the day were distressed. Adultery was spreading rampant as plague among the people. The authorities were at a loss as to how to curb this powerful drive. Finally, driven to desperation, they began to pray. For three days they fasted, weeping and pleading with God, "Let us slay the sexual drive before it slays us."

Finally God acquiesced. The masters then witnessed a lion of fire leap out from within the Temple's Holy of Holies. A prophet among them identified the lion as the personification of the primal sexual drive.

They sought to slay the lion of fire. But the result was that for three days thereafter the entire society ground to a standstill. Hens did not lay eggs, artists ceased creating, businesses faltered, and all spiritual activity came to a halt.

Realizing that the sexual drive was about more than just sex, that it somehow echoed with the Divine, the masters relented. They prayed that only its destructive shadow be removed while retaining its creative force. Their request was denied on high with the insightful psychological response: "You cannot have only half a drive." The greater the sacred power of a quality, the greater its shadow; the two are inseparable. So they prayed that the lion at least be weakened, and their prayer was granted. The lion, less potent but no less present, reentered the Holy of Holies.

The text is alive with myth, magic, and mystery. The most startling revelation is the radical claim of the text as to the originating place of the sexual drive. Why does this drive, personified as a lion of fire, emerge from the Temple's Holy of Holies? Apparently this is its eternal abode. Thus, remarkably, the text is telling us that *the seat and source of the sexual drive is none other than the Holy of Holies.*

In fact the Holy of Holies is often depicted in the mystical sources as the marriage bed. The tablets and the ark are depicted respectively as the phallus and the vagina or the clitoris. This sexual model of eros and the virtual identity between the erotic and the holy are perhaps the most vital and provocative insights of the Kabbalists. They teach it implicitly in a thousand different ways in their writings. They would rarely say it overtly for fear the message would be misunderstood, leading to a kind of sexual anarchy, which would bring in its wake the collapse of the family. So the dominant impression we are left with is that while sex is good, as it is created by God, it is exceedingly dangerous and is to be handled with great caution. One gets the impression that the attendant dangers may even override the essential good. Thus nothing as audacious as the secret of the cherubs was written about openly. And yet, once you see it, you realize it is there, subtly calling out, whispering from the folds of literally hundreds of texts.

Sex in the temple!? Sexually entwined cherubs atop the ark, and a fiery feline sexual drive living in the Holy of Holies? What are these mythic images trying to express? At first blush they seem to describe sex as a central preoccupation of the Holy of Holies, portraying the Temple as some kind of ancient Hebrew *Playboy* mansion. While Hebrew mysticism may wholeheartedly embrace a positive and healthy sexual ethic, one would not have thought that sex is the essence of the sacred!!

The answer lies in the story itself.

When the lion is subdued, the world does not wake up to just its sexual drive lobotomized. Rather, the world wakes up to an overwhelmingly dull and drive-less existence. All passionate engagement in any activity has suddenly withered and vanished. Whether it be in sex, art, work, or creativity, the thrill is gone. Clearly, that fiery feline inhabitant of the Holy of Holies represents not merely sexuality. Rather, she is the incarnation of a more potent energy force. She is the embodiment of the Shechina.

The Shechina is the feminine Divine. Her name means Indwelling Presence, "the one who dwells in you." She is presence, poetry, passion. She is the sustaining God force that runs through and provides a womb for the world. She is the underlying erotic, sensual, and loving force that knows our name and nurtures all being.

Shechina captures an experience, a way of being in the world, for which we do not yet have an English word. For this is a way of being that we in the West are hard-pressed to articulate. It is the experience of waking up in the morning full of utter joy for the arrival of the day. It is weeping over the splendor of the sunset or the scent of the ocean or the fragility of a newborn. It is a way of living in love.

Indeed, it is one of the great failures of love that we do not possess such a word for this fully charged way of living. The main reason we lack a word for the type of love we will be exploring in this book is that such an expanded notion of love is still so foreign to the fabric of our lives. Our vocabulary reflects our reality. Just as the Eskimo has an ample supply of words to describe different types of snow, a society infused with love would likewise have a menagerie of terms for different types of love. We should wonder over the paucity in the English language for our "terms of endearment."

Our best move in the English language is to turn toward the term Plato introduced in the *Symposium*: eros. For Plato eros is love plus. It is precisely the kind of fully charged life experience that is evoked by the Hebrew term "Shechina."

But over time the term "eros" has been so narrowed and limited that it has lost most of its original intention. Usually when we hear the word *erotic* it evokes only the sexual. And although the sexual is a part of eros, it is only a limited part. The type of full eros we will be describing in this book is way beyond the merely sexual.

Together we will work to reclaim this original meaning of *eros*, a meaning infused by its Hebrew counterpart, Shechina. May the claiming of our erotic birthright in these pages in-form a richer and deeper life for ourselves, our loved ones, and our communities.

TWO

Eros, Not Sex: The Faces of Eros

A Tibetan story wonderfully evokes the erotic experience we will explore together.

Reports had reached the young Dalai Lama that a certain Master of Kung Fu was roaming the countryside of Tibet, converting young men to the study of violence. Rumors even began circulating that this Master of Kung Fu was an incarnation of Shiva Natarajah, the Hindu god in his aspect of the Lord of the Dance of Destruction. The Dalai Lama decided to invite the Master for a visit.

Pleased with the invitation, some weeks later the Master of Kung Fu strode into the Dalai Lama's ceremonial hall. The Master of Kung Fu was stunning indeed, with thick blue-black hair falling down over the shoulders of his black leather suit. "Your Highness," he began, "have no worries, I wouldn't think of doing you harm."

"Well, when you do want to harm," asked the Dalai Lama, "what kind of harm can you do?"

"Royal Highness, the best way to show you would be for you to stand here in front of me while I do a little dance. Though I can kill a dozen men instantly with this dance, have no fear."

The Dalai Lama stood up and immediately felt as if a wind had blown flower petals across his body. He looked down but saw nothing. "You may proceed," he told the Master of Kung Fu.

"Proceed?" said the other, grinning jovially, "I've already finished. What you felt were my hands flicking across your body. If I had done it in slow motion, extremely slow motion, you would have seen how each touch of my hand would have destroyed the organs of your body one by one."

"Impressive, but I know a master greater than you," said the Dalai Lama.

"Without wishing to offend Your Highness, I doubt that very much. Let him challenge me, and if he bests me I shall leave Tibet forever."

"If he bests you, you shall have no need to leave Tibet." The Dalai Lama clapped his hands. "Regent," he said, "summon the Dancing Master."

The Dancing Master entered. He was a wiry little fellow, half the size of the Master of Kung Fu and well past his prime. His legs were knotted with varicose veins, and he was swollen at the elbows from arthritis. Nevertheless, his eyes were glittering merrily and he seemed eager for the challenge.

The Master of Kung Fu did not mock his opponent. "My own guru," he said, "was even smaller and older than you, yet I was unable to best him until last year when I finally caught him on the ear and destroyed him, as I shall destroy you when you finally tire."

The two opponents faced off. The Master of Kung Fu was taking a jaunty, indifferent stance, tempting the other to attack.

The old Dancing Master began to swirl very slowly, his robes wafting around his body. His arms stretched out and his hands fluttered like butterflies toward the eyes of his opponent. His fingers settled gently for a moment upon the Master of Kung Fu's bushy eyebrows.

The Master of Kung Fu drew back in astonishment. He looked around the great hall. Everything was suddenly vibrant with rich hues of singing color. The faces of the monks were radiantly beautiful. It was as if his eyes had been washed clean for the first time.

The fingers of the Dancing Master stroked the nose of the Master of Kung Fu, and suddenly he could smell the pungent barley from a granary in the city far below. He was intoxicated by the aroma of the butter melting in the Dalai Lama's fragrant tea.

A flicking of the Dancing Master's foot at his genitals, and he was throbbing with desire. The sound of a woman singing through an open window filled him with exquisite yearning to draw her into his arms and caress her. He found himself removing his clothes until he stood naked before the Dancing Master, who was now assaulting him with joy at every touch.

His body began to hum like a finely tuned instrument. He opened his mouth and sang like a bird at sunrise. It seemed to him that he was possessed of many arms, legs, and hands, and all wanted to nurture the blossoming of life.

The Master of Kung Fu began the most beautiful dance that had ever been seen in the great ceremonial hall of the Grand Potala. It lasted for three days and nights, during which time everyone in Tibet feasted and visitors crowded the doorways and galleries to watch. Only when he finally collapsed at the throne of the Dalai Lama did he realize that another body was lying beside him. The old Dancing Master had died of exertion while performing his final and most marvelous dance. But he had died happily, having found the disciple he had always yearned for. The new Dancing Master of Tibet took the frail corpse in his arms and, weeping with love, drew the last of its energy into his body. Never had he felt so strong.

What a holy tale of eros. The darts and lunges of emptiness and violence become the erotic soarings of fullness and love. The great mystery tradition of Hebrew wisdom is about a radical and profound path toward becoming just such a dancing master. It is about the dance with eros, with Shechina, the dance with the Goddess Divine.

Eros has many expressions. Each expression is hinted at in the temple mysteries. There are four faces of eros, which when taken together, form the essence of the Shechina experience. These four faces are the very stuff of eros. In this chapter we will explore the erotic understanding that forms the matrix of the secret of the cherubs and informs every arena of our existence. We will unmask the four faces of eros and reveal why they are so vitally important for anyone who wants to experience the full joy, depth, and aliveness of being.

After we understand the eros that lies at the heart of the Temple mysteries we can then turn to answering our core question. If, as we shall show, the essence of the Temple—and of every journey of the spirit—is eros not sex, then why is sex such a prominent feature of the Temple? In response to this question we will unpack in chapter 3 the mystical secret of the cherubs. As we shall see, at the very heart of Hebrew tantra was a very precise and provocative understanding of the relationships among love, sex, and eros. This understanding will open us up to a whole new understanding of our sexuality. This understanding will show us the way to erotically reweave the very fabric of our lives in more vivid patterns, sensual textures, and brilliant hues.

The First Face of Eros: On the Inside

"What lies behind us and what lies before us are tiny matters compared to what lies within us."
—RALPH WALDO EMERSON

The cherubs in the magical mystery of Temple myth were not stationary fixtures. No, these statues were expressive, emotive. They moved. When integrity and goodness ruled the land the cherubs were face-to-face. In these times the focal point of Shechina energy rested erotically, ecstatically, between the cherubs. When discord and evil held sway in the kingdom the cherubs turned from each other, appearing back-to-back instead of face-to-face. Back-to-back, the world was amiss, alienated, ruptured. Face-to-face, the world was harmonized, hopeful, embraced. Thus in biblical myth text being face-to-face is the most highly desirable state. It is the gemstone state of being, the jeweled summit of all creation. Face-to-face, to be fully explicit, is a state of eros.

As we shall see, face-to-face means, first and foremost, *being on the inside.* Indeed the God force said to rest between the cherubs in the Holy of Holies, the Shechina, is no less than the radically profound experience of being on the inside. Eros is aroused whenever we move so deeply into what we do, who we are with, or where we are, that its interiority stirs our heart and imagination.

Being on the inside is of course not about a geographical place but about a soul terrain, a place inside ourselves. Plato writes at the end of the *Phaedo:* "Beloved Pan and all ye other Gods that haunt this place, give me beauty in the inward soul, and may the inward and outward man be at one."

For the Temple mystics, exile is when one's inside and outside are not connected in day-to-day living. Or, said differently, exile is nonerotic living.

The first, although by no means the only, problem with exile is that it is extraordinarily difficult. When I am not living from the inside, I am not living naturally. My choices, reactions, and responses do not emerge spontaneously from what Teresa of Avila called one's "interior castle." I am not in the flow of my own life.

Eros is to be in the flow of the fountain, what the Zohar calls in its oftrepeated evocative mantra "the River of Light that flows from Eden."

There is a wonderful Zen story about two mountain climbers. The first, old and slightly bent, slowly makes his way up the mountain. The second, young and in good form, bounds past him, racing confidently to the summit. In late afternoon they meet again. The older man still climbs gently, step after step, toward the summit. The younger man lies exhausted, unable to move, at the side of the path. As they pass each other the younger cries out to the older, "I don't understand—what do you know that I don't?" Responds the old man, eyes twinkling with compassion and laughter, "The difference between us is simple. You come to conquer the mountain but the mountain is stronger than you, so you are conquered. I come to merge with the mountain—so the mountain loves me and lifts me to her summit."

To merge is to traverse the chasm that separates object and subject. It is to become one with your reality, to be on the inside of the experience.

Erotic living is living on the inside. The opposite of eros is therefore alienation. To be alienated is always to feel that you are an outsider with no safe place to call home.

The result of nonerotic living is always bad choices, betrayals, and pain. When I am not in the flow I wind up always having to watch my back. I am on the outside—exiled from my inner castle. I have lost face.

The face is the truest reflection of the erotic. To lose face is to become deeroticized.

THE SPELL OF SPELLING —*PANIM*

In the Hebrew mystical tradition, language is not merely a random designation of sounds and letters in a particular pattern. For the mystic, words are vital portals to meaning. Language is the spiritual DNA of reality. Thus when one root word is used for seemingly disparate ideas you can rest assured that these different ideas are in fact integrally related. So let's watch for a moment as the magic of language dances before us.

The Hebrew term for the Holy of Holies is *lefnai lefnim*. Literally rendered into English this means "the inside of the inside." This was not merely a reflection of the physical fact that it was the innermost point in the Temple. Indeed, teach the mystics, the opposite is true—it was situated in the inner-most physical point in order to evoke the sense of interiority that is the very key to eros.

In another architectural expression of this idea, the temples of the Masonic order have doors that open only from the inside. You must insert your hand through an opening in the door to grasp the handle on the inside. The point is that in order to open the portals to mystery, one must approach it from the inside. What's more, this opening was shaped like a heart. Eros—the yearn-ing for the inside—is the essence of love. The Masonic order, of course, springs from the Templars, a monastic order of Christian mystics in Jerusalem who fell in love with and understood deeply the eros of the Temple.

That, however, is just for starters. Hold on, for the magic of language, the spell of spelling, has just begun. The Hebrew word for *inside* is *panim*, but it has two other meanings as well. The first, not surprisingly, is "face." The face is the place where my insides are revealed. There are forty-five muscles in the face. From a biological standpoint, most of them are unnecessary. Their major pur-pose, it would seem, is to express emotional depth and nuance. They are the mus-cles of the soul. Every muscle of the face reflects another nuance of depth and interiority. When I say "I need to speak face-to-face," I am in erotic need of an inside conversation. At this point all of the cell phones and sophisticated Inter-net hookups won't give me what I need, for while amazingly efficient and effec-tive, they are nonerotic. True erotic conversations rarely happen on the Internet.

The spell continues. There is a third meaning to the Hebrew root *panim*. In a slightly modified form it means "before," in the sense of appearing before God. Specifically, the biblical myth text in Leviticus tells about how on the biblical Yom Kippur, the Day of At-one-ment, the Temple's high priest appears *Lifnei Hashem*: "Before God."

Read in the English, this appears similar to a summons to appear "before" a judging court, generally not a joyous occasion. For the Hebrew mystics, however, rooted as they are in the magic and spells of language, it is an entirely different affair. Remember that these three English words, *face*, *inside*, and *before*, share the same Hebrew root. The essence then of the Day of At-one-ment is not a commandment to appear "before God" in the magistrate sense. It is rather an invitation *to live on the inside of God's face.* Once the journey *to* God is finished, the infinite journey *in* God begins.

EVERYMAN'S EROS

The eros experience is the province of mystics, artists, and scholars. But not only. It awaits all of us in all our endeavors.

Have you ever gone jogging? You get up not at all enthusiastic about running but somehow feeling obligated. You reluctantly get dressed and begin your route. Slowly the discomfort fades and you begin to enjoy yourself. You find yourself in the rhythm. And then, on good days, at some point you break through an invisible barrier and begin to fly. Ecstatic, you lose yourself in the wind. Your body, the earth, the wind, the rhythms of your pace, the sound of your feet, all merge into one. It is no longer accurate, even if but for the briefest of moments, to say "I am going running." Rather, you are the wind, you *are* the running.

IN EVERY STITCH

It was the middle of the nineteenth century. Heaven was joyous, hell was in an uproar, for it seems that one Hanoch the Shoemaker was about to usher in the Messiah. The Master of Rishin tells the story to his disciples something like this:

"Hanoch the shoemaker used to sit every day intent in the stitching of his leather shoes. It was known that with every stitch Hanoch was meyached yichudim elyonim. *That is, he was unifying higher unities. Now yichudim, my holy disciples, in Kabbalah always means zivug (coupling).*" [Zivug is an ultimate erotic term. It refers not to the sexual person, but to the cosmic love affair between the masculine God presence and the feminine Shechina presence. It is a love affair brought about by human action.]

"*Now the strange secret of the story, my holy community, is that Hanoch wasn't doing anything that should have caused such ecstatic* yichudim. *He wasn't fulfilling any religious commandment, he was engaged in no ritual or pious act.*"

"*Perhaps,*" *said one of the disciples,* "*he was meditating on a passage of the Holy Zohar as he stitched.*" *Another chimed in,* "*Perhaps he was doing the spiritual exercises of Luria's Kabbalah, which cause pleasure above.*"

"*No, nothing of the sort,*" *replied the master.*

"*Then what was he doing while he stitched?*" *pressed the disciples.*

"*Nothing!*" *responded the master with a slight smile.* "*Hanoch was doing nothing… nothing other than being fully inside in every single stitch.*"

"*Fully inside in every stitch?!*" *Duly impressed, the eager disciples now had another confusion.* "*So then, Master, why is it that the Messiah has not yet announced his arrival?*"

The Master of Rishin sighed and said, "*The force of evil discovered the cause and countered it. Sadly he seems to have gotten the best of our holy shoemaker.*"

"*But how?*" *the crestfallen disciples asked.*

He replied, "*With plenty of good business.*"

And so it was. Rushing to fulfill his flood of orders, Hanoch had become the busiest and most prosperous cobbler in the region, mindlessly producing shoe after cookie-cutter shoe, and the Messiah still has not yet come.

POETESS, PROPHETESS, AND PRIESTESS

Eros is the birthright of every man and every woman. Though we may search long and hard for priests and prophets who can guide and counsel us, in the end we must return time and again to our own inner sanctum. The priest and prophet we seek sleep in our depths, waiting to be stirred and finally woken.

I will never forget one of my early dates with my wife, Cary. We were walking Jerusalem's streets. It was late, the silence was luminous. It was one of those moments when intimacy lets you enter for a moment. I asked Cary, "What do you pray for, in your heart of hearts, what do you most want to be?" She became very quiet. I could tell she was deciding whether or not she was ready to offer up her truest, most vulnerable self by answering me. We walked on. She started a sentence but faltered, silent. Finally, mustering a whisper, she told me, "When I pray for who I most want to be"—she glanced over at me uncertainly—"I pray…to be God's poetess, prophetess, and priestess." Her sincerity was so precious, so deep. I knew she felt silly and that her innermost place was exposed. I also knew then this was the woman I would marry.

In our deepest erotic longings, so many of us do want to be God's poets, prophets, and priests. Yet we are ashamed to admit it—sometimes even to ourselves. We fear appearing ridiculous or grandiose even in our own eyes. Yet the biblical myth insists that we are all potential priests and prophets. We can all enter the Holy of Holies, for it is within us. In contradiction to the priestly class and prophetic elites of the ancient Near East, biblical myth talks of a kingdom of priests and a people who are all prophets.

Life itself is the only real Temple of the spirit. Eros is everywhere. Churches and synagogues are a pallid, even if sometimes important, compromise for our disenchanted age.

The Zohar teaches that every erotic inside experience is a Shechina experience of the Holy of Holies. It occurs when we become one with the way, when we have moved from the outside to the inside. It is in this sense that the Temple is called in Hebrew the *bayit*, which means, quite simply, "home." The holiest place in the world—is home. Eros is about coming home. We all live split off from our selves. All too often we feel like imposters in our own lives, wearing masks and wondering when, and if, we will ever start to feel at home with ourselves. That is what it means to live on the outside.

COMING HOME

Once a year in a spine-tingling mystery rite the priest would enter the Holy of Holies. On this day, every person was forgiven. On this day, every person was to reexperience themselves in the depths of their own true innocence. For on the inside we are all innocent. This day is called in biblical myth tradition the Day of Atonement: At-one-ment.

The core erotic idea of the *Bayit*—the Temple—was that every person could and needs to access the Shechina experience. Every human being needs to live erotically in all facets of being. Every human being has a primary erotic need to move beyond being the impostor and into his or her own deepest place of oneness, a oneness not only with the self but also with others, and ultimately with all of existence. The Zohar refers to the exile from one's deepest self as *alma depiruda*, the world of separation. The most tragic separation is not from mother, not from community, but from the self. The journey of a lifetime is to move from *alma depiruda* to *alma deyichuda*, from separation to oneness—At-one-ment. Love is the path back home. We are not talking about superficial love, not merely sexual love, but erotic love.

The litmus test of an erotic lover is this: Does this person lead you back to your inner self? Are you able to share with him or her your most vulnerable, fledgling, faltering dreams? Every person has a Holy of Holies which, in those most intimate of times, we let another enter as the priest to worship at our altar. And in the gorgeous paradox of the spirit, by letting a lover enter we ourselves are let in as well. For when the Temple door is open and the lover enters, we ourselves trail behind. We gain uncommon access to our inner selves, a place that we are often unable to reach alone. *The true lover always takes you home.* As Emily Dickinson wrote,

> *Eden is that old-fashioned house*
> *We dwell in every day*
> *Without suspecting our abode until we drive away.*

Love lets us realize the Eden we are dwelling *in* every day. That is what it means to feel at home in your life, which is the greatest feeling in the world.

SIT DOWN

Teachers taught the Zoharic masters can take us home, but only if they teach from the inside. It is reported that Ziv Hirsch of Zhitomir, a charismatic nineteenth-century mystical master, would occasionally in the middle of his speech sit down, abruptly ending his address in midthought. When pressed for an explanation he responded, "My master—the Maggid of Mezritch—taught me, 'If when giving a *sicha* [spiritual lesson] you can hear yourself talking, sit down.'"

In *A Moveable Feast*, Hemingway remarks on the difference between his telling a story and the story telling itself. When *he* begins to tell the story, he knows it is time to quit for the day. This is a true echo of the temple tradition. Sit down when you can hear yourself speak.

EROS AND ZOHAR—
EXPANDING OUR LIMITED VOCABULARY

As we have seen, in his wonderful dialogue the *Symposium* Plato describes this inner state as eros. To be a lover, implies Plato, is to passionately enter the inside of reality. Eros is love but not in the casual, pallid, and sometimes anemic way we often talk of love. On the inside of things all is aflame.

Kabbalah scholar Yehuda Libes suggests that the word *Zohar*, the name of the magnum opus of Hebrew mysticism, is roughly synonymous with the Greek word *eros*. For the authors of the Zohar were not dry medieval scholastics; *they were rather men of great passion and depth who believed that by entering the inside of a moment, or a text, or a relationship, they could re-create and heal the world.* Zohar, like eros, is powerful, intense, and deep. It is the source of all creativity and pleasure.

Let us take a moment to see the full beauty of where we've gone on our journey thus far. We have understood that the Temple is the archetype of eros and that eros, the Greek term for loving, is the experience of being on the inside. This is the name of the Temple's Holy of Holies—*lefnai lefnim*—the inside of the inside, the face of all faces. The experience of Shechina—the sensual divine force that rests between the cherubs in the Holy of Holies—is the erotic experience. In fact the mystics often use the word *Shechina* as a synonym for eros.

Now lets add one dramatic step: The Hebrew word for *Temple* is *Mikdash*—which literally translates as "Holiness." If you put it all together it is radical, revolutionary, and overwhelmingly relevant to our lives.

What it means is that the erotic and the holy are the same thing, or to put it in more mathematical form:

$$\text{Eros} = \text{Shechina} = \text{the Inside} = \text{Zohar} = \text{Holy}$$

Finally, we have a definition of holiness. So many people use the word *holy* but virtually no one knows what it really means. Ask someone for a definition and you will likely get a fuzzy, nebulous response that will leave you no richer than before. So here—at last—is a definition of holiness. *To be holy is to be on the inside.* The opposite of holiness therefore is not un-holiness or anti-holiness. It is not impurity or demonic possession. *The opposite of the holy is the superficial.* Eros is about depth. Depth is an inside experience. It has its own unique nuance, texture, and richness. The superficial is bland and common.

Holiness is eroticism. Sin is superficiality.

The Second Face of Eros: Full Presence

The second face of eros is the "fullness of presence." This is not a quality that is distinct and different from the erotic qualities of being on the inside. It flows naturally and even overlaps with it. And yet it is not quite the same. Of course being on the inside requires the fullness of presence. But we can experience full presence even when we have not merged with the moment or crossed over to the inside. Full presence is about showing up. You can show up and be fully present in a conversation without necessarily losing yourself in the encounter's flow. Full presence at work can mean that you derive joy, satisfaction, and self-worth from your vocation. It means you feel full and not empty.

When I lead prayers at our retreat center overlooking the Sea of Galilee in Israel, we often do a face-to-face prayer. In this prayer, people sit in twos and read Psalms to each other. They each are singing praises to the God point in the other. Before we start the chanting, I begin by asking each pair to look deeply into each other's faces. "Begin by being wordlessly present for each other. Experience the full presence of another waiting for you."

After those uncommon sessions of looking into another's face many people have come up to me in tears, in joy, in awe, each with a different story. But they all share a common theme. "First I felt uncomfortable. I kept shifting my gaze. Looking at her necklace, her earlobes, her hair, but it was so hard to look at her face. Finally, our eyes fell into sync. It was uncomfortable, but we kept at it. Eyes—brown, with freckles of color. A funny, imperfect face. And then suddenly, something gave. A rush of emotion. A moment of release into the other person's gaze." Sometimes it happens, sometimes it doesn't. But when it does, you never forget it.

Have you ever looked, really looked, into another person's face? Have you ever witnessed that moment when the soul comes rushing up from its inner chambers and opens wide the windows of the eyes to see you, seeing her? To greet you like the daylight? This is the mystery of love, of the eyes and their eros.

I ask the participants to feel the face of their partner as a sculptor would his clay. "Run your hands—erotically, not sexually—over the skin, the bone structure, and then look again deeply into the eyes. In the eros of face touched and felt, the God point of the other emerges, and we are moved with full heart to sing praise." At the close of the exercise I often tell a particular mystical tale that I love very much.

The Hassidim, adherents of a powerful Kabbalistic myth movement that reached its apex in the mid-nineteenth century, tell of a girl—Sarah—who had run away from home to a convent. Now convents are beautiful for nuns—but not for Sarah. Everyone knew where she was, yet no one could persuade her to leave the convent and return home. Finally the distraught parents turned to the Baal Shem Tov, the Master of the Good Name.

It is reported that the Baal Shem went and sat behind a tree not far from the convent. He brought with him no books, no ritual prayer objects, and only the bare amount of food necessary to sustain him. One day goes by, and Sarah does not come. A second day—no sign of her. A third—no girl ... But wait, the sun is setting—Sarah runs out, looks around, and eventually finds her way to the master, who is sitting quietly behind his tree. They look at each other wordlessly, and she goes back home, ultimately growing up to be one of the great holy women of her day.

Late in life she was asked what the Baal Shem did to make her leave the convent. She responded, "On the first day I felt him there, waiting, and I was angry with him. What right did he have?! On the second day I was no longer angry, just curious—who was he, and why is he waiting for me? But I was determined not to let him trap me with my own curiosity. On the third day I felt him waiting and I was engulfed by an overwhelming sense of love. I tried to resist it, but my desire grew and grew until I could resist it no longer. And I ran outside to see his face."

What a magnificent moment of eros! To live erotically is to be fully present to each other's richness, complexity, and ultimate grandeur. It is to fully wait for the other to appear. The Shechina in the Temple is termed the indwelling presence. The erotic is always the experience of full presence. The Shechina, say the mystics, is waiting for us to show up.

The Shechina is presence waiting for us to be present. Standing outside our window, she is eros, waiting. Waiting for us to feel her presence. Waiting for us to be overwhelmed by her love. Waiting for us to run out and behold with wonder—her face.

EMPTINESS AND ADDICTIONS

Eros is about feeling the fullness of being, the opposite of emptiness. Every human being has met emptiness, that feeling we experience late at night, home alone or in the hotel room we return to after a long day's work on a business trip. We enter the room and are often overwhelmed by intense feelings of emptiness. We flip on the cable or order up dinner and entertainment—anything not to stay in the emptiness. Indeed the sentence that I probably repeat to my students more than any other is: "*Life is what you do with your emptiness.*"

In our society, which sadly defines human beings as consumers and not lovers, denying the emptiness is the primary strategy for coping with it. We are sold ful-fill-ment at every turn and in every guise. We buy buy buy, hoping that one of the hawked elixirs might finally full-fill us. And yet the emptiness lingers.

This is the great paradox of emptiness. The first way to approach emptiness must be not to fill it but simply to be mindful of it. To notice the emptiness. The goal is to move beyond the void to the fullness of eros and Shechina. Yet paradoxically you can only access the fullness of being if you are willing to stay in the emptiness long enough to find your way. The path to eros is filled with detours to pseudo eros, but they are all dead ends. When we are so desperate for fullness, when the emptiness hurts too much, these detours seduce us off the path, often spinning us to painful places where we never wanted to go.

Addiction is, at its root, the inability to stay in the emptiness. So we rush to fill the emptiness with whatever gives us the quickest hit of pseudo eros. Pseudo eros is virtually always addictive. Pseudo eros has many disguises—sex, food, public acclaim, drugs, work. Goethe was right when he defined addiction as anything you cannot stop doing. We are all addicts.

This takes me to another image from the Galilee. At our spiritual retreats, which are not geared toward addressing drug or alcohol problems, people are thrown for a little bit of a loop by the opening talk that I give at orientation. It usually starts something like this: "I know you are all addicts—but I promise you it will be okay. You can break the habit. Indeed here at Bayit Chadash we insist you let the addiction go." At this point everyone is looking at one another and silently asking, What is he talking about? We're not addicts. Did we come to the wrong place?

I keep on in this vein for some time until someone is finally fully exasper-ated and shouts out, "But I'm not an addict!" At which point I suggest to check that claim, we need to define *addiction*. The definition that emerges is always something like, "Addiction is anything you are incapable of refraining from doing for twenty-four hours that is not essential to your physical health." After everyone agrees on the definition, I pose the following question: "How many people here believe casual gossip about other people's ostensible shortcom-ings is essential for your physical health? How many people have succeeded in going twenty-four hours in their lives without talking negatively about someone else?" The place slowly gets very quiet. We realize that almost all of us are addicted to negative gossip. We cannot go twenty-four hours—or much less time—without negative gossip! We are addicts!

When you think deeply about it, you realize that talking about other people is one of the easiest ways to engage others in conversation. Deeper still, it is one of the easiest ways to fill the emptiness. It is a form of pseudo eros, a shortcut to fullness. At our retreats, rather than maintain silence, we invite everyone to engage in mindful speech. Indeed, Kabbalah scholars point out that one of the defining characteristics of the Zohar mystics is that illumina-tion happened not in solitary retreat but in groups engaged in sacred conver-sation. Fulfillment comes not from escaping but from engaging.

So watch carefully and you will see that a millisecond before you are moved to casual slander *you touched a moment of emptiness in yourself.* Something in the mention of a person's name or in the topic of conversation subtly, almost invisi-bly, challenged your self-worth, adequacy, or dignity. Imperceptibly, your sys-tem moves to fill the emptiness with a quick hit of seeming fullness—gossip—which is only pseudo eros.

CHOCOLATE-COVERED RAISINS

The same thing happens every day with food but without our realizing it. Our bodies can be our most blatant teachers. Our bodies are talking, but are we listening? On a religious fast day a few years ago, I finally listened and realized what fast days were all about. I was sitting at my desk, reading an article. Suddenly chocolate-covered raisins popped into my mind and my appetite. I got up to find a handful. Remembering that it was a fast day, I sat back down. The craving persisted. I thought to myself, It's only late morning. I've only been fasting a few hours, I shouldn't be this hungry yet. Why did I so desperately desire chocolate-covered raisins?

I pondered the mystery, finally figuring out why. It was the article I was reading. It was written by a colleague of mine on a subject I myself had worked on extensively, but I had not yet published anything about it. Instead of my mind reading the article and screaming, Jealousy! Emptiness! it had read the article and blared out, Chocolate-covered raisins! Had I not been fasting I would have proceeded to pop a couple of hundred calories' worth of those chocolate pills into my mouth and gone on to the next thing, never truly realizing the cause.

There's a wonderful short blessing in the Hebrew liturgy that is recited after eating. Strangely the blessing begins with a unique formula that appears nowhere else in the liturgy: "You created many beings, *each with its own unique emptiness.*" Yet we have just eaten; we are ostensibly feeling well fed, full, happy, and thankful. So why are we talking about all these creatures having a unique emptiness!? Quite simply, because food and emptiness are the closest of intimates. Food can be used to fill the empty stomach, or it can be used to fill the empty soul. It can be used and it can be abused. Addictive eating is born from the emptiness. Emptiness is like a shrewd foreign agent who hires food, rather than a beautiful woman, to seduce you. You give in to food's chocolate-covered charm, and as you devour it, the emptiness devours you.

One of the beauties of a spiritual system that invites an occasional fast day is that you can't just jump to devour. Instead, you have to sit there in the hunger, in the emptiness. From there you can observe the moments when you crave, seek out the source of the craving, and then discern if this is wholesome or unwholesome hunger. Are you feasting or are you being feasted upon? Have you brushed up against the emptiness again? Did you fill it up with a quick fix or did you take that extra precious moment to pursue its deeper source? That extra moment is the infinite distance between surface and depth. Next time take the time to search out the source. Erotic presence is about going for the root, rather than snipping at the twigs.

AFTERTASTE

Now if we are courageous enough to walk one step further, we will see that sex follows the same formula. Every human being engages in two very different forms of sexuality. The first is, by whatever your own inner standard may be, sacred sex, and the second is fallen sex. Everyone's examples will be different, but everyone understands the distinction.

How to tell the difference? Aftertaste. The first leaves you with a wonderful aftertaste; the second leaves you with an uncomfortable feeling, which you try to shrug off as quickly as possible—a very minor or major spiritual hangover.

Watch yourself very carefully over an extended time (which is really the only path to enlightenment). You will see that shortly before you feel sexual arousal toward what is fallen sex, you somehow brushed up against your emptiness. It may be an old tape triggered in your head by some association, perhaps a tape from childhood that says you are not worthy. It could be a feeling of jealousy or incompleteness triggered by a friend's accomplishment or one of a hundred other things. As soon as your system receives that jolt of emptiness it moves frantically, yet imperceptibly, to send you symptoms of sexual arousal, hoping to quickly fill the void. Next time you find yourself following your sexual arousal, ask yourself if you are nourishing yourself with sexuality or are you filling up the hole inside you, desperately trying to avoid the void.

Now here is a wild idea. Biblical myth practice suggests that, just as a fast day is helpful in sensitizing you so you can distinguish between wholesome and desperate eating, regular short periods of voluntary sexual fasting can be ever so enlightening. Sexual fasting is critical in helping you to distinguish between fallen and sacred sex, between the sexually erotic and nonerotic. It is a brilliant spiritual practice for the clarification of desire and the purification of sex. As a side benefit, sexual fasting is also the best practice available for reclaiming passion in a marriage—for anything that is always available, such as marital sex, can soon become terribly boring.

EMPTY WISDOM

The cherubs once again serve as our guide. Remember that the vortex of Shechina in the biblical myth is no less than "atop the ark in the Holy of Holies, *between* the cherubs." "Between" is interpreted by the Kabbalists as a word that dances *between* the emptiness and the fullness.

In the first unpacking, *between*, which is *bein* in Hebrew, is understood as the "*empty space* between the cherubs." *Bein* is the emptiest place in the world— hence the place in which the Shechina dwells. This is a seeming endorsement of the emptiness.

In a second understanding, "between the cherubs" is said to be the place where there is no emptiness. That is the place of Shechina—that is to say, of erotic fullness, the radical intensification of presence from which wells up the voice of God. This is a seeming endorsement of the fullness.

The meaning underlying these paradoxically different understandings of *bein/between* is clear. *Only when we can hold the emptiness does it become filled with the divine voice.*

Beautifully, the Hebrew word *bein* also means "wisdom"—*binah.* For wisdom only comes when we are willing to stay in the emptiness long enough to hold our center and walk through it. When we try to fill it too quickly we always wind up shocked and deeply unsettled when the emptiness does not go away. Instead, the void gets deeper, thicker, more palpable, virtually suffocating us.

ECHOES OF EMPTINESS —
THE EROTIC AND THE ETHICAL

The arena where emptiness—nonerotic living—is most destructive is in the ethical. Every ethical failure comes from the absence of eros. It is their inability to stay in the experience of emptiness that moves people to violate their ethics. All crimes are in some sense crimes of passion. But this is actually a misnomer. What we mean is that all crimes are rooted in the fear of passion's loss! We cannot imagine what life would be like without the eros that we stand to lose.

Joel finds out that his wife is having an affair. The betrayal opens up the void within. Afraid that if he confronts her she will leave, he slowly becomes a workaholic to dull the pain. Work for Joel has become pseudo eros.

Or take Susan, who was verbally and physically abused by her mother. Never able to claim the dignity of her anger, she became gradually disempowered as a person. As an adult, she is constantly furious at her children, often lashing out brutally at them. She seeks to assure herself that she is still alive and powerful. For Susan, her displaced anger at her children is pseudo eros.

Or more mundane examples. We cheat on income taxes because we think that the extra money will paper over some of the fear of life. Money becomes pseudo eros.

Or we exaggerate our accomplishments because we are afraid that our real story is insufficient to fill the void. Self-aggrandizement is pseudo eros.

All of our inappropriate behaviors that violate our values are really us crying out, "Pay attention to me—I exist!" All forms of acting out are pseudo eros.

Life is about walking through the void. Every time we walk through and not around the void we come out stronger. Every time we are seduced by pseudo eros, ethical breakdown is around the corner. There is no ethics without eros.

The biblical myth text describes the pit into which Joseph was thrown by his jealous brothers: "The pit was empty, it had not water," reads the story. "But isn't this redundant?" ask the students. "If it had no water, don't we know that it was empty?" The master replies, "This was an emptiness which bred evil. Water it did not have, snakes and scorpions it did!" Emptiness always breeds in its wake ethical collapse.

Of course, the real pit at play in the biblical myth is not simply a pit in the earth. The pit is in Joseph's brothers' very ground of being. Their own gaping sense of emptiness makes them envy Joseph so. It is their inability to walk through their own pit (void) that moves them to project a pit in the world in which they would cast their brother. The snakes and scorpions come from the unacknowledged emptiness of the brothers.

No, Joseph is not perfect, but when we respond to a person viscerally, it virtually always tells us more about ourselves than about the person. The brothers' own deeply felt emptiness—their pit—moved them to the murderous rage of attempted fratricide.

You see, until this point in the book of Genesis one son has always been chosen as the inheritor of blessing. Abel was chosen over Cain. Shem over Ham and Yefet. Isaac over Ishmael, and Jacob over Esau. The brothers were convinced that Jacob, their father, was going to likewise choose Joseph over them. Joseph's existence called into question the integrity of their stories. When the value and dignity of our stories are called into question we brush up against the emptiness. The inability to walk through the emptiness to the fullness is the source of all ethical collapse.

Ethics without eros is doomed. Only from a place of fullness of being can we reach out in love to others. The first step to love is always self-love. If you don't fill yourself up with love, then you have precious little to dole out. But as long as your love is not rooted in your erotic matrix—the inside of your fullness—it is doomed to fail. You will have to rely on an ethical source outside yourself, which will always make you view yourself as a sinner. No one is ever able to consistently follow external rules that seem to violate their inner desire.

However, if ethics well up from the inside, if you are at the center, then sin is not disobedience but the violation of human well-being. *In the end all ethical failure is a violation of eros—your own or someone else's.*

The Third Face of Eros: Desire

When I am on the inside, when I am fully present, I am able to access the third face of the erotic experience—longing. Longing and desire are two essential expressions of love and eros. As long as I am on the outside I can ignore my deepest desires and stifle my longing. But longing is a vital strand in the textured fabric of the erotic. It is of the essence of the Holy of Holies.

We are filled with desires. Everyone has chocolate-covered raisins in their lives. How should we relate to them—as ally or enemy, teachers or tempters? Here again the cherubs hint at the way.

Here is the place to introduce another set of cherubs that appear in biblical myth. The first of course are the cherubs above the ark. The second pair make a dramatic earlier appearance in the biblical book of Genesis as the two cherubs that guard the way to the Garden of Eden. They stand with "a fiery sword which revolves, guarding the path to the tree of life." The Zohar speaks for much of the mystical tradition when it suggests that these are one and the same cherubs. The Temple in biblical myth is called the Garden of God. The mystics reveal that the Garden of Eden and the Temple are in mythical terms on the same plane of consciousness.

Remember the archetypal Garden of Eden story. Eve, overcome by desire, eats from the forbidden tree and gives Adam a taste of the fruit as well. When confronted by God Adam blames Eve. Eve blames the serpent. According to the sixteenthe-century mystic Isaac Luria, had they but waited three more hours the Tree of Life would have been theirs. Full erotic fulfillment in all the senses of spirit, soul, and body would have been realized. But they could not wait. Unable to stay in the emptiness, they required an immediate hit of pseudo eros. For their failure to take personal responsibility and for their inability to resist the blandishments of pseudo desire they are exiled from the Garden.

The goal of personal and cosmic history is to return to the Garden. The cherubs however stand at the entrance to the Garden with swirling swords of flame. Anyone who attempts to return to paradise through the drugs of pseudo desire is slashed and burned by the cherubic sword. The same cherubs stand above the ark in the Holy of Holies. They give instruction in the path of Hebrew tantra. If we are willing to do the work, the Temple cherubs will ultimately lead us back to the Garden. Pseudo eros will give way to true eros. For to be in the Garden, which is the Temple, is to live in full eros in every facet of our lives.

DESIRE IS HOLY

The biblical mystic lovingly counsels us to be with ourselves and gently watch our desires as they come and go. We are invited not to eradicate them, not to get off the wheel of suffering which they are said to create, but to engage in *birrur teshuka*, the clarification of desire. To love someone is to wait on their desire, to watch it stir and delight in its presence, to help it crystallize and form.

Eros is to be on the inside, including the inside of your desire. Being on the inside invites a person to clarify his desires, yet not transcend them. True desire is attained through the deep meditation in which you access the internal witness. This is a place of detachment, from which you survey with penetrating but loving eyes all of your desires. This place of internal witness allows you to move beyond an addictive attachment to any particular desire. At that point the person engaged in *birrur*—clarification—does not abandon desire. Rather she moves to connect to those desires that were truest to her deepest and most authentic self. It is in the empty space *"between the spasm and the desire"* that the person is born.

Detachment for the biblical mystic is a strategy, not a goal. In the end, you must not remain a spectator in the drama of your own existence. Rather you need to become the lead actor on your stage by always living on the inside and never getting lost in the luxury of distance or detachment, so you can fully merge with the part the universe has invited you to play. Longing and desire are good not because we believe that all of our yearning will be fulfilled or realized, but because the yearning itself fulfills us. The desire itself fills the emptiness. When we yearn to grow, when we are alive with desire, we touch fulfillment.

Hannah was a walking prayer, constantly calling out to God. People would see her on the streets, carrying her groceries with a light step, all the while with eyes facing upward, a soundless prayer on her lips. Pass by her window and you would see her by the stove or by the sink, lips lost in prayer, pleading with the heavens for something, for anything, for everything. A neighbor with a jealous eye one day came to her and whispered, "And so why hasn't God answered all your impassioned prayers?" Hannah was shaken. What if this neighbor was right? When will God answer, and why should I wait? And so Hannah abandoned her beseeching. She gave up on her yearning. And though the groceries seemed heavier, the stove colder, she refused to pray. Until one night a divine voice called out to Hannah in a dream, "Why have you stopped praying to me?" Hannah retorted, "Well, you never answered, so I stopped asking." To which the Divine replied, "Don't you realize, every call of yours IS itself my response? Your great yearning is my greatest gift." With this, Hannah's ceaseless prayer came back to her lips. Her burden was again lightened, her stove was ablaze.

Depression is at its core the depression of desire. When we lose touch with our authentic desire, we become listless and apathetic. There is wonderful eros in desire. It is what connects us most powerfully with our own pulsating aliveness.

'TIS BETTER TO BLEED

In a published dialogue between a well-known Buddhist teacher and myself, the teacher challenged me persistently on this issue of desire. "After all," he said, "if you give up the desire for life, then death will not be horrifying and painful."

"No," I responded, "if I give up the desire for life I would already be dead." Since the debate took place in a kitchen in Jerusalem, I picked up a knife. "If I took this knife and cut my arm, would it bleed?"

"Of course."

"Now what if I, with the same knife, cut my hair? No blood. Why? Because the cells in my hair are dead. And dead cells do not bleed." Part of the eros of longing is to experience pain as well as joy. That is why biblical mystics viewed the inability to grieve and weep as a sign of great spiritual illness.

From the day the Temple was destroyed all the gates are closed; the gates of tears are not closed. So reads a fifth-century Hebrew wisdom text. The eros of tears, an inevitable corollary of longing and desire, is the way back to the eros of the Temple, to the inside, and to a full sense of your own aliveness. Nachman of Bratzlav, an erotic master of the inside, writes, "A human being is like an onion: strip away layer after layer and all that remains are the tears." To reach the inner recesses of a thing one must be willing to weep.

THE YEARNING FORCE OF BEING

The mystical tradition tells of time portals, each capable of accessing different regions of our interior castle. The mystical masters understood that the Temple of eros was built not in space but in time. The Sabbath—a Temple in time—is patterned in its spiritual blueprint after the Temple in Jerusalem. The *axis mundi* of the Sabbath, its Holy of Holies, takes place near dusk as the Sabbath ebbs away into sunset. In the mystical tradition this is the time of tears. Not crying in response to personal sorrows but tears that well up from the yearning force of being. This was when the disciples would gather around the master's table and sing songs of longing—often well into the night.

This is what Viktor Turner called Liminal Time, the time between the cracks when all the gates are open. Here is one of its tales of eros.

It is near dusk as the Sabbath ebbed away. The disciples were gathered. The master Levi Isaac of Berdichev—holiest teacher—rises to speak. He wants to explain to his disciples not the wonder of creation, or the mystery of the chariot, but merely that God is the inside of the inside, the erotic life force of the universe, and that therefore each one of our lives matters.

He begins his discourse with an elegant teaching from the Talmud demonstrating the reality of God.

"Do you understand?" he queries.

"No," they answer... heads hanging.

He then takes them on a dance of light, intricately weaving the mysteries of the Zohar,
which illuminate God's presence in the world.

"Do you understand?" he queries

"No," they answer… heads low.

In desperation he begins to tell stories, tales revealing great mysteries.

"Now do you understand?" he queries

"No," they answer, heads still hanging.

So he becomes quiet and begins to sing a melody of yearning, of longing, of pining. For a
few moments he sings alone, then one and then another joins in, till they became one voice.

Yearning.

Pining.

Longing.

Levi Isaac did not need to ask. Their heads rose. They understood.

I YEARN, THEREFORE I AM

It is said that the Great Maggid would convene his inner circle every night to
teach them the sacred texts. All of his greatest students would gather. When
the Maggid would begin to speak "And God said…" Reb Zushya would leap
up, overwhelmed with desire. He would yell out, "And God said! God said!"
He would spin around and around like a leaf in the wind, and then faint,
unconscious for the rest of the teaching. Every night it was the same thing.
The other disciples would tease him, saying, "Zushya, you're missing all the
holy teachings!" This teasing went on for days and days until finally the master said, "Leave him alone; he's the only one who gets it."

For the Hebrew mystic, unlike his Buddhist or Greek cousins, desire and
longing are sacred. Eros is the yearning force of being. I yearn therefore I am.
To be cut off from the eros of yearning is to be left in the cold of nonexistence.
To yearn is to be aflame.

This longing is built into the very fabric of human existence. In both the
Hebrew story of the creation of humankind as well as in Plato's myth told

in the *Symposium,* all human beings were initially both male and female. "Male and female he created them," reads the biblical myth story. Then they were separated from each other. And now they yearn to reunite with each other.

According to the biblical myth recorded in the Zohar, this was the grand design of creation. First, human beings needed to realize that they are essentially interconnected. No human being stands alone. None are essentially alienated, lonely, or separate. Once this knowledge is embedded in the human soul and psyche, then they must be separated from each other. At this point the longing for reunion begins. That yearning will be the driving force in human growth and spiritual unfolding. The difference between Plato and the biblical wisdom is that in the latter it is a longing that can essentially be fulfilled. *Full-fill-ment* is a genuine option and not an impossible mirage situated over the next hill by a punishing and cruel universe. Yearning is the essential formula of the universe.

The Fourth Face of Eros: The Interconnectivity of Being

Longing, desire, and tears remind us of the fourth strand in the erotic weave. They whisper to us that we are all interconnected. No human stands alone. The word *religion* traces its source to the Latin root *ligare,* which, similar to ligament, is about connectivity. Religion's goal then is to re-*ligare*—to reconnect us. Religion's original intention was to take us to that inside place where we could indeed experience the essential interconnectivity of all reality. All of existence is one great quilt of being, and we are all patches in its magnificent multi-faceted pattern.

Eros is what allows us to move past the feeling of isolation and separation and experience ourselves as part of the quilt. To sunder our connection to eros is therefore to sin. Not only would we lose the source of life's greatest pleasure, but we would also undermine the building blocks of connection without which the world would ultimately collapse.

In the Kabbalistic myth, the great sin that caused what is called "the shattering of the vessels" was the sin of separation. Each divine force—*sefira*—held itself apart, autonomous and independent, free of any dependency on the other *sefirot*. The result was that each independent *sefira* was unable to hold its light and ultimately shattered, causing great cosmic disarray. The *tikkun*—the fixing of the shattering—occurs when every point of existence is in connection as part of the quilt of being.

In this sense mystics were often also magicians. Ecstasy and magic are in the end inextricably bound up with each other. Both seek to access the myriad lines of connection that undergird the wondrous web of existence. A child intuitively understands this magic. Psychology dismissively refers to this childlike intuition as magical thinking and sees maturity as the triumph of the rational mind over magic. Yet the mystic insists that the child is at least partially right. It is not for naught that the magical Harry Potter books swept the world with such speed. Children who had never read before were suddenly reading hundreds of pages—volume after volume. Children felt that they were finally given something to read that was true to their spirit. The sacred child in us understands that the world is filled with magic. The world is filled with invisible lines of connection.

Eros is another word for magic and enchantment, the knowledge that everything is alive and intertextured—interwoven and filled with meaning. The experience of sin is the feeling that things, and you, are not holding together, that you are falling apart. Eros is the drive to wholeness and thus to healing and health.

LOVE KNOWS NO DISTANCE — NONLOCAL LOVE

The interconnectivity of being is neither doctrine nor dogma. Rather it is the nature of reality and is fully accessible if we just take the time to notice it.

Being enmeshed in a web of connection is the essential erotic experience of mystics throughout the ages. But all of us catch glimpses of it as well. We have all known those moments of seemingly inexplicable coincidences—a mother having a piercing pain in her chest precisely when her daughter two thousand miles away has been in a car accident, or that time when you thought of an old friend only to come home to a message from that person on your answering machine. These subtle synchronicities are all part of our daily reality. They are the faint yet persistent whisperings of the universe saying, "You are not alone. Love knows no distance." The all is connected to the all.

In the last twenty-five years, an enormous amount of serious scientific investigation has been done into what is called nonlocal distance healing. It involves the ability of a person at great distances to affect healing. The effects of this healing have been verified through many scientifically sound experiments that measure indicators of health ranging from protecting red blood cells, to impeding the spread of cancer, to lowering blood pressure, and much more. What is critical is that these experiments reveal that we are not discrete units but rather interconnected nondiscrete "unities." Like a network of rivers that interweave along their way back to the sea, we are beings fully woven into one another and thus able to traverse all the frontiers of separateness, including space and even time.

Physics has for years been speaking about a nonlocal universe. One of the recent leaders in this work is the Irish physicist John Stewart Bell. Bell showed that if distant objects have once been in contact, a change in one causes an immediate change in the other. It is irrelevant how far apart they are. Even if they are later at the opposite ends of the universe, the connection is not broken. We have known forever that there is a deeper level of consciousness available when we allow ourselves to let go of our separateness even as we maintain the individual integrity so necessary for responsibility and ethical action in the world.

Similarly, the worlds of music, dance, and, most of all, orgasm, allow us glimpses of our higher reality. Here again the sexual models the erotic, the erotic being the experience on the inside of reality where all of being yearns for connection and every living thing knows that it has a patch called home that is part of the great quilt of the universe. Love is the eros of connection—

the underlying interdependence of things, the bond among all living things, the great emotional ether in which we all live.

LOVE LETTERS AND LOVE NUMBERS

In biblical mysticism love and oneness are identical. In Hebrew, there is a mystical technique called *gematria* in which each letter, and thus each word, has a numerical value. The Hebrew word for love, *ahava*, has a numerical value of thirteen. *Echad*, meaning one, also has a numerical value of thirteen. To the Kabbalistic mind, this is more than just a coincidence. It is as if a mystical law has been encoded into the letters of these words. Love is Oneness and Oneness is Love. *One* is but another word for the erotic interconnectivity of all being.

But the rhyme of mystical meaning continues, for these two words added together equal twenty-six. Twenty-six is a central number in Hebrew mysticism because it is the numerical value of God's four-letter name: Yud Hei Vav Hei—the divine name of healing and love. Thus, God is One Love. Love is the universe's way of embracing us and telling us we are not alone. We have a home, a *bayit*. We are connected.

One + One = One.

DO YOU KNOW WHAT I NEED?

Isaac Luria, the great Kabbalist writing in sixteenth-century Safed, teaches, "All evil is a failure of love and eros. I can only hurt you if I feel that you are not connected to me. Would the hand stab the foot to take revenge?" For Luria, love in its very essence is the erotic re-ligaring with all of being.

It always starts, however, not with all of being but with a friend that you already know.

The master Moshe Leib of Sassov said he never knew what it meant to be a lover until he learned it from a drunkard. It happened that the master was in a tavern and overheard a dialogue between two men deep in their drink. One was professing how much he loved the other, but the other argued that this was not so.

"Ivan," he cried, "believe me when I tell you, I love you more dearly than anything in the world."

"Not so, Igor," Ivan replied. "You don't really love me at all."

Igor gulped down a glass of vodka. The tears streamed down his face. "I swear, Ivan, I love you with all my heart." He wept.

Ivan shook his head. "Igor, if you really do love me, tell me why I am not satisfied in my life. If you really loved me you would be able to tell me what I desire." With this, Igor was silent. This time Ivan was the one who cried.

All the faces of eros show themselves in the tale: interconnectivity, desire, being on the inside, and the fullness of presence. If you really love me then we are deeply *connected*. You hear the deepest *desires* of my soul because their melodies resonate in your soul as well. You learn to hear my soul's music by being fully *present* in our encounter. Moreover you are radically empathetic to my needs. Radical empathy comes when the fullness of presence engenders a great yearning to move beyond the alienation that separates us. This feeling of emptiness and loneliness is what propels you to shatter the ego boundaries that alienate us and to enter the *inside* of my story. You are my erotic lover.

THREE

Sex Symbols

Now we are ready to unfold an absolutely essential if ultimately provocative dimension of the cherubs' secret. All great mysteries arise in response to powerful yet simple questions. So if we were in a classroom, with the blackboards whitened with sketches of cherubs and notes on eros, Shechina, and sex, I would at this point step back and ask for questions, for all good spiritual maps should give rise to questions. Slowly a hand would be raised in the classroom...a second hand...a host of hands. The questions would begin. "If all that we have said so far is true—if eros is all these things other than sex—then why in the Temple of eros is the centerpiece two SEXUALLY intertwined cherubs above the ark?!? Why sex?! Why wouldn't the Temple use some other image of eros? Wouldn't a statue of a runner who has become the wind or a painter engrossed in her colors be a more fitting figure to perch atop the ark? If eros and love are, as you say, more than sex, then why does the Temple insist on using a blatantly sexual image?"

I would add questions of my own. "What is the magnetism of the cherubs and ark, which has so exercised the fascination of the world for millennia?

Why, as we saw in the ancient lore, is the dwelling place of the sexual drive itself—the lion of fire—in the Holy of Holies? What are we seeking to recover in our quest after the Temple's lost ark?

The questions could fill up this page three times. Let us ride their strength into the inner chambers, to unpack the secret of the cherubs.

Hebrew Tantra

If we stop to think even for a short moment, we realize that sex really is *the* great mystery of our lives. Two opposing groups, however, suggest very different approaches to sex. One powerful group of forces is arrayed in culture to prevent us from getting it. They tell us that sex is somehow wrong, immoral, or sinful. Even when we think we have gotten free of them they pop up again somewhere inside of us, wagging their fingers disapprovingly. And of course they remind us constantly of all the trouble sex has created in the world— from the Trojan War to the Clinton/Lewinsky drama.

Religion wants to affirm love and passion as virtues but divorce them entirely from sex. So moralistic religion works hard to erect boundaries that will protect us from the pitfalls of sex. And yet while we acknowledge that sex certainly requires a dimension of discipline, most of us believe that the moralists are wrong and that sex is ultimately—and overwhelmingly—good. Which brings us to the second powerful coalition of forces talking about sex. This group tells us: "Sex is wonderful—if liberated, it is the panacea of all ill; if repressed, the source of all evil." Freudians in disguise, along with many other schools of modern psychology, sexual revolutionaries, and a host of other intelligent folk are working hard to strip sex of its undertones. They want to liberate sex from love, eros, and their myriad complexities.

Indeed Freud himself was the most influential modern cheerleader at this party. Rooted in a hydraulic model of the psyche, which slightly confuses human beings and steam engines, his approach taught us that if we would just find a balanced way to release sexual tension, we would be healthy and happy. And yet those who achieved this vaunted balance were shocked to find that the same feelings of alienation, depression, and emptiness still plagued them. Okay—hydraulic equilibrium achieved—now what?

Since the sexual revolution, ostensibly uninhibited sex has been available in infinite variety in almost every imaginable social or commercial context, and yet we do not seem any happier for it. So much sex and so little pleasure. So many orgasms and so little satisfaction.

A few decades ago sociologist David Reisman called sex the last frontier. If this is true then we have crossed it and found it wanting. Psychologist Rollo May reminded us many years ago that patients rarely complain about sexual dysfunction or repression anymore, while it seemed to be the most common complaint in the days of Freud. Rather the malaise of our time is the lack of feeling or passion. Sex is all around, and yet no one seems to be enjoying themselves.

What is clear is that neither the moralist nor the many masks of Freud honor the mystery of sex in our lives. At this point let's turn to the Temple mystics, who affirm a radically different vision of the sexual. The Secret of the Cherubs. *Sod Hakeruvim.* The Kabbalistic tantra of Hebrew mysticism.

Contrary to the tenets of classical religion and much of psychology, Hebrew tantra insists that sex is integrally related to love and eros. There is no disconnect, not just because it is always nice if you love the person you are sleeping with. But also far more powerfully—and this is the Secret of the Cherubs—because *the sexual is the ultimate model for eros and love.*

Thirteenth-century Hebrew mystic Isaac of Acco said it most boldly: "Whoever has not desired a woman is like an ass and less than an ass; the reason being that it is from the *Murgash*—the sexual—that one understands divine service." Sex stands as the ultimate symbol because it both signifies and models the erotic experience in all areas of life. The goal of life is to live erotically in all facets of being, and sex is the model par excellence for erotic living.

Sex Is *the Answer*

Is there anything else that so grabs our rapt attention, incessantly pursues us, occupies our daydreams, fantasies, and yearnings? The Kabbalists state the obvious: God is trying to get our attention. Now I am not talking about the God who sends good people to burn in hell because they slipped up on one of his impossible demands. Nor even the Grandfather in heaven who hands out chocolate to do-gooders. Forget that God. The God you don't believe in doesn't exist. The God that exists for us is the personal erotic life force that courses through reality. The God we believe in is the vitality of eros. The God we believe in is the force for healing and transforming the world. The God who knows our name. That is the God who so clearly calls out to us that sex *is* the answer.

When religion splits us off from our sexuality, we correctly intuit that something is deeply askew. But sex is not a panacea. Sex is not a drug that will soothe away the lurking feeling of ennui that this cannot be all there is. Good orgasms do not a good life make. Sex is the answer *as a model and not as the sum total* of eros. Sex, if we will but listen, is a great master of the spirit—better than any guru, psychologist, rabbi, or priest. Sex can teach us how to reclaim the erotic in every aspect and element of our lives.

That is the essence of Hebrew tantra, the Kabbalistic secret of the cherubs. The core of Hebrew tantrism was the cherubic mysteries, which taught that the sexual was more than a force to be merely controlled or merely indulged. Rather the sexual in all of its intense pleasure is the model for all spiritual wisdom. The goal of spiritual living is to become a lover and to engage all of life erotically. Sex is our most important guide, offering glimmerings of guidance that pave the way to illumination. In Hebrew *Zohar* means "illumination" and is achieved when one lives erotically *in every facet of being*. The cherubic mysteries—which in this book we will unpack systematically for the first time in two thousand years—teach you how. This tantric system was the hidden core of the mysteries in Solomon's Temple.

Eros Everywhere

In the hidden teaching of the cherubs, the sexual is the ultimate spiritual master. Thus, deep understanding of the sexual is the ultimate guide to accessing the spirit in every dimension of our reality.

We are not talking about sexual technique. Sexual technique, even when important, is technical at best. Sexual technique can never make you a great lover. To be a great lover in all facets of your being you must listen deeply to the simple yet elegant spirit whisperings of the sexual. Nietzsche got something right when he said, "The degree and kind of man's sexuality reaches up into the topmost summit of his spirit."

In the previous chapter you just read a glimmering of what Hebrew tantra might mean when it says, "The sexual models the erotic." There we explored the four faces of the erotic:

1. Being on the inside
2. Intense yearning
3. Fullness of presence
4. The interconnectivity of all being

All of these are modeled primarily on the sexual. All of these qualities are essential to great sex.

"Being on the inside" means not on the inside of your sexual partner, for that is limited to the masculine sexual experience. Rather it is about being on the inside of the experience itself. Yearning is the essence of the sexual. So much so that it is often thought by poets and psychologists to be more pleasurable and intense than the fulfillment itself. Interconnectivity is nowhere more clearly manifested than in the sexual drive. We are born with an urge to merge. Finally, it is in the sexual where—in its ideal expression—we are most fully present to each other. Every gesture, fragrance, sigh, and whisper ripples through us as we listen deeply to the erotic instructions that well up from the depth of our soul's body.

All four of the primary faces of eros are modeled on the sexual. However—and this is the key—they are not exhausted by the sexual. It would be a great tragedy of the spirit if the only place where we experienced full presence, interiority, yearning, and primal interconnectivity was in the sexual. That would be to relegate eros to the narrow confines of the bedroom, when it needs to soar through our kitchens, our offices, our carpools, our classrooms!

In erotic living, we seek the realization of these qualities in every dimension of our existence. From work, to play, to politics, to intellectual pursuit—in all of these we seek erotic experience. Erotic engagement could become our daily fare if we just freed our eros from its old casing. These hand-me-down ideas of an eros that is only about sex have become threadbare. We must reweave the fabric.

The full pleasure of living, the joy of fullness and creativity, can only come when we reeroticize our lives. Until then, human beings will turn to the shadows of eros—rage, abuse, and violence—to remind themselves, through the intensity of those experiences, that they exist.

Baby-sitting Maya

Recently I had the questionable privilege of baby-sitting my brother-in-law's twelve-month-old, Maya, who is in the classical sense of the term quite cherubic. The cherub mystery in this case was that Maya was inexplicably wailing at top decibels. She wanted something and I could not for the life of me figure out what it was. All I knew was that she kept on crying out "Nana. Nana." Now, "nana" I knew. It means "banana," the essential tool of baby-sitting. So I kept trying to stuff bananas into Maya's clenched hands, which she would repeatedly thrust away, as if I were some illiterate idiot who understood nothing about baby talk.

Finally I distracted her with my vast repertoire of ridiculous baby faces and spoonfuls of every soft food available. Nothing worked until a spoonful of smashed sweet peas suddenly, mysteriously, quieted her down. When my brother-in-law got home I told him, "We had a hard half-hour there. Maya kept screaming out for "Nanas." So I tried to give her bananas, which she adamantly refused."

"So you gave her the sweet peas, eh?" Brad replied nonchalantly.

I blinked. "How did you know!?"

Brad explained, "When Maya started eating real food her favorite thing in the world was bananas. She thinks 'nanas' are the yummiest things around. But over time the word 'nana' has sort of transcended being about 'bananas' and has just become a general appellation for anything that falls under the category of 'really yummy.' So when she wants something yummy, like sweet peas or sweet potatoes, she just calls out 'Nana.' And since I gave her some sweet peas this morning, it figures that that is what she would have had on her mind."

I was floored! The mystery was revealed! What a feat of linguistic brilliance! Not only is my niece cherubic, but she is also a genius. So what if it wasn't my amazing repertoire of baby faces that had so amused her. This baby had brought me to satori. Enlightenment! I suddenly understood the whole conundrum of eros that had been sifting through my mind. Eros and "nanas" are the same thing! We have a little taste of sex—it's inordinately "yummy." It is called eros. But then we get a taste of cross-country skiing. It too is inordinately yummy. It too is eros. And what about writing that poem the other day. Erotic! That new CD. Eros!

Just as I thought Maya was talking about bananas when she said "nana," most of us think we are talking about sex when we say eros. Yes, eros is sexual, but it also transcends the sexual. Eros actually means all the places where I am fully present, on the inside, yearning and connected. Eros takes the sexual and lets it stand as the model for all that fills our deep desire. We are all crying out for eros, but instead of feeding us on the sweet divine stuff our soul craves, society is trying to sate our deepest desires with sex, which is like trying to stuff a baby with bananas when she really wants sweet peas! Give bananas to a baby who needs sweet peas and she will continue crying, her hunger unabated. Our society is in need of eros. So being fed only sex leaves us hungry, desperate, and crying out. We are calling out for eros. Not sex, eros.

Exiled into the Sexual

Now let's go back to our lost ark and its cherubs situated in the inner sanctum of the Temple. The ark in particular and the Temple in general are the mythic symbols of the Shechina, that is, of the erotic experience. That is precisely what the mystery texts mean when they say the Shechina dwells between the cherubs atop the ark. The fall of the Temple is thus not a mere historical event. In myth, the fall of the Temple is the fall of eros. This experience is called by the Kabbalistic masters *the exile of the Shechina.*

Now open your hearts and minds to hear the next sentence.

The exile of the Shechina means no less than the exile of the erotic.

But where did it go? To where was eros exiled? The answer is that the exile of the Shechina is *the exile of the erotic* into *the sexual.* That is to say, when the sexual is the only place where you can access the core qualities of eros, then eros, or the Shechina, is in exile. When the only time you feel that you are on the inside is in great sex, then the Shechina is in exile. When intense desire is a feeling you touch only before exploding in orgasm, then your life is poor indeed. The Shechina is exiled. Eros has fallen.

The secret of the cherubs is that sex is our spiritual guide. The rest of this book will outline in every chapter a particular quality of being that is modeled on the sexual. These are the essential qualities needed to live a life of wonder in body, mind, and spirit. However, we have lost our access to them. These qualities wind up not only being modeled by the sexual but also, tragically, being accessed in our lives virtually only in the sexual. As a result much of our lives feel drab and vacant—a pale reflection of what we once dreamed life could be. Our work, our friendships, our relationship to nature, knowledge, and the spirit, and to our families, neighborhoods, and communities—all of these have been disenchanted and deeroticized.

However we cannot live in a nonerotic world. So unconsciously we seek compensation. We look to get our erotic fix in the sexual. But this doesn't work either. For when you deeroticize all of the world except sex, then the sexual collapses as well. You see, we all have erotic needs. These needs require attention in all parts of life, but if we ignore them in all the other parts of life then we demand that the sexual fill all of our erotic needs. And so sexuality shrugs, collapsing under the weight of an impossible demand.

So as you can now see, the fall of eros brings in its wake the collapse of sex as well. The modern zeitgeist has slain all the gods save Aphrodite, the goddess of sexual love. Yet she cannot survive alone. We wonder why she has abandoned us. Why is sex not working? we ask ourselves incessantly. Foucault in *The History of Sexuality* suggests mockingly that we vaunt sex as our great secret and yet talk about it incessantly. Behind all of our talk about sexuality we are all frantically asking, Why has the Goddess not redeemed me? I finally *got some*...and I am just as depressed, lonely, and confused as I was yesterday.

Exile within an Exile

In the language of Kabbalists, we are now in an exile within an exile. The first exile of the Shechina is the exile of the erotic *into* the sexual. The second is the exile of the erotic *within* the sexual itself. The erotic is exiled to a very limited domain within the sexual: transgressive or illicit sexuality *that breaks your own boundaries.*

We have gotten to the point where we cannot even find the erotic in most of the arenas of the sexual. In order to touch the intense desire that brings us to a place deep in the infinity of the moment—on the inside of the inside— many people need a sexuality that breaks the boundaries of their own authentic story. We either downgrade or upgrade sex. The result of the first is adultery, degrading forms of pornography, and all varieties of sexual abuse. The second expresses itself in the search for sex in the form of the ideal true love. It is of course so ideal that it is inaccessible, leaving us forever fantasizing about the perfect lover or reading endless varieties of the same sexy romance novel. *We are desperately searching for eros in all the wrong places.*

The fall of the Temple is the mythic expression of the exile of the erotic not only into the sexual but also specifically into boundary-breaking sexuality. Listen in on a strange and wonderfully mythic Talmudic discussion!

A man is struck by the beauty of a particular woman.

His heart becomes sick. He falls deathly ill. Doctors are consulted.

Their response: "He cannot be healed unless he has sexual intercourse with this woman."

The sages' succinct reply: "Let him die and not sleep with her!"

Urge the doctors, "So let her stand naked before him."

"Let him die and she should not stand naked before him!" the sages respond.

"Let her talk to him from behind the fence [erotic conversation]," press the doctors.

Reply the sages, "Let him die and not be engaged by her in erotic conversation."

This striking case becomes a locus classicus in the debates of the academy for many generations to come. One of the central issues debated and recorded in the Talmud was the identity of the beautiful woman. One school held that she was married, a second school held that she was single. According to the school that said she was married, it is understandable why there would be opposition to a sexual encounter between our lovesick client and a married woman.

"And if she were single?" queries a voice in the Talmud. "Surely we should allow her to save his life through some sort of minimal sexual engagement, verbal, visual, or otherwise?"

"No!" roars a second voice from the pages. "For if we did so it would undermine the personal integrity of women."

"Well then," offers a third voice, "if she is single and he is single ... let them marry!"

"No, for if he married her," responds the same voice to its own query, "she would not settle his spirit [she would not satisfy his erotic need], for it is written, 'Stolen waters are sweet.'"

"Stolen waters are sweet." This terse epigram means quite simply that after being married the man's sexual excitement will recede and he will not be fulfilled. Only in the context of "stolen waters"—the thrill of illicit relations—could this man be sated. He is only interested in her as an already married or unavailable woman; once she is available, he will quickly lose his lust.

This is not viewed as the peculiar weakness of the man in the story. Rather, the man is a symbol of the times. And here we get to the essence of the text, where the wisdom masters draw a most provocative conclusion: *"From the day the Temple was destroyed the taste of sex has been taken away and given to sinners."*

That is to say, the "taste of sex" is experienced only in an illicit relationship! On the face of it the passage makes little sense. What could the fall of the Temple in Jerusalem possibly have to do with the varieties of sexual satisfaction?

Once we understand the mythic nature of the text, however, it begins to open itself up to interpretation. "The taste of sex" is another term for eros. The Temple, remember, is the seat of eros. The fall of the Temple symbolizes a mythic shift in the erotic psyche of the world, the exile of the Shechina, of the erotic, not only into the sexual but specifically into transgressive sexuality. Adultery is the paradigm in this passage of boundary-breaking sexuality. So the text suggests that in the tragic post-Temple world of fallen eros, man feels he can find erotic satisfaction only in the sexual. And then only in illicit sexuality.

It is not by accident that a thousand years later, the great Western love story sung by troubadours is that of Tristan and Iseult, who personify the sweet and mad passion of love. Of course, Iseult is another man's wife. Stolen waters. Or in a modern reincarnation of stolen waters, a movie called *Unfaithful* asks in its lead advertisement: "Would you risk everything in a moment of passion?" Of course the premise is that the moment of passion, the taste of sex, could only be available in the context of being "unfaithful." Marketing executives are our highest paid and often best psychologists. Even if not all of us yearn for that moment, most of us understand all too well the hole that such a "risk" is desperately trying to fill.

The yearning for a rebuilt Temple is not an artist's or carpenter's fantasy. It is rather the dream of a world in which raw eros—which today has been

exiled to illicit sexuality—will be accessed in the context of committed relationships. This text suggests that at least one of the goals of Temple consciousness is "to commit adultery... with your wife." The goal is to move beyond the
need for stolen waters and to be able to access the full power and passion of
the sensual within the context of your own highest story, where your own
waters are satisfying and sweet.

Healing the Split

The Shechina is exiled whenever sex and eros are split. An example: Jake, age
thirty-seven, works as a claims adjuster in an insurance firm. Often he works
well into the night. He feels oppressed by the routine and drabness of his
work. On days when he comes home feeling particularly empty he flips on
some pornography. His work is not erotic, so he looks for his erotic charge in
sex. The devastating truth is that even erotic sex in the context of a powerful
and committed relationship would not fulfill him. Nothing can substitute for
his very real need for eros at work. Certainly most forms of pornography,
which are essentially deeroticized sex, cannot fill his erotic needs. So he
winds up with a hangover—the kind you get from drinking too much cheap
wine. And work the next morning feels all that much more dead and depress-
ing. The Shechina is in exile.

Now the moralist will be quick to say, "See, he's right! Sex isn't the answer!"
Yet I for one, as a teacher and a human being, do not go with the moralists.
That is precisely the point of the secret of the cherubs. Sex *is* the answer.

The secret of the cherubs was an explicit tantric mystery studied, taught,
and practiced by ancient Hebrew initiates. Solomon was the great tantric
master who honored the sacred feminine. It was Solomon who wrote the
Song of Songs—an explicitly sexual love story that is understood by the tradition to be the holiest book of the Hebrew canon. Indeed the Song of Songs
is referred to by the masters as the Holy of Holies. This is not merely a literary
turn of phrase to emphasize its absolute centrality in Hebrew spirituality. It

is that and much more than that. It is also a veiled reference to the cherubs in the Temple's Holy of Holies, who stand as symbols of the Hebrew tantric mystery.

The Tantric Pilgrims

Three times a year pilgrims would gather in Jerusalem from all over Israel. These gatherings were called the Holidays of Vision (*Chag HaReiya*). A careful reconstruction of the sources suggests that on these holidays the adept pilgrims practiced visualizations, chanting, meditations, and a host of other spiritual techniques. These were the core of Solomon's mysteries. Scholar Mircea Eliade notes that there are profound parallels between both the Hindu and Buddhist varieties of Indian yogic tantra and the Western mystery traditions from Hermetic, Gnostic, early Christian, and Greco-Alexandrian sources. What Eliade fails to note is the connection these traditions might have had to the mystery cults of Solomon's Temple. One can well imagine that these mysteries were passed from the Temple initiates in Jerusalem to the Greco-Egyptian community of Alexandria. The biblical text itself implies that Solomon's wisdom and the mysteries of his temple were disseminated to all of the surrounding cultures. Indeed two great nineteenth-century mystical masters, Mordechai Lainer of Ishbitz and his teacher Simcha Bunim of Pshischa, already hint at a program of spiritual teaching partially rooted in goddess mysteries, initiated by Solomon and his wives. The mysteries of the cherubs are then not a Hebrew version of Indian tantra. They are quite the opposite, the possible *source* of the Indian yogic traditions as well as much of the great Western mystery traditions.

So our return to Hebrew tantra is a return to a fountain from which all these great wisdoms sprang. There are, however, two enormous differences between Hebrew and Hindu tantra in their classical sources. First, in much of Hindu tantra it is the avoidance of sexual release that allows the adept to rechannel the sexual energy inward and upward instead of outward. In

Hebrew tantra, it is the natural flow of sexual expression, including release, that models the lover's path in all arenas of living.

Second, in Hindu tantra the sense of the sources is that the partner is almost a sacred object. Sacred, but an object nonetheless. She is a symbol of the feminine principle, but by being the symbol she is fully depersonalized— a kind of nameless yogini who is a necessary aid in the spiritual tantric journey of the male adept.

In Hebrew tantra the partner is both a Shechina incarnation and fully personalized at the same time. The sexual, existential fulfillment and pleasure of one's partner is the primary ethical and erotic obligation of the Hebrew adept. The spiritual tantric journey is sacred only within that highly personalized intimate context.

Moreover, in the Hebrew tantric path the partners must share a committed relationship beyond the sexual. Naturally then there is no danger of splitting sex from eros in all facets of life. In the Hindu tantric model there was no committed relationship between the man and woman. For the Hebrew mystic this is the exile of the Shechina. Classic Hindu tantra (not its Western offshoots) limited eros to the realm of spiritualized sex, effectively divorcing it from all other facets of living. Sex became a limited spiritual activity that did not spill over into a day-to-day partnership and lifelong commitment.

It's All Art!

Whenever we keep eros confined to one narrow frame of being while deeroticizing the rest of the picture, the Shechina remains in exile. Sex is only one of the places where we exile the erotic. There is a wonderful Balinese saying that goes something like, "We do not have art—we do everything as beautifully as we can." When we build ugly cities where beauty is abused and people are depersonalized and then build a beautiful art museum, the Shechina is in exile. We exile the eros of beauty to the constricted precincts of formal art. The same is true of music. Music is not limited to symphonies or rock concerts. We are all musicians, and life is overflowing with music. Are you familiar with the off-Broadway show *Stomp*? There is no dialogue; it is all music and dance. The catch is that no musical instruments are used. The "instruments" are adapted from the fabric of everyday living: pots, pans, brooms, sinks, faucets, garbage can lids, bottles, bags, newspapers, hands, feet, virtually every part of the body—all of these are used to make music. The implication is stunning: We usually limit art to formal work by people we call artists, just as we limit music to formal instruments and musicians. Formal music and art need to model the erotics of sound and beauty in all aspects of our lives and not just in their narrow provinces. Music and art need to pervade all of life. Every moment is a canvas and possesses its own melody.

Rumi knowingly instructs us:

> *Let the beauty that we love be what we do.*
> *There are hundreds of ways to kneel and kiss the*
> *Ground.*

So too with falling in love. Just as it is nonerotic for art to exist only in a museum, so too it is nonerotic for love to exist only in a small circle of caring. When we fall in love with one woman or one man to the exclusion of all other people, the Shechina is in exile. When you are truly erotically engaged then through the love of one comes the love of all. For true love partakes in the essential connectivity of being. Unity is not divisible; it is holographic; in every moment of love are all the lovers and all the love in the world.

Too often love is merely a synonym for a radically narrowed circle of caring. We let only the smallest possible group—sometimes only one person—inside to our Holy of Holies. We feel alienated, deceitful, or apathetic about the rest of our lives. The Shechina is in exile.

An Erotic Hero—the Falafel Priest

Once—and I will never forget it—I unexpectedly stepped into the Holy of Holies at a falafal stand. We were returning from visiting my sons Eytan and Yair in summer camp near the town of Hadera in Israel. As we were leaving, my wife, Cary, spotted a falafel stand. Now falafel is a fried Middle Eastern food that I am less than fond of, and I hadn't eaten one in years. But Cary insisted, so I went along. Surprisingly though, as we stepped up to the simple falafal shack, there was something about the shopkeeper that made me want to order a falafel.

I took one bite of the falafel, and I swear to you, it must have been made in the Garden of Eden. I looked up and was bathed in pure love. The shop-keeper beamed at my pleasure. When we went to pay, he asked for six shekels. My jaw dropped—everyone knows a falafel costs at least fifteen shekels. And his was so unbelievably good. How could he take only six shekels? So I asked him. To which he responded gently, "Because that's what I need." That, my sweetest and most wonderful friends, is eros pure and simple.

To be erotically engaged at work requires only that you fully enter the inside of whatever you might be doing. When you do—whatever your work may be—worlds open up, opportunity knocks at your door, the angels sing, and you are filled with joy. So full are you with joy that the delight has no choice but to spill over—into your fried falafal, into the person who stands before you, into the very earth at your feet. Joy joins joy, and the earth brims with a new peace. This man did not leave his eros in his bedroom, he brought it with him to work every day. Somehow, with this, he made his falafal stand a Holy of Holies.

Dostoyevsky's Dad

Freud of course would have had the falafel king on the couch in no time. Freud's understandings, which have so colored our own unconscious view of the word, are the precise opposite of the secret of the cherubs. *For Freud every-*

thing is a metaphor for sex. For the Kabbalists, sex is a metaphor for everything. Freud was interested in reduction, in breaking everything down. He lived in an era in rebellion against 1,700 years of church domination, which had crippled science, freedom, and beauty. As a result, like most of the intelligentsia of his age, he automatically rejected spirit as a serious force. So Freud reduced everything in the world to sex.

The mystical project, however, is not about reduction; it seeks rather to raise up all the scattered sparks of light and return them to their source. To the Kabbalist all the processes in the world, including sex, are erotic at their core. For the Kabbalists sex points to the erotic.

This points to an even deeper distinction between Freud and the Kabbalah. For Freud, sex was a human release valve that allowed for the release of tension and therefore assured more effective functioning. For the Kabbalist effective spiritual living was not facilitated by releasing tension but by holding eros. A perfect world for Freud would be one in which everything was desexualized; then sex itself could perform its natural biological function of being a release valve without creating neuroses and complexes. For the Kabbalist the ideal world would be one in which the sexual modeling of the erotic was made conscious, with the resultant eroticizing of all of reality.

Certainly Freud was important in moving us to look at ourselves and pay attention to our inner lives. Yet his insight blurs because he cannot free himself from a deep inner need to reduce everything to the sexual. This becomes especially striking whenever Freud moves to understand the "higher" aspects of mankind—what we would call the erotic or the holy. A striking example is his reduction of a mother's love for her child to sublimated sexuality. In doing so, not only does he violate common sense and our deepest intuition, but he also loses all that is sublime.

Freud said after reading Dostoyevsky, "Here, psychoanalysis must lay down its arms," so overwhelmed was he by the sublime and erotic power of what he had read. And yet Freud, unable to resist, soon returns to Dostoyevsky, trying to locate the power of his presence somewhere in the recesses of his relation to his father.

Freud missed the point. The notion of a core spiritual erotic energy cours-ing through life was simply too much for his materialist mind to absorb. Life is not sublimated sex. It is eros itself. Freud's theories remain a great symbol of the Shechina's exile.

Similarly Kinsey, the great sex researcher who in documenting the sexual habits of Americans took much of sexuality out of the closet, nevertheless radically split sex from eros. Admittedly, he did so with much less sophistica-tion than Freud. For him, sex was a more simple and happy affair not much different from the mating of animals he had been taught to observe in his zoological training. Yet while for Kinsey sex remains a bland, zoological func-tion, and for Freud a more dark and deterministic force, for both of them the sexual remains uninspired and unerotic. Both Kinsey's and Freud's views ignore the soul of sex. To split sex from Eros so dramatically is to exile the Shechina. Both of these thinkers are seminal expressions of our society's disenchantment.

Supermodels

The Shechina's exile is all too apparent even in *Webster's* dictionary. *Webster's* defines *erotic* as "tending to arouse sexual love or desire." The sentence would be perfect without the word *sexual.* In the secret of the cherubs, sex always points beyond itself.

Sex is a kind of meditative practice for the common man. It is that area of his life that most clearly points beyond itself to something higher.

Paradoxically the place that understands this erotic secret well is the world of advertising. Even when television programs are bland and insipid, advertising is often erotic. We all realized long ago that advertising uses the sexual as a primary tool in its campaigns. Somehow we are meant to associate the beautiful woman with the sleek car.

Moralists often accuse the advertisers of a great moral wrong in this kind of advertising. After all, advertising seems to falsely suggest that we will somehow get the girl if we buy the car. I think we have all figured out that the girl does not come with the car. Rather, the implication is far more subtle. On some level this kind of advertisement actually intuits the secret of the cherubs. The profound implication of the girl/car nexus is that the sexual eros expressed by the girl is a model of the kind of eros the driver wants in his means of transportation. This profound and true idea drives much of advertising.

It is perhaps more than a telling coincidence of language that these glamorous women are called models. An obvious shoo-in for our theme! For essentially they are illustrators of the metaphysical (and physical) fact that sex models the erotic. Their sexual allure is used to pull at the erotic strings of our soul. When we buy into the ad we are chasing not the sex it displays but the eros modeled there, the eros we so deeply if subconsciously quest after. Models then become a handy visual and linguistic reminder of the fact that all we are really after is some good eros.

Mind the Gap

The Gap's ad campaign in the fall of 2001 shows slender stylish young ladies with a caption underneath that says, "My First Love." The reader/gazer/consumer expects some sexually provocative image or story to follow. Then comes the wonderful twist that makes this ad stand out. We see a picture of the model with a book—"My first love—Anaïs Nin," or with a tape, "My first love—the Ramones" ... or a photo, "My first love—my mom." What the Gap ads effectively did is suggest an expansion of the erotic beyond the sexual to include art, music, and personal nonsexual relationships. The ad plays off the Western mind, which expects the sultry story to fill in the blank of what is "love" or what is erotic. The Gap is ever so subtly suggesting that the Shechina needs to be liberated from the merely sexual. You can live erotically in all areas of life.

While we give kudos to the Gap for intelligent, soul-broadening advertising, it is undeniable that all too often Madison Avenue goes wrong by manipulating eros rather than serving eros. That is to say erotic manipulation is used to sell us products we don't need or want. Madison Avenue feeds on our eros-starved soul purely for the sake of uninhibited profit. That is not the exile of the Shechina, for indeed sex and eros are not split. It would be more accurate to describe Madison Avenue as pimping the Shechina—making her a prostitute, selling her wares to support "the Man."

Akiva—Mystic and Lover

In the Kabbalistic tradition, Akiva is the archetypal lover. He is a poor shep-herd who lived and walked in Israel only a few years after the death of Jesus. He witnessed the destruction of the Temple and understood deeply that the Temple was the axis of eros, and that eros is the essential force of attraction—the clasp upon the jeweled necklace that holds the whole world together.

Akiva, however, initially learns of eros not from books or old wise mas-ters. His life journey begins as he is shepherding in the fields, playing his flute for his God and his sheep. He is beheld late one afternoon by Rachel, the beautiful daughter of Kalba Savua, patriarch of Jerusalem's wealthiest aristo-cratic family. She sees him and she *knows*. Great love and passion are kindled. They marry against the fierce objections of her family. For marrying a simple-ton she is disowned. But with love and eros as their spiritual masters, Akiva makes his way to the academy and emerges twelve years later as the greatest spiritual master the Hebrew tradition has ever known.

To all his disciples he makes clear: my true teacher is Rachel. Not just because, as is usually understood, she urged him to study for many years away from home in the academy; but also because the love and eros they have between them were the greatest teachers of the spirit he ever had. Indeed the Kabbalists understand Rachel to refer both to the real woman who loved Akiva and as a metaphor for the goddess, for the Shechina. So when the Temple falls, Akiva needs to make people understand that for all of its magnificence and even holi-ness, in the end it is but a symbol of something more: it is the symbol of eros.

Akiva taught that when a man and a woman come together in sacred union, God is a third partner in their intercourse. They participate not only in the potential creation of new life below in the visible world, but also in the creation of new life above, in the divine. They fulfill not only themselves in eros, but they also fulfill God. "The Shechina dwells between them." Akiva is suggesting no less than that the Shechina, which dwells between the cherubs in the Temple, now dwells between a man and a woman in sexual union. Sexual union in the Kabbalistic tradition is the great mystical act that heals all the worlds above and below. The Zohar in a typical passage writes of man and woman:

> They should prepare themselves to be of one desire and one intent so that when they join they become one in body and soul; they become one in soul by aligning their wills in cleaving; when they unite in sexual union they become one in body and soul.... It is then that God dwells between them in unified oneness.

Eros, we now begin to understand, is the primal desire from which the world springs into being. God's eros created the world. Our lack of eros could destroy the world. Love or die. The mystics of every religion—those who lived on the inside—understand that this is not a mere metaphor. Every act of union causes and participates in divine union. The human being participates in the divine love affair even as God participates in the human love affair. For beneath the veil of illusion all really is one!

Song of Songs, Holy of Holies

Akiva had a second teaching, which takes us one step further on the path of eros and love. Akiva participated in a great debate with the other sages over whether to include the Song of Songs in the biblical cannon of Sacred Books. The Song of Songs is written as a dialogue between two lovers. "Let him kiss me with the kisses of his mouth.... His fruit is sweet to my mouth.... His thrust is upon me in love." The man responds, "Your lips are like the thread of scarlet... Your breasts are like two roes.... Your closed garden, your secret fountain."

As you can imagine, the sages of the day protested. The song appears to be a sexual love song, perhaps to be sung in ancient taverns and beer halls; what place could it have in the sacred writ? To this argument of the sages, Akiva has a twofold response. First, he says, know that the Song of Songs is a *mashal*, an allegory. Second, know that while all the books are holy, the Song of Songs is the Holy of Holies.

One way to read the text, which is the way it is usually read, is that Akiva is saying two distinct things. First, he says, do not be afraid of the content of this book; it is not about sexuality. The sexual is but an allegory for the spiritual love between the human being and God. Second, know that this great spiritual love is central to the religious endeavor. This book therefore is not only holy but the Holy of Holies.

That reading however is but a cloak that allows Akiva to hide his truly radical esoteric doctrine. This doctrine is no less than the Secret of the Cherubs—the spring of enlightenment from which we have been sipping this entire chapter. When Akiva says that the Song of Songs is a *mashal*, he means it is not an allegory but a model. That is to say, the sexual story of the lovers in the Song of Songs is a model for the erotic. The erotic, as we have seen, is identical with the sacred itself. This is Akiva's intent when he cries out with such passion and pathos that "the Song of Songs is the Holy of Holies!" This is not a casual metaphor affirming the importance of the book. It rather contains Akiva's deepest mystical intention. The Holy of Holies in the Temple, destroyed just a few years earlier, was for Akiva and the people the personification of eros. The cherubs reminded the people that the sexual was the window to the sacred. The secret of the sexually intertwined cherubs atop the ark was, you remember, not that sex *is* the erotic and the holy but that sex *models* the erotic and the holy.

The power of this idea does not fall with the destruction of the Temple. The fall of the Temple, insists Akiva, must not be the fall of eros. For every moment when life is engaged erotically, the Temple is rebuilt. Moreover, Akiva reminds a people who have just been disempowered politically that in the end political power structures are but illusion. The human being is powerful because by living erotically a person participates in and creates the divine union—because human consciousness and action are the touchstone of divinity.

Eros Expanded

Erotic fulfillment is reached when you expand the realm of eros beyond the sexual to embrace all of your existence. Indeed the root of the Sanskrit word *tantra*—*tan*—means "expansion." True tantric energy expands into all realms of life. This expansion is the goal of Kabbalistic tantra.

The Zohar weaves this esoteric teaching into a seemingly innocent passage. The original quote is so striking that I decided to leave it virtually intact. Read it slowly, almost as a tantric meditation.

> Every person must find himself in sexual union [of male and female]...for in that way the Shechina never parts from him. And if you will say that one who travels [and is separated from his partner and therefore separated from sexual union] the Shechina departs from him, come and see. Before a person begins his journey, he should organize his prayer—from a place where he is in sexual union—in order to draw the Shechina down on him before he sets out on his path. Once he has learned the order of prayer—and the Shechina dwells on him through his sexual union, he should set out on his way—for the Shechina can now remain with him...in the city or in the field.
>
> As long as he is on the way, he needs to be mindful of his path in order that the higher union, the Shechina, not part from him. Even when he is not in sexual union...this higher union does not leave. When he arrives home he should rejoice [be sexual] with his partner...for she is the one through whom he accessed the higher union with the Shechina.

This passage, part of the cherub mystery tradition, makes the merging with the Shechina *dependent* on sexual union. Clearly then, they are not the same thing. The goal is "higher union with the Shechina." The higher union takes place when someone has been able to move beyond the bedroom to transpose the sexual to that person's broader world—to greet the Divine at every doorstep, every crossroad, in every sparrow along the way. When the traveler returns he is instructed to again be sexual with his partner in order to recast his life once more in the model of the sexual. In this way sex leads him to Shechina.

It is in the move through the sexual to the erotic that we achieve the ultimate goal of the spirit: higher union with the Shechina, which leads to erotic fulfillment in every arena of living.

As Rilke aptly wrote of the ability of love to travel with us: "Believe in a love that is being stored up for you like an inheritance, and have faith that in this love there is a strength and a blessing so large that you can travel as far as you wish without having to step outside it."

Sensuous Study—The Erotic Text

Israel, Master of the Name the Baal Shem Tov, founder of the eighteenth-century Hebrew mystical movement called Hassidism, writes that the ecstatic swaying motion characteristic of Hebrew prayer is the swaying and rocking of a couple in lovemaking.

The Zohar writes that when one prays he must be aroused and become the feminine waters of the Shechina. Again the requirement is not for men or women to be sexually aroused when they pray, rather that all four qualities of the erotic modeled in the sexual find expression in prayer. It's about eros, not sex! Prayer is erotic.

We are used to thinking of intellectual pursuits as being somewhat dry. And even if ideas excite us it is clear that the mind is the primary faculty engaged in the pursuit of intellectual depth. Well, as you might expect at this point, the myth masters of Jerusalem had a markedly different idea. For them the engagement with wisdom was a more passionate and erotic endeavor.

Source after source uses sexual analogies as a way of describing the erotic nature of study. Elijah of Vilna, the founder of a great Kabbalistic school in the latter part of the eighteenth century, writes that one can study only if one has an *ever chai*, a throbbing phallus. Clearly the sage of Vilna did not mean that one has to have an erection when one studies. It's about eros, not sex! What he was suggesting is what I refer to as the textualization of eros. That is, after the fall of the Temple, the sacred study of text became for the Hebrew masters one of the primary places for erotic expression. So textual study became the place where one experienced:

- the fullness of presence
- the entry into the inside of a text, where student and text merge into one
- the yearning for divinity expressing itself in the yearning for deep understanding of the sacred text
- and finally the deep interconnectivity of being, realizing that all of reality is somehow expressed in the sacred word.

The Textualization of Eros

When the Temple was destroyed the masters knew that the holy writ of biblical myth needed to be expanded and deepened. The Temple, which was the archetypal object of erotic desire in biblical writings, was no more. Where was holy eros to be found? The ingenious and revolutionary answer for the masters, whispered to them from within the folds of the tradition itself, was the *textualization of eros!* The sacred text itself became the Holy of Holies in the Temple. Every student was potentially the high priest. The text itself was regarded as a living organism whose soul could be erotically penetrated by all who loved her sufficiently. From the inside of the text the word of God could be heard and a new Torah channeled.

The model for eros is virtually always the sexual. Mystical sources abound with the ritualized eroticism in the Synagogue service. Here is one image that unpacks itself from several Zoharic passages. The Torah scroll is taken out of the ark for public reading and study. She is undressed. Her lavish coverings are removed, revealing a scroll of bare animal skin. She is then laid on the altarlike reading table and rolled open. The reader places a phalliclike pointer on the spread parchment between the two scrolled sides and begins to chant the text aloud. The esoteric erotic mysteries are hidden in the most open of places.

In a tour de force the process of study is described in the Zohar much in the way the twelfth-century troubadours a hundred years before described their flirtation with their loves. In the romantic ideal of courtly love, though, the beloved remained forever beyond reach. In the more life-affirming image of the Zohar, the lover ultimately merges erotically with his beloved. (The following text, like most medieval texts, is written from a male perspective. New mystical texts need to be written today by women manifesting the Goddess.)

The Torah is like a beautiful woman who is hidden in a secluded chamber of her palace and who has a secret lover, unknown to all others. For love of her he keeps passing the gate of her house, looking this way and that in search of her. She knows that her lover haunts the gate of her house. What does she do? She opens the door of her hidden chamber but a crack and for a moment reveals her face to her lover, and then hides it again immediately.

Were anyone with her lover, he would see nothing and perceive nothing. He alone sees it and he is drawn to her with his heart and soul and his whole being. He knows that for love of him she disclosed herself to him for one moment, aflame with love for him. So is it with the word of the Torah, which reveals herself only to those who love her. The Torah knows that the mystic (the wise of heart) haunts the gate of her house. What does she do? From within her hidden palace she discloses her face and beckons to him and returns forthwith to her place and hides. Thus the Torah reveals herself and hides; she goes out in love to her lover and arouses love in him.

...Only then, when he has gradually come to know her, does she reveal herself to him face-to-face and speak to him of all her hidden secrets and all her hidden ways, which have been in her heart from the beginning. Such a man is then termed perfect, a "master," that is to

say, a "bridegroom of the Torah" in the strictest sense, the master of the house, to whom she
discloses all her secrets, concealing nothing.

The image in this text and the other sources cited above both in regard to
prayer and study are clearly erotic but not sexual. That is to say, the sexual is
quite literally not only a metaphor for, but as in this last image, also a model
for the fully erotic. To say that the Zohar's description is accurate is superfluous to anyone who has ever engaged a text in the serious and exciting business of holy amorous play.

Courting the Sacred

When I sit down to prepare a teaching the process goes something like this.
First is the attraction. I generally teach only what attracts me. I must have an
almost unquenchable longing to explore the subject. Second, I must be fully
present in the impassioned pursuit, in the investment of energy and attention, in learning its contours and plumbing its secrets. Finally, on the good
days, there is the ecstatic merging with the wisdom, when all the disparate
pieces fall together in an elegantly interconnected whole.

I once had such a romance when preparing a series of talks on the topic
of laughter. I had decided to give a lecture series on laughter, a topic that had
always fascinated me. To prepare, I gathered my ancient texts, bringing them
to a friend's apartment in the old city of Jerusalem. I barely emerged from the
apartment for days. I read source after source, but somehow they did not
make any sense to me. Ancient sources are very different from the modern
essay. The modern essay is too often "a lot that holds a little." The ancient
Hebrew wisdom sources are koanlike in their quality and are usually "a little
that holds a lot." Moreover you can only understand them if they decide to let
you inside. So I danced with them and flirted. They teased me, lead me on,
but then demurred and withdrew. Somehow it wasn't clicking.

Finally, one night I arrived at the apartment at 2 A.M., very tired and about
ready to give up. No, not just yet—one more time, I said to myself, and if not,

I am through with this topic. And as I slowly, gently read the text for the last time, it was as though light, a soft white light, illuminated the room. The words seemed to read themselves, and a single elegant sentence offered herself to me. And then thunder and lightning as I felt a wild erotic ecstasy and the text dropped veil after veil until she stood naked before me in all of her sensual splendor. I was on the inside of laughter. All the sources organized themselves in an instant and unfolded beautifully, as two distinct forms of laughter distinguished themselves in my soul and mind. Knotty issues that had troubled me gently untied themselves. And then, not more than six or seven minutes later, it was over. I was spent but happy.

But the story is not quite over yet. Exhausted, I gathered my books, and after sitting for a while I walked to the old walls of the city to find a cab back to my own apartment. I got into the cab, and the driver, Ari, wanted to talk. Truthfully, a quiet ride would have worked just fine for me, but such was not what the universe had in mind.

"So what are all those books about?" Ari asked. I knew I could not share with him the whole story so I said nonchalantly, "Just books I was studying."

Undeterred, he pressed on. "Well, what were you studying?"

Having little choice I answered, "I was trying to unpack the ontological and existential essence of laughter."

Now usually that is a conversation stopper. But Ari was undeterred; he went right on. "Laughter—the essence of laughter—that's easy. My grandmother told me about that."

At this point I was both bemused and interested: bemused because I had just spent three days in intense erotic encounter with this idea, and if he thinks he can just throw out a few words about such a profound topic, well... And yet interested, because I know that grandmothers are often wise and almost always worth listening to. And to my chagrin, even as I half expected it, he did it. He articulated in different words, in his grandmother's name, that great sentence of illumination that I had experienced but an hour before. Tears gently rolled down my cheek. It was much more than the affirmation of an idea. I knew that God was in me. I felt completely loved and embraced by the universe.

Everything I have described to you has nothing to do, and yet everything to do, with sex. I promise you that during this entire story, the sexual was absolutely the furthest thing from my mind. And yet the process of study was no less than a loving courtship leading to intimacy. The sexual models the erotic, but it does not begin to exhaust the erotic. At least for a few seconds on that night, I was on the inside of God's face in the Holy of Holies between the cherubs.

Where You Let Him In

Erotic experiences are available to us in every facet of our lives. We cannot live without them. To access eros we just have to make a decision to live high. This is the teaching of the Master of Kutzk, who once asked his students, "Where is God?" (In our terms, I would reframe the question: "Where is the sacred—the erotic?") One student pointed to heaven and another to nature and the third to the sacred writings. "Yes," replied the master, "yes, but where is God?" The students were silent.

Answering his own question, the master said, "God is where you let him in."

Why Is This Essential Now?

For many years the cherubic mystery tradition was not taught publicly and often not at all in the Hebrew wisdom traditions. This was not accidental. Hebrew tantra is an inseparable part of the whole Hebrew gestalt. In marked contrast to some of its Indian stepchildren and pagan antecedents, the Hebrew worldview was primarily rooted in a commitment to ethics. At the center of sacred works ethical action was seen. It was ranked far and above any other dimension of spiritual practice. So for the last two millennia after the Temple's fall the major focus of spiritual work has been making ethics an integral part of human life. As my grandfather used to say, "The most important thing is to be a mensch (Yiddish for "person with integrity"). For him, and for the tradition that produced him, ethics always trumped all other cards. *The problem, however, is that once we have incorporated ethics into the fabric of our lives, we find that they are not enough. We have still not filled the emptiness.*

If we do not reclaim the erotic for the spirit and the good, then its shadow will seduce us and our world to the worst of places. Fundamentalism is on the rise in the world because it offers a pseudo-erotic experience of community coupled with a pseudo-erotic worldview. Particularly sacred fellowship, with all of its passion and interconnectivity, is a key feature of the fundamentalist experience. Whether it be the community of mosque, church, or synagogue, the eros of communal belonging and caring is intoxicating. Communal ritual with its participatory song and drama, together with an all-embracing worldview that seems to explain away alienation and uncertainty, is undeniably seductive.

Fundamentalism is only pseudo eros, however, because ultimately it denies true interconnectivity. Too many all-embracing worldviews are built on excluding the "unredeemed" from their embrace. Fundamentalism in both its secular and religious varieties offers salvation only to the elite group that subscribes to its set of dogmas. Everyone else is an outsider and usually damned to eternal perdition of some variety. This is a violation of the core quality of eros—being on the inside. When you can be an insider only by making someone else an outsider then there is no interiority and no eros. This is precisely what we have termed pseudo eros. In your need to fill the emptiness, the other is degraded in order to attain the erotic feeling of being on the inside.

A second type of fundamentalist fellowship is seen in the communities of greed and accumulation. Greed and consumption move our lives because when the center doesn't hold, the pseudo eros of money seems the easiest means to fill the emptiness.

Paradoxically, more enlightened communities and individuals often seem weak and insipid, leaving us unmoved and uninspired. We turn to Yeats:

> *The best lack all conviction, while the worst*
> *Are full of passionate intensity.*
> *Surely some revelation is at hand.…*

The revelation at hand, that which we yearn for, is the secret of the cherubs—how to transform sexuality from a force to be controlled or a mere indulgence into the spiritual master that teaches us how to live erotically in all of the nonsexual dimensions of our lives. The old suspicious approach to sexuality is insufficient to create a world that is holy.

Imagine that a great sage from the twelfth century is resurrected. He rises from his grave and hears that there is a terrible war raging. He says, "I'll help you win this war. Hand me my sword and I can fight off a hundred people!" People would say to him, "Are you crazy? These are not the weapons of today. Today we have more sophisticated weapons. You push a button and you kill millions in one second." The potential for destruction is greater today than it ever was. Never has man felt so empty, rootless, and estranged, both from himself and his world. The old staid conventions are not enough. We need to return to the wine of ancient teachings but in the flasks of modernity. We need the Secret of the Cherubs.

Nachman of Bratzlav taught that new teachings are always hidden in a story. So allow us, like R. Nachman, to write a new story for you that reminds us we need to change our whole way of approaching the sexual.

There once was a king with a most magnificent wine cellar. It was said that this wine cellar had been stocked and guarded for forty generations. It was also said this cellar held carafe after carafe of a wine whose potency paralleled the elixir of life itself. Yearly the king and his men would partake of the treasured nectar.

One year during the ritual wine tasting, the king noticed that the flavor of the wine had changed. It was still the same sumptuous nectar it had always been, yet something had altered. Perturbed, the king sent for his wise men, his chefs, and his wine experts to taste and explain. All praised the wine's bouquet, its remarkable taste, but no one sensed a hint of change. Only the king knew that something uncanny had happened, and the wine was not the same. So he sent his messengers out across the kingdom to every vineyard and fine restau-

rant, to every wine garden and connoisseur. A small complimentary bottle was given to each with a request that all should send back a full review of the wine.

Not long thereafter the castle was flooded with reviews. "An astounding mix of musk and fruit." "The rarest of tastes." "A sumptuous bouquet." All rave reviews. All, that is, except for one. It read, "An extraordinary, unparalleled taste. But it has fully matured and will surely go sour within the year." The whole court gasped. Who would dare say such a thing about the royal vintage? The king roared, "Bring the writer of that review to me!"

The next day the royal court gathered to behold what rogue would dare criticize the king's vaunted wine. Imagine the surprise when they saw standing before the throne a young woman looking like nothing more than a barmaid. And indeed, a barmaid she was. The daughter of a tavern keeper, she managed the small vineyard on his property.

"Your Highness, I have spent my life among grapevines. When I taste wine I can tell you where and when it was made, how much rain fell that year, how much frost. Sometimes I can even tell what song the maidens were singing when they pressed the blood from the grapes. Or what thoughts the young men were thinking when they hoisted the crates. And when I tasted this wine, Your Highness, I knew it was the finest wine there had ever been. Each grape was nurtured with rapt attention. The soil, the climate, the whole atmosphere surrounding it was ideal. Yet I know that with all of its incomparable succulence, within a year it is destined to go sour. It has reached its peak, its perfection. It has been flawlessly aged. After this, its greatness will only decrease."

Amid the court's murmurings of disapproval the king considered long and hard. "What do you propose, then, that we are to do?" Without batting an eyelid, the woman replied, "Drink it all before it goes bad!" The king protested, "But there are thousands of bottles in that cellar! Each one is exquisite and irreplaceable. It has taken generations to deplete even a fraction of the treasure-house that is there! How are I and my men to drink it all within a year?"

" 'You and your men,' you say?! Your Highness, if you really want to know the intention behind this wine, the reason it has been so guarded and passed down through your royal line, I will tell you. Your ancestors who reaped this wine knew that it would one day be the greatest vintage ever made. And so they stocked the royal cellars with it, set guards around it, and created this yearly ritual of tasting in which the king and only his closest group of men would partake. Yes, you have been the honored guardians of this exquisite stock. But the wine was not made so that it would be cloistered away from the people all these hundreds of *years. The wine was made and it was guarded so that after these hundreds of years, when it had finally reached its perfection, it could be shared—with the entire kingdom. You have been the guardians, not the owners. That wine belongs to the kingdom, not to the king."*

The court was aghast. How dare anyone speak so presumptuously before the king? But a slow smile was spreading over the king's face. "So tell me, clever one. The point is just that the wine be consumed? The royal cellars will lie empty, the tradition of the yearly wine tasting will be lost. That is it, this whole magnificent ritual of wine will in one year's time be finished forever?"

The woman closed her eyes, as if listening to a far-off strain of music and said, "Tell me, Your Highness. If you go behind your castle, beyond your pleasure gardens, beyond your stables and hunting grounds, what would you finally find?"

"Nothing really. Just acres of overgrown, bramble-gnarled fields."

"If my intuition is not mistaken, Sire, those gnarled fields are no less than the grounds that birthed your precious stock of wine. Those fields could again be cultivated into a most glorious wine country. The tradition does not have to end. It could very well begin again. The conditions here are perfect, the land is well rested. It is calling out to again be fertile. It is in your hands to plant and reap this vineyard anew."

"No, my friend, it is not in my hands. It is in our hands. I appoint you overseer of the royal fields. You will direct the clearing and cultivating of the land. The royal vineyard will bear fruit again!" And so it was. The young woman became overseer of the richest vineyards the world had ever known. And within the year a great feast was had. It was no less than the celebration of the wedding of the king and the wine woman. The entire kingdom was invited. The treasure-house of wine was opened and emptied. For forty days and forty nights there was nary an empty glass.

It is time for the secret to be revealed and the wine to be drunk. It is time for a holy Dionysus to emerge and claim his place alongside the cherubs in the Holy of Holies. We've had enough of the sexual pathologies that poison our society—the violent fundamentalism, the abusive sexuality of the church, the vicious McCarthy-like witch hunts that falsely accuse, and the desperately empty sexuality of the everyday. These are all pathologies of the spirit that haunt our time. It is time to heal the split and reclaim the sexual as the master who can teach us how to access the erotic in all of life.

* * *

We have completed the first stage of our journey. Before we continue, let's retrace our steps to make sure that we're on firm ground.

We are unraveling the Temple mysteries. The Temple is the seat of eros. We have touched the four faces of eros—being on the inside; fullness of presence; yearning; and interconnectivity. These are all Shechina qualities. The words *Shechina, erotic,* and *holy* are virtually synonyms. We understand that the Temple in Jerusalem was the center of the mystery cult that taught that erotic living was the core goal of the life of the spirit.

We know that eros is very different from sex. Yet beyond eros, we also know that sexual symbolism was central in the Jerusalem Temple. The most striking of these symbols was the sexually entwined cherubs perched atop the Ark of the Covenant in the Holy of Holies. Yet why should this be so if the Temple is the seat of eros, and we know that eros is something very different from sex?

The answer is simple yet elegant and powerful. Sex and eros are different but essentially related. The relation is that sex models the erotic. That is to say, within the sexual itself are the most important hints of eros. From the nature of the sexual we learn what it means to live erotically.

Sex is neither our enemy nor our playmate—though it is sometimes both. Primarily, however, sex is our teacher, always hinting at the way.

When sex becomes virtually the only arena in which we experience erotic fulfillment then the Shechina is in exile. The exile of the Shechina is the exile of the erotic into the sexual. The redemption of the Shechina is therefore the reexpansion of eros from the narrow confines of the sexual back into the broad expanse of living. The goal of life is to live erotically in all facets of being.

Sex models the erotic but it does not exhaust the erotic. Sex at best can fill our sexual needs; but it can never fill our erotic needs. When sex tries to do what is beyond its power to accomplish, sexuality implodes on itself. We begin to find ful-fill-ment only in boundary-breaking sexuality, which becomes the only way we can experience eros. This is the Shechina in exile. The redemption of the Shechina is manifested when the taste of sex—eros—once again becomes part of the fabric of all the dimensions of our lives.

"Okay," you say. "I want to live erotically. So what are the specific qualities of the erotic, of being a lover, that the sexual models? Bring it down for me and make it real in my journey. How do I become a great lover in every dimension of my life?"

In the next stage of our journey we will outline ten paths of Hebrew tantra. In each of these paths the starting point will be the sexual. In each chapter we will identify a unique quality of the sexual that models the erotic. These include creativity, pleasure, imagination, transcendence, surrender, union, and many more.

These erotic qualities are manifested in our world most powerfully in the sexual arena. Sex tells us that these qualities are a genuine option in our lives. Once we know they are possible—for we have experienced their potent presence in our sexuality—we can begin to realize them in other aspects of our lives. We need to be lovers beyond the bedroom, even as the sexual hints at the way. This is the redemption of the Shechina. The end of the exile.

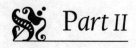 *Part II*

FOUR

Imagination

Sex models the erotic, but it does not exhaust the erotic. One of the core qualities of the erotic is imagination. The Zohar, the magnus opus of Hebrew mysticism, says explicitly in many places, "Shechina is imagination."

In common usage "imagination" is implicitly considered to mean "unreal." Indeed *unreal* and *imaginary* are virtual synonyms. To undermine the reality of an antagonist's claim we say it is "a figment of his imagination." In marked contrast, the Hebrew mystics held imagination to be very real. Indeed it would not be unfair to say that they considered imagination to be "realer than real."

The power of imagination is its ability to give form to the deep truths and visions of the inner divine realm. Imagination gives expression to the higher visions of reality that derive from our divine selves. Language and rational thinking are generally unable to access this higher truth. But the imagination is our prophet, bringing us the word of the Divine, which speaks both through us and from beyond us. This is what the biblical mystic Hosea meant when he exclaimed their God said, "By the hands of my prophets I am imagined."

But who are these prophets who so handily imagine God? Why don't *we* have access to the experience of prophecy? Because the Shechina is in exile, respond the mystics. The erotics of imagination have been exiled into the sexual. The sexual is the one place where virtually everyone is able to access the full power of imagination. This means that the core erotic quality of imagination no longer plays in all the arenas of our lives, where she is so desperately needed. For it is imagination that allows us to access the wisdom and vision we need to rechart our lives.

This exile of the erotic Shechina power of imagination is reflected both in our language as well as in our most intimate experiences. Our English word *fantasy* derives from the Greek word *phantasia*. It derived from a verb that meant "to make visible, to reveal." For the Greeks this fantasizing had nothing to do with sex. It meant "a making visible — through imagining — the world of the gods," the realm of pure spirit and forms.

So why in modern usage does the word *fantasy* first and foremost conjure up images of the sexual? We very rarely talk about economic, political, or social fantasies. We don't even talk about food fantasies. But we do talk about sexual fantasy . . . all the time. Just like the adjective *erotic*, the verb *fantasize* has found itself relegated to the narrow confines of the merely sexual. The reason is clear. In modernity we have lost much of our ability to make visible — to imagine — the deeper visions of the spirit. It is mainly only in the sexual where we use imagination to conjure up images of that which is hidden or not revealed.

The Exile of Imagination

Some years ago at a retreat on eros, I was trying, unsuccessfully, to get across a subtle point about the erotics of imagination. Desperate at my inability to transmit this idea, I decided to go for broke. The following day, I began with an exercise in imagination. You know the kind — "Imagine white light flowing through you, then let it turn to blue light, see yourself walking through a meadow with a beautiful streaming brook, see your grandfather come out to greet you," etc. I continued through a fairly complex imagination exercise for about twenty minutes.

I then asked, "How many of you had a clear experience?" Almost all the hands went up. I then, somewhat impolitely, challenged this assertion and accused my surprised audience of being a tad dishonest. After a funny and sometimes intense argument, most of the crowd admitted having much less of a clear visionary experience than they had initially claimed. We realized together that the New Age, with all of its good qualities, also fosters spiritual inferiority complexes. "What do you mean you can't see my aura? No ESP at all? I'm sorry but this just won't work."

I then proceeded to do a second kind of imagining with the crowd. A sexual visualization. Without being fully explicit to the group I invited them to imagine a sexual scene.

At the end of the process, I asserted my complete certainty that virtually every single person in the crowd was able to sustain, in graphic detail, a complete sexual visualization for a significant period of time. We all laughed. Slowly everyone realized that we had just grasped the point we were struggling with the previous day. Imagination, that gorgeous erotic quality, has been exiled into the sexual.

The simplest evidence of this is that we all have no problem accessing the power of imagination in the sexual. But we have enormous difficulty accessing that same faculty of erotic imagination not only in a nonsexual visualization but also in all aspects of our nonsexual lives. *The Shechina—eros, incarnate in imagination—has been exiled into the sexual.*

Mirrors of Desire

Fantasy and imagination hold the keys to many gates, not the least of which is the gateway to our freedom.

A story of the wisdom masters suggests that it was the erotic imagination of the Hebrew women in Egypt that set into motion the process of their liberation from slavery.

Pharaoh had insisted that the male slaves sleep in the fields separated from their wives. The women, in defiance of the pharaonic decree, visited their men in the fields. Their men, though, wilting under the oppression of slavery, had lost their potency. In response, the women found tools to evoke their men's desire—mirrors. With these they engaged the men's imagination, even when their bodies would not respond. The women, holding the mirrors in ways that reflected their physical beauty, would tease the men, saying, "Look, I am more beautiful than you." The mirrors are a symbol of women's erotic play, which resulted in the men reclaiming their potency. Fascinatingly, throughout the ages sex play has often involved using strategically placed mirrors.

The mirror can amplify the quality of imagination. As with the imagination, the mirror offers us an image, allowing us to see in a way that was previously hidden. If you hold a mirror in front of you, then you can suddenly see behind you. A rearview mirror is so helpful precisely because it shows you something your normal eyes cannot see. Or position a mirror at a sharp curve in a road and you can suddenly see around the bend, catching a glimpse of something to come that would otherwise have been hidden.

In the women's mirrors of imagination the men were able to reclaim vision, to see the lost images of their women's sexual beauty, which the oppressive burden of slavery had rendered invisible. It was, however, not primarily the women's bodies that were made visible by the mirrors; it was the men's. The women taunted them to see their own beauty. "Look, I am more beautiful than you." Mirrors are a tool of imagination because they allow us to see images of ourselves that would otherwise be inaccessible. To see oneself making love reveals a whole other image of the erotic self. According to one biblical tradition, this erotic play was itself the beginning of the liberation. In erotic play the imagination is engaged. Once the men were able to reaccess their imaginations, the images of freedom were not long in following. The Exodus from slavery became just a matter of time.

Sexually erotic imagination was then the model and catalyst for politically erotic imagination. About this the Talmud writes, "In the merit of the righteous women of the generation, the Hebrews were redeemed from Egypt!" When we think of typical "righteous" women, we rarely imagine troops of women with sexual paraphernalia going to seduce their men in the fields. But that is the precise righteous act to which the tradition refers. The fact that our idea of righteousness is at odds with the sexual is yet another sad example of the Shechina in exile.

Crisis of Imagination

The greatest crisis of our lives is neither economic, intellectual, nor even what we usually call religious. It is a crisis of imagination. We get stuck on our paths because we are unable to reimagine our lives differently from what they are right now. We hold on desperately to the status quo, afraid that if we let go, we will be swept away by the torrential undercurrents of our emptiness.

The most important thing in the world, implies wisdom master Nachman of Bratzlav, is to be willing to give up who you are for who you might become. He calls this process the giving up of *pnimi* to reach for *makkif. Pnimi*, for Master Nachman, means the old familiar things that you hold on to even when they no longer serve you on your journey. *Makkif* is that which is beyond you which you can reach only if you are willing to take a leap into the abyss.

Find your risk, and you will find your self. Sometimes that means leaving your home, your father's house, and your birthplace, and traveling to strange lands. Both the biblical Abraham and the Buddha literally did this. But for the Kabbalist the true journey does not require dramatic breaks with past and home. It is rather a journey of the imagination.

In the simple and literal meaning of the biblical text Abraham's command is *Lech Lecha*—"Go forth from your land, your birthplace, and your father's house." Interpreted by the Zohar, it is taken to mean not "go forth" but "go to yourself." For the Kabbalist this means more than the mere quieting of the mind. The journey is inward, and the vehicle—imagination. For imagination is the tool that allows us to image a future radically different from the past or even the present. That is exactly what Abraham was called to do—to leave behind all of the yesterdays and todays and to leap into an unknown tomorrow.

It is only in the fantasy of reimagining that we can change our reality. It is only from this inside place that we can truly change our outside. The path of true wisdom is not necessarily to quit your job, leave your home, and travel across the country. Often such a radical break indicates a failure rather than a fulfillment of imagination. True wisdom is to change your life from where you are, through the power of imagination.

Think "Cookies!"

Virtually every crisis at its core is a failure of imagination. Some years back, I took off three years from "spiritual teaching" to get a sense of what the world tasted like as a householder. I took a job at a high-tech company and from that relatively nondemanding perch began to rethink my life and beliefs.

During this period, I did a bit of consulting with Israeli high-tech start-up firms. Truth is, I had little good advice to offer, but some of the high-tech entrepreneurs who had been my students would call me anyway. At one point, I received a call from a small start-up firm in Ramat Gan, Israel. The problem: They were almost out of venture capital, their market window seemed to be rapidly closing, and their research and development team was simply not keeping pace with their need for solutions.

Apparently, the problem lay with the elevator. The company was on the top floor of an old warehouse. The elevator was small, hot, and inordinately pungent. By the time the R & D teams would get through the daily morning gauntlet of the elevator they had lost some of their creative sparkle. The president was convinced that this experience dulled their edge just enough to slow down the speed and elegance of their solutions. What to do? I have to confess to you, dear reader, that I had not the slightest idea.

Our meeting was on Friday. As was my custom, I went home for the Sabbath and consulted with my own private consultant, my then-eight-year-old
son, Eitan. When I asked him what I should tell the company, he laughed and
said somewhat mockingly, "It's simple, Dad—cookies." I did not find this
particularly funny. I raised this subject with him several times, to which he
would only respond, with maddening gravitas, "Cookies."

Finally I gave up on him. Several days later I went to tell the president I
had found no solution. I was going up the same malodorous elevator when
in a blinding flash I realized what Eitan meant. Cookies! Of course! We had
all been focused on elaborate ways to fix the elevator or to move locations.
Eitan—with the simple brilliance of a child—reminded us of the true issue
at stake. The crux of the matter was not the elevator, *it was how the R & D
team felt when they left the elevator.* So what to do? Cookies. We set up a table
with juices, fruit, and healthy cookies right outside the elevator. So even
though the ride up the elevator was terrible, people would spend the whole
ride eagerly anticipating the goodies that awaited them. No one else
could envision Eitan's simple yet elegant solution because their imagination was "stuck in the elevator." A simple paradigm shift was inspired by
re-imagining.

Like so many of eros's expressions, we fear imagination, for imagination
holds out the image of a different life. It challenges our accommodations to
the status quo. It suggests that all of the compromises upon which we have
based our lives might not have been necessary. Our fear of imagination is our
fear of our own greatness. So we work hard to kill it. We tell children to grow
out of it. "It's only your imagination," we tell them, as if this was somehow an
indication that "it" was therefore less real.

It was Albert Einstein's gift of imagination that allowed him to formulate
the concept of relativity. Einstein literally imagined what it would be like to
travel on a beam of light. What would things look like? What would another
traveler, on another beam of light going in the opposite direction, look like to
him? Without leaps of imagination, no growth is possible and the spirit pet-
rifies in its old frozen masks.

Free to Dream, Dream to Be Free

Erotic imagination is about the ability to see beyond the status quo. This is the deep intent of a second group of wisdom masters who, like those we met earlier in the chapter, also credit the liberation from Egypt to the power of imagination.

The great Exodus began with a man who had a dream. He was a man by the name of Nun, a Hebrew slave under Egyptian rule. One morning he awoke, stunned by his night imaginings. He had dreamed what seemed to be the unimaginable: He saw a time when the Hebrews were free! More than free, they were courageous warriors responsible for the dignity of their own destiny. News of the dream spread. It is said that the hope inflamed by this vision unleashed the dynamics of revolution, which ultimately led to freedom.

Although it would take many years for it to become real, this dream was the true beginning of the Exodus. Slavery ends when we can reimagine ourselves as a free people. Nun was none other than the father of Joshua, successor to Moses, who led the people into the Promised Land. All freedom begins with our willingness to stand and say, "I have a dream!" And even if we don't get to the Promised Land, we may well set into motion currents of redemption that will eventually heal our world. If we don't get there, perhaps our children will. Nun's entire generation died before reaching Canaan. Yet all of his grandchildren grew up in the Promised Land.

The Possibility of Possibility

Nikos Kazantzakis, a prophet of imagination, writes, "You have your brush and your colors, paint paradise and in you go." This is a near perfect description of the spirit that animates the biblical myth ritual that yearly celebrates the Exodus from Egypt. Every year on the anniversary of the Hebrew Exodus, people gather for Passover, a uniquely dramatic biblical myth ritual. Unlike the Fourth of July or other freedom anniversaries, it revolves around not commemoration but imagination.

The guiding principle of the holiday is: Every person is obligated to see him/her self as if they left Egypt. This Talmudic epigram, the guiding mantra of the ritual, is explained by the Kabbalists as an invitation to make a personal re-imagining of the most fantastic kind. You are in Egypt—your own personal Egypt. The word *Egypt, Mitzrayim* in Hebrew, literally means "the narrow places," the constricted passageway of our life's flow. *Egypt,* which Kabbalistically is said to incarnate the throat, symbolizes all the words that remain stuck in our throats; the words we never speak and the stories of our lives that remain unlived, unsung, unimagined.

We are slaves. Slavery for the Kabbalist is primarily a crisis of imagination. Consequently, healing slavery is a ritual of imagination. For an entire evening, we become dramatists, choreographers, and inspired actors. Our first step on our path to freedom is to reimagine our lives. As George Bernard Shaw reminds us, "Imagination is the beginning of creation. You imagine what you desire; you will what you imagine; and at last you create what you will."

God is the possibility of possibility—limitless imagination. The first of the Ten Commandments is "I am God." When this God is asked to identify himself, he responds, "I will be what I will be." That is, "You cannot capture me in the frozen image of any time or place. To do so would be to destroy me." It would violate the second commandment against idolatry. Idolatry is the freezing of God in a static image. To freeze God in an image is to violate the invitation of the imagination. It is to limit possibility.

Homo Imaginus

Bachelard was right when he wrote of imagination, "More than any other power it is what distinguishes the human psyche." Or listen to Norman O. Brown, the twentieth-century prophet of eros: "Man makes himself, his own body, in the symbolic freedom of the imagination. The Eternal Body of Man is the Imagination." We turn to the Hebrew mystical master Nachman of Bratzlav. "It is for this reason that man was called Adam: He is formed of *adameh*, the dust of the physical, yet he can ascend above the material world through the use of his imagination and reach the level of prophecy. The Hebrew word for 'I will imagine' is *adameh*."

For Nachman, the core human movement that gives birth to our spirit is the evolution (within the same root structure) from *adama* to *adameh*. *Adamah* is ground, earth, Gaia. Yet it can also be read as *adameh*, "I will imagine." Man emerges from Nature to live what philosopher Joseph Soloveitchik called "a fantasy-aroused existence."

Imagination is not a detail of our lives nor merely a methodological tool. It is the very essence of who we are. We generally regard ourselves as thinking animals, *homo sapiens*. Descartes's "I think, therefore I am" is hardwired into our cultural genes. Yet biblical myth offers an alternative understanding of the concept of "humanness." The closest Hebrew word to *human* or the Latin *homo* is *Adam*. The word *Adam* derives from the Hebrew root meaning "imagination" (*d'mayon*). The stunning implication is that the human being is not primarily *homo sapiens*, but what I will call *homo imaginus*.

At the very dawn of human existence, man is described as being created in the divine image. "Divine image" does not mean a fixed and idolatrous copy of divinity. God has no fixed form. God is, instead, the possibility of possibility. Recall that we understood the biblical opposition to idolatry as being grounded in precisely this refusal to put God in a box. Consequently, human beings being created in the divine image needs to be understood in two ways. First, humanity is not so much "made in God's image" as we are "made in God's imagination"—a product of the divine fantasy. Second, the human being himself participates in divine imagination—*homo imaginus*.

How different this understanding is from the bleak depression of modern existential thinking! Our longing for the good is dismissed by Sartre as a "useless passion." Human imagining, writes Camus, condemns us to misery, for it is absurd. We long for goodness, beauty, and kindness in a world perpetually marred by ugliness, evil, and injustice.

But for the biblical mystic, our erotic imaginings of a world of justice and peace are the immanence of God in our lives. Our creative discontent, which drives us to imagine an alternative reality, is the image/imagination of God beating in our breast. The cosmos is pregnant with hints that guide our imaginings. We are called to heal the world in the image of our most beautiful imaginings. The eros of imagination is the elixir of God running through the universe.

Creating God

Imagination is powerful. Very powerful. "Think good and it will be good," wrote Menachem Mendel Schneerson, the last master of Chabad mysticism. This is true not merely because of the psychological power of positive thinking, but also because every imagining gives birth to something real that eventually manifests itself in the universe.

Imagination is transformative not only on the human plane; it has a powerful effect on the divine scale as well. Kabbalists teach that each dimension of divinity, known as a *sefira* in Kabbalah, has a color that incarnates it. By ecstatically imagining the colors of the *sefirot* and combining them according to the appropriate mystical instructions, one can actually have an impact on the inner workings of the divine force. The Zohar is even more audacious, portraying man creating God in his image—that it to say, in his imagination. Unlike for the philosopher Feuerbach, who called human imaginings of God mere projection, for the Zohar such imagination simply reinforces the substantive reality of God. Or to put it slightly differently, while there is a limited truth in saying that God is a figment of human imagination, we need to remember that imagination is a figment of God.

The difference is simple. For the Kabbalist, imagination is not childish fancy. It is the spiritual reality called forth by the sacred child within. The God we do not create doesn't exist. Yes, there is a divine force that exists beyond us. Yet there is also a powerfully manifest current of divinity that is nourished by our being. The act of nourishing, sustaining, and even creating divinity is called by scholars of mysticism theurgy. The term expresses the human ability to dramatically impact and even grow God. One of the great tools of theurgy is imagination. In fact, theurgic imagination is the medium and message of a Kabbalistic rereading of "In the beginning." This first string of letters in the Bible, *"bereshit bara elokim"* can be reread as *"b'roshi tbara elokim"*—in my mind God is created.

A Pilgrimage Beyond Routine

If imagination can change God, it is certainly a sacred path and vital tool in our everyday lives. Remember that the path of imagination is the path of the prophet. "By my prophets I am imagined." The prophet symbolizes the divine energy of transformation that reminds us that the status quo is not holy. *What is* is not necessarily what needs to be.

One wisdom text reads, "Had God not taken us out from there, we, our children, and grandchildren would still be slaves to Pharaoh in Egypt." Clearly this is not a reasonable claim to make for the descendant of a Hebrew slave. After all, the Pharaohs are long gone, leaving behind only their pyramids to be remembered by. Rather it is a statement about the tyranny of inertia, the idolatry of the status quo: "This is the way things have always been, son...don't rock the boat." It is divine imagination that breaks the status quo, freeing us from our Egypts.

The prophetic imagination, with which we are all potentially gifted, insists that things can be different and better. Three times a year, taught the biblical myth masters, at least one member of every Hebrew family should make a pilgrimage to Jerusalem. The purpose of the pilgrimage was to access the Temple energy of eros in which imagination played an essential part. In the ecstasy of the Temple service, particularly during the autumn Feast of Tabernacles,

Sukkot, nearly all of the participants flirted with their prophet selves. The Hebrew word for these tri-annual Temple pilgrimages is *aliyah le'regel*. Literally this means something close to "going up, ascending, by foot." Closer reading reminds us that walking—or going "by foot"—is our most automatic activity. Hence the Hebrew word for *routine*, a virtual synonym for the status quo, is *hergel*—deriving from the Hebrew root *regel*, which also means "foot." Just so, our English word *regular* is a direct and obvious descendent of *regel*. And so a better translation of the Hebrew term for Temple pilgrimage—*aliyah le'regel*—might be "transcending routine, going beyond the regular, the status quo." How? By accessing the prophet archetype within, and with that prophetic strength reimagining life beyond its ruts and routines.

In the areas surrounding the Temple there were imagination chambers designated for prayer, meditation, and visualization. There the temple mystics would chart their journeys into the depths of imagination and soul where God is found.

Yet we are beyond the day when the spirit of imagination is reserved for spiritual elites. In our divine core, we are all prophets, architects of our own Temples. Remember that Bezalel, artisan of the mini-Temple in the desert, was a master of imagination. The very word Bezal-el is a play off an earlier biblical phrase, *bezel-em El-ohim*, meaning "in the image of God." In our unpacking, human beings participate in divine imagination and are thus invited to be the artisans of their lives. The raw materials, colors, and dimensions of your life's canvas are a given. How you mix the colors, weave the material, even choose the picture to draw on the canvas, are your artistic privilege and obligation. To be the artist of your own life—to be your own creator—is both the highest level of the sacred and the most profound expression of our glorious, our wondrous, humanity.

In a paradoxical set of mystical texts, Bezalel, the master craftsman of the book of Exodus, receives no clear blueprint from God or Moses on how to build the tabernacle. And yet he builds it in accordance with "God's will." For the Kabbalists, this is a hidden allusion to the power of holy imagination to intuit cosmic truth. When the mystics suggest that Bezalel is "taught by God," they speak in code. The artist is "wise of heart," "filled with the spirit of wisdom, intuition, and intimate understanding." All of these draw their inspiration from the breath of divine imagination.

Temples of Imagination

In the mystical tradition, God shows Bezalel a vision of a tabernacle of flames. This apparition fires Bezalel's imagination and guides him in erecting the desert Temple. The careful reader of the Exodus myth cannot help but notice the other image of gold that emerges from the fire, namely the golden calf.

The golden calf emerges from the fire of uncertainty. The tradition tells us that Moses is to come down the mountain toward evening on an appointed day. He has made a rendezvous with the people. Moses is the parent figure. He is security and comfort for the newly freed slaves. But Moses is late. The biblical commentators tell us there has been a miscommunication. Moses thought they had set the time for Wednesday evening; the people thought it was for Tuesday evening. They enter a twenty-four-hour limbo. What happens in this crisis of uncertainty? Can the slaves reimagine themselves as free people without Moses?

Their anxiety as they wait for Moses to come down the mountain is a test of their freedom. Will they be able to hold the center in the emptiness of their uncertainty? The answer is no. The people are not yet free. They are overwhelmed by the prospect of being free, yet responsible, actors in their own drama.

So they build an idol, the golden calf. An idol, you recall, is a "graven image." An engraved fixed image is a false certainty, a failure of imagination. In the language of the mystic Tzadok the priest, who expresses a theme that runs throughout Hebrew mysticism, they fixate on the face of the ox. The ox is only one of four images that, according to Ezekiel, are engraved on the cosmic vehicle, God's chariot. The others are the faces of an eagle, a lion, and a man. The chariot is the ultimate Hebrew mandala image. It is the locus of mystical meditation on the Divine. Tradition has it that during the theophany of mystical encounter at Mount Sinai the people were gifted with this precise vision of the divine.

They actually saw the four faces on the chariot. The only problem is that later they chose to focus on only one of the images—the face of the ox. The golden calf is a manifestation of the ox face. It is precisely such exclusive focus on only one image that short-circuits the imagination. "Getting stuck" is often caused not by imagination's absence but by the overbearing presence of one image. The Zohar teaches that the sin of the golden calf was that the people became so transfixed by one image that all other possibilities were blocked. This narrowness of vision is the unifying theme in the story. Initially the Hebrew's fixation was on Moses; they literally could not imagine life without him. When Moses disappeared, they were unable to wait for his return and transposed their Moses fixation onto the calf.

What Are You Waiting For?

There is much in our lives that evokes images of waiting. We are not fully realized—we await some future which we believe holds the secrets of our transformation and healing. But that future is fully available to us in the present. The secret is in how we wait. One image of nonerotic waiting was given to us by Samuel Beckett in *Waiting for Godot.* That play captures the all-pervading sense of ennui, despair, and hopelessness that comes when one loses all sense of present and presence, waiting instead for a fantasy messiah. This is the shadow of imagination: the inability to heal and repair the world because we are paralyzed by imaginary redeemers whom we await, hoping that they will finally make everything all right.

It is easy to get stuck in imagination. I am reminded of the story of a meditation teacher who gave an assignment to his students to sit in isolation and imagine themselves as something radically different from what they had ever imagined themselves to be. When the time came for the students to emerge from their meditation, one student didn't appear. Hours passed. The ashram was searched. Finally finding the young initiate in a broom closet, they invited him to come out and join the group. He said he could not emerge, for he had imagined himself as a bull. His horns were simply too wide to fit through the door, and so he sat.

Every facet of eros has its own shadow. We must be careful not to get lost in imagination. On the contrary—imagination needs to be the place where we "get found."

The essential act of imagination is transformative in and of itself. For as the contemporary biblical mystic Abraham Kook wrote in the early twentieth century, "Whatever you imagine, exists." Your imagination discloses the way things could be and, on an inner level, the way they already are. An alternative image of waiting is supplied by the biblical mystics. This is not the passive and resigned waiting for Godot, but waiting for Messiah, not as some future event that will make it all better, but as a reality, available in the full presence of the present. Messiah waiting is a process of active imagination that brings in its wake the social and spiritual activism of *tikkun*, the healing and transformation of the planet. In "waiting for the Messiah" we give birth to the first level of the existence of a better world.

In-Fancy

Little Jane comes to us in tears. "I wished Tommy would get hurt and he did. But I didn't mean it." We comfort little Jane, wanting her to know that she is not responsible for the accident that happened to Tommy. And we are partially right, but only partially. The essential intuition of the child needs to be validated and not explained away. Our kids need to know that they are powerful. They can reimagine the world, for good or for evil—to hurt or to heal.

Imagination is an essential part of responsibility. We need to nurture our infancy, our *in-fancy*, to encourage its power rather than undermine it with scoffing and ridicule. For this reason we intuitively look for our children to create a better tomorrow for all of us. Hebrew tradition interprets the word *banim* to mean both "children" and "builders." Children are always building imaginary realms and constructing fortresses and castles with such exquisite imaginary aptitude. Children are always dashing around as superheroes, saving banks from robbers, and creating elaborate family scenarios with a few dolls.

We have long since forgotten our true nature as agents of transformation. We have forgotten that we are superheroes. At the backs of our closets and eaten away by moths, our capes are long forgotten. Birds don't fly because they have wings; they have wings because they fly. We are what we imagine ourselves to be. The wings always come in good time. We need to reclaim our capes of holy imagination and heal our fear of flying.

The Twilight Zone — the Capacity to Be

One of my favorite, even if occasionally frightening, television shows when I was growing up in America was *The Twilight Zone*. Embedded in my memory is an episode about a boxer who loses a fight as his young son watches the contest at home on television. The son believes what the father does not, namely that Dad really can win the fight. So with his passion, his conviction, and the great love of a son for his father, he summons up all his inner concentration and tries to reimagine the fight. Lo and behold, we see the fight being replayed on the TV screen, and this time Dad wins.

When Dad comes home a few hours later, the son tells him what happened. Dad, of course, thinks this is sweet but childish nonsense. "No!" his son says desperately. "You've got to believe. You've got to believe." The father ultimately cannot bring himself to believe, neither in himself, his son, nor the power of imagination. For the third time we see the fight replayed on the screen before the father and son. The father loses as his son cries.

When raising a child, the parent often has to teach the distinction between the real and the illusory. And yet the child also must raise the parent, reminding him that imagination is real and possibility is infinite. Such is the deep wisdom of the following wonderful story told by the mystical master Nachman of Bratzlav.

The king's son seemed to have gone mad. He sat, stark naked, underneath the king's table, claiming he was a turkey. For quite a while, he had not come out from under this table where, making soft gobbles, he took his meals and slept. Oh…I forgot to mention—he was stark naked because, as he explained, nobody ever saw a turkey in human clothes. All the king's analysts and all the king's therapists couldn't put his son back together again.

Finally a wise old man, who was really very young, came and offered to heal the prince. Well, no one had heard of this old man, but the king, being rather desperate, consented to his offer. The old man promptly went and, much to everyone's consternation, sat under the table, stark naked, with the boy.

"What are you doing here?" asked the very confused and surprised prince.

"Why, I am a turkey," responded he old man.

"Well…I guess that's okay."

And the two became friends, as only turkeys can. Some days went by and the old man put on a shirt.

"What are you doing?!" cried out the boy, "I though you were a turkey."

"Why, I am," said the man, "but is there any reason a turkey cannot wear a shirt?"

The boy thought, and truthfully, although it did seem a bit improper, he could think of no substantive reason why a turkey couldn't wear a shirt. And if a turkey could wear a shirt, well, it was a bit chilly, so he put on a shirt as well. And so the process continued to pants, shoes, and eventually to sitting at a table, until the prince was fully healed.

Often a child seeks to compensate for the pathologies of society. The kingdom suffers from a lack of imagination. A lack of imagination is a lack of soul. So the child rebels and seeks healing through an increase of imagination. Yet it does not always hold that an increase of imagination is an increase of soul. Sometimes we overdose and lose ourselves in the very imaginings that were to be our healing. Often such overdosing is the key to the psychological reality maps of children. Then the child can only be made whole if we enter with them into the world of imagination. Our healing can only flow from that inner place. The underlying therapeutic principle can be summed up in two words: empathetic imagination, which is essential not only to psychological healing but also to all authentic relationships.

Next time you are in an argument, step out of the circle of conflict and imagine yourself as your beloved. Try to experience the argument through his or her psyche. Similarly in biblical myth tradition, amplified by the Kabbalists, God is radically empathetic to the suffering of every individual. To be a lover is to be like God—to enter into the space of your beloved so you can receive the full depth of their story, including their loves and triumphs, but especially their hurts, fears, and vulnerabilities. For the mystic this is the essence of our relationship to the Divine, both within and beyond. To feel the pain of the Shechina in exile is to exercise imagination; it is to enter divine space and feel what God feels.

Whenever I see my two kids arguing I am greatly pained. I imagine through my fathering experience how God must feel when his children kill each other. In doing so I participate in the pain of the Shechina in exile.

Just so in joy. When my sons love each other I am overjoyed. I imagine how God must feel when we are good to one another. In doing so, I touch ecstasy. I participate in the rapture of the Shechina redeemed.

FIVE

Perception

The tantric secret of the cherubs teaches that love and eros are skills that are modeled by the sexual. Sex is our teacher. Those very qualities are what teach us—in all aspects of our nonsexual lives—how to be great lovers. We rise in love when we learn the art of eros.

We do not need to wait for love to happen to us. We can choose to be lovers. The reason we can choose is because love is not an emotion. At least not in the sense we are used to thinking about emotions. We are taught that an emotion is something that happens to us. We are love-struck. Blinded by rage. Falling in love. We experience emotions, negative and positive, as external forces with which we have to contend; we are victims of their venom or recipients of their nectar. We are plagued by emotion, wracked by guilt, paralyzed by fear, heartbroken, carried away, smitten. We are wounded by Cupid's arrow, poisoned by bitterness, or driven insane.

The first great truth of Hebrew tantra is that love at its core is not an emotion. It is a perception of the other that often arouses in its wake great and powerful emotion. Love and eros are modeled by sexuality. The sexual always

THE MYSTERY OF LOVE

begins with a perception, usually external in nature. It is often an external perception of beauty or power. It might be the perceptive faculty of sight that arouses sexual attraction. But it could just as well be touch, hearing, smell, or taste. Any of these may arouse an emotional, intellectual, or even chemical attraction. As with sex, so with love. Love is also a perception, albeit an internal perception. It is the ability to see, to intuit, to sense, the infinite divine specialness, the divine point, in the beloved.

The Path of Hebrew Tantra

The mystics understood that sight—the core perceptive faculty of the sexual—models and can even lead to the more profound perception of love. The great myth master the Maggid of Mezritch was very young and had just begun his teaching path. He was sitting one day minding his own business when a "loose woman" came walking by, provocatively dressed in a way that was simply impossible to miss. Apparently the master had a momentary sexual response, a fact that agonized his soul. A great revulsion began to rise in him, so he started visualizing the lowly, physical origin of the woman, reminding himself that from the earth she was made and to the earth she would return. He repeated the mantra "from dust to dust," frantically conjuring up images of formation and decomposition until with this visualization he broke through the sexual attraction. He even started throwing up in utter disgust.

Clearly at this stage in his life the sexual was for the master, as for the Buddha, Jesus, and virtually all the saints at some point in their path, a trap to be avoided at all costs. The good news is that this is not the end of the story.

Many years later, after the master had deepened greatly in his service, he taught a very different teaching about our relation to the sexual. He tells the story of Akiva, the master who witnessed the destruction of the Temple.

Akiva was at the time a well-known teacher who often represented his community to the Roman powers. One of the Roman leaders, Turnus Rufus, returned home one day greatly distressed. "I just debated Akiva," he told his wife, "and as usual he made a fool of me."

"Let me deal with him, my dear," coolly replied his wife. So Mrs. Turnus Rufus—one of the ravishing beauties of the time—invited Akiva for a meeting. She alone was present. The candles burned seductively low. The most arousing and intoxicating incense was lit. The finest wine to drug the senses was served. The wife of Turnus Rufus was dressed in the most elegant yet reveal- ing of clothing, the curves of her body more sexually alluring than one could ever dare imagine.

Akiva saw her; he spit, he laughed with joy, and he cried.

Akiva spits to avoid being seduced *only* by the Roman woman's allure. He laughs with joy and pleasure because her sensual beauty opens the door for him to see her inner gorgeousness. He cries because her beauty moves him in the very core of his soul.

The Maggid wrote, "In beholding her great beauty, Akiva saw how this beauty was but a reflection of the greater beauty of the Shechina—the femi- nine Divine."

The feminine Divine to which the Maggid referred is not Venus or Aphrodite sitting in Olympus, nor is it merely the Platonic "form" of beauty. Rather Akiva by seeing her sexual beauty was moved to a deeper kind of perception. He saw her body in all of its immense beauty and then he looked in her eyes and there he saw—Shechina. He saw not merely the dust that she was composed of and the dust to which she will return, but rather the Divine which she was suffused of and the Divine to which she would return.

With this interpretation of Akiva's ancient story, we see that the Maggid has done a 180-degree turn. In the first story, sexual seeing was a trap to be avoided at all costs. In the second story, with Akiva as his teacher, the Maggid recognized that sexual seeing is a door of perception, which, when cleansed, opens us up to the infinite perception of love. When done consciously, sexual gazing leads to a deeper lover's perception. Love is the perception of the Shechina in the other.

All this and more is understood by the Maggid later in his life. In a parallel source he makes a religiously radical suggestion: "The spiritual initiate should seek out sexual beauty in the marketplaces." Why? In order to practice the cherubic mystery that transposes sexual seeing to the soul's perception. Sexual seeing can either be avoided, neurotically crushed, or expanded as a door to the higher seeing of love. In picking which path to walk you must employ common sense. Clearly there are times for avoidance and discipline. Yet in the higher world for which we strive, it is only the path of expansion that will lead us back to love.

"All eros from the sexual to pure love is of the same essence," wrote the nineteenth-century mystical master Nachum of Chenobyl. It is therefore possible to transpose sexual looking into the wondrous perception of love. The sexual models the erotic; this is the secret of the cherubs.

Receiving the Shechina

A strange teaching of the wisdom masters is: "If you are in the middle of meditation—rapturously receiving the Divine Presence—and guests that need greeting beckon at the door, first greet your guests and then finish the meditation." Why? Because the wisdom teaching instructs, "Greater is receiving guests than receiving the face of the Shechina." Now let's suggest a deeper reading. Greater is receiving the Shechina *in the face of your guest* than receiving the Shechina in meditation. Receiving the Shechina, suggests the teaching, is perceiving and receiving the divine point of beauty that dwells in each person. Eros and ethics become one.

Now back to Akiva. The master Akiva is one of the important sources of our great understanding that sex models eros and love. He teaches a simple if elegant truism.

If sexual perception is so powerful, then it must insinuate something greater. It must model love. Love, teaches Akiva, is not merely an emotion that happens to you; love is also a perception that allows you to see the inner gorgeousness—the Shechina—in the other.

In this passage we are not told of the outcome of the meeting between Mrs. Turnus Rufus and the master Akiva. In a different passage, however, we are

told that they fall in love and Akiva marries a second time. Isaac Luria explicitly implies that this is a bond that grows out of the power of sexual seeing
transmuted into pure and deep love. He makes the radical assertion that Mrs.
Turnus Rufus is an incarnation of Lilith, the provocatively sexual first lady of
ancient Hebrew myth. In the encounter with Akiva both he and this Lilith figure are transformed. Akiva is powerfully moved by the potent divine spark that
burns in her eros. He sees her. She feels seen. Mrs. Turnus Rufus becomes Mrs.
Akiva. Leaving Rufus and the pomp of Rome behind, she marries Akiva, the
first man who really "saw" her.

Celebratory Seeing

My wife, Cary, tells me that in high school, she and her friends always said that
one of the things they loved about hanging out with their African-American
male friends was that "they knew how to look at a woman." Now Cary did not
mean that they were ogling or rude, or that they looked at women in an inappropriate sexual manner. What she did mean is that when she and her friends
were with this group they felt seen and appreciated in a special way. "They
didn't just pay attention to girls most guys would think were good-looking.
They knew every woman was beautiful, and were more than happy to let her,
and anyone else around, know it as well."

Allan Bloom in his erudite work *Love and Friendship* is correct in critiquing
a society that has lost its natural eros. We have lost our ability to distinguish
between celebratory looking and inappropriate, invasive looking. This fall of
eros, in Bloom's phrase, cuts us off from the natural and sacred vitality that is
one of the essential passageways to love.

The Babylonian wisdom masters speak of a blessing that one would recite
upon encountering a beautiful person. And it is worth remembering that a person's beauty and virtue are not determined by the artificial impositions of a
centerfold culture; it is determined as beauty must always be—in the sacred
eyes of the beholder.

Circus Clowns and County Fairs

Love is a perception; to be loved is to be seen. I remember when I was a kid, I was little, scrawny, not worth a moment's notice by anyone or anything—or so I thought. I was at the County Fair in Columbus, Ohio, with my parents and brothers, who were otherwise occupied. I had wandered off—as kids do—seeking amusement or at least distraction. And there Distraction stood, draped in a long suit of glitter—a six-foot circus clown. He was amusing a crowd of candy-sucking, entertainment-hungry fairgoers. Being small, I squeezed my way toward the front and crouched down so that I could look up at the glittery spectacle from between people's legs. And from that crouch I watched and whooped with laughter along with everyone else.

When the show had reached its finale and the clown was about to quit his stage, he looked down. His eyes locked with mine and lit up with a great warm smile. Perhaps I amused him, a scrawny thing crouched on the ground. Perhaps he pitied me, or perhaps this was just part of the act. Or just maybe it was spontaneous, real, and loving. Whatever the case, he held out his shimmering arm and motioned for me to stand up and join him. Surprised, terrified, delighted, I stumbled out into the center of the circle. With a great extravagant gesture, he pulled out a large red envelope and handed it to me. I opened it and read: "Free Ice Cream—All You Can Eat." I was sure it was either magic or a miracle. "For me?" I asked dumbfounded. "For you—and no one but you," the clown said, grinning into my bedazzled eyes.

I bounded back to my family to show off my newly won ticket to ice cream paradise. So what if the three double-scoop cones left me sick in the morning? I had been seen! By a jumbo circus clown no less, who had looked out into the crowd and seen ME. From then on, I had a habit of lingering around fairgrounds, hoping to duplicate that magical encounter. Well, it never happened again. But it had happened once, and that was enough.

It's the kind of moment that makes a person want to go to clown school, just so that somewhere along the way you could change some little kid's self-perception. But we need not don a clown suit to peer into a crowd of faces and perceive the divinity of a person's uniquely gorgeous soul. We don't need to give out free ice cream on the street, but we do need to give out all the love and attention our eyes can muster. We do need to become lovers, masters of erotic perception.

It is not by accident that the common term for dating is "seeing someone," or that the somewhat outdated but no less expressive term for trying to pick someone up is to "make eyes" at them. Our language reveals that being seen is essential. It is really what being loved is all about. We then know that love is a perception. A great lover is one who trains, refines, and excels in perception. When a lover is with you, you have the wonderful sense of having been seen.

The Need for Piety

Many years ago, when I was nineteen, I broke up a relationship with a woman whom I loved with all of my heart. Though not yet a rabbi, nor even a teacher, I felt powerfully called to the spirit. I believed, as I had been taught, that only a full curbing of sexuality would allow me to be sufficiently pure to answer my spiritual calling. My teachers at the seminary reinforced my desire for piety and "purity" and lauded my decision. I broke off the relationship abruptly—honestly citing my need for purity as my primary motive.

Although I was completely unaware of it then, it was—in retrospect—probably the greatest sin of my life. Paradoxically it was the fear of what I thought to be sin that brought about the greatest sin—the inability to see one I loved and who loved me. About six months after we broke up I received a letter from her that had apparently been written six months earlier and gotten lost in the mail. It was a beautiful note. I cried for two hours when I read it. I did not cry again for twelve years, when I was thirty-one.

At that time I was married and needed to make a decision about getting divorced. I went to the person who had been my primary teacher for many years. The first words out of his mouth, before he really had a chance to think, were, "But you will ruin your career." It was the first in a series of moments of clarity that set me off in search of a deeper truth. I decided to reject the counsel of my teacher and follow my heart into the unknown.

I understood then that a teacher who is not a lover, who cannot see their students but only the students' "careers" is not a teacher. I knew that I needed to leave such teachers behind.

Disappearing Spouse Syndrome

There is a wonderful premarriage ceremony in biblical myth called *tenaim*. It represents the mystical merging of the two souls that occurs even before the wedding. It is a spiritual prenuptial agreement in which we read a bill of mutual commitment where both sides commit "not to run away and not to disappear." It seems redundant—if you do not run away then of course you will not disappear! That is, unless you remain physically present yet are not available. Or worse, you cause your partner to disappear. You do everything you are supposed to do—in the kitchen, in the bedroom, and in the family room— but your partner has long since disappeared from your consciousness.

There is a fantastic story by Ray Bradbury that captures beautifully the Disappearing Spouse Syndrome. It is set in the year 2500. Robotics has developed into a fine art. A woman wants out of her marriage but doesn't want to hurt her spouse, so she contrives the perfect escape plan. She will have a robotic replica of herself made, substitute it for herself, and be free. There was just one small difficulty with robot replicas. Humans have a heartbeat, but robots give off a sixty-cycle hum. When her husband gets close he will hear the hum and know it's a fake. The woman has a brilliant idea. She programs the robot's first action to be to record her husband's heartbeat and incorporate it into the robot's own system. It's an ingenious idea, insuring that her husband will never know the difference. All is prepared. The robot goes to the husband and takes the necessary recording of the heartbeat…only to find out that the husband himself gives off a sixty-cycle hum!

A chillingly comic tale to be sure, and all the more potent in its twisted irony. It is the modern tragedy of the "disappearing spouse," who, although present in person, has long ago fled in spirit. A dearth of perception is bound to turn any healthy heartbeat into a sixty-cycle hum.

Our all-too-well-founded fear of being replaced by robots is no less than a fear of a world robbed of erotic perception, of the ability to be seen for ourselves, instead of being seen as interchangeable cogs in the world machine. But we can reeroticize even the most sterile of modernities. As Bradbury hints, it begins with the heartbeat, with hearing and perceiving the unique rhythm of the person who stands beside us. This is eros, no robots necessary.

Yada, Yada, Yada

To fully ground our point that love is a perception, we need to summon up the evocative English phrase "carnal knowledge." It is an idiom that is rooted in the translation of the Biblical word *yada*, which in Hebrew means "perception" and "knowledge." Yet it is used in biblical myth first to describe sexual knowing—carnal knowledge, as in "Adam knew Eve his wife"—and only later to describe noncarnal erotic perception.

The first biblical text says, "Adam knew Eve his wife." Carnal erotic knowledge. Only then does the text later say, "You shall know God with all your heart." Noncarnal erotic knowledge.

This is because sex is the first level of seeing. It models the perception of loving. It is often the most potent realm in which we access perception. Thus sexual seeing can guide us to a much deeper form of perception.

IS LOVE BLIND?

Love to faults is always blind,
Always is to a joy inclined,
Lawless, winged, and unconfined
And breaks the chain from every mind.

—WILLIAM BLAKE

> Whoever said love is blind is dead wrong.
> Love is the only thing that lets us see each other
> with the remotest accuracy.
>
> —MARTHA BECK

Beck is right, and Blake is wrong. Love is not blind! Infatuation is blind. Love is in the details. Not in the sense of the petty particulars, but more as Abraham Kook, a twentieth-century biblical mystic, writes, "Love is 'the great art of the spirit.'" Art is where each magnified detail is part of a harmonized whole. An artist is a master at perceiving.

What is so special about the artist's eye? It is always open to the new, the never before noticed. Emily Dickinson says it best:

> Not "Revelation"—tis—that waits
> But our unfurnished eyes—

What a gorgeous phrase. We don't need to wait for Godot—an external God—who will redeem us with a great new vision of truth and beauty. We merely need to *unfurnish* our eyes. Our eyes are furnished with old trauma, competition, greed, and jealousy. We can't see. The blind man is literally leading the blind man. Blake taught us that love was blind, but in truth it is not. If anything, love is a magnifying glass. We notice more about the person we love than anyone else, for good and for bad.

Of course, criticism can certainly be the shadow side of perception. Every great quality of the spirit has its own unique shadow. We all know that the second we decide to love someone, we start noticing virtually every detail of their dress, habits, idiosyncrasies, all the wonderful and the not so wonderful. But love is much more than just a magnifying system for petty particulars. Dickinson invites us to a revelation that awaits "unfurnished" eyes. The artist's eye, the lover's eye, is unfurnished. It is not blinded with the opaque trappings of preconceptions and misconceptions. Of course Dickinson is not referring merely to the very narrow realm of interpersonal relationships. The quest of eros is for each of us to be a lover in *every* arena of our lives.

For this reason we often equate the lover and the poet. Indeed it is love that moves all of us to be poets. Who has not at some time picked up a pen to write poetry for their beloved? And if you haven't yet, you should now. Poetry and love are intimately related because poetry, like love, is an art of perception.

Poet Allen Ginsberg is in the tradition of the great lovers when he reminds us of the need for "clear seeing and direct perception." My wife, Cary, always begins her poetry classes by quoting Ginsberg: "Don't treat an object indirectly or symbolically, rather look directly at it and choose the aspect more immediately striking... and then write."

Love is about noticing the details. Baudelaire understood this well when he moved poetry from the ethereal and the abstract to the concrete and the real. All of a sudden, the poetic consciousness of the nineteenth century started to include the city, real estate, carriages, machinery. It was the great lover, Walt Whitman, who said, "Bring the muse into the kitchen."

To be a lover, writes Chogyam Trungpa, a Zen master, is to know that "things are symbols of themselves." What Trungpa means is that if you perceive a thing directly, it's completely there, completely revelatory of the eternal universe that's in it. In the lover's vision, perception is first narrowed, concretized, and then expanded into the realization that in the ordinary resides all of the extraordinary.

The lover's eye is open, ready to receive the Divine in all it sees.

Revealers of the Divine

Ever been to a wedding? They can be pretty beautiful. There is a moment when the bride and groom walk down the aisle or look at each other for the first time under the wedding canopy where you just gasp and quietly say, "Oh my God—this is gorgeous!"

It is the image of this moment that will help us understand the enigmatic

Kabbalistic koan "The bride and the groom are revealers of the Divine." We all know that special and wonderful feeling we have as we witness the vows of the bride and groom on their wedding day. Something different, something divine, is in the air. God, holiness, the force, the numinous—all of these become felt presences at a wedding.

You may ask, What is so special about the bride and the groom that their hearts are able to uniquely reveal the divine forces of beauty and goodness in the world? The Kabbalists explain magnificently: On their wedding day, the bride and groom reveal God by revealing the Divine in each other. The bride sees something in the groom—a glimpse of his infinite specialness, his divinity—that no one has previously been privileged to witness. And the groom likewise perceives something in the infinite specialness of his bride, something that no one—not her parents, not her best friends—have been able to fully grasp. We stand moved, humbled and quietly ecstatic as we witness the revelation of divinity—of the God who walks among us. The highest truth and the highest potential in each other is revealed through the prism of love's light that is the nuptials.

To say then, for example, that the bride loves the groom is consequently to say that the bride perceives the infinite specialness, the divinity, in the groom. In that perceptive experience, she is pleasured and feels the grand rapture and beauty of loving.

All lovers are revealers of the Divine in each other. God seeing God.

> All love is the love of God.
>
> —RECANATI, A RENAISSANCE MYSTIC

Love is to perceive another person unmasked, in the pristine beauty of their spiritual and emotional nakedness. Love is the pleasure produced by such a perception, when our loving awareness strips the beloved of all outer coatings until she stands fully revealed before the perceiving mind.

Love is a perception of the full divine wonder that is your beloved.

It is like Dante's description of his first sighting of Beatrice: "Something like the glory of God walking towards him." Or for those of us who don't speak in the bombastic language of "the glory of God," we turn in *Anna Karenina* to the more personal existential description of Tolstoy's Levin on the night his wife, Kitty, gives birth to their child. Levin

> …jumped out of bed, hardly conscious of himself and without taking his eyes off her for a moment, put on his dressing gown and stood still gazing at her. He had to go but he was unable to move, so struck was he by the look on her face…her flushed face, with soft hair escaping from under her night cap, was radiant with joy and dissolution. Little as there was of artificiality and the conventionalist in Kitty's character, Levin was still astonished at what was laid bare to him now when every veil had been removed and the kernel of her soul shone through her eyes. And in this simplicity and in this baring of her soul he could see her, the woman he loved, more clearly than ever.

Tolstoy understands that love is the perception of the soul's nakedness. To love someone is to see them in all the rawness of their authenticity, that is to say, in their divinity. It is about Levin the lover that Recanati, a Renaissance mystic, wrote, "All love is the love of God."

D. H. Lawrence adds:

> What's the good of man
> Unless there's a glimpse of a God in him
> And what's the good of woman
> Unless she's a glimpse of a Goddess of some sort.

That is precisely the point! To love is to perceive the God and Goddess in the other. And the desire to be loved is the great desire for that God or Goddess to be seen.

Inside, Insight

Love is all about insight—in-sight. It is the ability to see in, to the inside of the inside, to the Holy of Holies that is your lover. Eros is being on the inside. Thus, love is an erotic perception of the highest order. Naturally you have to move way beyond sexual seeing. Sex only models eros. To be an erotic lover you have to understand that "what is essential is invisible to the eye."

When something is far from you, you have to open your eyes really wide to see it. As it gets closer you squint your eyes; when it gets really really close, you close your eyes. Seeing with closed eyes is when we perceive way beyond seeing. The adjective *close* and the verb *close* are the same word. Closeness—intimacy—higher vision—all happen when we close our eyes. We move beyond sight and invite the other faculties of perception to guide us. Smell, sound, touch, and taste all become alive in a deeper way when we cloak our eyes.

The central mantra of Hebrew tradition is a daily meditation on the unity of God It is called the Shema, the listening prayer. Tradition requires that it be recited with hands covering the eyes, because it is only with eyes closed that we no longer see the world of distinctions and differences. Only then do we appreciate the fact that the boundaries between us are but illusions. For we are one and all is one. This is the meaning of the universal religious epigram "God is One." We close our eyes in order to let drop those screens that so distort our perception.

It is also why when making love, in the moment of rapture that moves us beyond sexual seeing to lovers' union, we close our eyes. For the Zohar, Shema is the Lover's Prayer. Its goal is to achieve erotic union with Being precisely in the same way sexual love achieves erotic union with the beloved. The highest perception of loving is the realization that you are part of God.

Trailing Clouds of Glory

A number of years ago I was teaching at a spiritual retreat center in California. Teaching was beautiful. Yet I was also in the midst of what I would call a "deepening" in my relationship with two good friends there, Ronit and Gil, the married couple who were organizing the seminars. As in every authentic relationship, there are pivotal moments where it either deepens and blossoms or wilts away. Well, we were at such a point, and I was having a hard time fully appreciating their point of view. That is until orientation the second week, which, as always, was being masterfully led by Ronit.

In the midst of this evening I caught Gil watching Ronit as she was talking to the group. A little later I glimpsed a momentary expression on Ronit's face as she watched Gil doing his presentation. Both had such looks of utter love on their faces that I was jealous. Clearly they saw in each other a light and a divinity that, much as I loved them both, I was not able to see on the same level. I prayed to be open to seeing just a fraction of what they each—in the private images of lovers—saw in each other.

Wonder of wonders, my prayer was granted. Even if but for a moment I was actually able to enter Ronit's love and get a glimpse of how she saw Gil. Conversely for a millisecond, I was privileged to see Ronit as a flash of light reflecting off Gil's eyes. What a glory it was to behold. The verse that found its way to my mind was Wordsworth talking about how we all, as newborn babes, enter the world:

> *...not in utter nakedness,*
> *But trailing clouds of glory do we come*
> *From God who is our home.*

We are born so beautiful, and the beauty never fades. Our eyes just get tired and we stop looking. It is this wisdom of love that psychologist philosopher R. D. Laing, one of my favorite modern thinkers, understood so well.

What we think is less than what we know
What we know is less than what we love
What we love is less than there is
And to that precise extent
We are much less than what we are.

On In-laws and Love

In the end we all want so desperately, so deservedly, to see and be seen. This is one of the best reasons to get married: to reveal and be revealed. Much of the tension in a family between the newlyweds and each set of in-laws is based on this dynamic of perception as well. The parent who so loves her child is convinced that she sees him or her like no one else could. "Then along comes this young woman—who did not give birth to him, nurse him on sleepless nights, worry, weep, and wonder over him for twenty-five arduous years—and she knows how to love him!? She sees him, knows him, in a whole different way than I do? Unfathomable!" And yet it's true. The mother and father intuitively know that the lover of their child perceives their child in myriad ways that they cannot.

Listen to this story of perception.

The Malach was in search of a wife. They called him the Malach, the Angel, for his appearance was so stunning, his wisdom so immeasurable, he seemed a divine presence among common men. Word spread throughout the shtetls and cities, the search for a wife began. They came to the town of Shalom Shachnah, a great master in his own right, who was famous for his intense study. He would sit before stacks of books, consumed in the words, sweating with concentration, moving for nary a bowl of soup or a stoke of the fire. Shalom had a daughter who, rumor had it, had inherited more than a little of her father's intensity.

The Angel had found his match—the shidduch *(match) was made. A buzz went out far and wide—the Angel was marrying the daughter of Shalom Shachnah.*

Crowds gathered for the celebration. Everyone was there. A great host of people. But the host of the party? The father of the bride—where was he? He simply did not show up. Indeed, back at home, he had not stirred from his study, engrossed as he was in his great stack of books.

The wedding went on without him—and how it went on! It was ecstatic, enlightening, with dance and drink, canopied as if by a bow of divine light, as befit the joining of the Angel and his bride.

After the wedding, the mother of the bride went home to her book-bound husband and screamed, "Where were you?! Do you know what you just missed? A wedding like you wouldn't believe! Your own daughter's wedding… and she was wedded to an absolute angel, a celestial soul! And you, you honored your books over your own blood! I refuse to speak to you until you go to their house in Mezritch for a proper Sabbath to give them the respect they deserve."

And what is a man to do when his wife protests so? He set out the next week for the three days' travel to Mezritch. He arrives for the Sabbath. The Sabbath prayers commence. The Angel starts to sing. His voice rises and rivets the room, a voice unparalleled in earthly and heavenly spheres. A light fills the prayer hall, a light so enormous and magnetic that Shalom is overcome by its brilliance and faints. The song finishes and Shalom awakes.

The Angel approaches him and asks, "Tell us, Shalom, what did you see?" Shalom answers with a whisper of awe, "I saw your angels. I saw all of your surrounding angels dancing about your shoulders! They were exquisite, amazing sights to behold. It was too much to bear. I passed out."

The Angel, shaking his head, replies, "Dear father-in-law, it is a good thing that you passed out when you did. For if you had beheld your daughter you would have perceived an even mightier and more majestic host of angels surrounding her. Their brilliance would have so overwhelmed you that you might not have woken up at all."

An incredible tale. At first glance Shalom seems tragic; but in the final analysis, he is redeemed. Quite simply, Shalom, with all his study of the sublime, could not perceive the sublime nature that sat before him in the form of his own daughter. But that's okay, because the Malach could. The Malach—with his acclaimed celestial radiance—saw in his wife an exquisiteness even greater than his own. And this beauty was not for her father to perceive. He would not have been able to bear it, and indeed, it was not for him to bear. Parents, with all their immense love, are privy to a different perception than what the lover beholds.

This story relates what the Hindus called *bhakti*, to truly see the other bathed in their divine radiance. "Love your neighbor as yourself," cries out the famous quote in the biblical book of Leviticus. But loving your neighbor is not the whole story. That quote is three words too short. What all too often gets left out of the passage are the three last, and perhaps most crucial, words. For the complete verse is: "Love your neighbor as yourself—I AM GOD." To love your neighbor is to know that the "I"—the essential self—is God. To love your neighbor is to reveal, to disclose, their ultimate divinity.

A Perception-Identification Complex

Even when we say that love is perception, we do not mean it is *merely* perception. The beloved not only *perceives* the divine, the soul print of her lover, but she also identifies him with that divinity. She understands that as his essence. She sees and *identifies* her beloved with his infinite specialness. This stage in the art of loving I have termed "the perception-identification complex."

This notion of perception *identification* is most clear in reference to parents and children. You love your kids. The neighbor's kids however—well, they are just so incredibly rambunctious, annoying, and immature....

In fact, we all recognize that there may be no appreciable difference between our kids and the neighbor's kids. Why then do we love our children and not the neighbor's? Not merely because they're *my* children, but rather, *because* they are my children, I am invested in them. This investment causes me to focus on them more intensely than on other kids. The result—I am able to perceive them in ways other people are simply unable to do. I perceive *my* child's beauty in a way that no one else is quite able to do. But perception is not enough. If I am a good parent, I know my child also has faults, and those shortcomings are real. They need to be addressed forthrightly and never swept under the rug. Remember, love is not blind. Infatuation is blind. Love is a microscope. Parents should be madly in love with their kids—but they should never be infatuated with them.

Having said this, how is it that I love my children even after I know their long laundry list of faults? The answer is the second step in the formula—identification. I perceive both my child's goodness and her not-yet-so-goodness—but I identify her goodness as the true core of who she is. All the rest I will deal with in whatever way necessary, but I know that at her core the trailing clouds of glory are the essence of my child, and I love her for it. With kids not our own, what we often (wrongly) tend to do is to identify the child with his failing or acting out instead of with his infinite specialness and grandeur.

Mirari

Have any of your friends ever gotten engaged and everybody's response was something like, "I can't believe it—SHE is going to marry...HIM? Candice is going to marry...Tom??!!" We don't understand what she sees in him. But see in him she does. She perceives him, sees him, discloses him, in a way that we are unable to access. Our eyes are too "furnished" to see the miraculous, infinitely unique gorgeousness that is Tom. But let there be no mistake about it—Tom is stunningly gorgeous. To Candice, the man is a miracle. The word *miracle* comes from the Latin *mirari* meaning "to behold with rapt attention." Candice has beheld the glory of Tom and found him to be divine. She has seen his infinite uniqueness, the snowflake essence of his soul that most miraculously never melts. To love is to witness the miracle of your beloved.

Parents' Love

And yet parents are our first lovers in this world. When that love is missing, then we spend the rest of our lives searching for it. "Three partners are there in creation," read the wisdom texts, "mother, father and God." Just because parents aren't privy to the same perception of us as our lovers, they nevertheless take center stage in our love lives for many crucial years. A parent's obligation to a child is, above all, love.

"What does one do with a child who has fallen under negative influence?" a parent asked Master Israel of Good Name. "Love him more," the master responded. Love is not an abstract emotion with which parents are automatically endowed upon the child's birth. Love is about the work of revealing the infinite specialness and beauty of the child. The audience for this revelation is not, as is commonly assumed, the world. The father who carries around baby pictures to show to anyone who will look is sweet, but he has offered no evidence of his being engaged in real parenting. Real parenting is realizing that the one who needs to see the picture most is the child herself. The sacred task of the parent is to reveal the unique beauty of the child *to the child.* Not to flash her picture to the world, declaring her beauty in broad boasting statements, but to reflect her gorgeousness back to her in a loving gaze or quiet words of confirmation.

The parent's ultimate mission is that the child knows—beyond a shadow of a doubt—that she is infinitely special, that her ray of light is unique and precious to the planet. The parent needs to be a prism that refracts to the child the infinite love that God feels for her.

Parents and lovers can't and don't need to make us beautiful—but they can and must remind us that we already are. And in so reminding us they move us through the ultimately motivating power of love to express our beauty in our every step, at every second of the day. They give us the confidence to walk on tables, to talk to God, to be ourselves.

Years back I gave a talk at a summer camp in one of the wealthier enclaves of Long Island. The kids in the camp were between ages five and twelve. After my official talk, I had some extra time, so I asked if I could perhaps have a casual talk with the kids alone. The camp director, being more creative and flexible than most, on the spot canceled that afternoon's activity and brought the kids together for a *kumzits,* a chat/singing session with the teacher. I sang with them, horsed around—thought I was outrageously funny, but wasn't getting the kind of gut response I wanted. Laughter, participation—yes...but real presence—soul sharing—wasn't happening.

Out of nowhere, I asked them, "When was the last time someone told you that you were beautiful?" Silence. "We need a first volunteer," I said, pushing them.

So one brave nine-year-old gets up and with a tremble of hesitation says, "My mother told me on Saturday that I was the ugliest little girl she knew." Silence—this time the quiet was worlds sadder but somehow more real. Then a little boy—looking not more than ten—raised his hand and, in his own words, said, "My mother was in the Holocaust. And she says that if she had known that I would be her son, she wouldn't have worked so hard to survive."

And then the stories came tumbling out. Of parents, so many parents, who weren't lovers, who didn't know how beautiful their children were. Stories of so many parents who broke the commandment to love. My heart broke. So right now, before you do anything else, before you go on to the next page, before you turn on the TV...turn to your child, call up your friend, call out to your lover, and tell them just how beautiful they are.

Let your eyes mirror their splendor; let your mouth remind them of what wonders they already are.

As You Love Yourself

Of course, to remind another of their full beauty you have to be fully aware of your own. The Baal Shem Tov has a wonderful teaching on the biblical mandate "love your neighbor *as you love yourself*." First it is a statement of fact— you love your neighbor precisely as much as you love yourself. For in the end, you can only perceive another's greatness if you have glimpsed and believe in your own. Self-love is self-perception.

If this is so, then a powerful question arises. How do you love yourself when you know all of your foibles, pathologies, and blemishes? Isn't self-love self-perception? And does not honest perception yield forth all of the reasons why we are not lovable? And yet most of us manage, at least to some degree, to love ourselves. Is it just self-deception? No, not at all. Love is not merely perception, it is a perception-identification complex. Self-perception means that although you are aware of the full complexity of your personae—the good, the bad, and the ugly—you identify the essence of who you are with your good—your good, loving, giving, creative, and generous self.

That does not mean that you deny your beast. It is, of course, critical to integrate all of you into your self picture. But the essence, the core of who you are, remains your goodness, virtue, and beauty. To love yourself is to identify yourself as part of the Shechina. Writes the Baal Shem Tov, "To love yourself is to love the Shechina." Not to love yourself is to send the Shechina into exile. So proclaim the Kabbalists, to which Rumi adds:

> By God, when you see your beauty
> You will be the idol of yourself.

In your deepest nature you must know that you are the hero of your story. In your deepest nature you are love and grace and strength and splendor. *Now you must decide to identify with your deepest nature.* Do you focus on your innocence or your guilt? Do you focus on your ever-inevitably dirty hands, or on your ever-eternally pure soul? To love yourself or anyone else, you need to know that your innocence is your essence. That you always remain worthy of love. That your innocence is never lost.

The Deep of the Deep

Biblical myth consciousness teaches us that we have three faces. The first face is the social you. It is called in the Zohar the "revealed world." The second face is the secret you. This is the primal raging of the subconscious. The Zohar calls this the "hidden world." Neither is your truest face. Your truest face is your third face, what the Kabbalists call *umka de umka*—the deepest of the deep. In the language of Abraham Kook, the twentieth-century mystical philosopher, "The truth of your essence reveals itself in your moments of greatness." It is those moments of greatness that set the standard that defines you, that *are you. Who* you really are is you at your best.

During my first year as a rabbi in Palm Beach, Florida, there was one bar mitzvah boy I will never forget. Louis was his name, and he was the first child to be bar mitzvahed during my tenure. He and his parents came to my office just a few weeks after I arrived. It turned out to be quite a disturbing meeting. You see, Louis was not a happy kid. He was overweight, awkward, and socially ill at ease. None of these traits were easy for a twelve-year-old to have who was trapped in the superficiality of a culture that idolized body, grace, and cool.

But to add to the taunts of his peers, his parents seemed to be doing their fair share of damage to Louis's self-esteem. The parents informed me that Louis was not the brightest kid, and that he probably would not be able to read the usual portion from Prophets read by other bar mitzvah boys. They figured that it would be enough for him to recite the blessings and be done with it. In their infinite wisdom, they said this in half-veiled sentences with him in the room. When they left my office I was bewildered, angry, and near tears. Perhaps it was his parents' insensitivity, or perhaps his awkwardness reminded me of myself at his age, but I resolved to do something.

In the ensuing six months I met with Louis approximately three times as often as I would have met with any other bar mitzvah boy. To my extreme delight I found that Louis had a beautiful singing voice and would have no problem reciting the usual bar mitzvah requirements. But I also believed that he could do more. Thus we prepared for not only the standard reading but the entire biblical portion for the week, no mean feat for a thirteen-year-old by any standard. We practiced and practiced and practiced.

On the morning of the bar mitzvah, I tell you that angels carried his every word. Louis shined! He glowed! The room and the heavens stood still in awe and wonder at the beauty and grace that was Louis. I got up to give the speech that I had prepared, but only one thought filled my mind. I had to speak directly to Louis. I had to make sure he realized the full magnificence—and significance—of that moment. The whole congregation seemed to disappear as I turned to Louis and let the words flow from my mouth. "Louis, this morning you met your real self. This is who you are. You are good, graceful, talented, and smart. Whatever people told you yesterday, and Louis, whatever happens tomorrow, promise me one thing. Remember…this is you. Remember, and don't ever lose it."

Several months after his bar mitzvah Louis's family moved away, and I lost track of him. But two years ago, I received a letter from Louis. He had just graduated from an Ivy League university, was beginning medical school in the fall, and was engaged to be married. The letter was short. It read, "High school was a nightmare. Sometimes I didn't think I would make it through. But I kept my promise—I always remembered my bar mitzvah morning when you said that this is who I am. For this, I thank you."

The essence of who you are is you at your best.

At a certain point in my life I realized I was meeting too many people who desperately wanted to be someone else. More than anything this makes me sad. I wanted a way beyond declamation to share with people the power of self-love. So I developed a very simple yet very powerful practice on self-love that I would like to share with you!

Close your eyes. Imagine going to a land where the things most highly prized are the very qualities that you happen to possess. For instance, if you are short, then in this land, shortness is the most ideal size…if you have red hair, then red hair is considered the most beautiful of colors…if you are a dreamer, then dreamers stand at the top of the social and economic ladder…if you are a runner, then running is the most acclaimed activity. Now soak in the sensation of being absolutely accepted, appreciated, and admired. This is the land for you, literally for you. Realize that you carry that land inside of you. Whoever you are, you can always find inside of you the best of you. Now visualize, inch by inch, that your inner land starts stretching, spreading, seeping out from within you until it completely surrounds you and it becomes the real world as well. Open your eyes and believe it, and it will be.

Self-love or Narcissism

Whenever I talk to people about self-love—which is, after all, according to most authorities, the most important injunction and the goal of the entire biblical project—there is always a group that gets upset. It sounds narcissistic, they claim, or it will lead to selfishness.

So let's take a moment to make two clear distinctions. Narcissism is to be in love with your external self—your mask. This is not a good idea because sooner or later masks fall off, and then you are left loveless. Self-love is to love your insides—your Holy of Holies.

Selfishness is to narrow your circle of caring until it includes only yourself and perhaps those who directly affect your well-being. Selfishness is then a narrowing of your identity. It stems from the failure to see your interconnectivity with circles beyond yourself and ultimately with all of being. That is definitive nonerotic thinking. Self-love, by contrast, is not self-centered at all; rather it is ultimately expansive.

Self-love is radically erotic in that it is the experience of being interwoven within the great fabric of being. It is the deep intuition that the world is a unified, loving consciousness in which you participate. The only true sin, from which all else flows, is to deny your greatness. Ultimately the answer to who I am is "I am part of God." It is the only *humble* answer to the question you can give. To think you are not lovable is the ultimate arrogance because it assumes that you are independent of God.

The Creative Gaze

The Kabbalists were often referred to as *mistaklim* or *chozim*, roughly translated as the Lookers or Seers. To get a handle on what that might mean, just imagine how we feel when someone looks at us with erotic, loving eyes. We feel energized, uplifted, and embraced. We become more vibrant, audacious, and alive. We feel safer in the world. The sense of alienation, separateness, and loneliness of our empty days and painful nights seems to lift.

The more steady the loving gaze is, the more we can steady ourselves and chart our direction and purpose on the path of being. It begins with the loving eyes of mother and father—our first lovers—and continues throughout our lives. Love's eyes sustain us, nourish us, and connect us to the essential aliveness that courses through the universe. Being seen makes us alove and alive. The same is true of God. The gaze of the mystic sustains and even "creates" God.

Once a few years back, my son Yair walked into the room. He sat and started playing with his Gameboy. I began looking at him, but really looking, perceiving him, loving him, with all my heart pouring out through my eyes. I was seeing every beautiful detail of his being as he sat there innocently playing. Suddenly he started singing. Yair singing?! A rarity. Could it have been from my love pouring out in his direction? He got up and sort of danced his way out of the room. Yair dancing?!

Well, proper scientific data it is not. But it was enough for me. It was exhilarating! Since then I have done this practice in a thousand different places—in streets, lecture halls, pubs, churches, libraries, and synagogues. As a result, the world has been much more full of singing and dancing. I realized that a loving gaze can transform reality. We call this in formal theology *imatatio dei*, the imitation of the divine force. Just as God looked lovingly into the darkness and there was light, just as God's gaze made it good, so too can our loving perception transform darkness into light and chaos into harmony. Try it!

The Festival of Seeing

We return now full circle to the cherubic mystery of love. When the pilgrims came to the Temple in Jerusalem three times a year, the biblical verse tells us that they came to "see and be seen." The festivals are great gatherings of eros and vision.

Ecstatic dance, camaraderie, overflowing joy, and Temple ritual characterize these great convocations. If you could imagine a rock concert or a sports event held with sacred intention and ritual, you could approximate at least something of the erotic energy that pulsed through these festivals.

The grammar in the biblical text is unclear—"The holiday of seeing." But who is seeing whom? The deep inside understanding is that two different mystical processes are happening at the same time. In an erotic circular loop one feeds into the other. On the first level the pilgrim comes to be seen by God. To be seen is to be loved. When the pilgrim would make his entrance into the Temple, one of the priestly greeters would call out, "So and so has arrived from village such and such to bring the appointed offering." His name would echo through the Temple. Perceived upon entry!

In the ecstasy of the festival the pilgrim reaches the consciousness which moves him to cry out, "If I am here all is here." The Zohar explains that if I who am the Shechina is here then all is here. The description is one of virtual *unio mystica*. A shift in perception takes place in which the individual leaves his isolating identity behind and imagines himself as part of the divine body. This results not in a loss of self but in the total reinvigoration of self as an infinitely unique reflection of God's face. When the pilgrim feels seen and loved he is then able to open his heart and let it overflow in joy. He himself becomes a lover. That joy and love, writes the medieval sage Maimonides, must express itself in acts of kindness and love, which he in turn does for others.

The pilgrim becomes a lover once again. He is able to love himself, God, the world, and most importantly his community and family.

This is the essence of the Holy of Holies: to become a lover and a seer. *To love is to become God's verb. To love is to see with God's eyes.*

Feasting on the Vision

The model of love's perception remains the cherubs sexually intertwined atop the ark in the Holy of Holies. The cherubs were not only in the Holy of Holies. They adorned the curtains, walls, and vessels of most of the Temple. At every turn they confronted the eye.

Part of the spiritual work of the priest in the Temple involved erotic gazing and its transformation into love. The priest envisioned, through both meditation and visualization, the sexual merging of the divine masculine and feminine.

This spiritual practice was fraught with danger. One could get caught in the intense erotic pleasure of the sensual and not know how to translate it into loving and ethical action. In biblical myth this is the failing of the sons of Aaron—Nadav and Avihu—who are described as *"Zanu einehem min haShechina."* Usually this is translated as "they feasted on the vision of the Shechina." It could also be legitimately translated as "they were harlots with the Shechina," as *feasting* and *harlotry* share the same Hebrew root.

The point is that Nadav and Avihu, driven by their erotic desire to love, attempted the practice of the cherubs and failed. Nadav and Avihu, the text relates, are consumed by the fire of the Holy of Holies. They are mythically "burned out" by their erotic drives. Moses by contrast is described as "taking pleasure from the rays of Shechinah." Here also the implication is erotic; Moses however was able to move from the merely sexually erotic to eros and love beyond the sexual. Nadav and Abihu remained transfixed by the sexual. They were unable to take that energy and expand it to all of life beyond the sexual.

The sexually intertwined cherubs, which so defined the Temple energy, clearly invite sacred sexual gazing. Yet great care is taken in order to insure that the sexual did not override the love eros and ethics that lay at the core of the Temple.

Only the high priest was permitted to see them once a year during the mystery of the incense offering on the Day of At-one-ment. Except! Except for the three love festivals. On each of these three auspicious gatherings, the curtains guarding the Holy of Holies were gently opened and the people were invited to behold the entwined cherubs. Erotic gazing!

The sexual gaze, teach the cherubic mysteries of love, is but the model. With it you can only see the outside. Now look deeper—look on the inside. Become a lover. Learn the art of erotic perception and you will see beauty and experience pleasure far beyond even your wildest dreams.

SIX

Giving: Self-Transcendence

The sum which two married people owe to
one another defies calculation. It is an infinite debt,
which can only be discharged through all eternity.
—GOETHE, *ELECTIVE AFFINITIES*

Sensual Saints

In his classic work *Love and Will*, Rollo May correctly bemoans modernity's overemphasis on performance and technique at the expense of feeling and passion. He tells one story of a patient who used ointment on the tip of his sexual organ because it dulled feeling, thus increasing his ability to perform. May viewed this as a kind of pathology symptomatic of his time, a telling example of the wanton willingness to forfeit feeling for the sake of achievement. And Rollo May may well be right.

Yet a second look reveals a deeper message in this story. Actually, this patient's goals are not necessarily worthy of our contempt. After all, the achievement he is after here is fully based upon *giving* to another, even at the expense of his own pleasure! How often in life is the standard of "success" based on how much you give, rather than on how much you've got? Imagine if everyone's greatest goal was to give the optimal amount of pleasure to other people. What a radically brighter, more alive world we would live in! So the patient in May's example actually sets the highest standard for what the moral/honorable heights of life might be.

You see, built into the sexual is an enormous desire to give, particularly to give pleasure. In virtually all arenas of living, most of us are perpetually on the prowl for "the great deal." The great deal is always about getting the most while giving the least. The great exception is the sexual. In sex, being a great lover is taken to mean that you give your partner an unbelievable, unforgettable experience. This ability to give pleasure (and the more, the better) is considered a great honor, a virtual badge of merit. As well it should be! Yet we need to expand this desire to give to apply to so much more than just sex. Sex models eros. It should not exhaust eros. The erotics of giving must engage every facet of existence.

Imagine if we brought into every realm of life this standard of giving. Imagine if all of us were willing to forfeit feeling some of our own pleasure, our own comfort, in order to further the pleasure and comfort of another. People who behave this way consistently over long periods of time are called saints, they are the Mother Teresas of the world. Paradoxically, it is in the sexual that the glimmerings of sainthood first appear. For it is in the sexual that the greatest hero is the one who gifts his/her beloved with the greatest pleasure.

Transcendence and the Gradual Widening of Self

It is through the *consistent commitment to the growth of the other expressed through regular and spontaneous acts of giving that you become a lover.* Slowly over time—in a gradual expanding of self—you are able to regain and surpass even the initial ecstasy of falling in love. The ego boundaries dissolve, self is expanded to include other, and the true intimacy of shared identity is achieved. This is the spiritual dynamic between lover and beloved. It is of course important to remember that the beloved could be a man or a woman, a child, a community, a vocation, location, animal, or cause. The principle remains the same. There is no loving without giving. *Love always involves the willingness to transcend self for the sake of the growth of an other.*

For the Hebrew mystic, love is self-transcendence. Transcendence means the ability to break the walls of your narrow persona in order to embrace a wider understanding of self. To love an other means to create a new shared identity that is larger than your individual identities. And yet the integrity of each independent other is maintained. Love is the great and wonderful paradox of shared identity and powerful individuality. So self-transcendence is the widening of self through consistent giving and commitment to the growth of your beloved.

For the Hebrew mystics, the word for *love* itself expresses this notion of giving, which they so cherished. *Love* in the original Hebrew—*ahava*—is derived from the word *hav.* The primary meaning of *hav* is "giving." Wonderfully, in the original Hebrew, *love* and *giving* are the same word.

Every human being is born incomplete. True birth takes place in the course of a lifetime and not at life's inception. There is nothing more tragic than to die before being born. A lover is a midwife. To be a midwife is to be committed to helping your beloved birth his or her highest self. This is the great gift of love.

THE BARON LOVES PIKE

The one proviso for the type of giving that is truly loving is to make sure that your focus is really on the growth of your beloved. Too often giving is but the most sophisticated disguise for taking.

There was once a fisherman who caught a large pike. Seeing what a substantial catch this was, he said out loud, "I won't eat this fish. He is such a great catch that I will take him to the baron. The baron loves pike."

Hearing this the fish breathes a sigh of relief. "There's some hope for me yet!"

The pike is brought to the manor house. At the gate the guard asks, "What do you have?"

"A large pike!"

"Wonderful," responds the guard. "The baron loves pike." The fish is by now sweating profusely and gasping for breath, but he is relieved. A few more minutes, and he will be safe with the baron. The baron loves pike.

The pike is brought into the kitchen. The baron himself enters with a big smile on his face. "I love pike," says the baron.

As the fish, with its ebbing strength, wiggles around to ask for water, he hears the Baron say, "Cut off the tail and head and slice it down the middle."

In his last breath of terrible despair, the fish cries out, "Why did you lie? You don't love pike—you love yourself!"

To love is to be committed to the growth of the other. This always requires at least the temporary ability for self-transcendence.

We are divinely hardwired for giving as self-transcendence. God in the meditations of the mystics reveals herself as a giver, not a taker. According to the Kabbalah the very formation of the world is motivated by a divine love expressed in an infinite desire to give. If there is any need in God, it is the need to be a giver. Our own deeply felt need to give is our overwhelming desire to incarnate the God point in our lives. To give is to be like God.

A LIGHT MOTIF

Usually, when I give you something, it means that you now have it and I do not. Not so in reference to light and love. One candle can light a hundred candles without losing any of its own brilliance. It is for this reason precisely that light was held to be the incarnation of love.

The core intuition of all the great systems of the spirit is that love and eros are captured best by the image of light. The Kabbalah teaches that the light that fills the vessels of creation is love. The word *Torah* itself—an all-encompassing Hebrew term meant to refer to all divine wisdom—means "light." (The root of *Torah* is *orah*, which is the Hebrew word for light, which is also the basis for the English word *aura*.)

When you give in love, much like a candle, you are able to illuminate many people without ever losing any of your own luminescence. Giving love only creates more.

SMALL DEEDS OF GREAT LOVE

The paradigmatic biblical myth tale of love and giving is the story of Abraham, who sits, sick, at the entrance to his tent, in the heat of the day. He is greatly saddened for there are no guests to grace his house on that day. Tradition tells the story of God who, having compassion for Abraham's suffering in his sickness, made the day especially hot so as not to disturb Abraham with guests. Yet Abraham has a deep need to give. He gets sadder and perhaps sicker because there is no one to serve. Until—lo and behold—in the distance, he spies three men.

The biblical myth narrative describes in great detail how Abraham rushes to greet them and hurries with great alacrity to wash their feet, prepare them food and lodging. In reward for his hospitality, tradition records that Abraham merited many wondrous divine gifts. One contemporary mystical teacher, Chaim Shmuelivitz, dean of the greatest Talmudic academy in Jerusalem, asks a simple but highly provocative question. "Big deal!? So Abraham was generous in his hospitality. So am I. So are many other people. What was so special about Abraham that his hospitality earned for him such an abundant divine reward?"

Responding to his own question, Shmuelivitz writes, "There are no great deeds of giving; there are only small deeds performed with great love." When

Abraham served his guests, he was doing it from a place of unending and pure love. All of the infinite love in the universe was contracted into his every small deed of hospitality. When the infinite and the finite merge in a small point of goodness all of the worlds are raised higher. A smile. A good word. Abraham is the master of "small deeds with great love." This is why only Abraham, of all the biblical myth heroes, is called by the text a "lover." For to be a lover is to be a giver.

Give First, Love Follows

"Giving is not only the litmus test of love; it also leads to love," teaches the Baal Shem Tov. "If you want to be loved, be a lover." Raised on the love ethic of Western capitalism, we view feeling love as the necessary prerequisite for caring. Only when you love someone will you be ready to really give to them. But for the Hebrew mystics, it is precisely the opposite. Don't wait to be a giver until you are a lover. Be a giver and you will become a lover. In the act of giving to another, you invest yourself—literally!—in them. They become, in a small way, part of you. This allows you to focus on them in a far more concentrated and sustained fashion. Remember that love at its core is perception. Care, concern, and giving are inextricably intertwined with passion and ardor. Once you give to a person you always start to love them. Is there someone you simply do not like at work but have to "put up with" all day? Bring them a present. And witness the subtle shift in your own, not to mention their, attitude.

To be a lover, then, means to be there even when the feeling is not, in the good months and the bad months, in the heat of passion and in the cold dreariness of life at its toughest. When you say "I love you," what you are really saying is that you will stay even on the days when you can't fully access the depth of that passionate love. That is the gift of true love. Eventually it is only in the dynamic of commitment that the heart opens in a way that outlasts the vagaries of time and the fickleness of human emotion.

What's Yours Is Ours

Another Hebrew word used for *giving* is *tzedaka*. Usually mistranslated as meaning "charity," it really means "justice." The difference is enormous. Charity means that the money is mine, and because I'm feeling magnanimous, I give some to you. Justice, the correct translation for *tzedaka*, is understood by the masters to mean that your money is not owned by you at all. In Hebrew law, a portion of your money is in reality *owned* by the poor in the community. According to one legal school, the Tosafists, the only right you have to the money is to determine which poor person will receive it.

Wow! This law reminds us of *the* great truth of nondual thought. *You are not separate from everyone else.* The accumulation of property and possessions in this lifetime is overwhelmingly due to sets of circumstances entirely beyond your control. You may have worked hard, but there are a million people who worked just as hard and the universe did not allow them to accumulate your level of wealth. Those possessions are not essentially yours. And so, a portion of your possession, according to Hebrew mystical doctrine codified in law, belongs to those less fortunate than you, not because the government legislated taxes, but because nonseparateness is the essential metaphysical truth of reality. "Charity saves from death" is the koan of Hebrew wisdom masters. Not to experience the interconnectivity of being is to live a nonerotic, dead existence. I must give not out of charitable altruism but because of the metaphysical fact that you are part of me and I am part of you.

Jerusalem's Holy Beggars

In Jerusalem, my home, the streets are filled with beggars, men and women who for all sorts of different reasons make their living by asking passersby to "share the wealth." In almost any other city in the world, these people would be deemed panhandlers and consigned to the bottom of the social ladder. While I cannot yet tell you that these people are Jerusalem's elite, there is a strong sense that they are holy people. We invite them to our weddings, we wait on their blessings. We talk to them like they are family. For they are.

The holy beggars of Jerusalem, city of lovers, are an essential part of her spiritual fabric. One has the sense that the beggar is doing the passerby a favor. After all, their open hand is affording us the opportunity to give. The ancients taught that when the human being is possessed of a desire to give, the universe will give him wealth so he can fulfill that desire. Such spiritual physics turns our common understanding of the nature of reality on its head.

For many Western tourists coming to Jerusalem, the beggar scene is hard to bear.

Often I am asked by tourists who come to my lectures, "But do we have to give money to people who look like fakes?" An understandable question to be sure, yet it is still based in that possessive part of us that is pained by the thought of parting with something that "belongs to me." I usually give the startled tourist three different answers. "First, you should know that every time you pass a person whose hand is outstretched and you ignore them, something closes in your heart. The love-channels in your being begin to clog up. Not only will it become more and more difficult for you to give love out, it will also become increasingly difficult for you to receive love back.

"There is a teaching that if you have a hundred different coins, you should give them to a hundred different people. Even though the money will have little real life impact on the recipient's economic reality, the very act of giving to every hand you meet could have a real impact on your reality. Simply put, giving is at least as much for the giver as it is for the receiver. 'The rich need the poor more than the poor need the rich. Unfortunately, neither is conscious of it.'

"Second," I say before my tourist friend can run away, "let me tell you a story of the Great Master Zusia of Onipol."

Zusia had a disciple who would visit him occasionally and donate funds toward his support. It seemed that the more he gave to Zusia the more wealthy he became. At some point, the disciple discovered that Zusia himself had a master whom he would go visit, the Master of Mezritch. The disciple reasoned that surely the master is greater than the student.

And with that he stopped visiting and supporting Zusia, switching his allegiance to the master.

From that point on the disciple's business began to fail, getting worse and worse as time went by. Realizing this was no coincidence, he went to visit his original master, Zusia. "Holy master," he said, "surely even you agree that your teacher from Mezritch is greater than you. So why should I not be allowed to give my support to the higher master!?"

Zusia responded with a twinkle in his eye. "You see, my son, God is our shadow. His dealings with us are but an imitation of our dealings with others. As long as you gave without first judging to see if the person was worthy or not, as long as you would support someone as undeserving as Zusia, then the universe imitated you and was willing to support you without checking exactly what you deserved. But once you became selective and began to support only those who you thought deserved it, the universe also became more selective in choosing where it sends its support."

Third, for those who are still unsatisfied and find it too painful to give undiscriminatingly, I ask a simple question: How would you like to be asking for money on the street? Much as we honor the holy beggar, it certainly is not the easiest way to make a living. To be a lover, you have to engage in the spiritual practice of *harchavat hadaat*. Literally translated, this means the "expansion of consciousness." Taught by the nineteenth-century mystical master Nachman of Bratzlav, it involves widening your narrow field of vision to incorporate more of the other person's story.

Say that someone smashes into your car from behind. You jump out of the car and furiously race to the door of the offending vehicle. Fuming, you open the door, see the other driver, and exclaim, "MOM!!" Your anger cools in an instant because the faceless offender has recovered a personality. Mom! She has a story. When you open yourself up to her story, your feelings of love and empathy overcome your anger. You want to give and support her. You have been transformed into a lover.

When you encounter the beggars on the streets of Jerusalem, you have to open yourself to their stories. Imagine them as a relative, a child on their birthday, or a person on their dying day! Envision in a millisecond the imaginary details of their story. Allow them to have a face!

Social Transformers

We have, all of us, an erotic need to give, to contribute in a meaningful way to individuals as well as to our larger communities. We are driven not only to small acts of giving but also to great acts of sacrifice and heroism. We all desperately need to feel that our lives matter, that they are possessed of something essential, meaningful, and valuable. The unheard cry for meaning is always a desire to give. We are hardwired for giving. We long for not so much what we do not have as for what we do not give. We are unable to feel that essential sense of fulfillment that comes from living a life that matters unless we feel we are making some significant contribution to our larger community.

Happiness is not a goal; it is a by-product of a life well lived. That life must include profound loving/giving or it simply cannot satisfy us. Life cannot be lived without a cause that is larger than life itself. There is a profound human need for sacrificial action for the sake of the larger community. We ignore this need at our own peril. If we do not honor it with creative and ethical expression, then we or our children will be seduced to sacrifice to the manifold pseudo altars of repression, fundamentalism, and extremism.

That does not mean that we all yearn for lives of public service. It does mean that we need to feel that in our corner of the world we are doing our bit for society, above and beyond caring for our immediate circle. We all know, after all, that giving to our immediate circle, who are in effect extensions of ourselves, is really but a form of self-preservation. It is important and vital, but insufficient.

We yearn to widen our circle of caring to include at least some broader sense of community. When we are denied the right to serve a higher purpose, or when that essential need is denied or even ridiculed, make no mistake about it, we are being oppressed. We are living in a socially induced denial of our basic humanity. Denial and oppression create a psychological time bomb that sooner or later will explode in our faces.

CIRCLES OF CARING, CIRCLES OF INFLUENCE

The major reason that we stop giving and loving beyond our circle of protection is that it hurts too much. We know that if we open our hearts, they will all too often get trampled and trashed.

We basically feel powerless and that we cannot really change anything. Once that belief is internalized, a self-protective mechanism kicks in. We cannot tolerate a situation in which our circle of caring is far larger than our circle of influence. When we feel that our ability to experience hurt is far greater than our ability to alleviate the pain, then we simply turn off. The dissonance becomes too great to bear. The gap between our perceived ability to be hurt and to help is simply too wide to traverse. So we narrow our circles of caring to only those we feel we have the ability to help. But to do so, especially in a world where graphic images of pain daily invade our lives, we need to shut down our hearts. Powerlessness corrupts. We need to know that each of us by ourselves, and even more powerfully as a community, can make a difference for love.

THE GENESIS FESTIVAL—
I REFUSE TO BE INSCRIBED WITHOUT YOU!

In the hills of Galilee in Israel today, I am engaged with a holy troupe of seekers in nurturing the seedlings of a new activist mystical movement. We call it Bayit Chadash. Together with wonderful partners, students, friends, and teachers we are trying to reclaim the holy impulse of both Hebrew mysticism and social activism. We are radically underfunded and understaffed—often to the point of absurdity. Yet we hold to the belief that a future vision of Hebrew thought needs to be reborn from the same hills that birthed the Zohar and Lurianic Kabbalah. We realize how truly silly it is that common folks like us should set about this task, but in the words of the ancient Talmudic sages, "In a place where there is Nobody, try to be Somebody."

Over the last several years, as the *rosh bayit*, somewhat of a cross between the president of a college and the leader of an ashram, minus the salary of the first and guru implications of the second, I have been invited to lead the opening ceremony of what is called the Genesis Festival. It is a wondrous gathering of some 25,000 people that takes place at the time of the Hebrew New Year. Several years ago we started a custom of blowing one hundred *shofarot* (ram's horns) accompanied by 360 drummers to bid farewell to the past as we usher in the future. In the middle of all this, I give a short talk, which is always the same.

"On the New Year, our tradition teaches that those who merit are inscribed in the Book of Life. At this moment, the universe is judging who will live and who will die. Here at the Genesis Festival of love, we will not allow God or his angels that choice. We will not allow judgment to separate us from each other. So I ask each one of you to turn to the person next to you and say—'I refuse to be written in the Book of Life...without you!'"

Thousands of people turn, and with pure love flowing from open hearts, they embrace the person next to them, and we all say together, "I refuse to be inscribed in the Book of Life without you!"

At this moment, I feel like we are in the Temple, in the inner sanctum of the Holy of Holies. It is worth being born just to experience these minutes. The people who attend these festivals and Bayit Chadash give me great hope. They are the best in all of us. They remind me that we can transform our world into something more!

THE POSSIBILITY OF POSSIBILITY

We need a politics of love! We need to know that it is possible. We are taught that what human beings want is money and power. Anyone in close contact with people knows this is not true. Human beings want to live in a world based on love and caring, awe and radical amazement. Everyone knows that having more is not being more.

The great credo of faith for religion today is not dogmatic assertions about the metaphysical quality of divinity. Rather it is the belief that God is the power for love, healing, and transformation in the universe. God is the belief in possibility. In fact it is the possibility of possibility—which is affirmed by lovers everywhere—that ultimately love will win out and we will be able to create a better world. There is a covenant not only between the human being and the Divine, but there is also a covenant between generations. Each generation commits itself to living so that we can show our children a way that is a little more loving, a little more compassionate.

This is possible because the underlying reality of the universe is relationship and interdependence and not loneliness and alienation. We are born into loving hands. Left alone, we would die. It takes a world of cruelty and greed driven by fear to produce a reality where so many people die alone.

It is possible, as Robert Kennedy reminded us in the 1960s, to change the bottom line. Instead of a gross national product measured in purely economic terms, we could have a bottom line in which loving, human dignity, value, and uniqueness were factored into the equation. A company that was highly profitable financially but insensitive to human dignity in measurable ways should not be given the same benefits or should be taxed at a higher rate!

We think this is absurd because we have internalized the pathologies of our generation. Erich Fromm and Viktor Frankel have already reminded us that entire societies, including our own, can be profoundly imbalanced. We need to remember their teaching—otherwise we will experience the pathologies of spirit of our generation as our personal failures. If we feel emptiness in the mad drive for success, it is not because we are neurotic but because the success is an empty goal. If we feel powerless and frustrated, it is not because we need treatment. Quite the opposite; because our societal norms need to be changed it is often a symbol of our sanity and inner balance when we have not succumbed to the superficial values touted by our society.

We must know that our deep desire to give—to be lovers—is the most profoundly normal human state of being. We cannot have a delusion of grandiosity, for we *are*, in fact, grand. For the Kabbalists, the natural human condition is to feel wholly dissatisfied unless we feel we are meeting a cosmic need. Meir Ibn Gabai, a Renaissance mystic teaches, "Only with the knowledge that our gift is needed—that the universe 'needs our service'—can we touch fulfillment." This is what it means to be a lover of God and man. It is our calling to embody love and giving in our lives.

We are God's language in the polis. There is no split between politics and love. Love, eros, and politics are one! We understand that on the inside we are all interconnected. Politics is usually about protecting our rights, particularly our right to be separate. It needs also to be about obligation and love, chovah and chibah, which derive from the same root word in Hebrew. Both affirm the erotic interdependence of all life. We experience an intense yearning and desire to be of service in our communities. Through that loving service, we experience the fullness of being.

SMALL GROUPS WITH A SHARED VISION

To move toward a politics of love you do not need to found a new political party or national social movement. You need just a small group of people with a shared vision who are willing to stand together. As the anthropologist Margaret Mead said so succinctly, "Never doubt that a small group of thoughtful, committed people can change the world. Indeed, it is the only thing that ever has."

Your political spiritual lovers should be chosen the same way you choose your spouse: shared visions and values.

The philosopher Maimonides, taking his cue from Aristotle, teaches that there are three kinds of friendship communities. First, there are the pragmatic friends that help one another through life. Whether carpooling or giving a hand at the office, or rounding out a doubles game in tennis, these friends make our lives more practically feasible. The second group, more psychological in nature, is empathetic community. It is a place to share your woes, sorrows, triumphs, and victories. The third, and by far the highest kind of fellowship, is one based on shared vision and values. This is what philosopher Abraham Joshua Heschel calls "a community of concern."

If you think that you are only a small band of committed individuals who can't change the world, know that you are the only ones who can. It is the gift of commitment and love between holy friends and communities that can bring healing where there would otherwise be only sickness, and life where there might otherwise be only death.

TO LIFE, L'CHAIM

A famous mystical tale is told about the Seer of Lublin, a mystical master who lived in eastern Europe 150 years ago. Everybody knew that the holy seer could see from one end of the world to the other. For him, past and future were transparent in the present moment. Well, one day Levi came to the Seer to be with him for the holiday. However, as soon as he came in, the Seer said to him, "I am sorry, Levi, but you cannot stay with me this holiday."

"But why?" protested Levi. "I have come so far to be with you!"

"The angel of death surrounds you, Levi. I see that you are destined to die this holiday. It would be better for you to go to one of the surrounding villages and die quietly there."

You can imagine the shock and despair that overcame Levi. He had only one day to live. He took his belongings, and with tears streaming down his face, he began walking out of town toward his death. On the road, Levi saw a coach full of the Seer's students traveling toward Lublin. They were singing with great joy, obviously on their way to the Seer for the holiday. Spying him on the side of the road they stopped the coach and invited him in.

"Holy friend!" they called out. "Jump in! The holiday is soon, and you are walking the wrong way!"

Levi could barely talk and motioned them to continue. But being mystic initiates in the art of loving, they could not just leave him on the road, so they pressed him for an explanation of his strange behavior. Accordingly, Levi related to them what the Seer had told him and how he was going to die in a nearby village. The students glanced wordlessly at one another and then back at Levi.

Virtually in unison they responded, "The Seer is not always right. You do not have to die alone in a village. Come with us to Lublin; that way, if you do have to die, we can at least make you comfortable and help you in the crossing. Yes," they insisted, "you must come with us, and let us rejoice in the holiday together."

So Levi got in and they continued on toward Lublin. On the way, they passed a tavern, which prompted one of the students to say to Levi, "Since you will die tomorrow, surely you do not need your money. Why don't you buy us all drinks at the tavern and we can have a preholiday celebration." Levi agreed that this made sense, and they all piled into the tavern.

They bought a great deal of good whiskey. Each time one of the students was to down a shot, he would first turn to Levi, who was, after all, footing the bill and say, with great passion, "L'Chayim, Levi! Levi, to Life!"

What a time they had. They got higher and higher, and soon Levi got caught up in it all. Each time a student would drink and cry out, "Levi, L'chayim tovim aruchim—Levi, a good and long life to you," he would respond by downing another shot and returning the L'chayim. Before long, tomorrow seemed eons away. Round after round the blessing of L'chayim poured fourth.

They lost track of time and arrived at the Seer's prayer service only minutes before the holiday, happy, more than a little inebriated, and deeply bonded. After the service, which was overflowing with people, Levi, unsteadily but respectfully, edged his way to the Seer to wish him a good holiday.

The Seer smiled at him with great love and said, "Levi, the angel of death has left you! A master's protection is not as powerful as the love-filled blessings of L'chayim that the students give to one another. So Levi," he said, lifting his holiday wineglass, "let me add my blessing to theirs. L'chayim! To life!"

You see, my sweetest readers and friends, it is when we come together in holy community, when we stand for life together against the forces of fear and greed, that we can indeed change the world.

Giving and Receiving

THE MATHEMATICS OF EROS

May you have what you hold
and hold what you give
loosely, so it flows.
—PATTI NIEHOFF

Take a break from reading and stop by your local bank. If there is a particular teller you know, talk to him, because you may need some inside connections for this assignment. Ask him to withdraw fifty dollars from your account. Then very politely request that instead of listing a withdrawal from your account, would he kindly list the exchange as a fifty-dollar deposit to your account. He will probably think that he misheard you and ask you to repeat yourself. Say this again slowly, firmly, and with utmost gravity. When he laughs do not respond but repeat your request again ever so politely. Do not budge until he fulfills your request. Of course he will never do so. In all likelihood he will call his supervisor, and at some point you will be—more or less decorously— escorted from the bank.

Now, the people in the bank were right.

Giving and receiving are two completely different actions and never the twain shall meet. It's first grade math. Everyone knows that.

This is true in nearly every sphere of our lives. And yet the lover seeks to infuse this sharp and angular world with the softer curves of intimacy. The lover seeks to transcend and transform the rules of first grade math. The model for the lover? The sexual. In the sexual, giving and receiving follow very different rules of math and flow very differently.

The Blurring between Giving and Receiving

Not only is sexual love the model for radical giving, but it also personifies a very particular kind of generosity—one that defies all other giving patterns. In the sexual, we transcend the world of win-win, common goals, give-and-take, or getting even. The sexual models a different order of reality, where giving and receiving are indistinguishably one.

Everybody knows that sexuality at its highest is when your partner not only knows how to give you pleasure but is also a master of receiving it as well. In your beloved's receiving of pleasure, you are given a great gift. In the sexual, the rigid boundaries between giving and receiving are so dramatically blurred that the two become virtually indistinguishable. Sexuality at its highest collapses the separate spheres of giving and receiving into an undulating rhythmic flow of union. It is a great leap beyond the give-and-take of business into the virtual identity of giving and receiving within every pleasured gesture.

The sexual models a reality where the giver himself is deeply aware of how, in the very act of giving, he has received. Similarly the receiver herself feels that in the very act of receiving, she has been privileged to give. In erotic living, withdrawals become your deposits...and giving is the greatest gift.

SCORE SHEETS AND GIFT LISTS

The sexual teaches us how to be lovers in all facets of being. To be a lover, I need to stop keeping score. Who did who the last favor? Who cares!

When I was growing up, I remember how most of the families in my neighborhood had gift lists. This meant that your parents kept a chart that included the names of all the guests invited to your confirmation, bar mitzvah, or wedding. Next to every name there were three columns. First—did they attend or not. (If they attended it means you spent money on them and thus expected a commensurate gift in return.) The second column was an estimation of the cash value of any gift they gave. The third column listed what they should be given in return when we get invited to their celebrations. Of course we would NEVER give in excess of the amount we received, for, God forbid, the generosity might just topple the whole balance of the universe!

The mystery of love, the Kabbalah's secret of the cherubs, teaches something else. It teaches us to throw away the gift list, to tear up the score sheets. The total dichotomy between giving and receiving, which guides our economic and political lives, is in the end false. It misses the true eros of giving and receiving modeled by the sexual. In the erotic, every act is simultaneously invested with both giving and receiving.

When giving and receiving are split we remain deeroticized, loveless, and, worse yet, not satisfied. The reason of course is elementally simple. I can only be satisfied when I have received something. Only then can I be fulfilled. When I take I have not received anything, so even though I have tried to fill up, I remain on empty. The art of the lover is not only to know how to give pleasure in the world; but it is also to know the secret of receiving pleasure and thus being full.

THE BAOBAB TREE

In every act of receiving there is a gift. Taking, however, is fully distinct from receiving. To take is to acquire without receiving. The spiritual definition of *theft* is taking without being willing to grant the gift of receiving. We seek gratification of all forms without wanting to give of our souls in return. Mutual using has become the norm. Natural trust between people is effaced as everyone seeks to take maximum advantage of the other. Giving and Receiving is replaced by Taking without Receiving. Of course people get hurt much more than need be in such a world. At a certain point—after repeated emotional battering—our hearts close down, much like the baobab tree in the tale I will now share with you. When that happens we simply become less human.

The day was hot, the air was thick, the ground was hard, and the mouth was dry. The hare was making his way home when he came across the baobab tree. "Baobab tree," he calls out, "you are old and wise and generous. Please let me rest in your shade." The tree answered, "Hare, your request is true, come sit in my shade." The hare sits and thanks the baobab tree. But the air is still thick and the ground is still hard and the mouth still dry. The hare calls once again, "Baobab tree, you are old and wise and generous, allow me to drink from your sap." And the baobab says, "Hare, your request is true, please drink from my sap." The hare drinks from the sap, is refreshed, and thanks the baobab tree.

Some time goes by, and the hare calls once more, "Baobab tree, you are old and wise and generous, won't you allow me to enter your heart?" And the tree answers, "Hare, your call is true, come enter my heart." The tree opens her heart, and the hare enters. Inside he sees unimaginable beauty, lights of all colors, sparkling dewdrops, onyx and emeralds, diamonds and sapphires—all glittering and glowing. The hare calls to the baobab, "You are old and wise and generous, won't you allow me to take one of your stones to my wife as a present?" The tree answers, "Your request is true, won't you take one of my stones?" The hare thankfully takes a single crystal, steps out, and the heart closes behind him.

Now the hare takes the stone to his wife, who places it on a chain around her neck and walks around town, showing it to all. That night, the wife of the hyena says to her husband, "Go, get me a stone from the heart of the baobab tree."

The next morning, the air is thick, the sun is hot, and the ground is hard. The hyena comes to the baobab tree and says, "You are old and rich and beautiful—let me enter your heart." The baobab tree opens her heart. The hyena enters and sees lights of many colors, sparkling dew, and precious stones. And the hyena starts to grab—a diamond, a sapphire, a ruby. He grabs more and more, frantic with greed. He is out of control, taking from every corner of the baobab's heart. The tree, trembling and terrified, calls out to him, but the hyena cannot hear her. So, with a great shudder, the baobab closes her heart, trapping the hyena inside. The hyena dies. From that day on, the baobab tree has not been willing to open her heart to anyone, even to those whose call is true.

They say that we humans were once like the baobab tree, that all one had to do was call and immediately we would open our hearts. Is there a hyena trapped in your heart today?

THE SECRET OF THE KISS

The Kabbalists viewed kissing as the highest model of eros. Referred to among the initiates as *sod haneshika,* meaning "the secret of the kiss," this teaching suggests two modes of communication. The first is speech. Although there are many levels of speech, they all suffer from one weakness: the subject-object dichotomy between giver/receiver, or speaker/listener remains in place. The very act of having to speak implies the sharp separation between two souls.

When the Zohar teaches "*Daat* [intimacy] is only found in the mouth," it refers not to speech but to kissing. Kissing is the level where speech should naturally flow into in the context of a sacred relationship— the ideal communion.

In a wonderful rereading of a Talmudic text, one mystic reads the rabbinic admonition of "you shall not talk too much to women" to mean "don't talk when you should already be kissing." In the kiss, the yawning gap between subject and object—giving and receiving—is bridged. The split dissolves. This is the erotic model of union. Thus the great love epic of biblical myth— the Song of Songs—opens with the fantasy, "Kiss me from the kisses of your mouth, for your love is more wonderful to me than wine."

In the mystical reading of this verse, what is intended is a yearning for erotic union *beyond* the sexual. There is a longing for the life of the kiss where the hard and brittle boundaries of ego are softened and smoothed into the lovers' flow of the kiss. This happens only in the secret of the kiss, where in every transaction both parties give and receive simultaneously.

TWO RUBLES' WORTH

Yet sometimes it is excruciatingly hard for people to receive. For some people—and this is often the case with women—it is simply more comfortable to give than to receive. This creates an imbalance in their lives, which at some point always exacts a painful price. For others—often men—having a liability of gratitude hanging over one's head becomes too heavy a burden. Instead of receiving gracefully and graciously, they sometimes strike out violently at the very bestower of the gift. My grandfather used to say to me, "Mutty—you should know, some people don't know how to be *mekabel a tova*." Roughly translated, it means "people who don't know how to 'receive a favor.'" Or as the wise maxim goes, "No good deed goes unpunished." Hebrew mysticism is called *Kabbalah*, a word that means, very literally, "receiving," in recognition of the great spiritual art of love implicit in reception. Indeed sometimes it is exceedingly difficult to receive, and doing so requires both discipline and art.

Two men board a train in Kraków returning to their native village of Stanislav. One gentleman has somehow lost his wallet. Having no money, he asks the other, whom he recognizes from the village, for two rubles. The second man gladly obliges, and they are seated together on the train. The man who borrowed the money keeps fidgeting around uncomfortably in his seat. Unable to calm him down the second man takes out a ledger book and writes in bold letters: "On such and such a date I lent Mr. X two rubles" and requested that the first man sign it.

At this point the first man becomes exceedingly annoyed. "What's your problem—why are you making such a big deal? It was only two rubles."

"Aha," responds the man. "That is just my point. You see I have done you a favor. But I see you do not know how to receive a favor. So I am sure that you will try and hurt me eventually. When that happens, I want to able to remind you that you only have the right to hurt me two rubles' worth."

THE FUTILITY OF TAKING

Stealing breaks the intimate covenant of giving and receiving, violently redrawing the line of separation. It reinforces the illusion that we are separate from one another and that therefore my good can only come at your expense. Stealing is a form of rape.

One of the great biblical tragedies is the story of Amnon and his half sister Tamar. They are both children of King David. Amnon, smitten with Tamar, feigns sickness in order to lure her to his bedroom. He attempts to seduce her. She rebuffs him, pleading that he ask David for her hand. He cannot wait and rapes her. After the rape, all of his love for her turns to hatred, and he moves to throw her out of his quarters. Again she beseeches him, saying that to be cast out with such disdain is worse even than her rape. He is unmoved and throws her out of the house. In the tragic end to this unhappy story, Tamar's brother Absalom avenges her honor by killing Amnon.

Clearly Amnon is "taking" Tamar. He is neither giving to her, nor is he receiving anything in return. Yet what is important to notice in the story is not only its immorality. Biblical philosopher Joseph Soloveitchik observes correctly that this greed-driven immoral act doesn't even work. Amnon is not satisfied after taking Tamar. He feels his alienation even more acutely. The very person whom he craved in order to fill his void now becomes the new symbol of his emptiness.

Similarly, the corporation that may have cost thousands of families their jobs seeking to fund a hostile takeover, creating untold despair and pain, does not feel fulfilled by its acquisition. Rather it prowls on, seeking yet another victim for its insatiable greed.

The sexual again models all of life. To be a lover is to merge giving and receiving. That is erotic living. Anything less, in the final calculation, is not only immoral but also futile.

"EAT, BE SATISFIED, AND GIVE BLESSING"

There is a wonderful biblical myth epigram: "You shall eat, be satisfied, and give blessing." The biblical law professors read this to mean that you only have an obligation to give blessing if you have eaten enough to be full. And then, as legal scholars are wont to do, they go on to argue just how much food you need to have eaten to be "legally" defined as full. The mystical psychologists reread the text more deeply. "You shall eat—and if you are satisfied with what you ate—that itself is the blessing!" Following this way of reading, it would be fair to say that feeling happiness—truly the greatest blessing—is to be satisfied with what you have. Feeling miserable is to be satisfied only with what you do not have. Happiness then is fulfillment—mastery of the lover's art of becoming full, of receiving and thereby achieving satisfaction.

EVEN AN OLIVE'S WORTH

There is a passage that most stunningly captures this notion and takes it one step further. Recorded in the Babylonian wisdom texts, it is a strange symbolic conversation between God and his angels. "Why," the angels ask God, "do you accord the people of Israel your favor even when they are not deserving?" God responds, "How can I not? After all, in my Torah it says, 'And you shall eat, be satisfied, and give blessing.' And the children of Israel give blessing even if they have only eaten an olive's worth of food."

The text refers to the biblical myth text injunction we just mentioned above, which seems to indicate that one is only required to give blessing in thanks for food if one is fully satisfied. Nonetheless, continues the Talmudic passage, the children of Israel give blessing over food even when they are not satisfied, even when they have only eaten an olive's worth.

Mystical master Aaron of Karlin unpacks the powerful wisdom of the passage. What the text suggests is that if you wait to be satisfied, to be ful-filled until you have everything you desire, you will never be able to give blessing. Moreover, you will never experience your life as a blessing. Spiritual greatness is about being able to experience satisfaction and blessing even when you have only an olive's worth of fulfillment. The feeling of blessing emerges from the ability to experience the fullness of divine reality in every fraction of goodness. When I fully receive anything, no matter how small, it is enough to make me full. This is the lover's art of receiving and giving blessing. It is the secret of fulfillment.

Story Exchanges

We yearn—in our deepest hearts—not to take but to give, and in that giving to deeply receive. Sexuality is the model for this, because one single act contains within it both giving and receiving. The same is true, however, in all of our relationships. Every interpersonal relationship is an iridescent web of exchange. We each have a piece of each other's story. A lover's exchange is when I invest myself in our relationship sufficiently that over time I share with you the piece of your story that I carry with me, and receive from you the piece of my story that you carry with you. It may be an idea, an experience, a perspective, a song, a moment of intimacy, or a thousand other possibilities. The nature of the world is that every significant meeting we have is choreographed in order to return to us a precious missing piece of our being.

The Baal Shem Tov said to each student, "I am dependent on you; without you a part of my teaching can never be heard in the world." And so it is with us. For we are all teachers and all students. And so it is with God. Every human being is a prism that can uniquely refract a particular color in the spectrum of divine light. We are all God's faces.

God needs us to be revealed in the world. God needs us as we need him. Giving and receiving define our relationship as lovers with the Divine.

God's gift to you is your life. Your gift back to God is what you do with your life. God's gift to us is infinite love. Our gift to God is to receive that love. In our receiving we love God in return.

SOUP STORIES

Two images conclude our meditation on the lover's path of giving and receiving. Both are images of the deathbed—and soup(!).

A man lies on his deathbed, minutes away from his death. His son says, "Dad, is there anything I can get you...anything at all?"

"Yes, my son. I smell your mother's apple strudel in the kitchen. Perhaps you could bring me a bowl."

"Dad, of course. Wait just one second." Well, two or three minutes go by until the son returns. He has a crestfallen look on his face and no strudel.

"Son, what happened?" asks the father with his last breath. "Sorry, Dad," mumbles the son. "But Mom said the strudel is for the shiva."

Many times we are so concerned with external forms—with pleasing the mourners, as it were—that too often we lose sight of the true object of our giving. When that happens, our giving is not giving—it is rather a subtle form of taking for ourselves.

Contrast that with the second tale—one of the great erotic stories of the Hebrew masters.

The master Elimelech from Lishensk was on his deathbed with only a few weeks left to live. His son asked him, "Father, is there anything I can bring you?"

"Yes there is, my son. Many years ago I passed a tavern where there was a woman who made the most marvelous soup. It had the taste of the Garden of Eden. I would like to taste that soup again."

Now I have to tell you that this was a strange request indeed. Reb Elimelech was from the old school of ascetics who ate little and certainly did not remember women from taverns from years ago. Yet that was his father's request, and so off went his son in search of the tavern. Well, he located the tavern. Sure enough the same woman still worked there. He asked her to prepare the exact same soup that she prepared for his father years ago. He was sure that she would not remember him, but lo and behold, she did. In fact she seemed overjoyed at his request.

Unable to resist, he asked her, "Please tell me what was so special about that soup."

"Well," replied the woman, "this was many, many years ago. When your father entered I knew immediately he was a very holy man. In fact I loved him very much the moment I laid eyes on him. I wanted so much to do something for him. But what could I give him? We had just opened the tavern. We served only drinks. We didn't even have any money for food.

"Sensing my despair he came and asked my name and ordered some soup. 'Put everything you have in it,' he said, 'and it will be wonderful.' But I had nothing. So I boiled water and put in salt and cried and cried as I prepared the soup. So much I wanted for him and so

little I had to give. Well, I brought it to him. With the first taste he lit up, jumped up, and began dancing all over the tavern, crying out at the top of his lungs, 'The taste of the Garden of Eden!'

"I thought he was mocking me, but he motioned for me to taste it as well. Without a doubt—I couldn't believe it, but it was the most heavenly soup I had ever tasted. With tears in both our eyes we thanked each other and I never saw him again."

As the woman finished the story, both she and Elimelech's son were drenched with tears. Tears for the father and saint who lay on his deathbed, tears for how deep and holy life can be. With these tears they made a pot of soup for the dying man. And the taste… well you can imagine.

The woman in the tavern really had nothing material to give. But she was a lover and she wanted to give with all of her soul. So she gave her love. Reb Elimelech truly wanted to give. He knew his greatest gift was the ability to receive. And yet there was nothing to receive. But he loved so much that he received anyway. And what a gift it was.

Reb Elimelech, who was from the old school of severe ascetics who would scarcely look at a woman, understood the difference between the sexual and the erotic. This is the story of a great encounter between two lovers. It of course has nothing to do with sex. The complete blurring of giving and receiving is but modeled by sex. To be a lover is to leave behind the old and brittle distinction between giving and receiving and claim eros in all the arenas of our lives—from our soup bowls to our baobab trees, on trains to Kraków, and yes, even on our deathbeds.

SEVEN

Giving Up Control

Human beings are educated to always be in control. Many of the messages we receive, beginning with early childhood, are that we *must be* in control. The first conflict with our instinctive natures is, for most toddlers, toilet training. We are taught to control our bowel movements. This is but the first step in a lifetime that will constantly demand we be in control. From early on in life we are rewarded for maintaining control. We get painful disapproval, or worse, when we fail to exercise control. One of the most damaging assessments one can hear about a person is, "He's out of control." The mantra hammered into our psyches is: "Get a hold of yourself. Control yourself!"

While all this control education could be accomplished a bit more gently, we all recognize its importance. Going with the flow has its limitations. Few of us want to live in a world where people let their bowel movements (or any other impulses) flow naturally without any restraint whatsoever. Civilization is built on the lucid understanding that the world cannot survive without systematic self-control. In the life of the individual, the ability to delay gratification and channel energy and impulses is the key to a richer and deeper life.

As all jelly bean devotees know, five jelly beans are delicious. On the other hand, uncontrolled consumption—300 jelly beans in one sitting, for example—will make you very sick.

"Who is a hero?" ask the wisdom masters. "He who controls his impulses." In the hero's journey, control and discipline are what create ethical human beings.

Moreover, exercising tight control is at least one stretch in the road toward transformation. It is true that initially control adds some pressure to our lives. It is worth remembering, however, that coal only becomes a diamond when subjected to significant pressure. Control is and should be part of our understanding of the heroic life. However, this is where the popular Western educational myth usually ends, when in truth, this is really just the beginning of the story.

Loosing and Loosening Control

He who binds to himself a joy
does the winged life destroy;
But he who kisses the joy as it flies
Lives in eternity's sunrise.
                    —*William Blake*

The master who saw it as his role to reclaim the erotic at the core of life was the Baal Shem Tov, or Israel, Master of the Good Name. We have already met this master of eros in this book, and we will encounter him many more times along the way. The Baal Shem Tov was an eighteenth-century magician, mystic, and healer who founded the movement of spiritual renewal that swept eastern Europe in the 1700s. The story is told of a fateful meeting between Jacob Joseph of Polnoye, a well-known religious master of the time, and the Baal Shem. The master from Polnoye had apparently heard of the Baal Shem before but had refused to join his ecstatic movement. The following is the

story of their meeting. It is a story of surrender. It is about the need to sometimes give up control. I invite you to read it as a personal call to yourself as
well.

Jacob Joseph of Polnoye heard that there was a lone individual in the marketplace
telling stories. His stories were preventing people from coming to the prayer house for morn-
ing prayers. He had his attendant summon the renegade storyteller with the intention of
severely reprimanding him. The Baal Shem came to him, smoking his pipe.

Before Master Jacob could begin his scolding, the Baal Shem managed to say—"Allow
me to tell you a story." Jacob's voice caught in his throat. Against his will, he was silenced.
The Baal Shem began. "There was a man who had a fine carriage. It was pulled by four great
stallions. Unfortunately, all of the stallions were stuck in the mud. Try as he might, yanking
at the reins with all his human strength, he could not get them to move. A farmer passed him
traveling in the opposite direction. The farmer called out to him, 'Loosen the reins, loosen the
reins!'

"Do you understand, Jacob Joseph?" asked the Baal Shem.

"Yes, I understand." Jacob Joseph began to cry. He cried and cried. He finally under-
stood.

This is a story about eros. Jacob Joseph is a religious leader who views his
job as enforcing the rules. He is angry when people stop to hear a storyteller
in the market and miss morning prayer. He is often angry, and his carriage is
going nowhere because his horses are stuck in the mud.

In Plato, biblical consciousness, and much of mythology horses are
symbols of vitality—both erotic and sexual. Our horses are stuck in the mud.
To get them out, we need to listen to the farmer, who is a man of simple but
elegant wisdom. "Loosen the reins," he tells us, "and let the horses lead the
way."

The sexual, as we see through this book, is the model for becoming a
great lover in all of life. In the sexual we all know that we need to loosen the
reins yet not let go of them—and let the horses lead.

Now we are ready to unfold the next layer in the mystery of love. *To be an*
erotic lover we need to know not only how to give but also how to give up. Most specifically,
we need to loosen the reins, to give up control.

The Invitation to Love and Vulnerability

Great sex is not about being ethically out of control. The rapist and the abuser are no heroes. Nor is unbridled and uncontrolled promiscuity a cultural ideal. We all agree that for sexuality to be both ethical and sacred, it needs to have limitations.

Yet within the context of ethical sex it is the letting go of control that is the very essence and ideal of the experience. The level of passion and intensity of pleasure is directly related to the degree to which the lovers allow themselves to lose control. Great sex cannot be fully experienced without yielding some significant measure of control, not only in orgasm but in the earlier and more gradual unfolding of desire as well. Sounds, facial expressions, body movement, and raw emotion are all freed from the tight reins of our internal regulators.

What is unique about sexual love is that lovers not only let go of their internal controls but they also invite their lovers to witness their surrender. In the invitation to the other to both participate and witness, there is not only a giving up but also a giving over of some dimension of control to the other. To love—in all arenas of living—is not only to relinquish control but also to grant a measure of control to another—that is to say, to be utterly, openly, vulnerable.

The moment Cary and I crossed the line into the world of love, I had to let down some of the walls and grant her a level of control. I was vulnerable. She could hurt me. I had invited her into my Holy of Holies in the trust and faith that she would tread gently. The uncertainty (and vulnerability) inherent in giving up control is inseparable from the invitation to love.

Control, Power, and Mixed Messages

Control is most often used in the world as a tool of power over others. When we say a person is powerful, we essentially mean that they have direct control over other people's lives. We label a person powerless in modernity when they exert no obvious control over destinies other than their own, and often not even that.

So we receive mixed messages. On the one hand, we know that to be a lover you need to give up control. On the other hand, we are driven by a society that worships control as the elixir of the gods and the implicit goal of living. Driven by fear, we seek to exercise maximum control and wield maximum power. This ambivalence reflects itself in the comic absurdity of much of therapy. We go to our shrinks to learn how to "let go" *and* how to "get control of our lives." We want them both. We feel constricted, tight, trapped, at the same time we feel we are losing control.

Deep down, the knower in us understands that love and what society labels as power are two very different, virtually opposite, modes of being. To love is to give up control and to expose our vulnerability. Power is to maintain control and hide vulnerability. In love, my gain is your gain. In power, my gain is your loss. In love, the goal is to serve and the grail is intimacy. In power, the objective is conquest and the trophy domination.

Love is inspired by the desire to give even as you give up control. Power is motivated by the desire to take even as you exert control.

Ultimately, the refusal to retreat and accept limitation and loss of control is the source of evil. Only the human ability to step back and give up ownership and domination holds out hope for a good, kind, and gentle world. This is what it means to be a lover.

Here again, sex models the spirit. The greatest gift a lover gives to his beloved is to relinquish his vaunted self-control in her presence. To be sexual is consequently to trust in the presence of the beloved. Just so for the lover in all facets of human life.

VICTORIOUS SURRENDER

Lindsey was a bright-eyed eight-year-old. One day at the grocery store, she saw a plastic pearl necklace priced at $2.75. How she wanted that necklace! How she begged her father for it! And what father can refuse the determined enthusiasm of an eight-year-old? Those pearls became her pride and joy. She wore them, flaunted them, polished them lovingly.

One night, after reading her a bedtime story, Lindsey's dad leaned over and asked her, "Lindsey, do you love me?"

"Yes, Daddy, you know I love you," the little girl answered.

"Well, then, give me your pearls."

"But, Daddy, not my pearls! You can have Missy, my favorite doll. Remember her? You gave her to me last year for my birthday."

"Oh no, darling, that's okay." Her father brushed her cheek with a kiss. "Good night, little one."

A week later, after the bedtime story her father asked once again, "Lindsey, do you love me?"

"Yes, Daddy, you know I love you."

"Well, then, give me your pearls."

"Oh, not my pearls! But you can have Randy, my toy horse."

"No, that's okay," her father said and brushed her cheek again with a kiss. "Sweet dreams, little one."

Several days later, when Lindsey's father came in to read her a story, Lindsey was sitting on her bed, a few tears trickling down her cheek. "Daddy…here," she said, and held out her hand. She opened it and her beloved pearl necklace was there. With one hand her father took the plastic pearls and with the other he pulled out of his pocket a blue velvet box. He opened the velvet cover, and inside was a string of beautiful, genuine pearls.

He had had them all along. He was just waiting for Lindsey to give up her plastic pearls so he could give her the real thing.

When we first read the story, Lindsey's father seems cruel, even sadistic. Often God appears the same way until we realize that God is waiting for us to give up the imitations in our lives so that we can receive the real thing. We all recognize imitation personalities, imitation happiness, and even imitation loving. Imagine what would happen if we really opened up to the knowledge that there is a force holding things together without our being in control. What if we surrendered to that force and allowed it to guide us in our lives? What if we stopped to realize that the planet is constantly supporting our lives?

The very air we breathe—unless we interfere with our planet's ecosystems—is constantly made available to our lungs by plants and ocean plankton through the remarkable process of photosynthesis. The universe is consciously supporting us and breathing life into our souls at every moment. For the Hebrew mystic, creation is not a one-time event. It is instead a continuous process, hinted at by modern quantum physics, in which the universe re-creates itself in love at every second.

This essential giving up of control does not mean that we do not expend enormous effort and energy in trying to chart our destinies and repair the world. It does mean that we need to do so in such a way that we understand that even as we labor mightily, we know that it is simply not all up to us. Knowing that, we consciously invite the universe to be a partner in our efforts, breathing its life and energy into and through us.

The spiritual process of giving up control is called by the Hebrew mystics *bittul*. Usually, this is explained as self-nullification to God. In reality, it means something quite different. Rather than abnegation, it is a way of making ourselves *transparent* to God. We give up lower self-control because we desire the higher divine self to flow through us. This is the experience of eros modeled on the sexual. We can access it in creativity, prayer, sexuality, study, and any other arena of life in which we are willing to be lovers.

THE KEY—AIKIDO

One paradigmatic example of giving up control to let a higher force infuse us is the martial art of aikido. Randoori practice in Aikido is a form of freestyle training in which the student is attacked by multiple assailants. In this kind of attack—as is so often true in life—there is no way for one to control the outcome through raw power, no matter how skilled you are.

The key to randoori is to become an erotic lover of yourself and the universe. The student steps deep inside to access an interior center of calm and balance. Everything slows down, and when it happens you feel what the

Japanese call *ki* and the Hebrew mystics call *shefa* (divine effluence or flow) gently coursing through you. You do not decide which response or technique to offer your attackers. That would be an attempt to control the situation. Rather, from a deep place, you feel your attacker's energy and you visualize the outcome of the combat before it has even begun. The student is always grounded and centered even when swirling to meet the next attack. The key to randoori is paradoxically to give up control, to be a lover. Here is the description by one Western randoori practitioner of his black belt test.

I bowed to my attackers, giving them the signal to begin. They came rushing in, far faster than I was prepared for, and almost without thinking, I dropped to my knees directly in front of my first attacker, destabilizing him enough to completely throw off his balance and attack. When I rose to my feet again, although I knew my attackers were moving very quickly, my perception of time had changed. I discovered I had the space to take a few steps, the leisure to feign a strike to an attacker, the opportunity to pivot and lead an attacker into a fall. Yet during these chaotic moments I was more deeply attuned to my breath than to my attackers. The sound and rhythm of my breathing filled my ears more than the cries and grunts of my opponents.

Because I spent a fraction of a second too long throwing one of my attackers, two of the other opponents converged upon me, seizing my arms at the same time in an attempt to immobilize me. I knew that they were far stronger than I was, and that if I did not do something, the other attackers would descend upon me in a moment. In a fraction of a second of panic, I discovered that I could not dislodge them with my strength alone. In that moment, my panic subsided and I gave up my ego. I did not even try to struggle with them. I ceased caring whether or not I would emerge successfully from this situation; I stopped caring whether my teachers would promote me or what my friends who were watching would say if I failed. I let go of my sense of self, and for the briefest moment in time, I was happy not to care. I centered myself and exhaled deeply, whirling around, shaking all of the tension and anxiety out of my body like a dog shaking off water after a swim.

I could have said "abracadabra" and the effect would not have been any less magical—my attackers flew off me as though we were magnets whose polarities had suddenly been reversed. In that moment of shock and amazement, my trance ended. I found myself gasping for breath and drenched in sweat. My test was over, and suddenly, everyone in the room was clapping.

This could well be the archetype of the experience of *bittul*—transparency—taught by the Hebrew mystics. The soul longs for loss of intention, consciousness, and control. There is a part of us that wants to give up the charade of being in control, constantly thinking, planning, and directing our lives. In addition, we sense intuitively that there is some deep part of us that can only be revealed when we "loosen the reins" and give up control.

The Music of the Temple

One of the places where we overcome alienation and step inside to an act of surrender is the sacred realm of music. Song and music are erotic. We plunge into our depths even as we surrender ourselves to the music. Eros cuts through ego and touches essence. We feel alive and totally present in the fullness of our longing. Mastery in song and music takes place precisely at the point where radical discipline and control are transcended. At the intersection between control and surrender the singer or musician gives herself up, allowing herself to be played by the universe. It is of course not an accident that an essential component of the Temple service was music. The biblical myth text reads, "If you are searching for Shechina" then come to the Temple with its symphony of holy song. Through music from exotic instruments and songs that opened the heart, the people were aroused to the erotics of desire and personal surrender.

"A Helpmate against Him"

It is however in the music of relationship that giving up control is most important. Man is lonely. In biblical myth God makes him a helpmate, *kenegdo*, opposite him, or, in some translations, a helpmate against him. Now what does that mean, a partner who is against him asks virtually all of biblical commentary? The Hebrew word used is *ezer*, a "helper." If she is a helpmate then how can she also be *kenegdo*, against him?

Adam is lonely. The only way beyond loneliness is love. Love is the oppo-site of control. If the relationship is one of domination and control, it will fail on two levels. First, both sides will remain lonely. Second, they will not help each other, for an equal partnership is premised on giving up control. It is only if he respects her *kenegdo*, her opposition, her "no," that there can be love and partnership.

Whenever you insist on control in a love relationship, there are two reasons why you ruin the love. First, because only mutuality can redeem you from loneliness. Second, because love is a perception, and domination always blurs perception. This is why I often refer to our Edenic couple as "Adam and Even"—for the point of Eve being a helpmate "against" is that Adam must view her as Even to himself, or the relationship is doomed. When you are not *kenegdo*, when you are not face-to-face at the same level, you simply cannot see each other with clarity.

Naming, Nakedness, Cleaving, and Kenegdo

Sometimes it helps to survey the results of past relationships to understand the deep necessity of giving up control. God brings to Adam the animals to name. Naming, in this context, is a symbol of control. These are not intimate, affectionate names. It is more similar to the taxonomist naming animals zoo-logically as an act of classification and control. Eleventh-century interpreter Rashi suggests that he did not merely name them. Mythically, "naming" implies that Adam had sexual relations with all the animals. The image sug-gested in this myth is then sexuality as conquest. It is an image of sexuality without giving up control. The animals, in this reading, become symbols of sex divorced from love and eros. Adam wanted to know if sexuality by itself was sufficient to redeem him from his loneliness.

The answer? "Man did not find among all the animals an *ezer kenegdo*—a partner opposite." The sex was great while it lasted. But when it was over he merely felt his loneliness all the more acutely. So God causes Adam to fall asleep, a powerful myth image of vulnerability. Then in the first recorded surgery in history, God removes the rib from which Eve will be formed. The point is clear: only by giving up control and being literally opened up and exposed can an authentic relationship be formed. What's more, it is only by giving up a part of your being, in this case symbolized by Adam's rib, that you can hope to overcome the infinite ache of loneliness. Only vulnerability and sacrifice can create the connection and lift you out of your loneliness.

Man and woman are described as being "naked and not ashamed." With each other they are able to be totally vulnerable and exposed without feeling shamed. To be naked means to let go of the need for posturing. If you fall in love with my outer facade, you remain lonely because deep down you know the person your lover adores is not you at all. British philosopher Adam Phillips said it beautifully: "It is only when two people forget themselves in the presence of the other, that they can remember each other."

Only then does it say, "Man cleaved to woman and they were one flesh." "One flesh" is an obviously sexual image. *Cleaved*, which is a translation of the Hebrew word *devekut*, is a word of the spirit connoting eros and deep love. Once man gives up his striving for domination and control, once he is ready to create a relationship of mutuality where each side challenges the other in love to higher growth, only then is loneliness transcended into union and love. Love is a surrender, a relinquishing of control. Love of God is responding in trust to the loving force of being—the God-flow in the universe. Love of an other is responding in trust to the divinity of an other.

Where Lovers Gaze

Love means mutuality. Neither side can have a controlling vision.

I heard recently of a mother whose son very much wanted to be a writer. For years though, for not fully understandable reasons, he was unable to get it together and write. Finally, one day, on the verge of despair, he broke down crying to his mother. He told her that he was going to abandon writing. To his surprise, she said to him, "I have been waiting for you to give up writing all these years. I know it isn't right for you. Indeed I pray every day that you should not write."

This is a story that sends shivers down my spine. Of course the poor guy can't get a word out! And his mother, of course, does not love him at all! We are told that Saul, the first king of Israel, loved young David very much. Yet when he tells David, after the latter has slain Goliath, "You shall not return home but shall eat at the king's table," the reader knows that something is amiss. If Saul is attempting to control David, then he cannot love him. Trouble lies ahead. In due course, the jealousy emerges and Saul spends much of his later years in pathetic attempts to have David killed. As soon as the desire to control entered the story, it was only a matter of time until love failed.

In the classic lover's model, the two lovers look deeply into each other's eyes. This lasts for as long as they are still head over heels in love. But eventually that fades and then the struggles for control begin. Looking into each other's eyes too often becomes staring each other down. Usually the dominant personality in the relationship determines the controlling vision that guides them forward.

For the biblical mystic, though, the initial relationship needs to be based on something other than long, melting looks as you gaze deeply into each other's eyes. Lovers must begin by looking at the horizon together. They must come together based on shared values and vision. Only after looking together at the same vistas of spirit can they turn and look at each other. Lovers who refuse to yield to a higher vision wind up in ferocious battles for control. Love happens when each side gives up its controlling vision of reality. This allows each side to forge its connection in the raw fires of untainted love.

The Etrog

Hebrew mystical initiates like to tell the story of Reb Mikel's *etrog*. Now an *etrog* is a very specific kind of citrus fruit used in the ecstatic rituals of the biblical harvest festival Sukkot.

Reb Mikel loved the ecstatic ritual of the etrog fruit. As such, he was greatly saddened at not having sufficient funds to purchase a proper etrog. He grew even sadder when he heard that there was one beautiful etrog available at a very high price in town. He went to see it and was taken by its particular beauty and precise measurement that fit so perfectly the legal requirements for the ritual. But alas, he had debts and obligations. There was no way he would ever have such money.

Well it happened that before Sukkot, a wealthy merchant gave Reb Mikel a particularly fat envelope to give to his wife. For some reason, perhaps the thickness of the envelope, his curiosity was piqued, and he opened the envelope. Imagine his surprise when he saw a very large amount of money inside. He was overjoyed. Surely this gift was directly from God. He literally ran into town and used all the contents of the envelope to buy the beautiful etrog for the Sukkot ritual.

He came home overjoyed and showed his wife this wonderful etrog. She was silent for a moment. Then, with a voice quivering with rage, she asked him, "Where did you get money for such an etrog? We are so poor and have no savings. Where did you get the money?"

Just as she feared, he was oblivious, overjoyed as he was at his etrog, and answered gaily, "Why a wealthy merchant gave me an envelope. You won't believe this, holy wife, but it was filled with money. A gift from God! I ran back to return the money to the merchant and he seemed taken aback. He told me that it was a gift from God as well and to do with it as I please. Isn't that wonderful, my dear?"

His dear, naturally, realized that he had spent all of their charitable food money for the entire holiday on his etrog. She was both furious and brokenhearted at the same time. She stormed over to the table where the etrog sat, picked it up, and hurled it against the wall, where it smashed to bits.

His face went white and there was dead silence in the room for about sixty seconds. Brokenness. He then slowly walked over to her and said, "Before, we had the money, then we had the etrog, now we have only each other. Let us, sweet wife, dance together." They both burst into a mixture of tears and laughter and danced in the bliss of love all through the night.

Truly this is a love story. Both Reb Mikel and his wife had visions of how life should be lived. For years, each had attempted to impose his or her own perception as the controlling vision that guided the relationship. (Mikel was more otherworldly and mystical; his wife was more practical.) Finally it all came apart as the *etrog* exploded on the wall of their tiny home. Money gone, *etrog* gone. At that point, each realized their own inability to impose their vision on the other. It was a Zen moment of turning and illumination. In the same instant they both, in a fit of despair, gave up control. But once they let go, something opened: the gates of love. For the first time in so many years they were able to see each other again, to give, to love, to dance, to laugh.

Divine Failure, Divine Miniatures

Maybe the most important Kabbalistic teaching on love comes from the realm of cosmology, where the biblical mystics introduce to us a beautiful and important idea that enormously effects how we live our lives. The idea in two sentences: The world does not come into being through divinity stepping forward in a creative gesture. Quite the opposite—God steps back in a movement of sacrificial withdrawal in order to create the world. God creates an empty space, and only then, in that space, can the world emerge from the divine womb of being! "But how could that be?" we ask the mystics. "Isn't the whole point of the God idea that divinity is infinite and everywhere? How can God just step back?"

"This," respond the biblical mystics, "is precisely the mystery of love."

This can be explained by two images, in which the second expands on the first. In the first image, Raphael of Barsad tells of his meeting on the road with eighteenth-century Eastern European mystical master Pinhas of Koretz.

"Please," says Pinhas to Raphael as his coach pulls up alongside where Raphael was walking. "Please get in and ride with me."

"But master, there is no room!" protests Raphael.

Responds Pinhas, "Don't worry, let us be close friends and there will be enough room."

In the second image a sacred conversation takes place between fourth-century Babylonian wisdom masters.

It is written that God withdraws his presence from the world to dwell in the empty space between the cherubs in the Temple. But how could this be? Is it not also written that all of heaven, indeed all the space in the cosmos, is not enough to contain divinity? "Ahh," says Master Yusi. "It is to be likened to lovers. When they quarrel, even a palatial home is not enough for their needs, but when they love, they can make their bed even on the edge of a sword."

The mystery of creation, of existence itself, is *tzimtzum,* meaning "withdrawal." God creates the world by withdrawing to make space for the world. What is the motivating force of *tzimtzum?* Both of our images give the same answer. *The motivating force of tzimtzum is love.*

Love is the force in the cosmos that allows God to step back and allow room for us. As with God, so with us. We are *homo imago dei* who participate in the divine image—divine miniatures. In order for us to create a world, a relationship, we need to step back and create an empty space in which there is room for *other,* in which there is a place for the relationship to unfold. "Let us be close friends and there will be room." If I love you, I need to know how to step back and make space for you. *Tzimtzum* is God saying, "You can choose—even if you choose against me." This is the gift of love.

S-mothering

Just as God steps back and allows us room to be and to choose, even when we choose against God, so a parent needs, at a certain point in the child's development, to step back and allow the child room to choose, even if it is a choice against the parent. The litmus test of love is not only giving but *giving up* control. Can you, as a parent, step back to make room for your child's growth, even if it is sometimes growth away from you?

There is something tragic yet beautiful in this moment of love. A mother begins by being bonded to her child. Her primary gift of love in the early months and years is radical presence. It is the presence of the mother that allows the child to become psychologically healthy and spiritually sound. Yet as time passes, it is the mother's job is to become more and more absent. This is the nature of Shechina love.

Remember the biblical story about the two mothers who come before the wise King Solomon? Each claims the same baby as her own. Solomon moves to cut the baby in half to give part to each mother. One woman protests, "No! Give the baby to her...only do not harm him." Solomon knew immediately that the true mother had spoken. The story is about loving and giving up control. True love gives life while pseudo love smothers and strangles.

In the biblical myth, we are told that Rebecca loves Jacob. This is the only place in *Genesis* where we are told of a mother's love for her child. It is also the only place in *Genesis* where we see a mother sending her child away. Rebecca sends Jacob far away from Canaan, to her brother Laban in Padan Aram. As they part, she promises to bring him back. She never does. Rebecca never sees Jacob again.

She sends him away in part to protect him from his brother Esau, whose birthright Jacob has stolen on Rebecca's instructions. Yet she primarily sends him away so he can begin his hero's journey. For she knows that only if she lets go can her son find his own voice, "the voice of Jacob." Not only mothers, but also lovers need to give up control—to step back and withdraw their presence to allow room for the beloved. The husband who claims to love his wife cannot refuse her desire to go to school, even if he is afraid that it will allow her to go places where he cannot follow. Love is commitment to the other's growth without controlling the direction and nature of that growth.

Presence in Absence

Love is the revelation of another person's freedom. The body of the beloved may be penetrated, but on some level you know that your beloved's consciousness can never be fully penetrated. In the biblical wedding there is a custom where the husband covers his future's wife face with a veil. It is as if to say, "I know that I can never fully know you. Even as I commit to spend my life trying to understand you, I promise always to honor the mystery."

However, even when parents, partners, or lovers withdraw their presence, they are still there. They never go away. I say to my lover all the time—even if I am not with you, I am always on your shoulder. Paradoxically, the moments of greatest love are sometimes the moments when we are least obviously present, when we have absented ourselves because we know it is essential for our partner's or child's growth.

Mom is teaching her son to walk. She holds on to both of his hands above his head as he takes the first step. She lets go. He takes the first steps on his own. Who among us does not understand that the mother is closer to her son at the moment she lets go than she ever was before? It may take a long time. He falls, rises, walks a few steps, and falls again. Love is a commitment to growth and giving up control even if it takes a very long time.

Letting Go of Perfection

Perfectionism is but another disguise for control. Self-love then means giving up on your own need to be perfect. Self-love allows room for imperfection and failure. Emerson was right when he wrote, "There is a crack in everything that God has made."

It's like the old Japanese tea masters. When they made their utensils, they'd make sure that something, be it the tea scoop or the bowl, would have a flaw. A really nice and well-placed flaw, mind you, but still a flaw. If the thing was flawless, they'd fix that. For as every wisdom master knows, nothing is flawless.

The Baal Shem Tov was asked by his disciples, "After you have gone, how will we know whether another spiritual master is true or false?"

"If he promises to teach you pure prayer, know that he is a false master."

So the first movement of love is to let go of the need for purity, which is really just a cover for total control.

Even God Didn't Get It Right

My grandfather loves to tell of the man who orders a suit from an excellent tailor for his upcoming business trip. The day before his departure, he goes to collect the suit, but it is not yet ready. Unable to postpone his journey, he travels, returning after many months. Again he goes to collect his suit, but the tailor says, "Sorry, another four days."

In fact, four days later the suit is ready. The man tries it on and is overjoyed. The cloth feels so wonderful, and the suit is both beautiful and an incredible fit. When he wears it, he feels wonderful currents of energy and confidence. But he cannot resist asking the tailor, "Why did it take you so long for one suit? After all," he adds, "even God only took six days to create the world."

The tailor, not batting an eyelash responds, "Yes that's true; but look at his world and look at my suit!"

For the Kabbalist, failure is built into the very fabric of existence. Ultimately, that means that God is both the source and model of failure. One of the least understood and most radical dimensions of Kabbalistic teaching is the model of a God who cannot seem to get it right the first time around.

Remember that in Renaissance Kabbalah, the primary image of creation is God force emanating light into vessels. For whatever reason, these vessels are structurally flawed. "Structurally," of course, is not a physical term but refers to the diagram of the spirit on which the vessels are patterned The flawed vessels are unable to hold the light streaming into them from the divine emanation. They shatter. Shards of vessels fall and disperse throughout reality. Many of the shards retain sparks of light. The purpose of existence is to gather the sparks of light, called *nitzotzot*, and reintegrate them with their divine source.

What is essential in this Kabalistic image is the centrality of failure. God tries to create the world. It doesn't work because the vessels shatter. Our whole lives are then spent trying to return to the original pristine state before the vessels shattered, the only difference being that this time when we return, we are humbler, wiser, and able to transcend even the initial perfection with which we began.

An image from Talmudic mysticism is the God "who creates worlds and destroys them." God is dissatisfied with his creation. He is the artist who tears up draft after draft until one spills from his brush that seems right.

We are imitators of divinity. We participate in divinity. Just as God stood on the abyss of darkness and said, "Let there be light," so do we stand on the abyss of darkness and say, "Let there be light." Just as God failed in his creative gesture yet reached deep within to find the love to create again, so do we.

Businesses fail, love is on the rocks, theorems and theories are exploded. Yet built into the original design of our being is a special reservoir of inner strength, which allows us to pick ourselves up off the floor and start again. And the second creation, be it an idea, a marriage, or what have you, is always potentially more beautiful and more complete than the first. The question is not did you fail—but rather did you try again?

Failure is part of the hardwiring of the system. Failure is structurally embedded in both the Divine and ourselves. There can be no creativity without it. When a business fails, a marriage falls apart, or a dream shatters, we are playing out the primal drama of creation, which repeats itself time and again from the beginning of history to the end of time.

Broken Tablets

We return to the ark in Solomon's Temple. In the ark are two sets of tablets. In the language of the masters "tablets and broken tablets rested in the ark together." This is a stunning image. The broken tablets were received by Moses at Mount Sinai in his first valiant but failed attempt to bring God's law to the people. When he realized he has failed he smashed the tablets. The second tablets are from his second more successful ascent of Mount Sinai. The broken tablets are the symbols of our failures.

Most of us tend to leave our failures behind, to delete the names from our Palm Pilots and to excise whole chapters from our sacred autobiographies.

Biblical myth comes to gently remind us: Your broken tablets are holy. Love them. Sparkling manuscripts only come from rough drafts. The rough drafts too must be given a place in your sacred ark, in the Temple of your life.

The primary job of the parent is to teach us that we are worthy of love even when we fail. Parental love is distorted in the parental urge to control the child. Often such distortions are motivated by a genuine desire to save a child from failure. Even so, it does not show real love. Often parents avoid coming to grips with their own stories by attempting to control the lives of their children. To love is to give up control and make space for the other. But when we lack an inner center ourselves, it is nearly impossible to make space.

Controlling God—Cosmic Vending Machine

Just as God must give up control of us to be a lover, so must we give up control of God.

One reason that biblical myth was so powerfully opposed to idolatry is precisely because it was a method of controlling God. The basic idea in much of ancient idolatry was that the gods could be manipulated. If you said the right prayer or incantation, or performed the right sacrifice, then the god would do whatever you willed. Divinity becomes a cosmic vending machine where the key is having the right change.

Prayer also can be a form of controlling God. Prayer healers abound both within and without organized religion who promise that prayer can bring healing. Now, there is little question that prayer does affect wellness. Dr. Larry Dossey has collected many studies and written important books on the subject. But as Dossey himself cites from numerous sources, the prayer that is truly effective is the one in which we ask for healing without specifying a particular outcome. We are not sure what the best outcome is. We cannot force the universe's hand.

What we can do through prayer and spiritual practice is to open up what the Kabbalists call the channels of energetic flow. In Kabbalah these are somewhat like the heart valves of the universe, which get clogged when we do not clean them through prayer and practice.

We try to control God with theology all the time. When preachers, imams, or rabbis give explanations as to why people suffer in the world, they are refusing to give up control. It is an act of hubris motivated by a desperate desire to maintain control. A Jewish example is the Holocaust, in which most of my family was killed. There are voices in Judaism that seek to explain why the Holocaust happened; usually, they are based on pointing to the spiritual failings of a particular group of Jews. It is of course never the group with which the explainer is affiliated. A Christian example is Jerry Falwell's explanation of why the September 11 terrorist attacks happened. They were punishment for the underlying moral malaise in America.

I can promise you that God did not inform Falwell or the Holocaust explainers of his plans. The explanations come from a desire to control and even own God. But they do not come from a real love of God—quite the contrary.

In truth, we do not know why people suffer. And no explanation can suffice to justify the horrors of war, hunger, and disease. The lover seeks not to explain or control, but to become a partner in the healing.

Involuntary Systems

Our bodies remind us that we are neither the masters of our fate, nor even the sergeants of our destiny. Actually although we identify with parts of our bodies, we disassociate from most of our physicality. Language always reveals the secrets of the psyche. We say "I moved my hand" but we do not say "I circulated my blood." Your ego can identify with your arm, but not with your circulatory system. We identify with our voluntary systems and detach from our involuntary systems.

The reason is as simple as it is obvious: We fear loss of control. We disassociate from the body, for it is essentially not under our control. Most of the body is a well-organized collection of involuntary processes—that is, processes beyond our control—metabolism, digestion, growth, circulation, respiration. We distance these from our identity. We do not call them "self" because they are uncontrollable. Yet isn't it strange that we call only half of our organism "self?" To whom does the other half belong!?

When I was eighteen years old I was close friends with Dafna, an incredible Israeli woman. She taught me far more about life and its mysteries than most of my teachers.

Early one morning, a terrorist bomb exploded in the café in which she was having breakfast. She was paralyzed from the neck down. I went to visit her in the hospital the first day she was allowed visitors. She kept repeating to me the same words: "I am trapped in my body, I am trapped in my body." My heart was breaking and tears streamed down my face as I understood that our bodies, sources of wonder and pleasure, were also terrible prisons over which we have little control. Our lack of control is brought home again by the body's vulnerability to severe damage and pain.

Paradoxically enough, the body is also the seat of pleasure. The major locus of pleasure is for most people sexuality, which models, as we have seen, the spiritual ideal of giving up control. Our unwillingness to lose control in the sacred contexts of pleasure can have devastating results. The loss of control will inevitably come but take the forms of pain and pathology.

While initially the decision to have sex is voluntary, once engaged, we have very little control. As the sexual experience climaxes, all of our illusions of control are swept away in spasms of pleasure. Hebrew tantra, unlike its Hindu counterpart, revels in the loss of control. Yet the pleasure is not complete. Sexuality has many shadows: the sexual scandals that rock our world on a regular basis, the false accusations driven by the complex ulterior motives of piety, and the very real abuses like child pornography. The list is nearly endless.

Besides all that, in the realm of healthy sexuality there is still an undercurrent of disease. It expresses itself mostly in the legions of off-color jokes as well as in our general embarrassment when talking about sex. The source of all this unease is that sexuality reminds us that we are not in control of our bodies and therefore not in control of our lives. In a society where control is so vaunted and worshipped, that reminder is a deep dark secret we don't want revealed to anyone, least of all ourselves.

The Sage and the Courtesan

The wisdom masters tell a wonderful story of the sage Eliezer, son of Dordaya, who had visited every courtesan in the land. He was a great master, yet he was driven by something deep inside, a sense of deep emptiness and futility. Even as he began to teach in the Academy, he continued to visit the great prostitutes of the land.

Once he heard that there was a prostitute by the sea who took a pouchful of dinarim (a very large amount) for her fee. He took a pouchful of dinarim and went in search of her. He crossed seven rivers to find her. In the midst of their sexual engagement, he passed wind (expelled gas). She said, "Just as this gas will never return to its source, so too Eliezer Ben Dordaya will never return to his source."

Eliezer is electrified by her words and leaves immediately. He runs to the forest and says to the trees, "Plead mercy for me," and they refuse. He turns to the stars, to the earth, to all of nature. Each time he cries "Pray for me," and each time he is refused. In the end he realizes, "It depends only on me." He places his head between his legs and prays.

What does this strange myth mean? Eliezer is out of control. Driven by emptiness he seeks out sexual encounter after encounter. He wants to stop but cannot. While deeply ashamed by his lack of control, there is little he can do. What the myth suggests is that his healing cannot come through fighting for control. Paradoxically it is only by embracing his essential lack of control that he can change.

The key to the story is in the passing of gas. Did you ever sit in a meeting and need to "pass wind" and yet work mightily to hold it in? Why? Of course we are mortified at "passing wind" because it punctures our false, inflated projection of control. When we give our essential fragility and lack of control a place of respect, then we are less threatened by apparent emptiness and futility. Slowly and gently we can begin to invest our lives with meaning. Honoring our lack of control is the only way to return a measure of control to our lives.

Sexuality can become a sacrament modeling our true position in the world. We no longer need to chase it compulsively to remind us that we matter. We give up the need for obsessive control. In that surrender, the world comes alive.

 *Part III*

EIGHT

Circle and Line: The Dance of Male and Female

The lover's art most clearly modeled by the sexual is the merging of the masculine and feminine. Although it is often expressed in the merging of man and woman, it is by no means limited to that expression. For to the Hebrew mystics the sexual union of man and woman both models and participates in the more primal union of Shechina (the divine feminine) and *Tiferet* (the divine masculine). Masculine and feminine express the two essential forces of the universe.

In Chinese Taoist thought we would call these forces the yin and the yang, whose integration is the source of all harmony. In Hinduism we speak of Shiva, the male fire deity, and his consort Shakti. Their union brings blessing to all the worlds. Nicolas of Cusa, the Christian mystic scholar, labeled this universal merging of the masculine and feminine *coincidentia oppositorum*, the union of opposites.

For the Hebrew mystic, *Tiferet* and Shechina are not disparate forces in the world that occasionally come together for a one-night stand. Instead, they are different faces of the greater union, the force of divinity that courses through the cosmos and beyond. Their integration is the highest erotic expression of a healed world.

The Zohar reminds us that both principles exist not only in every human being but also in the successful flowering of any activity. In every arena of engagement, personal as well as public, success is largely dependent on the appropriate integration and balancing of these two forces.

The Personal and the Cosmic

The Kabbalistic archetype of the integrated male-female are the two cherubs in the Jerusalem temple. Kabbalistic sources are replete with references to the cherubs as the male and female expression of the *yichud*—the merging— of Shechina and *Tiferet*. The mystery of the cherubs is to achieve this unity in all facets of existence.

So cosmically divine is the act of sexual union that the mystics would go so far as to recite a blessing before sexual relations. In ancient tradition the bride and groom are joyously led in dance and song from the wedding canopy to the *heder yichud*, the room of "union," where the newlywed couple are alone together, presumably for the first time. Mystic tradition has it that the community would stand outside the *heder yichud* so that upon hearing the groom recite his blessing before "unifying" with his wife, the joyous clan would raucously call out "Amen!"—and then ecstatically dance off toward the wedding feast, leaving the couple alone. The *heder yichud* is the paradoxical realm where the couple is fully intimate and alone, yet fully exposed to the witnessing of the entire community! There is an open recognition that their merging is deeply personal as well as radically universal and cosmic. While the custom has been discontinued, we desperately need to reclaim the symbolism behind it if we are to reclaim our birthright of erotic sexuality.

Each touch during sexual joining is invested with parallel erotic mergings in the spirit worlds. In the explicitly tantric writings of the Kabbalist Cordevero, each limb corresponds to a different manifestation of the divine body-spirit. Cordevero speaks of the intention that accompanies the union, explicitly guiding the reader through the mythic "seven kisses," the embracing of head and arms, the entangling of legs, the meeting of thighs, sexual penetration, reception, and climaxes. Thus the sexual movement of any limb, every stroke or caress, has the power to integrate that corresponding cosmic limb in the universal force, effecting the healing of God and world.

For the medieval Kabbalist Joseph Hamdan, this is the deep meaning of the mantra *Adonai elohenu—Adonai echad*, the core phrase in the Shema, the most well known and central of Hebrew meditations. "Hear O Israel—the Lord our God is one."

That is to say, the Lord (Adonai), which is the masculine principle of the divine, and our God—Elohenu, the feminine divine principle—*are* one. On the deepest level, all who unite the masculine and feminine principles are part of Israel. Hear O Israel—the Lord and Our God are One!

But now comes the truly radical insight. The human being is responsible for effecting the uniting of the masculine and the feminine in the God force. Entrusted to us is the sacred task of erotically merging the Shechina and *Tiferet*, the Goddess and the God. We are the erotic mystics invested with the magic to influence and affect the Force in powerful and profound ways.

For the Kabbalists, this is the essential intention when one chants the Shema mantra. The recitation of the Shema is not merely a witnessing of divine unity. Rather it is a creating of divine unity, a weaving together of the masculine and feminine forces in one mantric formula. It is a reaching toward the integration of our own internal female and male—a stretch toward healing, a stitch to mend the cosmic rent.

This is so because we reside in the undivided heart of God. So it is not that we have power over God. Rather we have power as part of God. By uniting, balancing, and integrating the Shechina and *Tiferet* poles within us we heal the split in divinity. We are bridge and balancer. It is we who bring home the exiled Shechina.

The Trinity Pattern

Does union of masculine and feminine mean that after total integration, gender will dissolve as an issue? That a kind of transvestite existentialism is the Kabbalistic dream of an evolved world? Well, yes... and absolutely not.

There is a core paradigm in Hebrew mystical sources and many other traditions that provides a clear reality map for integration. It is a trinity of stages: simple; complex; simple.

Simple: Before enlightenment: chop wood, carry water

Complex: Enlightenment

Simple: After enlightenment: chop wood, carry water

The linchpin of the idea is that the third stage and the first, although externally similar, are really worlds apart. For stage three deeply integrates the new consciousness of stage two. So while the simplicity of stage one might be symptomatic of someone who is naive, superficial, and even irresponsible, the simplicity of stage three is an expression of someone who is deep, wise, and responsible.

Another image of this pattern is drawn directly from the world of love and eros.

Stage one: falling in love. Initial ecstasy. Head over heals. Love conquers all. Fairy tale.

Stage two: falling out of love. Pain, alienation, disappointment, even betrayal. Boredom. Ennui. Yet if you have the courage to stay, you can return to stage one, but so much higher.

Stage three: Transcendence. Joy. Quiet bliss. Passion born of commitment. Ecstasy.

This cycle is also the model for the marriage of masculine and feminine that needs to unfold in each person. Let's look at a man who is predominantly masculine. His maleness is his natural vitality and energy. It is his eros. This is the first stage. In the next phase, he needs to distance himself from his masculine eros in order to incorporate feminine energy. This is absolutely critical to his development. However, the deep knower in us understands that if he remains at level two he will be a decidedly nonerotic man. He needs to reclaim his deep masculinity.

Being deeply masculine, however, clearly has little in common with being macho. For after the feminine has been integrated, the new eros that emerges in stage three will be more vital and powerful than the primitive eros of stage one, but not less raw, sensual, and erotic. This is the marriage of the *Tiferet* and Shechina within the masculine itself.

The same is true within the feminine. Let's begin with a woman who is primarily feminine. This is her natural eros. Yet this alone is insufficient for her. She yearns for an aliveness that she cannot access through her feminine self. She searches for the male qualities inside of her. On finding them, she is able to tap into whole new sources of vitality, power, and achievement.

Yet if she remains trapped in stage two, she becomes nonerotic. Men are attracted to women, not to men. (In archetypal terms this is true, whether one happens to be heterosexual or homosexual. Practically, this means that within the homosexual community there are "men" and "women"). The masculine yearns for the feminine.

To reclaim her erotic self, the woman must move to stage three, reembracing her primal feminine. This third stage is far more sensual, alive, and erotic than the feminine self of stage one.

"What's the Difference?"

We have now arrived at the heart of the matter. What is the difference between masculine and feminine?

The core cosmic intuition of the Hebrew mystic Isaac Luria offers a deceptively simple paradigm. Men are lines, women are circles. Or more accurately, a line is a masculine image and a circle is a feminine expression. In his language circle is *iggul*; line is *yosher*, or *kav*. Every man and woman is a unique interpenetration of line and circle.

First, we notice the sexual model. This image of a line and a circle is reflected in our sexual physiology. Men's sexual organ is a line, and women's sexual organs, both breast and vagina, are more circular. The sexual models the erotic! It is almost as if Divinity drew diagrams to help us understand the very core of reality. The message is also inscribed in our very bodies. God is pointing ever so gently, saying, "Just look at yourself. You yourself explain it all. Study the book of you and you will understand the All!"

Let's look at the nature of a circle. Circles are characterized by suppleness, intimacy, egalitarian sensibility, connection, and communication. Everyone has her place, no one is ahead of anyone else. Everyone can see one another. In Luria's language, everyone is face-to-face. Face is an eros term. Already it is clear to us that a circle is erotic. There is an intimacy to a circle. When you walk into a room set up with rows of chairs, the room feels masculine and nonintimate. When you walk into a talk where everyone is gathered in a circle, it signals that a more intimate process will be taking place.

A circle is egalitarian. (The Hebrew word for circle, *iggul*, is part of the etymological source for *egalitarian*.) The feminine circle is defined by relatedness. It surrounds, embraces, and envelops. It is a symbol of intimacy, loyalty, and a capacity to forgive and renew. The circle moves round and round, repeating the same motions time after time. It always comes home again.

The masculine line is far more rigid than a circle. Judgment and distinction are natural linear functions. A line sets up a definite boundary between itself and the other. One is either higher on the line or lower. There is a clear hierarchy. If people are moving in the same direction on a line, then they will not be face-to-face. Instead, they will be face-to-back or back-to-face—a clear lack of intimacy. A line is forward moving, goal oriented, directed, and focused. It spends a lot more time looking ahead than looking around. The image of a line invites you either to move up or down; you rarely stand still. The line's natural movement is to thrust forward.

Luria writes, "Every world of world and every detail of detail in every world of world is made up of these two principles, circles and lines." Lines and circles in various permutations and balances are the DNA of spiritual reality. The unique blending of their energies gives contour, character, and depth to every unit of existence. It is a blending in which neither the circle nor the line ever disappears. Each is fully absorbed in the bliss of merging with the other while never losing its own integrity.

Both energies—that of the masculine line and the feminine circle—are essential. Each one held by itself has its own unique and terrible shadow.

Pacifists are usually circles. Lines correctly point out that had pacifism won the public debate at the time of World War II, the terrible evil of Nazism would now rule the world. Rigid fundamentalists are usually lines. A demarcating characteristic of fundamentalism is the belief that strict adherence to law is more important than compassion. In fundamentalist societies women and the feminine always suffer the most. This shadow is affecting the entire world today in the form of Islamic fundamentalism.

Many cultural and political debates today revolve around lines and circles arguing with each other. George Bush and many Republicans, for example, are lines, while Ralph Nader and the environmentalists are circles. John Lennon is a circle, while Rush Limbaugh is a line. Each side thinks the vision of the other will bring disaster to the country and ultimately the world. Each accuses the other of being immoral and blind. Both are correct.

The deep truth is that only an integrated vision that holds both circle and line can be both moral and visionary. It is the line quality in George Bush that cancels a critical environmental treaty that could have protected the earth, and the circle quality in Ralph Nader that is so often morally blind to core distinctions between good and evil when unpacking his fanciful foreign policies.

In the following conversation we will be focusing on lines and circles as cosmic principles whose roots are in our souls. We will see clearly that neither New Age spirituality (circle) or the old religious orthodoxies (lines) alone have within themselves the power to heal our souls and our planet. It is only an erotic vision unpacked from both, the paradox of holding lines and circles together as one, that can heal us.

We need to fully embrace the truth of the line, then roundly challenge it with circle consciousness, only to reembrace the line from a more supple and rounded place.

Similarly, we need to rejoice in the circle, only to bisect it with the challenge of the line, all in order to come back to the circle in a more balanced, honest way. This is the spiritual pattern of the three levels that we introduced in the beginning of our discussion.

We begin in the middle — in the glory of the circle.

Jagged Lines; Erotic Circles

The circle is more naturally erotic than the line. Recall that we identified four faces of the erotic: interiority, interconnectivity, yearning, and fullness of being. The circle evokes each of these qualities:

Interiority — The circle, unlike a line, has an inside and an outside. Its very essence is in the creation of an inner circle.

Interconnectivity — In the circle, all are interconnected. All have a place. No one is ahead or behind, above or below. Because of this, the circle naturally invites cooperation instead of competition.

Yearning — Circles also bespeak our unquenchable longing. It is not a line, where movement is pragmatic and linear. In a circle one understands that no end will ever be reached. This longing participates in the yearning force of being.

Fullness — The circle attracts us to the fullness of its curves. Whether it be the round table, the swelling of a woman's pregnant belly, the curvatures of thigh, breast, or shoulder, the gentle slopes of a lush countryside, circles vibrate with fullness and energy.

Creation Stories

Lines and circles tell very different creation stories. The primary biblical creation narrative is distinctly linear and masculine. This is not only because the grammatical constructions describing God are male, but also because the process itself is an expression of line consciousness. Masculine sexuality is essentially external. It is a forward thrusting movement that creates something, expels something, ex-presses something, outside the male body.

In Genesis, chapter one, God creates a world outside himself. The light, plants, animals, and human beings may have been created by God, but they are certainly outside him. What's more, like the masculine image of the father, God can choose to stay and care for the world or simply to walk away. If God does care, it is a divine choice and not a necessity. In this first chapter, man—created in the image of God—is also primarily a masculine image. He is commanded to "fill the earth" and conquer it, to rule over the birds of heaven and the fish of the sea. Hierarchy is the order of the day. God is clearly above nature. As we shall soon see, this biblical line-consciousness understanding of creation is an incredibly important story in our spiritual development. However, it is not the whole story.

Temple mysticism told a primarily feminine circle creation story.

The feminine circle motif, however, is already implicit in Genesis, chapter two. Here the human being is more intimately addressed by God. He is invited to serve the earth and guard it, to be God's gardener as it were. In biblical myth, however, this feminine circle moment is only hinted at. The mystics took the hint and developed from it a full-blown worldview. They taught that the building of the Temple and the creation of the world are the same spiritual process. Not surprisingly then, the mystics loved to quote the biblical passage that describes the Temple as the Garden of Eden. For then, it is clear that the priest is the Gardener. And as the medieval Kabbalist Isaac the Blind and his school liked to teach, the mystics are the successors to the Temple priests. Their role, like that of the priests, is to serve the feminine circle eros incarnate in the Temple.

The Temple, remember, is the place where the Shechina dwells between the cherubs. The Shechina is known in the Kabbalistic sources as the great feminine. She is mother, daughter, and lover. She is the force that allows the human being to feel at home in the world. The Temple is the place of eros; it is the experience of being on the inside.

In the biblical line image, the world is God's place. God owns the world. God's relationship to world is that of father, king, or even husband. For the Temple mystic, however, the world is not God's place, instead, God is the place of the world.

To be in Temple consciousness is to be *in God*—eros pure and simple. This shift in consciousness is hidden within the folds of biblical myth text itself. We have already seen that the biblical term *Lifnei Hashem*, which is usually translated as "before God," can be more fruitfully understood as "on the inside of God's face." This allusion plants the seed for the much more radical move made by the mystic Isaac Luria in the sixteenth century. In Luria's graphic and daring vision, the world is *not* formed by a forward-thrusting male movement that creates outside itself. Quite the contrary—Divinity creates within itself a sacred void in the form of a circle. This is the creation not of the line masculine God but of the Goddess, of the Shechina! This is the Great Circle of Creation. The circle, unlike in the original biblical image, is within the Goddess It is an act of love that moves the Goddess to withdraw and make room for the other—paradoxically *within God*.

In this vision, all of being is within the womb of the Goddess. In the ultimate feminine, life is born not by expelling the baby but by making room for offspring within the eternal womb of the Goddess. Nature is not outside the Goddess but is a daughter expression of the Divine. This is of course precisely the power of paganism. In paganism, there is an understanding that the Goddess is "on every hill and under every tree."

The trees are part of the Goddess's erotic manifestation. The central symbol of much of the ancient pagan cult in biblical Canaan was the Ashera tree. The Ashera is the feminine earth goddess erotically expressed in the image of the Ashera tree. In a wonderful phrase of Keats, "Even as the trees that whisper round the temple become soon as dear as the temple self." For the pagan, the hills were literally alive with the sound of music. Nature is the music of divinity undressed to the human ear. Every hill, brook, tree, and blade of grass was invested with its own divine muse.

In our spiritual movement of Bayit Chadash in the hills around Israel's Sea of Galilee, we are committed to reclaiming the spark of sacred paganism. The pagan knows of the mother God. "Love your mother" means not only your human biological mother, but also mother earth, which nurtures you, balances you, and grounds you in her embrace.

Both the vitality and metaphysics of a pagan eros were understood by Abraham Kook to be essential to the reclaiming of a religious sensibility that reflected both the depth and need of modernity. It is in large part this pagan sensibility that we yearn for when we speak of the dream of a rebuilt Temple.

The Temple is the original Hebrew expression of pagan consciousness. Now, as we will see later in this chapter, the difference between Temple and pagan consciousness is very crucial. But it is a difference that is important only because of their profound similarity. Both the Temple and the pagan cults shared an intoxication with the feminine Goddess. Paganism was not a hobby, like modern religious affiliations sometimes tend to be. It was an all-consuming desire to be on the inside, to feel the infinite fullness of reality in every moment and in every encounter. Because the ancients were so deeply aware of the depth of reality, to live without being able to access the infinite was enormously painful.

Paganism is pure circle consciousness. One quality of paganism, suggests Kook, is that it overrides any and all other considerations, including judgment, evaluation, and distinction, which are line qualities. It is difficult for a modern person to imagine that kind of attraction or commitment. Difficult, that is, until one remembers the enormous power of infatuation and sexual attraction. All three are expressions of the same primal divine life force.

What Solomon Understood

The pagan felt that not to be able to touch the feminine sensual divine in every brook and on every high hill was somehow akin to death. The primal need for the feminine circle was understood deeply by King Solomon, spiritual architect of the Temple. It was Solomon who loved and cleaved to his thousand wives. They were surely expressions of his powerful intoxication with Shechina. With them he shared the holiness of the pagan intuition of God "under every tree and on every high hill."

Solomon understood that the cosmic existential embrace of the erotic feminine is essential to our sense of being at home in the world. Indeed, a reading of the Book of Kings reveals that the pagan goddess Ashera was an integral part of the Hebrew religion. The prophets, for all of their moral force, were incapable of convincing the people to abandon her.

One scholar concludes that of the 370 years that Solomon's Temple stood in Jerusalem, for at least 236 of those years—two-thirds of the time—the statue of Ashera was present in the Temple. Her worship was not some underground cult but part of what was understood to be the legitimate Hebrew spirit itself.

Indeed, the erotic passion for the Goddess was so essential to the people's spirit that when the great reformer Elijah challenged the pagan god Baal, he pointedly avoided challenging Ashera. Ashera had become too much of a Hebrew Goddess to be challenged even by Elijah. The spirit of Ashera in the leafy trees and on the high hills was so beloved by the people that it remained a potent force in the Temple experience until the destruction of the first Temple.

Paganism understood well the primal human need to feel at home in the world. For the pagan, every place was filled with divine presence. The erotic pagan imagination was able to uncover divinity in every nook and cranny of existence. Everything takes place in the great cycle of being. There is no place, no thing, and no person that is outside the circle. The pagan understood well the mantra of the Zohar: There is no place empty of God.

A powerful and radical passage in the Zohar suggests that the altar in the Temple itself was an Ashera tree!! The deep intention of the Zohar is not that this was an actual Ashera tree. Rather the Zohar is teaching that the Temple was deeply connected to the primal power of the sacred Ashera Goddess.

The Marriage of the Gods

The two cherubs are an evolved expression of the pagan Hebrew marriage between the biblical Yaw-weh and the pagan Ashera. That is to say, the spirit of biblical text, which rejected some of the essential dimensions of paganism, nevertheless accepted the core feminine erotic principle that powered paganism and recognized the essential need to integrate it with the masculine principle. So Ashera was transmuted into the female cherub in erotic union with the male cherub. Though the prophets rejected the Ashera, they embraced the cherubs. Indeed, biblical prophecy taught that the space between the sexually entwined cherubs was the source of prophecy.

The priest, archetype of love, would open the curtain to the Holy of Holies, showing the people the cherubs as an explicit model of the sacred sexual union between male and female. The erotic and pagan nature of the female cherub was clearly apparent to the wisdom masters of Babylon. They understood that the cherubs were the Hebrew embrace of the sacred moment in paganism and thought it essential to the Hebrew spirit.

The cherubs atop the ark went underground after the destruction of the Temples. The cherubs reappear in public consciousness centuries later as the masculine and feminine expression of the Divine in the Kabbalistic books of the Bahir, the Zohar, and in virtually every subsequent Kabbalistic text. This divine pair are called *Malchut* and *Tiferet*, Shechina and *Tiferet*, and a host of other names. They reach their apex in Kabbalistic consciousness in the mystical works of Isaac Luria and his one-time teacher, Moses Cordevero. The latter even says explicitly, in a passing comment in one of his works, "*Malchut* [shechina] is *Ashera.*" So we have come full circle. The Canaanite pagan Ashera has been reclaimed as a Hebrew Goddess. Now we need to reweave the circle consciousness that she embodies into the fabric of our personal and world soul.

Failed Lines

Phallic line consciousness has proved to be an outlook that is impotent for so many of us. It has not given birth to the reality for which we dreamed. We have competed, failed, and succeeded. Yet we have found the process debilitating and the prize woefully insufficient. Even if we've gotten what we were always supposed to want, we have realized that it isn't enough.

On the most personal level, the rat race of line consciousness has failed us. The radical focus on our place in the hierarchy has exhausted us. For many years we have ignored Lily Tomlin's truism: "Even if you finish first, you are still a rat."

On the global level, line consciousness has failed us as well. We live on the edge of unprecedented ecological disaster. The imbalanced ethics of "fill the earth and conquer" in Genesis, chapter one, is not innocent in this. The ecological disaster is driven by corporations who take advantage of the core emptiness in the heart of the West, by feeding it with an obscene over-abundance of goods and foods. Corporations driven by line consciousness form the crux of our world's economy. Sadly, these corporations are driven by basically only one desire: accumulating maximal power through maximal profit. Unhappily, the natural result of this posture is a virtual rape of the environment for the sake of climbing higher on the line's ladder. It is the line consciousness of probably not more than ten thousand people that is having this devastating impact on the world's environment.

The driving force behind the corporate ethos is fear of emptiness. When we lose the sense of the world being divine and full of meaning, we risk falling into the void in which we "lose touch" with our own essential self-worth and value. In order to stifle those voices we work hard at producing and climbing in the line world. Somehow the eros of productivity and competition gives our lives a veneer of meaning, at least until a crisis when our vulnerability is exposed and we plummet into the void.

Only by raising a new generation on the eros of the circle can we hope to truly effect a transformation in the world. Only by internalizing the erotic experiences of interconnectivity, interiority, and the fullness of being can we move toward healing and change. This is the call of circle consciousness. This is the ethos of redeemed paganism. This is Temple consciousness.

The Shadow of the Circle, the Ethics of the Line

If the circle is so wonderful, why not live in circle consciousness and just jettison the jagged and cutting line once and for all? The essence of the mystery of love—the secret of the cherubs—is that this is not possible. The line and the circle must be integrated. The failure to achieve that integrity would result in a great and tragic failure of love.

The primal feminine eros of the circle—connected with Gaia and the mother—is an essential erotic need of the human being. It expresses itself in different forms at various periods of history. Because it is a primal need, it never has nor is it ever likely to disappear.

Paganism drew that erotic circle archetype from deep within the unconscious. Since it served an essential need, it was honored and found its place in human hearts and practice. The nature of that pagan expression, however, had a powerful shadow manifestation in the ethical realm. It is this shadow that caused the Hebrew prophets to categorically reject paganism.

Intellectual historian Yehezkel Kaufman is correct in reminding us that the opposition to paganism may well be the singularly most important theme of the entire Hebrew biblical project. The opposition was based on primary ideas that are, as we will see, inextricably bound up with one another. Together they cast the great shadow of circle consciousness.

Nonetheless, the need for the erotic feminine circle continues. It remained to mystics of the postprophetic era—the Kabbalists—to reembrace the circle after purifying it of its cruel ethical aberrations.

The Closed Circle

The first great shadow of circle thinking stems precisely from its circle nature! The circle is by definition not open. It is a closed system. There is no way out. It is to this consciousness that the wisdom masters referred when they said, "Until the Exodus no slave had ever succeeded in leaving Egypt." This statement is not just an aggrandizing of the breakout skill of the Hebrew God. Rather it is an affirmation of the core breakthrough in Hebrew myth. In the pagan circle consciousness of Egypt, no one could ever leave his or her place. No one could break out of the closed cycle of life. You were born into your circle and destined to go round and round in it.

The Haggadah is a book that celebrates the Exodus of the Hebrew slaves from Egypt and is read by their descendants yearly on the anniversary of the night they were delivered from that enslavement. The Haggadah asserts that if "God had not come and redeemed you, you would still be there—slaves to Pharaoh in Egypt." Reading this as a child, it always troubled me simply because it did not seem to be true. Could it really be that we would still be in Egypt under Pharaoh? Why, the Pharaohs themselves were long ago trashed in the dustbin of history. Until one day many years later—I got it! God is the force of healing and transformation in the world who affirms that things can be different from the way they are now. God is the rejection of the status quo that is built into the cyclical pagan worldview. If the God force of progress, transformation, and freedom had not been introduced, the world would still be stuck on the same great wheel of suffering.

When Moses witnesses the terrible suffering in Egypt, the loving God voice exclaims that it does not have to be this way. "Moses, you can challenge the status quo. You can start a revolution!" Indeed, the great revolution of the biblical Exodus was the *very idea* of revolution. Things *can* change. They *can* be different. You can get off the circle and move forward.

The Line of Evolution and History

The line of evolution—beginning with the gradual unfolding of creation from simple to complex in the Genesis creation story—is essential to the biblical spirit. Biblical myth in the story of the Exodus introduces line consciousness into the mind and heart stream of the world. It is the creation of the very ideas of history, progress, and therefore hope. Love desires growth, healing, and transformation. For the circle to exist without being bisected by the line would be the greatest failure of love.

But for mystic Isaac Luria, the story of the Exodus is the story of the second great escape from the tyranny of the circle. The *first* great escape is the story of the first Hebrew, Abraham. In fact, it is precisely Abraham's ability to make the great escape that makes him the first Hebrew, for the very word *Hebrew* (*Ivri*) means the "one who crossed over."

Abraham is part of a nomadic Semitic tribe in ancient Mesopotamia. He wanders, as does his generation, round and round and round again. Nothing is original, new, or fresh. All that is has already been and will continue to be forever. That is until that fateful day. Or maybe it happened at night. Or perhaps it took a whole year, or even several decades. It doesn't matter. What is important is what the voice said. "Abraham! All your life is not a circle! Sunrise and sunset, day after day. You can go somewhere! You can progress forward toward a point and arrive someplace entirely new and original where you have never been before."

This is the line that breaks out of the circle. The line consciousness of Abraham introduces to the world the notion of journey. The clear implication, against all of pagan thought, is that you can actually go someplace. Line consciousness is history. The line of the Hebrews created the very idea of history, his-story. When you read the Sumerian story, there is no clear story line. The idea of a plot, suspense, and ultimate resolution so engrained in our maps today was unknown to the circle consciousness of the pagan.

In Hebrew, there is no word for *history,* instead the word is *zachor*—which means "remember." Not accidentally, *zachor* in Hebrew has a second meaning:

the masculine. History is a function of line consciousness, the masculine thrusting-forward property of the spirit. It is biblical mysticism that gives birth to the notion of *tikkun olam,* "the world's fixing"—which a very close reading of Isaac Luria's works reveals to mean the evolving and healing of all consciousness—human and divine.

What we are talking about is much more than the evolution of man. It was the Kabbalists who introduced the idea of an evolving divine consciousness. The unfolding of divine consciousness in not a purely intradivine process. The great privilege of being a human being is that we participate in the evolution and healing of God. We are God's healers. The evolution of the human spirit is what catalyzes the evolution of God. When God and man meet in an evolutionary embrace, redemption is achieved.

This is the great messianic idea, the climax of all history and evolution. "Messiah" in biblical mysticism is more than a person. It is a destination that we arrive at after the long and often arduous journey. It is the hope and the vision of a better tomorrow. It is the possibility of possibility.

Until this shaft of the line cut across human consciousness, human existence was fundamentally determined. All that happened was thought to be revealed in the astrological wisdom of the stars in their heavenly cycles, or in the guts of animals when you killed them. No matter. The key was that there was "nothing new under the sun."

Abraham did not deny the truth of the circle. According to tradition, he himself was a master astrologer of his age. He accepted that the cycles on earth reflected the cycles of the heaven. However, he understood that the God force was a line that could free him from the circle's oppression. For the God force was "above the sun" and indeed beyond all of nature and therefore not subject to her laws.

In one biblical description, we hear of Abraham's conversation with the divine voice. The voice has told him that he will have a son. Abraham—being the great astrologer that he is—knows that this experience is simply not in his stars. So God "takes him outside." The wisdom masters explain that the God voice takes him outside the circle. The stars reveal the seemingly inexorable circle pattern of your life, but if you listen closely you will hear a voice whispering a trace of transcendence. This voice calls you to journey beyond the circle—to break out of the pattern that your past and present seem to preordain for you. To be free.

The freedom implied in line consciousness means not only that a slave people can throw off the shackles of the oppressor. It also means that each of us can throw off the shackles of our own personal taskmasters. There is no greater slave driver than the idea that yesterday determines today. This is precisely the shadow of circle consciousness. The line sets us free. It pierces the circular bubble, shattering the "realities" that want to hold us back and keep us down.

Beyond the Family Circle

Many mental health professionals have written that the degree to which a person is able to emerge from the womb of family is the degree of their mental health. The family *circle* is a classic example of both sacred eros and the potential shadow of the circle. For many people, family is the ultimate experience of home. We feel safe, loved, and embraced. It is a Shechina presence in our lives. Yet family can also be oppressive, tyrannical, and suffocating. Often the same family will have all of these qualities at the same time. Without being able to climb out of our family dynamic, we might never be free to chart the unique destiny of our lives. This is the essence of the Abraham story. The voice calls to him. "Go forth from your land, your birthplace, and your father's house."

In effect, the voice says go forth from all your yesterdays. Know that today you are free. This is the same theme in the second "Go forth" story in Abraham's life. These two stories are the bookends of his life. The first begins his journey; the second is the final crowning milestone on his path. In the second "Go forth" story, he hears the voice tell him to sacrifice his son as a burnt offering. The reader knows however that Abraham's father had tried to sacrifice him to the local king deity, Nimrod. Thus Abraham is about to do to his son what his father did to him. Repetition compulsion! It is a cycle from which there seems to be virtually no escape.

Abraham hears the internal compulsion to sacrifice his son as the command of God. It is the inexorable force that drives him until, in the last moment, he rereads the text. He realizes that the voice said to him "Go forth." He remembers that "Go forth" means to leave your father's house. Leave the old pattern and mold that invisibly lock you in their hold. You are free. Abraham listens again. He realizes that the voice has said not to sacrifice your son, but that you and your son together should sacrifice a ram. The command to sacrifice Isaac—stated as such in the biblical text—is not the divine intent; it is Abraham's own compulsion, which he had misinterpreted as a divine voice. He puts down the knife. Tears trickle down his cheek. Isaac is sobbing. They embrace. Abraham is—for the first time in his life—truly free. The cycle of repetition compulsion is shattered!

God and Nature

We now come to the second great shadow of circle consciousness. The pagans insisted that divinity was in trees and in all of nature. But the essential biblical idea is that God is also *beyond* nature. God is the creator of nature and therefore not trapped within it. Biblical myth therefore opens with the Genesis story—"In the beginning God created the heavens and the earth." The powerful and revolutionary implication is that *God is not nature.* Unlike the Greek, Roman, pagan, or Buddhist pantheons, biblical myth insists on a God who is both within and infinitely beyond the circle, radically immanent as well as transcendent.

When we say that God is infinitely beyond trees, we are also saying that if you can connect to God he can free you from the ensnaring web of nature. The notion that a human being is created in the image of God means for the Hebrew mystic that a person has it within them to reach beyond the natural.

The reason this is so critical is because in biblical consciousness, the loving God's primary demand is ethical behavior. The single most important expression of love is how we treat one another, not how we think about one another. Perhaps the most important principle of Hebrew ethics is that although thoughts count, actions are infinitely more important. Moreover, in the formulation of sixteenth-century master Aron of Barcelona—"A person is formed by their actions." Treat a person lovingly, and you will love them in the end. Love a person passionately and treat them unethically, and you will be alienated from them in the end.

When anyone suggests that we need to act against our instinctive nature we get slightly uncomfortable. Isn't the unnatural intrinsically a violation of the right? The best antidote to the superficial aggrandizement of all that is natural is to keep toilet training in mind. Probably everyone who reads this book relieves themselves someplace other than in their clothes. This is, of course, decidedly "unnatural." Indeed as a kind of protest against the violation of the natural implicit in toilet training, the central ritual of one pagan religion— the cult of Peor—was that its adherents defecate on the Peor idol itself. Biblical myth explicitly sets itself up as the alternative to the Peor cult.

Ethical behavior always requires that we will be able to act against our primal instinctive natures. *If we were only part of nature, then clearly we could not be expected ever to control our nature.* We are both part of nature, and beyond nature. Only because of this paradox are we capable of self-control.

What this means is that values need to serve as a guide in training our natures. Biblical line consciousness insisted that the most important value was ethical behavior. To be ethical, one must be responsible. Response-able. Able to respond to the conflicting drives of nature and nurture by charting a course that reflects an ethical vision. One can only respond if one can step outside the circle. Responsibility stems from a person's awareness of their ability to control or transcend their instinctive natures.

A contemporary example: A priest can decide not to abuse a young boy if he is at least potentially able to resist his nature and say no! But in the pagan cult, the homoerotic attraction between priest and young boy was made sacred by being made part of the temple cult. In the context of a circle ethos, not only sexual drives are considered uncheckable. There can also ultimately be no accountability for doing evil. Mother Teresa and Hitler are equally innocent and equally guilty. Since there is no real possibility of choosing other than what you chose, you cannot be expected to do anything other than what you did. All the forces of nature acted upon you and produced the only possible result: precisely what you did. It is therefore not surprising that paganism is laced with deterministic overtones. Biblical myth insists that after all of the influences have had their say, we have a divine core that is beyond nature and can therefore choose against nature.

Circle consciousness claims that people are naturally the best that they can be. But the most important act of love, according to the Hebrew gospel, is to develop a training system for goodness. The problem, argues the circle, is not goodness but alienation. The great evil for the circle is to be cut off, distant, disenchanted, out of the circle. Line consciousness disagrees with the circle and says that people are potentially good but not naturally good. In biblical myth people are born innocent, but they are not born good. Goodness must be learned and even cultivated. The great evil for the line is to do evil.

The commonplace phrase "a good baby" is actually a misnomer. Babies are not born evil, but they are not born good either. In fact, as infant psychologists have pointed out, babies are actually minidictators (albeit adorable dictators). The ethical hero in the mother-baby relationship is most certainly the mother and not the baby. The baby presents his parents with a list of incessant demands, which he expects to have met no matter what else might be going on. Whether his parents are in the middle of a financial crisis, a medical emergency, or simply want to make love is irrelevant to the baby. Having been a kid who was very much the school misfit, I can tell you that kids are also naturally cruel. As a matter of fact, the level of raw meanness and sadism that kids are capable of inflicting on other kids is simply incomprehensible... that is, if you believe people to be naturally good.

For biblical myth the belief that people are naturally the best that they can be is not only wrong but also destructive. If people are naturally good, then evil must be the result of some set of external forces. These external forces could be anything from social environment, economic circumstance, hand-guns, parents, television violence, government cutbacks, or the devil. The result of this approach is that an enormous amount of energy is spent trying to fix all sorts of outside stuff while almost no time at all is spent transmitting the values that might change or develop our internal natures. This kind of think-ing is an extension of pagan thought, which held that the manipulation of external nature would bring the good. The Hebrew Bible, then as now, says no to this thinking. Hebrew gospel teaches that only the control and refine-ment of our internal nature can bring the good.

In the view of the Hebrew Bible, the essential demand of God was justice. It is Dostoyevsky who best captures the Hebrew God when he writes in *The Brothers Karamazov*, "Without God all is permitted." God was experienced by the Hebrews as a parent who is truly happy only when his children treat one another well. For this reason biblical wisdom insisted that God was beyond nature and that human beings were *homo imago dei*—created in the image of God. The power of this idea gives birth to the best of Western civilization.

There is another critical reason why the line-driven ethical prophet does not experience God as being exclusively in nature. If God were in nature and not beyond nature, then nature would be our source of ethics. It is clear, though, that for all of her splendor in reflecting a pale cast of divine beauty, nature is amoral. The law of nature is nearly always that the strong kill the weak. Certainly the helpless and the infirm have little chance of survival in the natural order other than as a dinner for a stronger adversary. If we were to transpose natural law into the human world, we would certainly live the law of the jungle. Social services, hospitals, and help for the disabled are all pro-foundly "unnatural," at least according to the law of nature in the nonhuman world. In fact, the hospital is a direct corollary of line and not circle conscious-ness. The morality of the line insists that those higher on the line—that is to say stronger and with more means—take care of those lower on the line. This is the faith and God experience of the prophets.

The Prophet and the Pagan

Let's frame the clash between circle and line in the most striking possible terms.

The prophet, the hero of the Hebrew Bible, represents ethics—the line. The pagan, hero of the ancient world into which biblical thought was born, represents eros—the circle. The clash between the prophet and the pagan—the circle and the line—is in the end the clash between the erotic and the ethical.

Obviously the prophet is not devoid of eros and the pagan not entirely oblivious of ethics. Yet the goal is their full integration. The erotic and ethical must merge. This is the secret of the cherubs and the model of the sexual.

What the prophet and the pagan respectively incarnate, however, is made manifest when the erotic and the ethical clash. An oft-quoted line from Jung, heir to the pagan myth tradition, is the best summation I have ever heard of the pagan position: "I'd rather be whole than good."

The importance of this maxim is evidenced by the many times one hears it cited by Jung's students. Apparently the circle will always seem more whole than the line. Circle and Shechina are the experience of eros for which we all yearn. The pagan yearns to feel whole. Indeed for the pagan the alienation from divinity is so palpable and painful that it must be overcome at all costs, even if ethics are the price. This is where the balanced scales start precariously to slip. It was Jung who was sadly seduced by the pagan goddess Ashera into a flirtation with Nazism, that menacing shadow of eros which horrifically darkened our world just a few short decades ago.

The prophet always responds, "I'd like to be whole. But if I have to choose, I'd rather be good than whole." This is why the prophet is the great critic of the Temple. The erotic fulfillment of the Temple experience was all too often a replacement for the kind of direct ethical action that could heal the world. It is the widow and the orphan, the vulnerable and the dispossessed, who must be the primary concern of the *homo religious*. This is the word of the prophets.

The prophets oppose paganism with all of their ethical fire and passion. Their opposition to paganism is based upon pagan cruelty and corruption.

Built into the pagan ritual are demands for parents to burn their children as a sacrifice to the gods. Hardly a mention of the pagan occurs in the Hebrew Bible without a reference to this practice. "They have set their pagan abominations in my house...to burn their sons and daughters in fire." (Jeremiah 7:30, 31.) The burning of children was not the exception in pagan worship. Rather it was the model of the pagan idea that erotic abandonment to the god must, by its very definition, overrun all intuitive human ethical boundaries.

Listen to the ethical cry of Isaiah in chapter 1:

> *I do not want your multitude of sacrifices*
> *I delight not in the blood of bullocks or goats or rams.*
> *Do not come to seek my face...*
> *as you trample my courts of justice...*
> *your hands are full of blood...*
> *wash yourselves, make yourselves clean...*
> *cease your evil doings...seek fair judgment,*
> *argue the case of the widow and the orphan...*
> *Zion will be redeemed*
> *by justice and...integrity.*

The ecstatic service of the Jerusalem temple, religiously powerful and important as it might be, had become primary. The reaching for Shechina experience overrode all; eros overrode ethos, and the prophet exploded in divine rage.

Having said that, we want to make a radical claim—which, as is often the case, is patently obvious once you see it. On the essential interpretation of reality, the prophet was actually a circle and not a line. The difference was that the pagan was a first-stage circle archetype and the prophet a third-stage circle archetype.

The prophet's line expression is a necessary corrective response to the pagan consciousness that dominated the world at the time. The prophet saw his role to overturn that pagan ethic, which was bound up with so much cruelty. Human sacrifice was but one of the outrages that prophecy sought to eliminate. The prophet was wildly successful and gave an ethical cast to the foundation stones of all Western civilization.

The Erotic and the Ethical

In the picture of the prophet as a social reformer, it is, however, too easy to lose sight that at his core, he was an erotic mystic.

Though the prophet insisted that nature was not all of God, he experienced with all his being that God was all of nature. Even as he decried the pagan claim that identified God with the Ashera tree, he knew and rejoiced in the truth that God was fully present and accessible "on every hill and under every tree." God was not only reflected in nature as the external creator but God was also fully present in nature. The later mystics used *mamash*, meaning literally "actually," to describe that God was actually present in nature and not just as a metaphor or symbol. The words of later Hebrew mystics capture accurately prophetic consciousness. Schneur Zalman of Liadi writes that "trees and stones are *mamash* divine." Nachman of Bratzlav told his disciples that "every blade of grass has its own (divine) song."

The Temple in its ideal state was supposed to manifest the third-stage circle moment in Hebrew consciousness. What the prophet realized, however, was that the people had not incorporated second-stage line consciousness. The erotic was overrunning the ethical. In principle, however, the Temple was meant to be a balance between line and circle, erotic and ethical.

Only a short distance from the seat of eros, the Holy of Holies with her sexually intertwined cherubs, was the *lishkat hagazit*, the "room of hewn stone." This was the Chamber of Justice, whose passionate concern was the ethical—the creation of a just society. On the face of it, its sensibilities seem so far removed from the erotic motifs of the sensual and the sacred that permeated the Temple's aura. What, after all, do ethics and eros have to do with each other?

The answer is—everything. In the short run we can train people through behaviorist rituals, social engineering, and a good deal of guilt to behave ethically. However, in the final analysis, we also find that nonerotic ethics will always collapse under the weight of contracts and contacts it cannot fulfill. The room of hewn stone must necessarily be housed in the eroticized Temple in order for its ethics truly to thrive.

Picture a house that has three consecutive rooms. In the first room is Master Schneur Zalman of Liadi, founder of the mystical Hassidic court of Habad, the grandfather in our story. In the second room is his son and successor, known as the Middle Master. In the third room is a small baby who will ultimately succeed his father and grandfather as the third master of Habad.

Father and grandfather are lost in erotic mystical rapture. They have crossed over to the inside; suffused with yearning they have entered the fullness of being. Eros. Suddenly the baby cries. Grandfather rises from his ecstasy, goes to pick up the child and rock him to sleep. Afterward he is unable to recapture his ecstasy. He smiles and falls asleep.

Come morning, father and grandfather meet at morning meditation. "Did you not hear the baby crying?" inquires Schneur Zalman gently of his son.

"Why no, Father. I was so caught in rapture I could hear nothing but the singing of the angels," the Middle Master replies, secretly hoping his father would be impressed, for it seemed that he exceeded even his father in the interiority of his en-trance-ment. "You have not understood, my son," responded Schneur Zalman, a tear slowly wending its way down his cheek. "Rapture that deafens you to the crying of a baby—such holiness is not kosher."

Another image: Abraham sits at the en-trance to his tent, deep in meditation. God appears to him in the heat of the day. Celestial fires encircle him. The breath of the Divine caresses him. Abraham basks in perfect Presence.

Abraham opens his eyes and sees in the distance three strangers passing by. He jumps up to greet them. Perhaps they are thirsty from the desert sun or in need of lodging for the night. He races after them. "But wait!" cries out God. "Where are you going...one second...we were just about to—"

"Hold that thought, God. I'll be right back." And off Abraham runs.

"How could it be?" inquire the fourth-century Babylonian myth masters in radical amazement. "Is not rapture with the Divine the point of everything? How could Abraham just run off and leave God hanging?!"

They answer their own question with a gorgeous Hebrew koan: "Greater is the feeding of guests than the receiving of the face of the Shechina." *Face* and *Shechina* are words that we recognize—virtual synonyms for the erotic. And yet the imperative is clear. In the clash between the erotic and the ethical, the ethical must take priority.

In order to foster a loving world we need to merge the masculine line with the feminine circle. Any attempt to maintain line or circle consciousness when they are independent of each other is doomed to failure. The deepest wisdom of Hebrew myth will require eros and ethics to interpenetrate. Prophet and pagan will need to merge into one.

When we unpack stage three we will see that the erotic is not opposed to the ethical. For the erotic to be full and life giving, the masculine and feminine must merge. Failing to effect this erotic merger, the Shechina remains in exile. The marriage of the masculine and feminine in the sexual models the merger of the circle and the line, the erotic and the ethical, in every facet of being. Whenever that marriage fails, there is a failure of love, and failures of love always produce evil.

Indeed, every ethical failure comes from the absence of eros. It is the painful experience of emptiness that moves people to ethical violation. The universe does not tolerate a vacuum. Ethics without eros is doomed. It is only from a place of fullness of being that we can reach out in love to the other. The first step to love is always self-love. If you don't fill yourself up with love then you have precious little to dole out. As long as my love is not rooted in my erotic matrix—the inside of my fullness—it is fated to fail. I will have to rely on an ethical center outside myself in reference to which I must always be a sinner. If ethics well up from the inside, however, and if we are at that center, then sin is not disobedience but the violation of human well-being.

In the end the only ethical failure is a violation of eros—your own or someone else's. The prophet in us needs to reclaim holy paganism. The pagan within must be open to hearing the call of the prophet. When the prophet and pagan meet, the Temple of the heart will be rebuilt.

I have long believed in my heart of hearts that ethics without eros cannot survive even on the ethical level. First, our erotic longing will not be assuaged by prophetic ethics. We can do the right thing our entire lives and still feel empty. The prophetic idea that God, and thus the God point within us, is beyond nature and can therefore act against nature is important. But it is only a stage in the unfolding ethical conscious of man. I was delighted many years back to happen across this passage from Abraham Kook, the greatest modern Hebrew mystic:

> We are filled with the emotion of ethics;
> we yearn toward a life that is pure
> Our imagination excites the desire in our heart
> With images of life that are most pure and most noble.
> Yet this desire cannot be realized
> except through inner and outer commitment
> to the light of being the Light of God,
> to erotic morality
> ...
> Morality not guided by the sacred is not deep,
> and does not enter into the inwardness of the soul;
> and even though a person might be drawn to it for good reason
> —for she recognizes the uprightness of logical things—
> this kind of instruction does not have a lasting hold
> in the face of... passions strongly aroused.
>
> Such a weak morality
> does not have the power to guide...
> the polis, the human community,
> to penetrate to the depth of the soul
> and to transform the heart
> of universal man and of individual man

from stone to flesh.
There is no alternative plan for humanity
other than that it be guided by the erotic morality.

And it is much better
that a person fall a number of times
on the journey
but establish his vision of world
   and the morality of his life
     according to that profundity of the erotic morality,
than if he has fewer failures
   but lives a weakly spiritual life
   at the hands of the superficial influence
   of secular morality.

Ethics that are not rooted in eros ultimately fall apart. We yearn for eros. By exiling God from nature and secularizing the sexual, we condemn ourselves to emptiness and vacuity. For example, the company "line" ethic of the 1950s in America produced the "circle" yearning for communes and free love of the 1960s. This is the recurrent pattern of the human soul. Eros cannot be denied. Any ethical collapse is ultimately rooted in a failure of love, a lack of eros.

When we talk only about a God giving rules that run counter to our nature, the rules cannot hold. The eros of our nature will always overrun them. But if we come to understand that ethics is an erotic expression of our deeper divinity, we are truly moved to the ethical. For that is when we realize it is an expression of our deepest selves, a response to the call of our own voice. To be compelling and powerful, ethics must be an expression of your erotic divine nature and not a contradiction of it. So when the prophets insist that God, which is also the God within you, is beyond nature and can therefore act ethically against nature, they are referring only to your first nature, not to your deeper second nature. Your deeper nature *is* God. This is the secret whispering in the leaves of the Ashera tree and in the embrace of the cherubs.

Opposing the Temple Prostitute

Now this transmutation of the Ashera energy to the female cherub was not just a superficial "biblicizing" of a pagan notion. To read it this way would be to miss the whole point of the Hebrew myth revolution. It was rather one of the first moves toward union, the ultimate integration between masculine and feminine, the ethical and the erotic.

Ashera was represented in most temples by both male and female prostitutes. These temple prostitutes were either sacrificed to the Goddess or engaged sexually by the king or priests as incarnations of the goddess. To say that the prophets radically opposed human sacrifice is obvious. What is more revealing is that they opposed the entire institution of the temple prostitute.

Here again it is critical to understand the nuance of the argument between prophet and pagan. Both agreed that human sexual encounter could potentially reenact and even catalyze the cosmic divine sexual encounter between the God and Goddess. The Zohar is replete with imagery in which the priest plays an essential role in arousing the feminine waters of the Shechina so she will be ready to receive her divine partner. Close readings of such passages make it deliberately unclear if the human role is only to sexually arouse the Shechina or actually to merge with her in ecstatic sexual union.

Yet the prophet passionately opposed the temple prostitute. The reason is clear. The temple prostitute was the classic case of the erotic overriding the ethical. The entire human persona of the prostitute was effaced. The sexual became an expression of the cosmic, which absolutely overrode the personal face of sexuality. The prostitute in the temple, as in contemporary society, has no name. She serves a cosmic function that "defaces" her. The prophet opposes anonymous sex because in his ethical mission his essential goal is the personalizing of the sexual. The ethical moment in sexuality of commitment and personhood needs to be seen as primary, overriding even cosmic erotic needs.

The great biblical myth affirmation is that for sex to be sacred it must be personal. Personal means connected to a story. The prostitute whose name you do not know, to whose dreams and vulnerabilities you are impervious, is the archetype of the impersonal. Impersonal (as we will see) can also describe sex that is used to weave a false story. It refers to sex that is detached from the web of soul print passions and commitments that is your life. It refers as well to sex that we reach for compulsively to cover up—even from ourselves— the dull throb of emptiness.

It is not that the biblical myth masters did not recognize the power of the impersonal and even cosmic erotic. They did. Indeed, in the myth of Luria, the world itself is re-created every moment. In every second and in every space, cosmic circles and lines erotically penetrate one another and existence is brought forth anew. Ecstasy, dance, music, prayer, study, and meditation were all part of the prophetic service. They were all practiced in a way that would allow the initiate to access the coursing eros of being as it washed and revitalized his soul. Impersonal cosmic eros was vitally important to the prophet. But not when it required the depersonalization of a human being, the temple prostitute. And yet we need to find ways to reclaim the power of impersonal eros in our personal lives and in the larger life of the polis. If we do not, the void will continue to be filled with abusive and degrading forms of pornography. We must find a way to reclaim the eros of the temple prostitute, cleansed of its shadow qualities, even as we affirm the centrality of sexuality rooted in personal commitment and shared dreams.

NINE

Lishmah, for the Sake of the Name

Stage One: For Its Own Sake

The next quality of love and eros modeled by the sexual is what the Hebrew mystics called *lishmah*, which is usually translated as "for its own sake." We are engaged in the erotic when we do something simply for its own sake; when we stop networking and let go of goal-oriented thinking; when the activity itself is the end and not the means. *Lishmah* is when loving is the motive, for the only ulterior motive of eros is love. Indeed the litmus test of true love is that it has no ulterior motive. It stands and endures for its own sake. *Lishmah!*

To be erotically engaged means to be on the inside, totally filled and satisfied by the activity itself rather than using it as a way of getting somewhere or something else. The model for this kind of radical "in and of itself" engagement is the sexual. The sexual invites us inside to its fullness, promising at its highest not a networking opportunity but the richness of the experience itself. Advancement is not the issue; *lishmah* is not goal oriented. Once you are in the erotic, you have arrived, you are already there. This is the endpoint. There is nowhere else to go. The process itself is the goal. It is this sense of *lishmah* which engenders ecstasy. Past and future melt away as the present swells to infinite proportions.

The sexual models *lishmah* and teaches us how to be lovers, living erotically in all facets of existence. Loving either a person or an activity is an end in itself and not a means. There is no expectation other than what is. There is a deep appreciation of the inherent value, wonder, and truth of each moment itself. The litmus test of *lishmah* for an interpersonal relationship is when the person you are with becomes more important than the activity you are doing. The process becomes the result.

Beauty is *lishmah*. A breathtaking vista, a rainbow, a sunset—they need no excuse for existing. They just are. They are beautiful and need not serve any other purpose. A perfect expression of this *lishmah* quality is the female breast. The rapture that the female breast has provoked in poets, painters, and biblical writers throughout the ages is fully self-validating. It is not *because of* infantile memories of nourishment or *because of* the fascination with taboo, it is just *because*. God is called *Shaddai*, a Hebrew wordplay on the word for *breasts—shaddaiim*. The point is not only that God nourishes, but that the essence of the Divine also lies in its being enough; it is self-validating.

Art is *lishmah*. It is the end itself and requires no external justification. So while we valorize the commercial businessman who is driven by profit we tend to frown upon an artist who shares the same quality. We expect him to carry the torch of *lishmah* for society. The same is true of a spiritual teacher who seems driven by commercial motivation. Yes, the teacher has a right to be compensated for his efforts. But somehow we expect him not to violate the quality of *lishmah*, which is so essential to endeavors of the spirit.

When we expect an activity to model *lishmah* we are collectively horrified when it does not. This is precisely why society never fully accepted prostitution. On a moral plane there are certainly more ethically serious issues to engage—slander, corporate corruption, manipulative advertising, to name but a few. Yet we hold prostitution to a different standard not because it is a violation of any overriding moral principle. Rather it contravenes, paradoxically, an erotic principle; sex for commercial profit violates the erotic quality of *lishmah.*

EMBRACING THE SACRED ANIMAL

It would not be incorrect to say that *lishmah* is an animal-like quality. Human beings are the only animals that are both blessed and cursed by their awareness of life and death. Awareness brings in its wake the potential of consciousness. Its shadow however is the non-*lishmah* qualities of past and future anxiety, obsessive planning and fear. By contrast, an animal lives not for the sake of past or future but for its own sake—*lishmah.* It is this contented *lishmah* quality of the animal that made Walt Whitman write, "Turn and live with animals...they do not lie awake in the dark and weep for their sins...not one is dissatisfied."

The place where human beings are most instinctive and animallike is the sexual. In its ideal expression, the sexual exists only for its own sake. The sexual therefore models the quality of *lishmah.*

In human beings, *lishmah* is manifested in both higher and lower expressions of consciousness. As we saw in our discussion of male/female, the spirit unfolds in triads: simple, complex, simple. In the context of our present conversation the unfolding would be: (1) lower *lishmah* (2) awareness (3) higher *lishmah.* While levels one and three are similar, they are worlds apart in their erotic quality. The classic expression of level one, lower *lishmah,* is sex when it is "merely animal-like." Eating as an instinctive, nonreflective activity would be another example of lower-level *lishmah.* Level one is characterized by a lack or loss of awareness. The second level is normal human awareness—in all of its negative (anxiety) and positive (self-knowledge, transformation) manifestations. Self-conscious neurotic sexuality would be included on this level. I have often said to my students that the word *neurotic,* when psychologically and linguistically deconstructed, is really just *erotic* with a "Nu?!"

The third level of *lishmah* is manifested by human beings when they do an activity for its own sake, such as sacred sexuality, as well as in all of the other non-sexual areas of life. This *lishmah* however is occasioned neither by a lack nor a loss of awareness but by the *transcending* of awareness into a higher level of consciousness.

THE TASTE OF THE TREE

The goal of the erotic life is to engage every area of our lives with the mantra of *lishmah* beating in our breasts. This means being fully present for each thing itself without needing always to justify our activity by recourse to some external gain. In the poetry of Hebrew mysticism this is referred to as *taam haeitz ketaam haperi*, meaning "the taste of the tree is as the taste of the fruit." This phrase has its source in the delightful biblical creation myth where God commands the trees to be "trees of fruit which bear fruit." The stunning implication of a precise reading of the divine instruction is that the tree itself, the bark, should also have the taste of the fruit. The point is, there should be no distinction between means and ends. A coarse tree that brought the fruit into being should share the very taste of its succulent fruit.

In a similar metaphor Schneur Zalman of Liadi talks about how "the source of the vessels is higher than the source of the lights." Just as a tree holds and sustains the fruit, the vessel holds and sustains the light. The usual distinction is that the vessel is the means to hold the light, which is the end. Luria suggests that this distinction is nonerotic and unreflective of the fullness of reality. The vessels themselves, teach Luria, are no more than "congealed" light.

The essence of *lishmah* collapses the distinction between fruit and bark, vessel and light, means and end. The idea that "the ends justify the means" is therefore not only unethical. It is also nonerotic.

SACRED PLAY

An open portal to the experience of *lishmah* is play. Play is very much for its own sake. If you play to win, you lose. Very often a game is defined by purely arbitrary rules governing purely trivial actions. The goal lies in doing the activity itself.

There are few better spiritual lessons than watching the enraptured play of two toddlers. Children are the archetypes of *lishmah*. Yet the same quality of *lishmah* should hold true for adult play. One of the tragedies of the institution-alization of play is that it has lost its very playful, and therefore erotic, char-acter. Sports play is often bound up with intense competition and betting. It has become a bottom-line, win-lose proposition. Competition always drives us harder. Where competition says, "Couldn't you try just a little bit harder," play says, "Couldn't you try just a little bit softer." *Lishmah* invites us to play softer and gentler.

In Hebrew, there is a whole set of words that feature the repetition of one syllable. The repetition expresses a particular intensity. One of the more powerful examples of this intensity through repetition is the word *sha'a shu'ah*, which is translated as the "delight of erotic play." The word is taken in Hebrew mysticism to refer to erotic delight in both its sexual and mystical forms *Sha sha* forms the core of the word. In Hebrew the word *sha* means "turning toward." *Sha sha* is thus explained by the mystics to mean "turning toward for the sake of turning toward." The same formula follows for the Hebrew word *ga'a gu'ah*, which means "yearning," again with both sexually and mystically erotic implications. *Ga ga* is thus understood as "yearning for the sake of yearning." The subtle wisdom of language reminds us that the erotic is *lishmah*, that is, for its own sake. Its goal is to take us to itself, to remind us that we are already there.

SACRED WORKPLACE

One of the central areas of our lives that has been most painfully deeroticized is work. The Western world has greatly succeeded in reducing the length of the workday. Yet we have failed terribly to erase the dichotomy between work and pleasure. It is clear that such a division can only make our lives miserable. No matter how wonderful it may be, the weekend is still far shorter than the workweek. If we do not transform our work into *lishmah*—that which we do for its own sake—then we are destined for depression. In Hebrew, the word for *work* is *avodah*. Wonderfully though, in Hebrew the first connotation of *avodah* is that of the service in the Temple in Jerusalem. The subtle linguistic association shows up in English as well. The words *work* and *worship* come from common roots in Old English. The implication is clear: all work—like the work in the Temple—should be erotic. That is to say, *lishmah*—for its own sake.

At the site of the ancient Sumerian city of Ur, archaeologists were surprised to find a golden harp buried together with a set of golden working tools. It would appear that the Sumerians, like the Hebrews, understood that there can be no division between eros and work.

Six days a week you shall work, and on the seventh day you shall rest on the Sabbath. We naturally assume that the sacred imperative is to rest on the Sabbath. The wisdom masters read it differently. "Six days you shall work—this is a positive commandment." The sacred imperative is not just to rest on the seventh day, but also to work for the other six!

No matter how noble a goal we claim as the purpose of our work, it is insufficient. We must search for the meaning intrinsic to the work itself. Only then can we have the erotic workplaces envisioned by biblical myth.

WHY ARE YOU RUNNING?

A story of yearning for a sacred workplace that I have loved since my youth:

The great master Levi Isaac of Berdichev was walking his usual route in the market-

place. Along came a man rushing madly to somewhere and bowled the master over. "Why are you running so fast?" asked Levi Isaac as he got up.

"Well," said the man, "I need to make a living."

Levi Isaac asked, "Why are you working so hard to make a living?"

Well, no one had ever asked our mad dashing friend such a question, and he was at a loss as to how to respond. "Well," he stuttered—and then a lightbulb went off. "I am working so hard in order to make a living for my children." It seemed to be a fine answer, and the master wished him good day.

Twenty-five years go by. Again the master is walking on the same path in the market-place. Again, he is bowled over by a rushing passerby. Masters are consistent, so the same conversation ensues. And again it concludes with the man saying, confidently, "I am rushing so much in order to make a living for my children."

Levi Isaac looks deeply into his face. He realizes that this is the son of the man who had bowled him over twenty-five years ago. Turning his eyes heavenward, he asks God, "When will I finally meet that one child for whom all the generations labor so mightily?"

These gentlemen running through the market each justified their labor in terms of their children. Though supporting children is a very good reason, it is still insufficient. Every "reason" is ultimately an excuse. Even kids may be used as excuses, a violation of the erotic quality of *lishmah*. It is only enough to respond, "I am running for the sake of running, working for the sake of working!"

The most common expansion of *lishmah* beyond the sexual to the erotic is study. Remember that for the Hebrew mystic, study is an erotic encounter. It is a flirtation with text, a wooing of wisdom that leads to the final full embrace of life-giving learning. A core requirement of Hebrew law is that the study of Torah (sacred wisdom) be *lishmah*. *Lishmah* means the Torah must be studied not for the sake of honor or prestige, but for the sake of the spirit. According to a second school, studying even for the sake of the spirit is not *lishmah*. Study of Torah must be totally self-validating—Torah *lishmah*, purely for *its* own sake.

Stage Two: For the Sake of the Name

The erotic quality of *lishmah* has a second layer of meaning, which takes us even deeper. *Lishmah* derives from the Hebrew letters spelling *sham*, meaning "there." In the first understanding of *lishmah*, acting for its own sake, when you give up getting there, you realize you are already there.

However *sham*, pronounced "*shem*," has a second meaning—"name." In this layer of understanding, *lishmah* means "for the sake of the name." In the ultimate expression of *lishmah*, which we will see in a few pages, it will become clear that this quality of *lishmah* is also modeled in the sexual. First however let's understand what this erotic *lishmah* quality means on its own terms.

Your name is the face of God that is you and you alone. *Lishmah* means living for the sake of the unique God expression that is you in the world—your name!

The second book of the Torah is called the book of Names—*Shemot*. (In English it is poorly mistranslated as "The Book of Exodus.") The book of Names opens with a description of the Hebrew people during their prosperous early days of sojourning in Egypt; at the time they were still free men and women. One major characteristic stands out in the description. The text here, like the genealogies in the book of Genesis, takes great pains to record for us individual names. A name is a symbol of personal identity. Unique among ancient chronicles, the Bible thinks individuals count. This expresses itself as well later in the biblical narrative, which tells of the great census in which people are individually counted.

The crescendo of this description of freedom is the seemingly superfluous last verse of the section "Joseph was in Egypt." Remember, Joseph, the son of Jacob, has risen to greatness as the viceroy of Egypt. He has an Egyptian name—Tzafnat Paneach—and yet the text tells us "*Joseph* was in Egypt." Joseph, not Tzafnat Paneach. This deliberate use of his Hebrew name suggests that Joseph has retained his authentic identity, his name, his roots.

In the very next verse, however, the shift begins. Individual names blur into anonymous pronouns. The text begins to swell with anonymity. Describing the Hebrews, it reads, "*They* multiplied, *they* increased, *they* became strong...the land was full of *them*." This is followed by the chilling announcement: "A new king arose who did not know Joseph." The name, with all its erotic implica-tions, has been forgotten. From this point until the birth of Moses, the text speaks almost exclusively in pronouns. The children of Israel are repeatedly identified as "they" and "them." "A man from the house of Levi marries the daughter of Levi." Names are effaced. Slavery is on the rise. "And they made *their* lives bitter with bondage, in mortar and in brick, and in all the work of the field...they enslaved *them* with brutality."

The essence of slavery is the deconstruction of identity and intimacy. Intimacy is dependent on identity. Intimacy, as we have already explained, is in its essence not the giving up of self for other but rather "shared identity." Undermine the name—the symbol of identity—and there is no possibility for intimacy. Slavery in biblical myth is the symbol of nonerotic living. The slave in the Bible, although later protected by a strict code of ethics to insure his dignity and safety, is nevertheless a means to his master's end. He does not make independent decisions. His evaluation of reality, his testimony, is considered inadmissible in a court of law; most critically, he may not initiate his own marriage.

Slavery at its core is nonerotic and therefore an affront to human dignity and holiness. The shift in the biblical story toward transformation and redemp-tion is signaled by the name. A new child is born. "His name is called Moses." A name breaks through the darkness of slavery with the intimacy of personal identity. The Kabbalists point out that Moses' Hebrew name spelled back-ward is *Hashem*—"the name." Slavery still rules—the name is still backward, but freedom is in the air. The name, a glimpse of godliness, has reappeared.

SPIRITUAL MARRIAGE — SPIRITUAL DIVORCE

The essential requirement in Hebrew law for marriage and divorce is that it be done *lishmah,* for the sake of the name. This is an affirmation that the full uniqueness of the other is being engaged in the marital relation. If this is not so, if the name is somehow effaced, then no relationship can be established or terminated.

Changes in personal status must be *lishmah*, that is, they require the full erotic engagement and presence of all the parties involved.

All of this is expressed by an almost exaggerated emphasis that is placed on the correctness of the name in marriage documents. Great ritual care is taken in researching the precise Hebrew spelling of the name as well as in the listing of any nicknames. The point is that marriage must be an affirmation on both sides of the unique soul root of the other, which makes the beloved an end and not a means. Marriage is a commitment to the *name* of the beloved.

Not just marriage but also divorce needs to be an erotic process. How many divorces are done with radical violations of name, of intimacy. What is petty "name calling" other than slinging "names" at a person other than their true soul-printed name. During the divorce process, how many couples refuse even to use each other's names...calling their former spouse "him" or "her" in a tone of disgust. Biblical wisdom attempts to assuage the bitter namelessness of divorce by inviting us to a ritual of spiritual divorce, whose essence is the requirement of *lishmah*, "for the sake of the name.".

WHAT IS IN A NAME?

A name is an expression of relationship, of intimacy. "What's in a name?" asks Shakespeare. "Everything!" answers the Hebrew mystic. Many of the most common Hebrew mystical sayings reveal the magic, power, and invitation of the name. "For the sake of the great name"; "May his name be blessed"; "May his name be blotted out"; "He is as his name"; "Name is primal cause."

In biblical myth there are two names for the book of redemption, which tells the story of physical and spiritual emancipation. One of the names, which we mentioned, is *Sefer Shemot*—the Book of Names. The other name is *Sefer HaGeulah*—the Book of Emancipation. Why? To remind us that finding our name is the beginning of getting free.

To be a lover is to know the power of the name. A slave has no name, which is why slavery is such a brutal violation of the spirit of biblical myth. And this is slavery of any kind—not only legal juridic slavery but also typological slavery.

Anyplace where you are regarded only as a function, where your name is not known and honored, you are a slave. Anytime you regard another as a mere instrument in your design, the other becomes a slave master and an oppressor. To be a lover is to know the name. It can be the name of the waiter, the taxi driver, of your accountant's son or of the mailman's wife. By remembering the name, you become a lover.

It is for this reason that the pet names by which we call our beloved are the stuff of beauty in our lives. The more you love someone the more you accumulate pet names. Now, just a sidebar. I need to tell you that nicknames sometimes go awry. Don't laugh, but Cary and I call each other Bootch and Bibble. I am not sure why. Anyway, at various times she is Bootch and I am Bibble, and vice versa. Frankly it is sometimes hard to keep track. One day about a year back Cary was getting into the car with her dad and I called out to her from the house. Now I didn't in that split second remember if she was Bootch or Bibble that week, so they sort of came out together. "Hey, Bitch!" I shouted out. Her father looked up and…all was silent…for a very long moment…until we all burst out laughing.

The converse of Bootch and Bibble that always comes to mind is from that old great movie *The Graduate*. Dustin Hoffman has an affair with Mrs. Robinson, his parents' good friend. Finally he tells her that he cannot go on with it.

"Why not?" asks Anne Bancroft. "I love you," she says with little conviction.

"I cannot go on," repeats Hoffman.

"Why not?"

"Because I don't even know your first name, Mrs. Robinson."

A final image. It was ten, eleven years ago, and I was giving a lecture in a rented hall on the Upper West Side of Manhattan. The topic was exciting and so the hall was full, far too full for me to speak without a microphone. And as Lady

Fate would have it, in the first two minutes of the talk the microphone system went out. The host of the event went running to find the custodian who, it was hoped, would help fix the microphone. He came back some seven long minutes later and whispered to me, "I'm really sorry, Rabbi, I found the custodian, but he's a really nasty guy and he refuses to help."

I looked at him and was blessed with one of those moments of grace that allows us sometimes to ask the right question. "What's the custodian's name?" I asked him.

Flustered, nervous, and impatient, he blurted out, "Rabbi, we've got five hundred people in here, how do I know what the *blank* his name is?"

"Ah ha," I responded, "perhaps that's the problem." Asking the audience to wait a moment I went out myself and found the custodian glaring in his office, apparently still smarting from his encounter with the evening's chairman. I walked in and said, "Hi. I'm Marc. What's your name?"

Taken aback, he said, "George." George knew exactly how to fix the microphone and did so graciously and immediately.

The power of the name.

The Name of God

Magnified and Exalted Be the Name
—THE KADDISH PRAYER (HEBREW LITURGY)

Lishmah, for the sake of the name, is a core feature of the erotic. The name is a symbol of identity, intimacy, and freedom. But a name is all of these in a way far more powerful than one might initially imagine. When we talk about acting "for the sake of the name" we refer to something far deeper than the technical name that we use to identify a human personality. Name is, as we said earlier, "the face of God that is you and you alone." Here is where we touch the deepest erotic core of *lishmah.* Your name is not just a reflection of God's face, it is also actually part and parcel of what the mystics called God's great name. In the deepest level of human identity, the distinction between human being and God collapses. It is here that we realize that each of us is part of God.

As with all good biblical wisdom…we begin with a question.

In the Hebrew myth tradition the prayer that is recited when someone dies is called the Kaddish. It opens with the words *Yitgadal veyitakadash shemei raba*, "Magnified and exalted be God's great name." Why, you may ask, is the central prayer of mourning so preoccupied with God's name? Why does God need us to magnify his great name? If his name is so great, why can't it take care of magnifying itself? Even more important, is this the best prayer we can say in the face of the open grave? Someone has died—we are sad. Sometimes we are truly broken. We then say Kaddish, "Magnified and exalted be the great name." Is this the most profound response we have, standing before death? Would not words of comfort and an embrace be more appropriate? The answer to this quandary holds one of the most sacred mysteries of love, which is rooted in the heart of the cherub mysteries.

I first asked this question about the Kaddish in a talk delivered in memory of Eish Kodesh Gilmore, the son of my dear friend, who was killed in a senseless terrorist attack in Jerusalem. His name, Eish Kodesh, means Holy Fire.

A full year after Eish Kodesh's passing (while the terror still raged), I gave a talk in his honor at two in the morning around a campfire. His dad and several of Eish's friends were there with me. It was there that we explored the Kabbalistic secret of the name. Someone sent me a transcript of what was said that night. It captures perfectly this next stage in the erotics of name—the merging between the name of the individual and the name of God. Allow me to share it with you. Be a little patient; it unfolds more like a Buddhist Dharma talk than a formal essay. So sit back—relax for a few pages—and follow the flow of the spirit.

A NAME WITH THE POWER TO HEAL

There is a story told about the great teacher who started the mystical Hassidic movement of the late eighteenth century. This teacher, Israel son of Eliezer, became known as the Baal Shem Tov, which literally translates as the Master of the Good Name. This appellation was a title given to only the holiest adepts of an eighteenth-century secret mystical tradition. This honored appellation suggests that the master had connected to the root of his name, to his unique divinity.

When Master Isaac heard of the marvelous effect of the Master Israel's holy healing amulets, he was angry. He thought that surely amulets can only have such power if they use the holy name of God. Since this would constitute improper use of God's name, Master Isaac decreed, "Because of improper use of God's name, the power of the amulets must pass away." And so it was.

When Master Israel realized that his amulets were no longer healing, he sought the reason. Eventually it was revealed to him on high that Isaac's decree was blocking their efficacy. Israel confronted Isaac. "Why do you stop my amulets, which are used only to heal?" demanded Israel.

"Because you have not the right to use God's name in this way," retorted Isaac.

"But I do not use God's name in my amulets."

"You must, or they could not have such power."

"I insist, I do not use God's name," persisted Israel.

So all the amulets of Master Israel were gathered and brought before a tribunal. When the first one was opened, there was an audible gasp. Then the second, the third, and the fourth. Master Isaac was in shock. For the name of God indeed was not used in any of the amulets. Instead, in every amulet, in the place where God's name could have been, it read, "Israel son of Eliezar." It was Israel's own name and not the name of God that gave the amulets their special power. Awed at this great wonder, Master Isaac restored the power of Israel's amulets. Some say that after this incident Israel son of Eliezar became the last and greatest master to hold the title the Baal Shem Tov, Master of the Good Name.

In the story we begin to sense a potent enmeshing of the name of God and the name of the person. Are they indeed separate names? Or perhaps in some mysterious way, the name of the individual and the name of God are one.

Oh God!

This second image is one in which we will see very clearly that the second quality of *lishmah*—for the sake of the name—is modeled most powerfully in the sexual.

What do we call out at the moment of sexual climax? Three common possibilities. The first is that we cry out "Oh God" or its equivalent in whatever the lingua franca happens to be. *Elohim*...Mon Dieu...etc. The second possibility is that we call out the name of our beloved. The third possibility is some combination of the two. Oh God...Jack! or better yet...Oh Goood Jaaaack...!!! (Some good pastoral advice: make sure to get the name right.)

And yet when bantering over this subject is said and done, we notice that something of utmost seriousness and wonder has been revealed. As in the story of Master Israel of the Good Name, at the moment of ultimate vulnerability—and thus authenticity—there is a blurring of names. The name of the other and the name of God become almost interchangeable. Here again the sexual models the erotic—this time in the most dramatic of ways, bringing us to the heart of the cherubs' secret.

Why do God's name and the name of the beloved seem to interchange at the moment when all the outer layers are stripped bare and we call out our highest truth? Because in the deepest place *it is the same name!* The name of God is no less than the name of every being from the beginning to the end of time.

IN THE HOLY OF HOLIES

Now let's go one step deeper. The high priest in the Jerusalem Temple would enter the cherub-crowned Holy of Holies once a year. What would he do there? What was the nature of this mystery rite that he performed? In the Hebrew myth the priest is the incarnation of the flow of love in the universe. This is the only rite that is witnessed by the sexually entwined cherubs. So undoubtedly the mystery rite in the Holy of Holies lies at the very heart of the mystery of love.

As we already know, this day of entering the Holy of Holies is called the day of At-one-ment. It is a time of radical ecstasy, union, and joy. The priest is described in the Zohar as the incarnation of the male organ, while the Holy of Holies is the feminine Divine, the Shechina. In some Zohar passages, Shechina is the archetypal expression of the vagina. So the mystery rite is the priest and Shechina *merging in erotic union.* What did the priest actually do in the Holy of Holies? Tradition answers unequivocally; he called out the name— "Oh God!!" Not just any name, mind you; he called out the unpronounceable name of God, the name that was so true and had so much power that it was never said except at this one time of great intimacy. In the ecstasy of the erotic spirit, the priest, the lover par excellence, cried out the name! Mystical orgasm—pure and simple.

In the language of Kabbalah, mystical orgasm brings the priest into the *Ayin,* no-thing-ness. *Ayin* is the bliss of leaving self behind in the rapture of orgasm. Yet when love is deep, orgasm gives way not to an empty hangover but to a sweet aftertaste. In that aftertaste the self is reborn. In calling out "Oh God" the lover also rebirths his/her own name. In the little death of orgasm, self is reborn. The name of God and the name of the person are one.

In a precisely parallel image, God's face is the totality of all human faces from the beginning to the end of time. The Zohar teaches that when all the root souls who form God's will have been born, it will be the dawn of a new age of consciousness. We will have entered the Holy of Holies—otherwise known as the inside of the inside—or in an alternative reading of the same Hebrew phrase, the face of faces.

When all human beings who form God's face will have been born, we will be *"Lifnei Hashem."* As we saw in chapter 2, this literally means "before God." The deeper translation, however, would be on "the inside of God's face"—or the most fully literal translation—on "the inside of the face of the name."

A DIMINISHMENT OF THE NAME

Now let's go one last step before we bring this all together. What do we do when a person dies? We say a eulogy and recite the Kaddish meditation.

First the eulogy. What is its deep intention? What spiritual service does it render us on the day of the death?

When I first became a synagogue rabbi many years ago, I was called to the funeral home all too often. I can still remember today, however, the occasion of my first eulogy. A forty-eight-year-old man named Jerry had passed away while jogging. His wife, Fern, called me to do the eulogy and funeral. I had no idea what to say. So I asked Fern and her kids, Doug and Wendy, to sit with me the day before the funeral.

We sat around Fern's living room for a few hours, talking about Jerry. At first the talk was just polite. But as time wore on, with a few drinks to help, it got far more honest and real. All the while, I jotted notes, trying to capture their precise phrases. I spent most of that night awake, trying to weave their own sentences and words into a eulogy that would honor Jerry.

What is a eulogy? It is the last—and sometimes the first—opportunity to recognize the soul print of the one who has passed. The eulogy is when we try to paint in fine brush strokes the person's radical uniqueness that was their life. It is when we "receive their name."

The next morning, I shared the eulogy with Fern and her family and friends at the cemetery. It was magic, plain and simple. All of us felt that Jerry had entered the room. Or put better, somehow his presence seemed to surround and encompass us. We were on the inside. At that very moment, I asked Fern and her children to rise and recite with me the Kaddish meditation. "Magnified and exalted be the great name!" Whose name? Why, God's name...and Jerry's. Of course! For in the deepest place, they are the same name.

Death in the mystical tradition of Ezekiel is called a *hillul hashem*. Usually translated as "a desecration of God," it more literally means "an emptying of the name." Death is a diminishment of divinity. One aspect of God in the world has suddenly disappeared. Death is tragic because a person dies leaving so much of their story untold. Each person is a unique name-face of God. Each death is a dimming of the divine visage.

This truth is not limited to Kabbalistic masters. Walt Whitman understood at least part of it when he wrote.

> *In the faces of men and women I see God,*
> *And in my own face in the glass,*
> *I find letters from God dropped in the street,*
> *And every one is signed by God's name.*

At the eulogy, we try to trace God's signature in the name of the departed.

Now, it all comes together! After the eulogy at the grave site we do the Kaddish meditation—"Magnified and exalted be the great name." Both the great name of the one who passed and God's great name. Someone has died. A potential emptying of the divine appellation. A diminishment of divinity. Someone may pass on without having their name recognized. To be recognized is the deepest craving of our soul. So we say eulogy in a last—and yes, sometimes a first—attempt to recognize the person. When we succeed, we are able to recite the Kaddish, for we have certainly magnified and exalted the great name. Not *merely* the name of the departed, but also the name of the departed, which is an infinitely unique expression of God's very own face and name.

Fixing the Name

In Kabbalistic language, Kaddish is a *tikkun hashem*, a fixing of God's name. God's name is healed when we fully recognize and receive the name of the one just passed, because the name of the departed is no less than the name of God.

In this light we can more fully understand a wonderful passage from Tennyson's memoirs:

A kind of waking trance I have frequently had, quite up from my boy-hood, when I have been all alone. *This has generally come upon me through repeating my own name to myself silently,* [emphasis added] till all at once, as it were out of the intensity of the consciousness of individuality, the indi-viduality itself seemed to dissolve and fade away into boundless being; and this is not a confused state, but the clearest of the clearest, the surest of the surest, utterly beyond words, where death was almost a laughable impossibility... the loss of personality but the only true life.

Tennyson, like Master Israel of the Good Name before him, understands that it is not the abandonment of individuality but rather its radical embrace that is the portal to the infinite. This is so because at the deepest level of our individuality, we participate in the name of God. One's own name is the por-tal to the name of God. They are the same name. It is in this sense that mysti-cal master Nahum of Chernobyl writes in the nineteenth century:

They are called by their names... for the name of a person is his soul. For the letters of his name is his soul root and divine flow and with these he serves studies and prays. Therefore a wicked person is one who does not know his name.

Name is intended—in this passage in particular and in this chapter in gen-eral—in the way I will use it in the upcoming discussion of the eros of story. Your story is your gateway to eternity. The litmus test of your story is *lishmah.* Is it for its own sake? For the sake of your name? For the sake of The Name?

For this reason reciting the Kaddish prayer at a funeral and throughout the mourning period was considered in the Hebrew myth tradition such a vital spiritual task. In Kaddish we recognize, sometimes for the first time, that the departed did not live to serve us. We affirm the infinite dignity of their story.

So often we don't really see those who are closest to us. We somehow view both our partners and our parents as extensions of our story. We are all too often unable to recognize the full and independent dignity of their lives. Often the pain of mis-recognition accompanies our closest loved ones to their grave.

Yet there is another chance. Kaddish! In saying Kaddish we declare for all to hear that the beloved who is departed lived not for our sake but for the sake of The Name—theirs and God's. Often this is what opens us up to a deeper love for them and begins the process of healing open wounds.

A Kaddish Story

In the following story it is not the details of the story line that are vital. It is rather to taste in the tale the full erotic beauty and power of Kaddish, where man and G-d merge into one in the spelling of the name.

There is an old story from the villages of Europe of a woman, Rebecca, who owed rent to her landlord. But owing rent then was not like owing rent today. Back then, the landlord had full right to take your possessions, your home, put you in jail or, even worse, sell you off to slavery. Well, Rebecca, her husband, and her beloved children owed thousands of rubles and were about to be sold into slavery. They would each be sold to different buyers. She would never see them again.

Imagine her grief. She is broken. She walks desperately through the town, door to door, begging for help. By the end of the day she has a meager three rubles to her name. Hopelessly, she heads home. She walks, weeping and weeping over her impossible fate. Weeping because she won't see her children grow up, weeping because she won't see her husband grow old.

In her despair a tragic thought arose in her mind—"I won't even be there the day my dear husband passes away. Who will say Kaddish for him?" The thought strikes her soul with a strange and desperate urgency. She runs over to a beggar on the road. Handing him one of her rubles she pleads, "Dear sir, please, say the mourner's Kaddish for my husband. Please, it means the world to me." The beggar is baffled but agrees.

Rebecca walks away but another desperate thought strikes her, "And what of all the anonymous people who die and nobody says Kaddish for them? What about them?" She runs back to the same beggar and thrusts the second ruble into his hand. "Please, please also say Kaddish for all the unnamed souls for whom no one has ever said Kaddish before." Again the beggar, moved by her impassioned request, also agrees to this. Rebecca turns to leave, her heart more and more shrouded in grief. But another thought arises. She turns back to the beggar, takes her last ruble, and places it in his hand. With tears streaming down her cheeks she entreats, "Please, sir, when you say Kaddish for all those lost souls, please please, say it with all of your heart, all of your soul, and all of your might. Hold nothing back!"

And as she turns to leave she hears over her shoulder the beggar beginning to pray. He begins softly at first but then growing with more and more strength. Like a trickle that becomes a stream that becomes a flood. He prays with all of his might, all of his brokenness, all of his pain. Rebecca listens, transfixed, drenched in tears. It is as if a fire enwraps her and lifts her to the highest heavens. There she has a vision of the beggar's prayers, ascending and crashing through the celestial gates, releasing the myriad souls of those who had long been awaiting their Kaddish to be said, their name to be called. There is a great surge of flowing energy and relief.

And then it is over, the flood turns back to stream turns back to trickle.

Rebecca somehow stands lighter, her heart more at ease.

As she continues down the road, the strangest thing happened. A beautiful shining carriage approached her. It stopped and a well-dressed man inside asked for directions. Then, quite unexpectedly, he asked her if she would like a ride. Rebecca, having never been in such a fine carriage before, declined. But the man insisted. And so she boarded the carriage and there entered into a deep conversation with the gracious man. Her whole story tumbled out effortlessly. How times were so rough and so many children to feed. How a cruel landlord had increased the rent, and debt had built up, and all had been lost, and now how the whole family was to be sold into slavery. The man listened thoughtfully, and as Rebecca left the carriage he did a most incredible thing. He took out of his pocket a check, filled it out for the exact amount of her debt, handed it to her, and before she could protest, he sped away.

The next day, Rebecca dashes to the bank. When she hands the check to the clerk he gives her a suspicious glance and asks her to wait a moment as he scurries away. Rebecca becomes nervous...perhaps the check was not real and this was all a cruel joke. Again distraught, she waits. Finally the clerk arrives and escorts her to the office of the president of the bank. She enters the president's plush office and sits before him, a large and forbidding man behind a sprawling desk. "Where did you get this check?" he demands. She explains to him the entire story, about the stranger in the carriage, about her debts and her family and even about the beggar who had prayed so mightily.

The president then asked her, pointing to the dozens of pictures hanging on the walls of the room, "Do you recognize anyone in any of these portraits?" Rebecca looks and immediately points to the large portrait behind the desk. "That man there—he is the man in the carriage who gave me this check!" The president turns pale. You see, the portrait behind the desk was of his father. And the check, it bore his father's exact signature. The only thing was that his father had died three years before. And his son, now the president of the bank, had never said Kaddish for him.

RETURNING TO THE CHERUBS

The way of *lishmah* is rooted in the mystery of the cherubs. The sexual models the erotic and teaches us how to be lovers in the world. The Name—of God and Other fully merged into one—is at the heart of the sexual. The sexual is the most exemplary expression of eros. For sexuality at its best is *lishmah*, for its own sake, and not to network some other advantage. It is, simply, for the sake of the name.

The cherubs themselves were held by many Kabbalists to be the masculine and feminine names of God. When united in sexual embrace, the cherubs were in effect engaged in a unification of the Name. Exile of the Shechina and the archetypal loss of the ark represents the fragmentation of the Name. Whenever the Name is made whole, the Shechina is redeemed from her exile. When one reclaims one's name, when one lives *lishmah*—for its own sake—stepping off the wheel of networking and superficiality, then the Name is healed. Whenever the calling out of the Name is limited only to the sexual, when the sexual is the extent of the erotic and not the model of the erotic, then the Shechina is in exile. The erotic—the calling out of the Name—is exiled into the merely sexual. The cherubs are separated from each other, and in the language of the Zohar "blessing does not flow in the world."

TO GREET WITH GOD'S NAME

Calling out "the Name" is evoked the world over in greetings. The Spanish hello—*hola*—originated in Arab Spain from the term *"O'Allah"*—Allah of course being the Arab appellation of God. In Austrian German they say *Grias God.* In Hebrew, the common response when asked how you are doing is *Baruch Hashem*—Praise God, or Thank God. The Hebrew greeting *Shalom* is actually a name of God. In English, we still follow this custom when we part from someone and say "Godspeed" or "God be with you."

In a wonderful and mysterious passage, the wisdom masters talk of a special decree made nearly three thousand years ago. It taught that one should greet his friend with the name of God. Although the Third Commandment proscribes such "idle use" of God's name, this new law legislated special permission to use the divine name in casual greeting. The source for the decree is said to be the verse "In a time to do for the Name (God) you may override the Torah."

The idea underlying the decree is very powerful. To greet a person, we are allowed to use the sacred name of God, which is never taken in vain, because to greet a person is to recognize them, to perceive them. Perception is healing through love, for there is nothing more painful than anonymity. Love, you remember, is the perception of the infinite divine specialness in other!

You come to a party alone. No one recognizes you for several long minutes. You feel forlorn, alienated. Then someone taps you on the shoulder and calls your name in warm welcome. The world is transformed. You have been recognized, perceived. Called by name!

Of course, true recognition is deeper than a mere greeting. It requires a true knowing, receiving, and even merging with the name. This is what happens when the Name (God's and the beloved's) is called at the height of sensual passion. If the passion is situated in the context of a shared story and commitment, then the calling of the Name in the cherublike embrace of sexuality is the ultimate transcending of loneliness, both for the lover and the beloved.

Minimally, however, the wisdom masters write that we must greet each other with the Name. The simple and correct reading of the text indicates that they are referring to the name of God. But on some deeper level, the Name they refer to is none other than the Name of the person being greeted. In this powerful rereading the new decree is that no person should remain anonymous. Every person should be called by their Name. Never allow yourself to be served by someone without knowing their Name. In knowing the Name of the waiter serving you there is a fixing and healing of God's Name.

It is a time to fix divinity. To create God. God is created by revealing the infinite divine in every person. God's name is emptied when people live without having their Names recognized, without being called by Name. So the wisdom masters decree, "Greet every man with the Name." The Name of God and the Name of the blessed and beautiful individual before you, for they are one and the same.

In the tradition it is taught that after the Temple fell the name was lost. The Name is erotic. The fall of Temple = fall of eros = fall of the Name. The exile of the Shechina is the exile of the Name. Shechina is the sound of your Name being called in ecstasy and love. Every time we call a person by Name we redeem the Shechina and rebuild the Temple.

Story, Voice, Creativity, and Pleasure

The path of eros is the path of living your story. To live one's story is very close to the modern expression "to find voice." Voice is that unique and infinitely special sound wave that only you can generate in the symphony of the world's voices. As we shall see in the course of our discussion, the unique voice of your story is the wellspring of both your greatest personal creativity and your highest personal pleasure. So before we finish this chapter we will devote a few words to creativity and pleasure as well. But our journey begins in the beginning—with the erotics of story.

In the path of story, as in the other paths of Hebrew tantra, sex models eros. As in sex, the degree of eros that imbues every facet of our existence is intimately linked to the degree to which we are living our stories. Sex divorced from story is fragmented, in exile, not sacred. When the sexual is "de-storied" then the erotic Shechina is exiled into the faceless sexual. When this happens, in the language of the Zohar, the erotic Goddess of Shechina becomes an *eshet zenunim*, a prostitute. In my reading of the Zohar a prostitute is the archetype of the person who splits her sexuality from her personal story. We never know a prostitute's real name. She is either anonymous or carries an impersonal trade name: Candy, Lolly, Sugar. Sex has been de-storied.

When life is "de-storied," the erotic Shechina is exiled into faceless anonymity. For to be anonymous is to live with your *true* name, your unique story, unknown.

When living your story even life's difficulties are somehow all right. When caught in a story not your own then even life's successes are never enough. There is no eros more satisfying or fulfilling than the eros of living your story. You can only fill the void of emptiness with the stuff of your own sacred tale.

To fully understand the de-storying of life, which expresses itself in the prostitute archetype in all of our lives, we must first reconnect to what it means to live one's story. So in order to proceed on this stage of our search for the lost ark, the erotics of story, we need to deepen the understanding we developed in our first soul print journey together. (*Soul print*, you may recall, is the term I use in my book *Soul Prints* to refer to your infinite uniqueness, the spiritual DNA of your soul.) Let's reexplore the core soul print mantra, "live your story."

The Candle of God

The image used most often in biblical myth to describe the soul is light. Light in Hebrew is referred to as *sapir*. You may be familiar with the English word *sapphire*, which is derived from the Hebrew. A sapphire, with its incomparable blue shine, is a stone of light. It should be no surprise that this word meaning "light" is also the luminous root of the word *sipur*—"story." Your story is your unique configuration of light. Your *sipur*, story, just like a wave of light, is flowing and streaming, the wave of events and emotions you experience in a lifetime. The incidents, details, images, and apparent coincidences of your life all weave a story unlike that of any other human being on the face of the planet.

Sipur is about being the hero of your own life. Dickens said it so perfectly in *David Copperfield*: "Whether I shall turn out to be the hero of my own life, or whether that station will be held by anybody else, these pages must show…" Being able to realize your destiny comes from your ability to follow the outline of your own story. This is why the tragedy of a disease such as Alzheimer's is far more than the ultimate physical disability it inflicts. What is so infinitely painful is the gradual yet conscious losing of the outline of your story.

Each of us sleeps, eats, loves, rages, works, and speaks. Not one of us, however, does those things in quite the same way. Living your story is about expressing the originality of your commonness. It is about making the ordinary extraordinary. *Sipur* is also your "calling," the human experience of being summoned to a specific mission or destiny, the revealer of your unique destiny. It is the unique weave, the blending and the melding of all the moments and encounters of a lifetime. For it is your own story, your unique story, that calls you forward, propelling you upon your path.

The soul's story says that you are singled out, unique, one and only, and that therefore you are called to a mission that you alone are charged to fulfill. This is the place of your light, where it shines brightest in the world. When we see someone living their story, we feel a great rush of love for them. This is because love at its core is a soul print perception. To love is to perceive the infinite glow and uniqueness of your beloved's story.

Appreciating Each Other's Purple Trees

This is a wonderful story about a girl who paints a purple tree. The teacher has drawn a tree on the board and asked the children to copy it. When she sees the girl's tree she disapproves. "You didn't copy my tree."

"I know," says the girl, "I painted my tree."

"But I've never seen a purple tree."

"Isn't that a shame," says the girl.

To which Hebrew myth master Abraham Kook adds,

Along come the learned teachers,
and focus their gaze on all that is outside,
they too distract us from the "I,"
they add fuel to the fire,
giving the thirsty vinegar to drink…
stuffing the minds with all that is external to them…
and the I is more and more forgotten.

Sometimes our educators, our leaders, our parents, haven't the eyes to read our insides. And so we write our own stories to fit their skewed sight, even if it means a betrayal of our own tales. Children are all naturally unique until they "try to be." They try to be in order to get us to notice them because we weren't paying attention to them when they were painting purple trees. The job of an educator, and we are all educating one another, is to impart basic skills to the student AND to honor their purple tree.

The purple tree is rooted in the part of us that cannot be fully expressed, cannot be narrowed into words, and cannot be subjected to laws. Ultimately, every person is completely free and has her own special salvation. No form of instruction exists, no savior exists to open up the road. No road exists to be opened. The road is you. Your soul story says, "I am more than that." You are the sum of your choices—but you are more than that. You are the sum of all your particular traits and dispositions—but you are more than that. The "more" is your soul story—that is, the unique constellation of loving that is you. The "more than that" is what makes healing and transformation possible. The "more than that" is the unique face of God that is your face.

When we die we are asked one thing—Did you paint your purple tree? Hebrew mystical master Reb Zusia used to say, "After I die and am in heaven I will not be asked, 'Why were you not Moses?' I will be asked, 'Why were you not Zusia?' And for that I will have no answer."

Try to be anyone else but you, and you will always be second best. But you are the best you there will ever be.

There is no higher calling than living *your* story. You are a messenger of God, sent to this earth as God's personal envoy. There is something in this world no one can do but you. Is there any other job that could be more special?

Soul Print Hints

A word in the Zohar used for those souls who are living their story is *lechisah*, meaning "whisper." To live your story is to be able to hear the intimate whisper of divinity erotically caressing your life. We are all recipients of cosmic love notes. Paul Tillich reminds us that we can only hear through the love that listens. Buber captured the spirit of biblical myth when he wrote, "To live means being addressed."

To live one's story is erotic in the resonance of its melody and the fullness of its canvas. The world, when we are in our story, is no longer empty. The soul is not here just to pay back karmic debts. It has a contribution to make from the depth of its infinite specialness. Through making that contribution a human being feels ful-filled. That is the eros of living one's story.

When you are in your story, the universe becomes full of what Nachman of Bratzlav called *remezie deorayta*—"divine hints." Interestingly the most important shared feature between lovers and schizophrenics is that they tend to interpret the world as if it is happening for them alone. So Plato terms love a form of divine madness. But who is truly insane? Often mild insanity is a refuge for the truly sane, and those of us normal folks marching to the beat of any drummer but our own are the ones who are disconnected from reality.

The universe is full of whispers, and they are talking directly to you. And here is the paradox—the more you act as if you are being addressed, the more you will be. The world is filled with soul print hints. It may be the lyrics of a song, a sign on a building, an old friend you meet after years of not seeing each other, or a book that grabs your attention and demands to be read.

British thinker Adam Phillips, in his wonderful work *The Beast in the Nursery*, understands well the slow and subtle eros of hints. The artist inside us, he

writes, is "all the time on the lookout for material to make a dream with...
inspiration means being able to take the hint.... It is not only a tuned respon-
siveness, it is also an unconscious radar for affinities, for what speaks to one
by calling up one's own voice."

There is a self-fulfilling circle: the deeper one enters one's character and
story, the more whisperings are heard and hints are detected. Of course, the
wink, the subtle gestures, the tilt of the head, all these are the language of
lovers; hints and intimations are the hallmark of intimacy.

Each person has their unique talent, pleasure, obligation, form of silli-
ness, and pathology. These are all personal soul print hints that direct you
toward living your story. (If this path is particularly compelling to you, then
allow me to invite you to read my first English-language book, *Soul Prints*.)

The Prostitute Archetype: The Storying of Sex

The great biblical myth affirmation is that for sex to be sacred it must be personal. Personal means connected to story.

Impersonal sex may mean sex that is used to weave a false story or it may
refer to sex that is detached from the web of soul print passions and commitments that is your life. It refers as well to sex that we use compulsively to
cover up—even from ourselves—the dull throb of emptiness.

The connection between sex and story is hardwired into our spiritual
operating system—so much so that we have a universal name for one who separates his or her personal story from the sexual. We call that person a prostitute. The essence of the prostitute archetype in every culture is the de-storying
of the sexual.

Of course, the prostitute archetype is not limited to our vision of the single woman soliciting her male client. When we talk of prostitution we can be
referring to any combination of man or woman. More important, it can refer
to sexual relations within a marriage or even nonsexual interpersonal relationships. There are many ways to be a whore.

The archetypal prostitute is willing to separate sex from her deeper personal story. The symbol for a person's story is her name. A name is the gateway to the personal and intimate contours of our life narrative. The prostitute makes up a name—be it Candy or Lola. The client is a John, and she is an anonymous body. She is the fantasy object of her client—object, not subject. This is their contractual agreement.

The classic expression of the de-storying of intimacy is the archetypal refusal of the prostitute to kiss. The kiss is the time when all distinctions between subject and object melt; the Zohar calls it *the merging of spirit in spirit*. She refuses because it is too difficult to depersonalize a kiss. She has sold her body, and even that is only for the moment. She has in no way sold her soul. The client has not earned the right to the intimacy of personal contact. She has placed a screen between him and her inner light. Though he may enter her physical space, he is denied entry into her story, which is her spirit.

When the divine Shechina Goddess achieves union with the divine male God it is called kissing. The human and the Divine mirror each other in Kabbalistic myth. It is in this sense that we say, when there is no kissing, the Shechina is in exile. She is eros exiled into the merely sexual. She is Shechina degraded to being a prostitute.

The Impersonal and the Transpersonal

The prostitute archetype manifests itself in two forms. The first is the classic prostitute with whom sex is nonintimate and impersonal. The second is the Temple prostitute, who expresses the sexual as transpersonal and cosmic. The Temple prostitute would engage in transpersonal sex both with worshippers and temple priests as part of the erotic service of the Goddess. What both share in common however is that the prostitute, whether man or woman, is not related to in personal terms. The prostitute is upgraded to a symbol. Once that happens degradation is sure to follow eventually.

For the slippery slope between the impersonal and the depersonalized is seductive and steep. Thus, as powerful and even necessary as a transpersonal erotic moment might be, the prophets disallowed the Temple prostitute. The prophet recognizes that the sexual model of the erotic courses with a powerful energy that is essential to human ful-fill-ment. However, they insisted on replacing the male and female Temple prostitutes with the male and female cherubs. This was their way of insuring that the transpersonal did not slip into the impersonal, which could slip into the nonpersonal, which could slip into the nonethical, which could slip into evil.

Remember, paganism allowed the mutilation and even slaughter and sacrifice of the prostitute as an integral and regular part of the pagan cult. Once the sacrifice of a human being who was seen only as a symbol occurred, all ethics broke down.

The prophets insist on the radical holiness of the individual. The individual is of infinite worth and dignity and can never be reduced to a symbol. It is this emphasis of infinite value—the personal story of every human being—that is the driving force of prophetic ethics. We see in our own culture just how insightful this prophetic intuition is. Everyday pornography and soft porn may play the role of the Temple prostitute and seem innocent enough to be on the counter of respectable newsstands or on the movie channel at the best and most established hotels. But the line—driven by profit and emptiness—between the impersonal and the depersonalized is very, very slippery. Eventually it may lead to the radical depersonalization that lies at the core of all evil. Pornography based on rape, abuse of minors, and even murder—"white snuff"—is now available all over the world.

Erotic and Ethical Entitlement

Personal eros comes from living your story. But though the prophet is fully identified with eros, he insists nevertheless on the merger of ethos and eros. Now what does it mean to be ethical? The answer: to behave in a way that supports a person's ability to live their story.

What is an ethical violation? It is to behave in a way that undermines someone else's ability to live their story. According to biblical myth, this could be an active violation—theft, deception, or violence. Or it could be a passive violation—failing to get involved in making the world a place where every human being has the opportunity to live their story. Since the primary ethical violation would be to violate someone's story, the ethical and erotic merge, because the underlying principle of ethics is to affirm and support the erotic integrity of every human being's story.

The only clash, then, between the erotic and the ethical is when my eros is at the expense of yours. Since biblical myth affirms that every human being is a *homo imago dei*, in Dante's phrase, a divine miniature, then all human beings are equal in their erotic entitlement. Any violation of that equality would be an ethical—and an erotic—violation. So all ethical lapses are really violations of eros.

As we saw earlier, the inner impulse for all ethical violation is a lack of eros. When we human beings feel empty, exiled from our stories, we try to feed off other stories. That is the core of every ethical violation: when another person becomes not an end, a story unto themselves, but rather a means of fulfilling your own story.

Moving one step beyond what we saw in our discussion in chapter 8, it now becomes clear that there is no possible distinction between the erotic and the ethical. In fact, the word *ethics* comes from the Greek *ethos*, meaning "the special nature of a person or group"—to be precise, their story, which is also the source of the most powerful erotic fulfillment.

The prophet insists that the erotic sexual affirm the stories of both partners in the relationship. To de-story the sexual destroys intimacy, which leads to the prostitute archetype, the exile of the Shechina, and the destruction of the Temple.

Sex models eros in that it must always emerge from deep within our story line. When it does, then we can embrace the full erotic nature of the sexual as the guiding spiritual model for all of the nonsexual dimensions of our lives.

Stolen Story

Remember the story on p. 52 with which we introduced the mystery of the cherubs? It was about a man who could be cured only by sleeping with a particular woman—if she was married. "About this the master said—from the day the Temple was destroyed, the taste of sex was taken and given to violators of the path—as it is written, stolen waters are sweet." This expresses how we have lost the core Temple energy, when the erotic was an integral part of a person's story. A person in exile feels that they need to violate the parameters of their story in order to touch erotic fulfillment. "Stolen waters" refers to something that is not part of your story, and "are sweet" means that they give you a quick pseudo-erotic charge, which allows you to forget the emptiness for a moment. By definition, this must be an illusion, for full eros is only available to a person who is living their story. Your story is the web of ongoing commitments, promises, and dreams that form the core of your narrative. The reclaiming of Temple energy is then no more than an expansion of consciousness allowing a person to realize the full eros of living their story; the sexual is an organic and holistic expression of all the primal power and passion of that story.

When you are not in your own story, the need for fulfillment becomes obsessive, overwhelming. But when you are living the depths of your story, freely chosen full sexual expression, which is both gentle and wildly erotic, can well up and fill you.

The Home That Is Holy

The symbol of your story is *home*. The place of the cherubs, symbols of the erotic, is *Beit HaMikdash*. Although usually translated as "the Temple," what it really means is the "home that is holy." The Hebrew myth image for the most sacred space—the epicenter of the spirit, the great Temple—is the home. In much of Hebrew literature it is not even called the holy; rather it's referred to as either the Mikdash or the *bayit*, meaning "the Sacred," or "the home." As if to say that to use both appellations would simply be repetitive. The cherubs, sexual symbols of the erotic, are in the *bayit*. This is precisely the notion we have been trying to unpack. The sexual needs to be connected to home and story, not to hotel rooms or hideaways (although at times hotel rooms can also be transformed into sacred homes). Have you ever been ashamed to bring a boyfriend or girl-friend home? This is not a good sign about the depth of the relationship. If it's not a relationship you can "bring home," then it's not a sacred relationship.

The eros of home and hearth, your story, provides a stable matrix for the full erotic power of the cherubs. The biblical epigram "*Ishito zo beito*"—"His woman is his home"—in the reading of the mystics has nothing to do with patriarchy or ownership. Rather it means his Shechina—his erotic self—needs to be rooted in his *bayit*—his story. So for woman, so for man.

Emily Dickinson continues the idea. "A home is a holy thing—/ nothing of doubt and distrust—/ can enter its portals." Home is created by love. My Jerusalem home where I lived for most of the past decade had two rooms. The only furniture was a double bed, one table, one chair, a closet, and a few thousand books, which lined the walls from floor to ceiling. In that place I first understood what "home" meant. I discovered my interior castle, where the secret of the cherubs revealed itself to me. It is where I grew up. It was my Temple and travels with me on all my paths. It was there that I found my other cherub—my wife, Cary. It is in the safety of this home that I seek to merge the eros of the sexual with the eros of *bayit*. That is what it means for sex to have a story. That is what it means for a home to be a Temple.

A beautiful poem by Mary Mackey, which Cary gave me upon our engagement, captures the intertwisting of sex and story.

Love comes from years
Of breathing
Skin to skin
Tangled in each other's dreams
Until each night
Weaves another thread

In the same web
Of blood and sleep

Leah

Now, lest my dear reader be all too confident that the prostitute lingers only at the outer reaches of society, in red-light districts and on dank street corners, let me share with you a vision of psychological prostitution, the de-storying of eros, which is far from marginal, and not far from many of our homes.

Who is the biblical myth archetype of the prostitute? Amazingly the wisdom masters identified Leah, the great matriarch, mother of six tribes, as an occasional manifestation of the prostitute archetype.

What makes her a prostitute is that she is disconnected from her story. She has no true home. Her existence is therefore nonerotic—an expression of the Shechina in exile. And a careful reading of the biblical myth reveals that not only Leah but also her husband, Jacob, plays the whore on occasion. The very heroes of the biblical narrative wrestle with their prostitution inclinations.

Let me briefly reconstruct the narrative.

Jacob comes to his uncle Laban's home. His uncle has two daughters—Leah, the elder, and Rachel, the younger. We are told that it has already been decreed by destiny that Leah was to marry Jacob's older brother Esau, while Rachel would be destined to the younger brother, Jacob. Leah, however, desperately wants Jacob. She feels that without Jacob her life would be drab, empty, unbearable. Jacob, on the other hand, wants desperately to marry Rachel. She is the woman for whom he lifted the great rock at the well. She is the woman he kissed and wept over.

But Jacob knows that Laban, the father of these two women, will attempt to deceive him. So the well-prepared Jacob gives Rachel signs that she should pass to him as she is escorted, heavily veiled, to the wedding canopy. She will covertly pass him the sign, and he will be assured that he is getting the right bride.

But as is often the case with the best-laid plans, something goes wrong.

In his bedchambers after the nuptials, Jacob finds himself with Leah and not Rachel. It was she and not her sister who gave him the coded signs under the canopy. "How can it be?" ask the reader and Jacob in unison. The answer: Leah, who so desperately wanted Jacob, manipulated her younger sister, Rachel, into giving her the codes. She cried to Rachel that she could not survive the humiliation of her younger sister being married before her, the older. She wept and screamed—perhaps even threatened to do herself harm. In the end, Rachel, unable to resist her sister's manipulation, relents and gives over the signs. Rachel will have to wait another seven years to wed Jacob.

On this night, though, it is Leah who marries Jacob. Leah, however, has violated the destiny of her story, intended as she was to Esau. She has deeply hurt her sister and made Jacob a pawn in her desperate bid to find fulfillment. But one cannot find ful-fillment by marrying Jacob in the darkness. We all know that! Have we not all, at one time or another, married Jacob in the darkness?!

She may now have Jacob, but she still does not have fulfillment, and so she tries to use her children to win Jacob. She has her first child, naming him Reuben, an acronym for "God has seen my affliction." Her second child she names Simeon, the biblical acronym for "God has heard that I am hated." Still, Leah flounders in her darkness. The next son is called Levi, biblical acronym for the pathos-filled "now maybe my husband will take walks with me."* Her fifth son she calls Zebulun, "maybe this time my husband will find me luxuriant and fertile." It is a tragic pattern that climaxes in the birth of her sixth son, Issachar. But first, the narrative leading up to Issachar's birth.

Leah's firstborn, Reuben, has brought her mandrake flowers from the field. Reuben brings his mother flowers because, like his brothers, he desperately seeks her love. Reuben, Simeon, and Levi internalized their mother's degradation as the unloved wife of Jacob. They are filled with rage toward their father. They desperately seek to fill their mother's emptiness, an impossible task for any child.

---

*Her fourth son, Judah, breaks this pattern. See my Hebrew book *Redefining Certainty* for the story of Leah and Judah and what I have termed "The Judah Moment."

So Reuben brings his mother flowers. Tragically, even in receiving his gift Leah can still not see Reuben. There is no recorded discussion between them. No "thank you," no embrace. She sees only the flowers, intuiting immediately that they might be a tool in her ongoing bid to win her husband's love. So Leah, still desperate to be filled by Jacob, struts about with her flowers in full view of her barren sister, Rachel. Rachel, you recall, is desperate for children. These flowers are the double symbol of motherhood. First, they are man-drakes, powerful fertility plants. Second, they are a son's doting gift to his mother. "Give me your mandrakes," pleads Rachel with Leah.

Which is precisely what Leah intended. "Is it not enough that you take my husband—will you also take my son's mandrakes?" Of course, Rachel falls into the manipulative web.

"I don't want Jacob," Rachel cries out. "Take him. I will give you my night with him but you must please let me have those beautiful mandrakes from your son." And the tragic exchange between two desperate sisters is done. Jacob comes home that night, thinking to go to his beloved Rachel's bed. But it is Leah who brazenly comes to greet him. "Leah goes out to greet Jacob; 'To me you shall come tonight, for I have hired you with the mandrakes of my son.'"

A humiliated but not innocent Jacob for the second time sleeps with Leah instead of Rachel. Born of this mandrake-purchased union is Issachar—mean-ing no less than "he [Jacob] was hired." On that tragic night Jacob became the prostitute. But not only Jacob. Leah "goes out" to greet Jacob. The wisdom mas-ters observe, "Leah our Matriarch was a whore that night." The interpretive key is "She [Leah] goes out." That is to say, she went out of her story. It is not about that night alone. That night is but the symbolic expression of Leah's tragic inability to embrace the fullness of her story. That is precisely the pros-titute archetype: the divorcing of the sexual from the fabric of an authentic personal story. The Leah figure of biblical myth is the proto-feminist story of a married woman who attempts to use her husband as her story. Jacob, she is convinced, can fill her emptiness. So painful is her hole, her emptiness, that she hires Jacob—turning him into a prostitute, if only to feel the fleeing libidinal illusion of being filled.

But prostitution occurs not only when we divorce sex from our story. More seriously, if we are sexual in a story not our own, if we use our sexuality to weave a false story, or if our sexuality is not integrated in our story, then we fulfill all too grandly the prostitute archetype.

The Erotics of Voice

> Ah! From the soul itself must issue forth
> A light, a glory, a fair luminous cloud,
> Enveloping the Earth—
> And from the soul itself must be there sent
> A sweet and potent voice, of its own birth,
> Of all sweet sounds the life and element.
>
> —COLERIDGE

Sex in its full erotic and sacred context has a story. So our lives too in their full erotic and sacred form must have a story line. To live in my story is to find my voice. Voice however is not only to have a story, but also to find the words to tell my story. Voice is our full emotional range and our ability to be fully present and expressive of our feelings. If the free flow of my story is blocked in the world, then I do not have voice.

Great and sacred sex is about the free flow of voice. Wonderfully, the Talmudic wisdom masters refer to sex as a form of speech. Perhaps that is why we get so hurt when, during sexual play, our partner says, "Shh! Keep your voice down."

Good sex comes from freely flowing emotions. Bad sex is when the emotional flow is blocked—when we are stuck in our throats.

The throat is the narrow passage connecting heart and head. Fascinatingly, the word Egypt—*mitzrayim* in Hebrew—itself means "the narrow places." So in Kabbalistic myth, to be in Egypt is to be with too many words stuck in your throat, too many sentences and paragraphs edited away in the censor-

ship of life. To be in Egypt is to have a blocked voice. To leave Egypt—
Exodus—is to find and claim your voice.

Voicing Desires

Sex is the place where you give voice to your truest self. It is not a coincidence of
biology that the female sex organ has lips and is essentially a mouth. "Mouth" is
one of the erotic mystical names given by the Kabbalist for the Shechina, symbol of
eros in all of our lives, for they are one and the same. Eros in the deepest sense is
about giving voice to our deepest desires, which need to be the ultimate guides in
our story. My true voice speaks my deepest desire, which is my soul print.
Desire, in Adam Phillips's phrase, is "what speaks to one by calling up one's
own voice." For Kabbalist Mordechai Lainer, finding true voice is called "Birrur."
The equation is simple. *Birrur* literally means "the clarification of desire." To identify true desire is to find voice. To find voice is to live your story. To live your
story is to be free. Freedom, voice, and story are the heart of eros and love.

Biblical myth writer Y. L. Peretz, writing at the end of the nineteenth century, tells the story of Bontsche the Silent, a story of disconnection from desire
and the exile of voice.

*All the heavens were in an uproar. Bontsche the Silent, the most righteous man, had
died. Bontsche, who never complained and always accepted his fate with graceful silence,
was coming to heaven—what a day! The angels exuberantly recounted the tales of humility
of this silent saintly man—how he never asked for anything, was always simple, accepting,
and sublimely silent! The angels rolled out the reddest celestial carpet they could conjure.
The celestial hosts were eager to honor their celebrity.*

*On his arrival to heaven, Bontsche was granted a meeting with God. This was more
than unusual—it was never done—but for holy Bontsche an exception was made. He came
before the throne and heard the divine voice say, "Ask for anything. Anything you want is yours."*

*Never had the celestial hosts heard anything like it. Every ear strained to hear—what
would Bontsche say?*

Bontsche was a little overwhelmed by all the attention. After all, he viewed himself as a sim-

ple man. He responded to God, "It would be wonderful if I could have a roll and butter every day."

When the Buddhists got hold of this story, they went wild. What a satori story, they said, what an example of total detachment and simplicity, the reduction of all expectations, the giving up of desire even when God offers you everything!

Yet from the perspective of biblical myth this story reads very differently. Hebrew mystics say—what a shmuck! God offered Bontsche everything, and all he could think to ask for is a bagel and butter? If he wanted nothing for himself, then what of a world that suffers so? For them as well he could think of nothing to ask? Was he so absent from himself that he could no longer feel the joy or pain of others?

Biblical mystics look at his life of silence and view it as a tragedy. Bontsche is totally disconnected from his own desires—from his own story. He is called Bontsche the Silent because he has no voice. His silence is a silence of absence.

Sights of Silence

But there is a different kind of silence from which our voices can truly emerge to express our story. In the biblical story of the Divine Chariot so beloved by Hebrew mystics, the prophet Ezekiel envisions what he calls *chashmal. Chash* means "silence" and *mal* means "speech," hence *chashmal* is speaking silence. Our silence enables the opening revelation of divine speech.

But it is even more than that. Our speech itself has two forms. First, there is speech that comes from speech. It is unconnected to the deep silence. We speak because we cannot tolerate the silence; its emptiness is painful and oppressive. The second kind of speech is *chashmal*—that is, speech that wells up from the silence. We all know the difference between conversing with a person who speaks from speech and a person who speaks from silence. Compare cocktail party chatter and the words of a Zen master. The speech that comes from speech is a desperate attempt to paper over the void. The speech that comes from silence wells up from having stayed long enough in the quiet to hear it become full of sound. In the words of Zen Master Dogen, "I have no need for my speech to come [only] from my tongue"—that is, his speech is connected to a higher sound: the sound of silence.

A person who speaks from silence is comfortable with the space between words. Imaginereadingwordswithoutanyspacesbetweenthem—it's not easy to comprehend what is being said, is it? What a jumbled, mumbled world it would be without the empty spaces! Words by their very nature need space; the silence surrounding them is an essential ingredient of their meaning. Someone who speaks from silence allows for emptiness.

The scroll of the Torah is black ink written on white parchment. According to the Zohar, the black-inked words represent the speech that comes from silence. The Zohar calls this Black Fire. The white spaces between the words are the silence itself, the White Fire. Master Levi Isaak of Berdicheu teaches that a Torah scroll is deemed invalid—that is, it cannot be used in ritual reading—if the black ink of even one letter spills over into the white space. According to one mystical text, it is because the White Fire is the source of the Black Fire and must always be protected, lest our words turn to ash. In a world overflowing with noise and nonstop words we need to take great care to protect the spaces of our silence.

Some teachers have taught that the revelation heard long ago at Mount Sinai when God spoke to human beings was an event that occurred only once in the lifetime of the universe, calling it, according to its biblical phrasing, "A great voice which did not continue." Again, the mystics insist that another reading is possible. In the original Hebrew, the phrase "did not continue" can paradoxically be read as "did not cease." The voice of Sinai is accessible even after the echoes of the original revelation are long since lost in the wind. The voice of revelation has never ended.

So if the voice still continues, in what form does it live on? It thrives in the voice of the human being who speaks from the silence. This is what I have termed Silence of Presence. When we listen deeply, we are able to uncover the God-voice within us. We become present in the silence. We are called by the presence—the God-voice within us—that wells up from the silence.

Learning the Language of God

When you attain voice and realize your soul print, fully becoming your name, you become one with God. When Moses did this, he found his voice. Moses is the ultimate contrast to Bontsche the Silent.

In the beginning of the book of Exodus, Moses is described as stuttering, unable to speak clearly. He asks God, "Who am I to go to Pharaoh, I am not a man of words." And yet by the end of the five books, Moses gives great and powerful speeches to Pharaoh, to the people, even to God.

The beginning of the last biblical book, called Deuteronomy (which in Hebrew is *Devarim*, meaning "words"), opens with the sentence: "And these are the words that Moses spoke." The transformation is easy to miss for the untrained reader. But when you catch it, it is simply breathtaking. Moses, who in the book of Exodus says, "I am not a man of words," has become the ultimate man of words. He now speaks the word of God. When we find our voice, when we connect with our inner soul print, then divine energy courses through us and we are able, each in our own way, to speak the word of God.

All of a sudden the intent of biblical and Kabbalistic myth becomes clear. Moses is the one of whom the Zohar says, "The Shechina speaks from his throat." Not surprisingly, then, it is Moses who finds voice and is called to lead the Hebrew slaves out of Egypt, for what is Egypt if not the narrow place, the throat. And what is a slave if not a person who has no voice, whose voice is usurped by his master. Any human being who has lost the courage to speak their unique story is a slave. Moses is the biblical hero because he dares to claim his voice and live his story.

For the Hebrew mystics, however, Moses is not merely a person. He is also a mythic archetype. Anyone who attains full voice participates in the Moses archetype.

The artist, writer, creator, businessman, doctor, gardener—anyone can tell you that when they feel merged with their calling, when they're no longer standing on the outside performing a task but standing on the inside, flowing with their action, then something higher is speaking through them. Remember what photographer extraordinaire Ansel Adams said? "Sometimes I get to places just when God's ready to have somebody click the shutter." I know that when I teach I often get lost, and I feel the words flowing by themselves, shaping and forming sentences almost magically before me.

It is in these moments that we access our soul print and realize fully our unique voice in this world. At those moments of actualized soul print we have learned to speak the language of God.

Eros and Voice

Now we have come full circle to the erotic and the sexual, for in a series of stunning passages Moses is described by the Hebrew mystics as being *Ish HaElohim*, "God's man." For them, that was an erotic term in all of its full power. Moses attains the ultimate mystical level referred to as *zivug* with the Shechina, erotic union with the feminine Divine. So Moses, who attains ultimate voice—so much so that his voice merges with the voice of God—is also the highest expression of erotic fulfillment, *zivug* with the Shechina. "When Moses comes, voice comes," says the Zohar in one passage. In a second passage, "The Shechina speaks through the voice of Moses." In a third passage Moses is "the Man of the Shechina." That is to say, Moses is pictured as erotically merged with the feminine Divine.

The Erotics of Creativity

The eros of voice and the eros of creativity are intimately linked. In the self-understanding of the Hebrew tradition the Torah, the sacred writ, is the word of God. Given that, the notion of Moses creating "new Torah" through his finding of voice powerfully expresses the eros of creativity. Moses is creating new divine words through the resonance of his own voice.

To say that the Shechina speaks through the throat of Moses is to claim that when the human being fully steps inside his erotic essence he touches divinity. Eros is divine. The human being in his full creative capacity becomes God-like and is therefore able to create new Torah—the ultimate creativity!

As we just learned, this creative capacity is not limited to Moses. Moses is an archetype that is available to anyone who can access their own Moses energy. In the words of the Zohar, "There is a Moses in every generation." To which Hebrew mystics add, "And in every person."

This radical embrace of human creativity is rooted in the secret of the cherubs.

It is not insignificant that according to Hebrew myth the world was created from the empty space between the two sexually entwined cherubs in the Temple. This "space between" is the *axis mundi*, the source of all creativity. The Temple, you remember, is called in the original Hebrew the "the *Mikdash*"—the place of holiness. It would not be unfair at this point then to say, Eros = Creativity = Holiness.

Even more dramatically the wisdom masters symbolically identify the Holy of Holies with the marital bed of King Solomon. The masters explain, "Just as Solomon's bed was fruitful and multiplied, so the Holy of Holies was fruitful and multiplied." Said differently, "Just as the bed of Solomon was sexually creative, so too is the Holy of Holies erotically creative." (It would perhaps not be superfluous at this point to remember that Solomon had a thousand wives. One would imagine that his bed was very much an epicenter of creativity.)

Solomon, fired by divine imagination, was the human architect of the Holy of Holies, the builder of the great edifice of eros. Solomon understood that there was an essential connection between the sexuality of his own bed and the eros of God's temple. This connection is precisely the secret of the cherubs. Sex models eros; our bedrooms model the temples of our lives.

In its archetypal mode, sex is the ultimate paradigm of erotic creativity. What could be more erotically powerful than the creation of a new life? Indeed creativity is so bound up with sex that many religions, classical Christianity chief among them, only sanctioned sexuality if it led to procreation. The breaking of the connection between procreation and sex was seen as a fundamental violation of the sexual ethos.

Hebrew mysticism shared the deep correlation between procreation and sex. Sex that created a child was considered ultimately sacred. However, the Zohar teaches that every sexual act is creative, whether it creates a child or not. The essential nature of the sexual is creativity.

Sex always creates a new reality. Sometimes that reality expresses itself in the visible material world in the form of a child. But even when there is no physical manifestation, there is always a spiritual creation. Every sexual engagement, no matter how seemingly meaningless, births a new spiritual reality. In the old spiritual language these new realities were thought to be either angels or demons. A deep reading of these sources show that the angels or demons are really manifestations of our inner soul processes. In this sense there is no such thing as casual sex. Sex always has meaning and creative impact in the world of the spirit. Thus sex models the eros of creativity.

Return to the Lion of Fire

Many of the great philosophers and mystics have gone so far as to view creativity and eros as being identical. For Plato in the *Symposium*, eros is the creative arousal that drives the world forward. Plato implicitly understands that eros is most powerfully symbolized in sex.

But the idea is more ancient than Plato. We return to our story from the first chapter, a Talmudic tale from about a century before Plato. Recall that the sexual drive was personified as no less than a lion of fire abiding in the Holy of Holies. When the masters attempted to slay this fiery feline they found very quickly that to uproot sexuality meant to uproot all creative eros. Chickens no longer laid eggs, businesses did not open, painters did not paint. The very life force of the world dried up.

Realizing that the sexual drive ignites more than just sex, the masters modified their request, asking for the sexual drive to remain in force but without its terrible shadow. The heavens refused, reminding us that genuine creativity cannot exist without shadow. It is a package deal. Understanding their mistake, the master prayed for the restoration of the sexual drive. Their prayer was granted, sexual drive and erotic creativity were restored. The world was revivified.

Sex and Creativity—Yetzir and Yetzira

The question we need to understand is—How does sex model erotic creativity? That it does so through a physical procreation is obvious. But what is it about sex that is so essential for our inner creativity?

The answer lies in the nature of the sexual. Sexuality models eros because sex takes us to the inside. There is a moment in sex where we let go of our observer status and fully merge with the sexual. In this moment we access our most primal self, the self that underlies our public postures, social masks, and even rational thought. This inner self is the erotic source code of reality. Sex opens the portal to the inner source of creative eros. All creation is generated by touching this *prima materia* of eros.

To access the inner operating system of the cosmos and be creative, any separate self must be temporarily suspended. We reimmerse ourselves in what the mystics called "the river of light that comes from Eden." This river is the flow of eros, the throbbing, pulsating primal energy that sustains the universe. One Zoharic passage teaches that this river is the semen virile of being, the source of all erotic creativity—sexual, intellectual, emotional, and spiritual. When the human being lets himself be reabsorbed in this river he attains the mystical level of *ayin*, no-thing-ness. From this place creative eros is aroused.

Not surprisingly, in the original Hebrew there is only one root word for both primal energy and creativity: *yetzer*. *Yetzer* means "primal drives and energy" and *yetzirah* means "creativity." The message is clear—one depends on the other. You cannot create without touching that primal place that is beyond knowing. Plans, logic, and information are all important for the creative process, but they can take you only so far. True creativity happens when the I, in Hebrew the *ani*, becomes the *ayin*, when the "I" gets out of the way.

The Eros of Tears

One of the places where this is most gorgeously apparent is in the creative arts. There is a wonderful documentary, *From Mao to Mozart*, on Isaac Stern's visit to China after the end of the Cultural Revolution. For many years Western music had been strictly forbidden in China. A resurgent interest in classical music had led to the formation of Suzuki schools where thousands of children were learning to play the violin. But all they had were the music scores—no one could get access to actual recordings of Western music.

Only the kids who were the very best players performed for Stern. There is an exquisite moment in the film when a young Chinese girl comes up on stage and, before a packed stadium, executes a technically flawless rendition of a Mozart piece. A storm of applause. Then Stern himself mounts the stage and ever so gently takes the violin from the girl's hand. He starts to play. In his hands the violin comes alive, the music sweeps and soars, and then finally climaxes in the most beautiful of cries. When he finishes playing there is silence in the auditorium. He turns to the girl and says, "You see, it is not you who plays the violin. The violin…it, it plays you. No, no, something larger plays you both."

When we surrender so much to allow for something larger to play us, when it is only by the infinite compassion of God that we return to play the next note, then we have touched the erotic God of creativity.

The medieval philosopher Maimonides suggests that deep study is a form of music. This is especially true of mystical study. A loving surrender is a prerequisite for any mystical study that engenders radical creativity. Scholars have dubbed the Zohar, "the Kabbalah that creates." Indeed in some mystical sources the word *Keshot*, meaning "truth," and the word *Chiddush*, meaning "original creativity," are virtually synonyms.

Master Nachman of Bratzlav teaches that the Babylonian Talmud, one of the great original unpackings of the divine mind, was created by the tears shed by the Rivers of Babylon. The words of the prophet Jeremiah are echoed in a great African-American spiritual: "By the Rivers of Babylon there we sat, and we wept." Nachman powerfully reinterprets the verse in order to suggest a new meaning. "The Babylonian Talmud was created through our tears... Through the crying which discloses the divine place—we are able to create new Torah which is the word of God."

From the tears that soak her face, I can always tell when my wife has created a special poem.

New Souls

The mystical tradition teaches that the destruction of the Temple is the spiritual archetype for the exile of creativity. In the symbolic literature of the Zohar this is expressed by saying, "There are no 'new souls' in the world since the destruction of the temple." A "new soul" for the Zohar means a wholly original soul. In the mystical reality map most souls that come into the world are reincarnating to finish their healing paths. However in order for the world to spiritually evolve to what is called by the mystics *bechinat mashiach*, "messianic consciousness," new souls must also be brought into the world.

The bringing down of a new soul is the ultimate act of human creativity. The catalyst for the creation of new souls is the mystic. In one provocative and powerful image from the Zohar, the mystic *becomes* the "aroused feminine waters" and seduces the masculine expression of the Godhead to erotic union with the Shechina. In a second Zoharic passage, unpacked by Kabbalah scholar Yehuda Libes, the role of the mystic is no less than to excite the clitoris of the Shechina.

Of course the description is not physical but mythic. To say that this is a mythic idea however is not to say that it is mere allegory. The Kabbalistic symbol is virtually always much more than allegory. It is an expression of a far more substantive relation between the symbol and the symbolized. What that means in the case of these explicitly sexual symbols is that sexuality accesses the same primal place that is the source of all creative eros. New souls are formed through the creative eros of the mystic expressed in meditation, study, and prayer. This is true however not only for the mystic. Whenever we touch the inside and access our creative eros we are also bringing new souls into the world and moving the world a step closer to consciousness.

What all this tells us is that creative eros is divine and thus participates with divinity in the very structuring of reality. Indeed the Zohar goes as far as to say that the human participates in the creation of God! That is not to say that God is a projection in the old Feuerbachian understanding of the idea (which we talked about in chapter 4). Rather that the human being is a divine miniature who is not only patterned after but also actually participates in divinity.

The key however to all of this is the realization that a dimension of divinity is created in human acts of self-creation! It is on the canvas of our internal spiritual, emotional, and psychological processes, as well as through our physical actions, that we create God. Our stories—each and every one of them—are part of God's story.

So to say we are creators of God, as the Zohar teaches, is to say that we are the creators of our own stories. To use an image from Hebrew myth, we are artists painting the canvas of our lives. The ultimate erotic creative act is *the storying of self.* The creative power of sacred originality needs to be channeled not only into writing new Torah, but also in writing your unique letter in the Torah. As Isaac Luria writes, "Every person has their own unique letter in the sacred scroll." Your unique letter is your story.

To create our stories is the same as finding our voice. *Voice* derives from the Latin *vocare,* which is a word of calling and destiny. To authentically create the vocations of our lives we must transcend all of the external influences that would have their way with us. We need to go deep inside the bubbling cauldron of eros and from there access the raw ingredients of our lives.

Our true birth is not our physical appearance at the end of nine months of gestation. Rather it is the person you are on the day you die. There is no greater tragedy than to die without ever having been born.

To be a great artist of self one must access the full erotic energy of the universe. Only this energy allows you to defy inertia and create the infinitely unique being that is you. Through inertia we tend toward imitation, to fashion our souls according to everyone's instructions except our own. The person of evolved consciousness is the one who creates his original self and transcends the overwhelmingly powerful urge to be an imitation.

Dark Eros

The mystics understood that all true creativity requires connecting to our primal and even shadow selves. The original source code of personal creative eros is referred to by Isaac Luria as either *prima materia* (*Chomer Hiyuli*) or primal chaos (*Tohu*). What is crucial to notice is that biblical mysticism describes the world as being created out of these same two places: primal chaos (*Tohu*) or *prima materia* (*Chomer Hiyuli*).

The point of the parallelism is captured succinctly by nineteenth-century mystic Tzadok the priest—"The human being is created by the same process in which the world is created." Just as the world is created out of the primal chaos, so too is the human being. In the mystical sources, primal chaos, *Tohu*, has two different expressions in the human context. First, it means the primal drives and urges that make up the inner human persona. Second, *Tohu* means the shattering, crises, and tragedies of our lives. Both of these are the matrixes of creativity from which human consciousness evolves.

In reality they are the same. Both are often expressions of shadow in our lives. Shadow means the primary energy systems that we keep hidden and locked away, often even from ourselves. Included in shadow are repressed sexuality, anger, or conversely, great unexpressed talent. Any part of our life stories that we deny expression becomes *Tohu* shadow energy. *Shadow is our unlived stories.*

The Maggid of Mezeritch likened creative eros to a seed falling into the darkness of the ground, a "down and dirty" place. It is there in the darkness that the seed is nourished with the ingredients it needs to sprout and blossom into the light of day. We can only engage in self-creation when we reaccess our inner energy sources and channel them toward our self-creation. It is the nature of the world that often only in the darkness do we find the access point to our greatness.

In non-crisis mode the place where we most regularly access this primal energy of light and darkness is in the sexual. It is precisely this accessing of erotic source code that gives sexuality its creative power. Similarly our life shatterings connect us to that same erotic fountain. Often it is crisis and transition that strip away the veneers of imitation and force us to confront and claim our original selves.

The sexual is the focal point where we touch eros. For not only does sexuality tie us into unmediated eros, but it also connects us to the darkness. It is through our sexuality that we meet much of our shadow. For this reason the sexual drive is commonly referred to in Hebrew sources as *Yetzer HaRa*. *Yetzer* means "drive" and *ra* is an all-inclusive term for shadow qualities and events in our lives. It is the *ra* in our sacred autobiographies that opens us up to the vital stream of *yetzer*.

As always, sexuality models the erotic, but it does not exhaust the erotic. The goal is to plug into these matrixes of eros and engage in the artistic re-creation of every dimension of our lives. This is the secret of the sexually entwined cherubs that stood at the epicenter of eros in the Holy of Holies in the Temple.

The masters pass down the story of David's attempt to lay the foundation of the Temple, which is a mythic image of the quest for consciousness. Realizing that the Temple is the seat of eros, David knew that its erection could only happen if he could access the primal chaos power of the universe. In digging the foundation of the Temple David discovered the *even shetiya*, which in myth is the cork stone that holds in place all of the primal erotic powers in the universe, the *axis mundi*. Overcoming his fear, David removed the cork stone from its place. All of the great and terrible power of the *Tehom*, the raging depths, the primal eros and chaos of creation, were unleashed. It almost destroyed

David and the world with it. Yet David knew that it was only through this direct engagement with the depths of eros that the Temple could be built and consciousness could evolve.

According to the tradition, the biblical six days of creation are only completed when the Temple is built. The point is that human and divine creativity merge, or at the very least complement and complete each other. "Man is God's partner" is the great erotic truth of biblical mysticism.

The Eros of Pleasure

There is another way that sexuality models creative eros. That is, of course, the way of pleasure. Sex and pleasure are virtual synonyms in the consciousness of humanity. Sex models the metaphysical truth that all creative eros is deeply pleasurable. *Noam elyon*, "the higher sweetness" and *oneg*, "pleasure," are but two of a veritable stream of Zaharic idioms that describe pleasure as the natural bedfellow of eros.

The *Sefer Yetzira*, our earliest known Hebrew mystical work, sets up *oneg*, "pleasure," as the highest level of good. In one wisdom passage the great question that is posed by God to every soul after death is none other than "Did you derive pleasure from my world?" This is the measure of a life well lived. To live erotically is to live in pleasure.

Pleasure of course is not the same as comfort. Pain is usually thought to be the opposite of pleasure. But probing more deeply, we realize that this is not quite true. The opposite of pain is comfort. The goal of comfort is to avoid all pain. Pleasure always incorporates a dimension of pain. Indeed the more profound the pleasure the more there is potential for necessary pain. Just ask a parent to name their greatest pleasure and their greatest pain and the point becomes abundantly clear. The answer to both is invariably "my children." The essence of wisdom is the ability to distinguish between necessary and unnecessary pain.

In classical sources the goal of the future world is to "receive pleasure from the Shechina." This future world however is fully available in the present.

The Maggid Mezeritch, for example, implies that conscious eating in which one merges erotically with the pleasurable taste of the food is a Shechina experience. In fact he teaches that the good taste of the food is the physical manifestation of the Shechina herself.

We have lost the power of transformative ecstasy, which is rooted in pleasure. Sacred hedonism is somehow associated with decadence. We have a new disease in modernity that psychiatrists call anhedonia, the inability to receive pleasure. We forget that the primary ritual of the major biblical holy day is to "eat and drink *before God*."

We return to one of the core cherub texts with which we began. Said Rabbi Isaac, "From the day the Temple was destroyed, the taste of sex [i.e. pleasure] was given to the boundary breakers [illicit sex]." The point of Isaac's koanlike observation is that the fall of the Temple led to the exile of the erotic quality of pleasure into the sexual. It becomes enormously difficult to access erotic pleasure as an integral part of our engagement in every facet of living. Pleasure becomes most easily accessed in the carnal, and then not even into the sexual but only into illicit sexuality. The redemption of the Shechina is therefore the reclaiming of pleasure as our human birthright both in committed sexuality and in all other facets of our lives.

In the next chapter, the conclusion of this section, the threads of pleasure, voice, story, creativity, and name will all be woven together in the fifth-century Hebrew myth tale, "The Harlot by the Sea."

The Harlot by the Sea

A Tale of Pleasure, Self-Creation, Story, Voice, and Name

All of the themes of the previous several chapters come into sharp focus in a fabulous but little-known myth told by the third-century Babylonian wisdom masters.

In the style of the Talmudic study hall, I will first tell the story. Then we will raise a series of literary queries that highlight what is strange and needs to be explained in the tale. Finally, together we will unpack its underlying mythical erotic themes.

Once there was a man who was very careful in his fulfillment of the law of ritual fringes. This man heard about a certain harlot by the sea who accepted four hundred gold coins as her wage. He sent her four hundred gold coins and fixed a time for their encounter. When the day arrived, he came and waited at her entrance. Her maid came and told her, "That man who sent you four hundred gold coins is here and waiting at your entrance."

To which she replied, "Let him enter."

When he came in she prepared for him seven beds, six of silver and one of gold, and between one bed and the other there were steps of silver, but the last steps were of gold. She went up to the top bed and lay down on it naked. He also went up after her to sit naked, facing her.

At that very moment his ritual fringes ascended the stairs by themselves and slapped him in the face, whereupon he slipped off the bed and sat on the ground. She also slipped off and sat on the ground. She swore, "I will not leave you alone until you tell me what blemish you saw in me."

He swore, "Never have I seen a woman as beautiful as you…however there is one commandment called 'ritual fringes,' and the ritual fringes have appeared to me. They represent to me a higher order of value—I cannot sleep with you."

She said, "I will not leave you until you tell me your name, the name of your village, the name of your teacher, and the name of the academy in which you study Torah." He wrote it all down and placed it in her hand. She then arose and divided her wealth in three parts. A third she used to pay taxes, a third she gave to the poor, and a third she retained. However, the beautiful bedsheets she used on her harlot's bed she kept with her.

She then came to the study hall of Master Hiyya (the man's teacher). "Give me instructions," she said, "so that I may convert."

"My daughter," replied the master, "perhaps you have set your eyes upon one of my students." (In which case her desire to convert may have been insincere and thus legally invalid.)

She took out the paper on which the man had written his name and the name of his village, master, and school. Upon seeing the note R. Hiyya agreed to convert her. "Go," he said, "and enjoy your acquisition. [You may marry him.]"

The very sheets she spread for the man as a harlot she now spread for him as his wife.

A strange and wonderful story, to be sure. In the way of the myth masters, let's reread, this time keeping our eyes and hearts open for *remize d'orayta*, "glimmering of light," and *lechisha*, "whispers of meaning."

First we have a man who is very careful about ritual fringes. The Hebrew word for careful is *zahir*, which means both "careful" and "illuminated or shining." Remember that the image for one's story is light. The word *zahir* derives from the word Zohar, which as we have seen, also means "eros" or "fullness." Your story is always the source of your fullness and eros.

In a different passage, the Talmud asks a wonderful soul print question about one of the spiritual teachers. "In what was the master most *zahir*?" Literally, in what spiritual practice was the master most careful? What was the source of his illumination? Or, in our language, what was his soul print? Our passage is playing off this set of allusions when it says, "He is *zahir*—he shined—in the *mitzvah* of ritual fringes." This indicates to us that his soul print—his special calling, perhaps even his particular struggle—was somehow connected to ritual fringes.

Biblical law speaks of a spiritual practice in which one places specifically designed ritual fringes on all four corners of a garment. The reason given for the injunction is "in order that you not stray after your hearts and eyes, which you tend to stray after." The word in Hebrew for "stray," *zonim*, plays with the Hebrew word *zonah*, meaning "harlot." Thus, ritual fringes are in some measure designed as a countermeasure to unredeemed sexuality. It is certainly not a thematic accident that the protagonist in our story, uniquely engaged in ritual fringes designed to prevent *zonim*, "sexual straying," is on his way to see a *zonah*, a "harlot."

The soul print of our hero is clearly bound up with his struggle with emptiness. He is going to a harlot not because he is overcome with natural sexual desire. He is not one who passes by a brothel or accesses an Internet site and is temporarily overcome by desire. This harlot lives far away by the sea. She takes four hundred coins as her wage. Four hundred in biblical myth means an enormous amount. She is the highest-paid courtesan in the land. He makes an appointment with her months in advance. He is looking for a peak experience, something that "will take him there," that will break through the emptiness that plagues his days. "If only I could have that experience"— whatever "that" may be—"then I would be satisfied."

He has heard of this harlot by the sea. The sea—water—is virtually always in myth the symbol of overwhelming passion. At this moment of intensity in his landlocked world, the visit to the harlot by the sea seems to be his only way out. He makes an appointment, and he waits with great antici-

pation for the meeting. The desire and yearning fill him, and at least temporarily his emptiness abates.

This is an encounter with shadow to be sure. It is a meeting with the
most primal of energies. He has paid not only with coins—four hundred
coins—but with gold coins. "In the shadow is the gold," writes Jung. In Jung,
as well as in the sources he draws from in alchemy and biblical myth, gold
always represents shadow. When the children of Israel leave Egyptian slavery
and begin their journey to the promised land—the mythic journey from sickness and fragmentation to wholeness and health—they take with them from
Egypt vessels of gold and silver, vessels that they have taken or perhaps even
stolen from the Egyptians—definitive shadow symbols. That shadow will
erupt in the flames of the golden calf, formed from those very vessels. In the
end, the journey can only be successful if that same gold can be melted
down and resmelted as the gold of the Temple, the gold of the ark, and the
two cherubs. These are the three stages in the journey of gold/shadow in biblical myth. So the gold in our story evokes images of primal energy and
shadow work—the alchemical process of turning darkness into light,
shadow into spirit.

But who is she, our harlot woman? At this point, she is an archetype, she is the
sexual incarnate. Relationship, depth, and commitment are not her trade. She
deals in fantasy, filling up men's emptiness with peak experiences that crash
the next morning. In the image of the Zohar, she is the Shechina in exile, the
lost princess.

The week of the appointment arrives. The man has been telling himself for
weeks that he should not go, but when the time draws near he simply cannot resist. His legs carry him almost magically to the village of the harlot by
the sea. He knocks on her door. In the Hebrew text, it reads, "He comes and
sits at her opening." A liminal place. A pivoting point. Surely a sexual image.

"Let him enter," says the harlot. She—master of her trade—sets up seven
beds, gold and silver, ladders between each one, gold and silver, which evoke
in us the shadow images we remember all too well from the Exodus story.

Seductively she climbs the ladder, naked, inviting him to follow. He does, and she sits *kenegdo*, facing him, or more literally opposite him. And yet the climb was not easy. The Hebrew text speaks of the ladder being *bein*—between—the beds. *Bein* is a word we are familiar with from the mystery of the cherubs. God rests in the space "between the cherubs," in the empty space between the cherubs. Only by walking through the emptiness—"between the cherubs"—can one touch the Divine. This is the emptiness that the Buddhist masters yearn toward and that the Kabbalists call *ayin*. He climbs the space "between the beds," reaching, yearning, struggling, hoping. "Life is what you do with your emptiness."

The story is about to reach its natural climax. But then something magically strange and unexpected happens. The man's ritual fringes somehow follow him, ascending the ladder through the emptiness. And as he stretches his hand to caress her cheek, the fringes slap his face.

He recoils. She draws back. Almost in unison they flee the elevated bed and sit on the ground, facing each other, still naked. She does not understand. For the first time, they speak to each other. Voice is introduced.

"Am I not pleasing to you?"

"No, that is not it," he responds gently, "You are more beautiful than I could've ever imagined. And your face is kind. But I cannot be with you. If I cannot be with you fully in the world, then I do not want you like this."

She is at first confused and then, when she realizes his intention, overwhelmed.

For the first time in all her years, during which her body has been exposed in all of its intimacies to so many men, for the first time she feels seen.

She says to him, "What is your name? The name of your master? Your village? Your school?"

A cacophony of questions about names spills from her throat and heart.

Remember, up until this point, the entire text used only pronouns and nouns to describe the subjects—the man, the harlot, the maid, that man, she said, he said, she said…no names. A desperate encounter—faceless, nameless, anonymous, and sad.

His ritual fringes interrupt them in the midst of it all. The biblical verse describing the function of the fringes is, "And you shall see and you shall remember and you will not stray." To see is perception. Sexual seeing models love—but love goes deeper. It is seeing with God's eyes, such as taking in a kind face or eyes that have suffered.

"What is your name?" she asks. *Lishmah*—for the sake of the name. The whole encounter turns around. How did we define *prostitution* earlier in chapter 10? Sex without a story. The prostitute whose name you do not know, to whose dreams and vulnerabilities you are impervious, is the archetype of the impersonal. She is de-storied. She lives in a world of pro-nouns. She is never "there" (*sham*). She has no name (*shem*). Both she and the man who seeks her services exemplify the prostitute archetype. The harlot in the Zohar's imagery is thus the Shechina in exile. And in the tale's beginning, both she and he manifest the prostitute archetype. Their redemption is when they move out of their anonymity and begin to weave the strands of shared story. The impersonal becomes personal.

As we saw earlier, it is not that the biblical myth masters did not recog-nize the power of the impersonal and even cosmic erotic. They did. Indeed, in the myth of Luria, the world itself is re-created every moment. In every sec-ond and in every space, cosmic circles and lines erotically penetrate one another, and existence is brought forth anew. Ecstasy, dance, music, prayer, study, and meditation were all part of the prophetic service. They were all practiced in a way that would allow the initiate to access the coursing eros of being as it washed and revitalized his soul.

Impersonal cosmic eros was vitally important to the prophet. However, it is the prophet who replaced the ancient cult of the Temple prostitutes with the cherubs. Though the cherubs themselves are explicitly sexual figures, they are not personal—that is to say they are not human beings who are depersonalized and transformed into symbols of cosmic eros. The Ashera god-dess was often thought to be represented and even incarnated by the Temple prostitute. The goddess and her prostitute were commonly referred to as "My Lady of the Sea." Ashera temples and their prostitutes were usually found in towns by the sea. It is very likely then that our passage about "a harlot who lived in a town by the sea" is precisely the Ashera temple prostitute arche-type. She is the manifestation of the powerful, impersonal erotic force. This depersonalized eros is what the prophet fiercely opposed.

In asking for the names, our harlot invites a story. By engaging a story, she is transformed from a prostitute into the Shechina. The merely sexual becomes erotic. What is your name, the name of your village, the name of your master, the name of your school? Four times. Each time, a hundred gold coins of shadow are transformed into a hundred gold coins from which the Temple may be built.

Remember that the Holy of Holies in the Temple, in the image of the wis-dom masters, is no less than the erotic marriage bed. It is that bed—the bed with a story—rooted in commitment and depth that she seeks. She has left the faceless world of the void and entered the world of the name.

The harlot, who is transforming before our eyes, asks for all of the man's names. She says, in a literal translation of the Hebrew: "I will not be comforted until you tell me...your name." Her comfort zone has been violated. She had lived her life being invisible even when she was in full view. She did not know anything else was possible. When he fled her bed because he wanted her in a much deeper way, she was shaken to her very core. All of the compromises on which she had based her life no longer seemed necessary. She knew she could never return.

So she broke her one great rule to which she had held fast all these years. She asked his name. In that moment she was no longer a harlot and he no longer a client. They became authentic, fragile, hopeful, scared, vulnerable...and real. Not naked of body, but naked of soul.

He does not respond to her request in spoken words. Language cannot hold in its weak and paltry vessels what he feels at this moment. It is not a silence of absence. It is silence of presence, pure and simple. "He writes and puts it in her hand." This is the very verse in the Bible used to establish the requirement of *lishmah* in issues of marriage and divorce. *Lishmah*—"for the sake of the name." He writes in silence and gives her all of the four names that she requests—his name, his village, his master, his school. In writing, the essential self is given over.

It is an act of trust and vulnerability. His writing identifies him. The harlot could use it against him, it could sully his name, the name of his teacher, of his school. He goes on his way. There are no words of parting. Silence again. She closes her business—liquidates her worldly possessions, pays taxes, and gives a large amount to the poor. Even at its height the erotic must never obscure the ethical.

The harlot travels to the village written on the piece of paper, to the school and to the master. He is a disciple of Master Hiyya—one of the great teachers of the day. It is not every day that a woman of her beauty and worldliness shows up at the study hall asking for lessons in conversion. Conversion in this myth is not concerned with the dogmas of religion but with personal transformation. The legal requirement for conversion is that it be *leshem shamayim*, "for the sake of heaven." Translated more literally, *leshem shemayim* means *lishmah*—"for the sake of the name." God's name. Master Hiyya doubts her intentions are "for the sake of the Name alone." Perhaps she is interested merely in marriage. He questions her. Again, silence. She does not have words that suffice to hold her truth. She takes out her slip of paper. It is filled with names. The name of his student—one of his best—of the village, of the school, and his own name, Master Hiyya.

A paper filled with names. From the scrap of paper, he understands everything. He smiles to himself. He is a true master. Yes, this conversion is *lishmah*—"for the sake of the name." He performs the conversion and perhaps officiates at their wedding as well. Remember that marriage, like conversion, is an act *lishmah*—"for the name's sake." The master understands that this conversion is her claiming of her deepest name.

Until this point in the narrative she remains anonymous. She is the harlot. She lacks a sense of personal story or name. She is first awakened to personhood by the man's last-minute refusal to engage her sexually. He is totally ready—throbbing with passion and desire. She is ready to receive him. And just then his ritual fringes, symbols of his inner story and commitments, step in. When they prevent him from acting sexually at the height of passion, she realizes that there is something in his personal story more powerful than her most potent allure. When she sits on the ground with him she feels seen for the very first time.

Part of what moves her toward conversion and transformation is the wondrous experience of being seen. To be seen is to be loved. Love is perception. This provokes for the first time her desire to see, to know her client's name, to be a lover, to connect sex and story. She blurts out her song of names. Yet he cannot call her by name. For in a conceptual sense she does not yet have a name in the story. The entire narrative is about her moving toward name. The word *lishmah* is most literally translated from the Hebrew as "toward her name." The story crescendos in her conversion. On the outside her conversion seems not to be "for the sake of God's name." After all, she wanted to marry Master Hiyya's student. On the inside however it was fully for the sake of God's name, for it is the encounter with Hiyya's disciple that prompts her journey toward the claiming of her name. In this deeper sense, the conversion can be said to be for the sake of God's name, for we manifest God's name when we live our unique stories.

The tale is almost over. One critical point however remains to be told: the satin sheets she used as a harlot. Those she did not sell. She remained the same seductive woman she had been. Her sexual allure and the magic of her body were not lost in her spiritual transformation. "The same sheets she spread for him as a harlot she now spread for him as his wife."

Remember in chapter 3 the passage we read while unpacking the secret of the cherubs? A man is smitten by a married woman, but he remains attracted only if she remains unavailable. "Stolen waters are sweet." The sexual intoxication quickly evaporates at the thought of a "licit" sexual encounter. Remember, the fall of the Temple is the exile of the erotic into the sexual. In the image of the Zohar, the Shechina becomes a prostitute.

The myth we just unpacked together now becomes clear. It is the story of the Shechina's redemption. The prostitute becomes the Shechina once again. The seductive thrill of the forbidden is rejected. Sexual fulfillment in all its raw and primal power is delayed. He wants her. She wants him. But only if they can share their individual stories with each other will they share their bed. The sheets of forbidden sex are now spread as sheets of erotic love. The transformation has been made. No longer are stolen waters sweet. The taste of sex is returned to the *bayit*, the home and hearth of depth and commitment. The full erotic sexual intoxication that he waited for on that day is fulfilled as husband and wife meeting on the marriage bed, the Holy of Holies where the Shechina dwells. The Shechina has been redeemed.

With all of this in mind, we understand the calling out of *the name*, which is our ultimate cry, both at times of intense pleasure and at times of great pain. We have talked in this chapter of pleasure, orgasm, the high priest, and the lover. And yet the world is also filled with pain. Then also we cry out, "Oh God!" Many times we reach for the Shechina, seeking comfort and wanting to be embraced, but understanding that ultimately we participate in God. For this is the ultimate comfort and the only embrace. We are part of divinity and are held in this deep and intimate knowledge. We know that God is the force for healing and transformation in the world, that eventually good will triumph, that in the end we will know that it has always been good. We trust the name. We are part of the name.

TWELVE

Time

Philo asks: What is the most holy and important day of the Hebrew calendar?
Is it Rosh Hashanah?—No. Yom Kippur?—No. The Sabbath?—No.
The answer—every day. Every day is the holiest day.
For God created each day, each moment, and that is the Holy of Holies.

If Not Now, When?!

—TALMUD

To see a world in a grain of sand
And a heaven in a wild flower,
Hold infinity in the palm of your hand
And eternity in an hour.

—WILLIAM BLAKE

Time, like all of eros, has line and circle qualities. To access the erotics of
time we must embrace both cyclical and linear time consciousness. In its

cyclical expression, time rolls round and round again. Circular time is oblivious of the demands of goals and destinations. It soaks in the glory of the eternally recurring moment. You can never be late. It's all happening now. But in its linear expression, time moves forward and progresses. Reality is experienced through datelines and time lines. The hero of linear time is the expert in time *management*, who *uses* his time well and is never late.

While the circle experience of time seems more obviously erotic, in reality both circles and lines are necessary for the full erotic experience of time.

Linear time is clock time. Clock time is important. It is a critical tool of measurement that allows us to create a sense of structure and pattern in our lives. It is the instrument we use to chart growth and set direction. Time is the power tool of progress. Deadlines foster the ability to set goals and standards that are vital to productivity and growth. Much of our technology, including the healing powers of modern medicine, rests on our ability to measure time with virtually infinite precision. There would be no science as we know it without the fully developed line quality of time.

Our psyches also need the assurance of linear time, that bygones are indeed bygones and that we are safe in the present. The line quality of time is critical when we get stuck in the past, perpetually reliving old rejections, old traumas, and old failures. The line quality of time assures us that it's possible to leave yesterday behind and move forward into the promise of a new day.

A sense of linear time is an essential human need.

Yet, taken on its own, line time casts a giant shadow that undermines love and eros. A line shadow: Someone is chatting with you and he keeps furtively glancing at his watch. Somehow time has come between you and the person before you, creating alienation instead of intimacy.

Modern man is a killer of time—circle time. His method of execution is obsessive measurement. Digital watches, diaries with entries by the hour, and fifteen-minute appointments are all accomplices in this modern murder of time. Line time is clock time. Using the clock and calendar we have divided time down so brutally it has almost lost its soul. And somehow in the subconscious of our culture, we think that if we measure time ever more precisely it will move slower and we will live longer. Or we hope that the rigor of our schedules will cover up the deadness of our nonerotic lives. Focusing on deadlines is the drug of choice in covering the emptiness.

Albrecht Dürer's picture *Artist Drawing a Nude through a Gridded Screen*, is a powerful metaphor for the deadening effect of clock time. An artist, a naked woman, and a gridded screen. The woman stands in her full sensual glory. The artist has placed the gridded screen between himself and the woman so that he can precisely plot her measurements and proportions. So meticulously involved is the artist with the grid on the paper that no woman is before him at all. He can only see the lines of his grid. Just so is the modern experience of time. We are so overwhelmed by our numbered measurements that we are often blind to the full erotic experience of time herself.

Meister Eckhart refers to this linear relationship to the passage of time when he said, "Time is what keeps the light from reaching us; there is no greater obstacle to God." We need to reach back to the circle teaching of the Hebrew mystics, who reminded us that time is alive, that time has a soul. To touch the soul of a moment is to know that the moment is not a notation of a fleeting second but a sensual perception of eternity.

Clock time is ultimately insufficient. Truly putting the past behind us is possible only when living in the eternal now. Only our presence in the present can free us from the ghosts of the past and the anxieties of the future. To fully experience eros we need to make the transition from clock time to eternal time. As helpful as line time might be, our race is always "against the clock" and our productivity and organization are but buffers against our fear of mortality. We can only overcome that fear when we transcend clock time and begin to live under the aspect of eternity.

Circle time invites us to walk through death and touch everlasting life. For this reason the great model of eternal time is called by some *le petit mort*. A little death. Sexual orgasm is the model for the ultimate eros of eternal time.

In our drive for sexual fulfillment we break free, in more and less noble ways, from the constraints of clock time. Often in the sexual we forget the constraints of yesterday and tomorrow. No less often we forget the commitment of yesterday and tomorrow. This seduction is an essential quality of what is sexual. In it, time slows down, softening its relentless grip, and seems to recede into some shadowy space. During sex every movement participates in forever, inviting us to the rapture and bliss of time transcended. In the sexual climax, time literally disappears as we melt into the fullness of the eternity residing in the moment.

Orgasm models the erotic movement by which we slip between the slivers of time and into eternity. The present is no longer bounded by the clock's chime—it expands to fill all time. An essential quality of the erotic, which is modeled by the sexual, is the boundaries of clock time collapsing into eternity. The sexual symbols our hunger for eternity in the moment. The word *orgasm* comes from the word *orgas*, which, like the Hebrew word for *marriage—hekdesh—*indicates that which is owned by God. Rapture means to be taken. Taken to a time beyond.

But it is not only the great sexual lover who can stop the clock and reach beyond. This stopping of the clock in an identifying characteristic of all erotic experiences. My first touch of eros with my wife, Cary, had nothing to do with the sexual. We met for dinner at a Jerusalem restaurant. We sat for five hours in a seemingly effortless and flowing conversation. We were both surprised when the waiter asked us to leave. We looked up; it was long dark, we were the only people in the restaurant, and it seemed like not more than twenty minutes had passed.

The intuitive understanding that being a lover is bound up with eternity is what moves us to seek the forever in love. In a moment of passion we say, "Tell me you love me forever," even if we know it might only be for tonight. The promise of love and eros modeled in the sexual is that of altered consciousness. Sex models a hunger of the soul and not merely of the body. That is the very essence of the secret of the cherubs.

Love promises to take us to the forever place, far from the ravages and mortality of time. All eros, whether it be in art, music, exquisite food, work, or play, flirts with that place beyond time. Isn't it true that a great friend is someone you haven't talked to for ages but when you see them the easy intimacy picks up just as if you spoke yesterday? That is because true friendship is deeply erotic. Every painter, poet, and artist knows and yearns for that moment in their art when time passes away and they stand painting or creating in the mystic cloisters of eternity.

The Mystic and the Strawberry

The word *time* means—in the original Hebrew—*invitation.* Time is an invitation to move beyond itself. The invitation is not to run away from the moment but to pass through it to the beyond. The mystic is the individual who accepts the invitation of time. The Zen master Seppo reminds us that if you want to know what eternity means, it is not farther than this very moment. Rumi taught us that the Sufi is the son of the moment. Hebrew mystics made the dazzling claim that the present moment manifestation is actually the name of God. *Yaw-weh*—the God point. The Hebrew God name is an impossible grammatical construction because it is simultaneously past, present, and future, indicating the collapse of time into the present moment.

A man is running very fast with a leopard in hot pursuit. He is running so fast that he doesn't see the cliff in front of him. Over he goes. He grabs a branch as he goes over. If he falls, it is to certain death. If he climbs up, it is to the leopard's jaws. The branch is not that strong. The branch begins to crack. Above, the leopard. Below, the void. Out of the corner of his eye, he spies a large and luscious strawberry growing out of the side of the cliff. Above, leopard. Below, void. He reaches out, gently plucks the strawberry. Pure eros. He takes a succulent bite, is filled with pleasure.

Eternity resides in the moment.

A Window to Eternity

When the masculine line enters the feminine circle, something happens, something larger than the mere technical or even psychological integration of these two expressions of life force. Something mystical happens—a window to eternity opens in the soul. One is able to step through a sliver in time and then touch the vast, fantastic expanses of the eternal. Such a line-circle moment is described, surprisingly, in terms borrowed from Hebrew mysticism by Carl Jung. In a little-known passage written in 1944, after Jung suffered a heart attack, he writes:

> It was an ecstatic state…everything around me seemed enchanted. At this hour of the night the nurse brought me some food she had warmed…for a time it seemed to me that she was an old Jewish woman, much older than she actually was, and that she was preparing ritual kosher dishes for me. When I looked at her, she seemed to have a blue halo around her head. I myself was, so it seemed, in the Pardes Rimmonim, the garden of pomegranates, and the wedding of Tiferet [Kudsha Brichu] with Malchut [Shechina] was taking place. Or else I was Rabbi Simon Ben Yochai, whose wedding in the afterlife was being celebrated. It was the mystic marriage as it appears in the cabbalistic tradition. I cannot tell you how wonderful it was. I could only think continually, "Now this is the garden of pomegranates! Now this is the marriage of Malchut with Tiferet!… We shy from the word 'eternal,' but I can describe the experience only as the ecstasy of a nontemporal state in which present, past, and future are one…nothing was distributed over time, nothing could be measured by temporal concepts.

Jung describes *hieros gamos*, the marriage of the feminine Shechina with the masculine *Tiferet*. These are unique terms of Hebrew mysticism, which describe the marriage of the cosmic line and circle who are united though their marriage within each one of us. When that union takes place, time's warp and woof shift, inviting us to slip through the portal between the cracks in time. It is the bridge to infinite peace and goodness—eternity.

This transition from the temporal to the eternal, from the interminably boring moment to the eternal Now, is a deep thirst of the spirit. It can be attained during periods of meditation when, seemingly without warning, you tumble/fall into the One. Everything changes even as it stays exactly the same. Somehow it is all alive, shimmering, gentle, and as it should be.

Sometimes this state is artificially induced through the use of mind-altering drugs or through a sudden life-threatening crisis. In crisis there are moments that last forever; everything slows down as if it were moving in slow motion. In just a moment you might have enough time to see your entire life—in a fair amount of detail—pass before your eyes. A peak experience is also often a peek experience—a glimpse, a glance, at the great expanse. As perception gently shifts into a higher mode, reality becomes bathed in luminescence and a door opens to a reality always present but rarely witnessed. In the image of the biblical writer "we peer between the lattice works" seeking the eternal.

We generally understand eternity to be a very long time. But this is only because modern man has lost touch with the concept of eternity. We have lost one of our most important faculties of perception—mystical insight. Without mystical insight we become afraid of time. She becomes an enemy. We sense, as Macbeth did, that life "creeps in this petty pace from day to day, to the last syllable of recorded time." Because we are afraid, longevity has become our goal. As the saying goes, millions of people long for eternity but do not know what to do on a rainy Sunday afternoon.

Knowing that we will die but having little notion of how to prevent it, we figure that a long life comfortably lived is the next best thing. Eternity, however, is not a long time, rather it is totally outside or beyond time. It is not so much that time stands still as it is that time disappears.

Full Presence in the Present

What we have described so far in this chapter is the experience of union, *zivug*, in mystical parlance—the erotic merging with the Shechina. Here is where you slip through the cracks in time to touch eternity. This is the melting point, when we dissolve into the divine.

The question is, How to get there? What is the path to union?

The portal to union lies in the fullness of presence itself. In order to slip through the cracks of time to eternity, you first need to enter time. To enter time is to enter the present consciousness. This is the first stage in our relationship to time.

Here again, the sexual models the erotic. It is the nurturing of touch that brings us back from our time disassociation directly into the pleasure of the present moment. In the sexual it is foreplay that brings the lovers into focus, grounding them in their full mutual presence. To enter the fullness of the moment we often need to throw away our clocks. Time only allows those to enter who have let go of their obsessive attachment to clock time. Only when we transcend the mechanical grid of time measurement do we first find ourselves in the deep presence of the moment.

Last year a group of us spent several days in the wilds of Maine. We brought with us no clock or any other time-measuring instrument. In the beginning there was an almost desperate need to know "the time." People were looking at their absent watches and constantly guessing what the clock time might be. Slowly however we began to let go. There was no schedule. We wandered the wilderness trails as our hearts moved us. We got up with the first light and slept when the sun set. The calls of the birds, the different winds that blew through the day, all became our friends. We talked about what was real to us—fears, hopes, dreams, and fantasy. There was much silence, even more laughter, and occasionally tears. By the third day we had entered a new shimmering world of sound smell and intuition. Touch was sensual, words seemed like magic spells, and eternity truly dwelled in every moment. On the first day out we were all secretly eager to get back as soon as possible to our safe and measured lives. But when we walked into base camp many of us were sobbing. Tears of ecstasy mixed with great sadness. The idea of returning to the world of schedules, clocks, and deadlines was physically painful, and yet we knew the great joy of our pilgrimage would remain with us as our guide.

In ancient Jerusalem the Pilgrim went to the Temple three times a year to touch divinity. These pilgrimages took place on what biblical myth calls Moadim—"Times." From here comes our English word holi-day or more accurately *holy day*. Much of the experience was about leaving behind the clock time of routine and schedule in order to touch a deeper way of living with time. The goal was not to transcend time into some abstract eternity. It was rather about merging with the full concreteness of the now. The week was filled with the meditations of eating, drink, sacred conversation, prayer, dance, and song.

Presence is only found in the present. The Hebrew term for indwelling presence is none other than Shechina. The first moment of feminine Shechina consciousness comes from full grounding in the present moment. Masculine line consciousness may be good at doing broad strategy sweeps and grand plans, but it is often woefully inadequate in the present moment. These two relationships to time—as a gateway to eternity and as full presence in the present—are not exclusive. Rather, they dance with each other, each a different face of the same experience.

The Mystical Erotics of Aging

The eros of eternity, the full entry into the pleasure of the present moment, is the glorious invitation of old age. This is the first face of erotic time. At some point however the fullness of the present moment yields as time collapses into eternity. This is the second face of erotic time.

The word for *elder* in the original Hebrew is *zaken*, which, according to the wisdom masters, is short for *zeh shekanah chocmah*, "the one who has acquired wisdom." For me, this understanding was best explained in an obscure passage by the Hebrew myth master Mordechai Lainer of Ishbitz.

The complex yet elegant passage offers a unique interpretation of the Talmudic assertion that Jacob never died. Clearly this is not to be taken literally, for in the humorous remark of the Talmud we are told, "But we were at his funeral, his eulogy and his embalming!"—We know he died! In Lainer's elliptical explanation, "Jacob never died" means that Jacob never experienced the horror of death, for the pain engendered by death stems from the sharp transition it involves.

All transitions are painful. Anyone whose dad ever changed jobs in the middle of high school can attest to that. The first day in the new school often remains one of life's indelible memories. The move from this reality to the next can also be traumatic, suggest the masters. One moves from a fleeting temporality to the infinity of eternity—from clock time to eternal time. Jacob, however, never underwent this painful transition, for Jacob was already able to taste eternity in his old age. "Successful" aging, implies Lainer, is the time when we are able to experience the eternity that resides in a moment within the daily routine of our lives.

My friend Fern was one of the most ambitious people I knew. She was always busy—planning, talking, doing, moving, and shaking. I lost touch with her for almost a decade, a decade that ended with her approaching her sixtieth birthday. I called to reconnect and asked how she was doing. "Well," she replied, "I am finally happy."

"Wow! What are you doing?"

"Oh, really, nothing that people consider *doing*. I'm with the grandchildren a lot. I have lunch with the girls every Tuesday. I walk. I feel wonderful." Indeed there was a calm and peace in her voice that I had never heard.

"You know, Marc," she said, "I think God lets us get old so we will slow down and experience the eternity that resides in the moment." My heart stopped. At the time I had just written an article that was the first draft of this chapter. I had called it—"Eternity Resides in a Moment."

Rahav! Rahav!

In order to unpack that pregnant and inviting phrase, let's return to Lainer's text for a moment. At this point, Lainer asks a seemingly unrelated question. In the passage in the Talmud that makes the claim that Jacob never died, there is an unusual literary flow of ideas. The very next passage discusses Rahav, the famous harlot from the time of Joshua. The Talmud says that anyone who knew (carnally?) Rahav, even if many years had past, would have an involuntary emission at the mere conjuring of her name.

An interesting passage to be sure, says Lainer, but what has it to do with Jacob's not dying? Lainer's implicit answer: Both passages are about the same topic—eros, which is understood by him to mean the ability to access the eternity that resides in a moment. The spiritual work of life, which climaxes paradoxically in old age, is to be able to experience the full infinity of every moment. Our lives, however, make this extraordinarily difficult. We can barely remember what happened to us yesterday. Moments blur into one another, their unique qualities obfuscated by the torrential flow of time, which menacingly threatens to sweep us away.

Old age is intended to slow the flow of time and allow us to go back and recollect, re-collect, the moments of our past. We realize that they have not passed or gone away. All that ever happened to me is still present—that is to say, available in the present. That is the true realization of memory. To re-live is to relieve the pain, pressure, and even bitterness of a moment gone. In the way I remember, or re-member, I can reconstruct and give new and different meaning to what was. For, in some deep way, it still is. In old age, we try to connect the dots of our lives in order to form a picture that we can understand. In old age we realize that tomorrow is fleeting, yesterday is past, and eternity is only in the now.

Before reaching our later years however there is one experience available to all that models for us the spiritual living that is our goal. This experience is sexuality. This is virtually the only arena where, for all of us, time stands still and eternity is present in the fleeting moment. (Meditation is the other experience. But it is still the province of a small select group; and even within that group, only a few meditators actually taste the eternity of the moment. Sex is the common man's meditation.)

Moreover, the moment does not get lost. If someone knew Rahav once, he can always recover the eternity and glory of that moment, even many years later. The litmus test of eros is: Have I held the day with me? Did it become part of the fabric of my life? Can I conjure it up in the magic of present memory as a living reality that informs my present experience?

An Invitation to the Present

Old age, implies the Talmudic text illuminated by Lainer, is when the erotic shatters the boundaries of the sexual and spills over into every facet of being. This is the great and wondrous invitation to be an elder! To be able to access the wonder of erotic time only through the sexual would be a great tragedy.

A major characteristic of the erotic and the holy is their ability to be fully available to the present. Through both you can experience time standing still as the eternity that resides in the moment cascades through your being.

Everything you could possibly need for the now is available in the now. The great art of the feminine is to be able to completely receive the full power of the now. In this sense the mystic Isaac Luria writes of the *Aliyat HaNukva,* (translated as "the Rise of the Feminine"). In the future the feminine will be the primary source of power. In Luria's messianic archetype, power derives not from the brute strength of masculine aggressiveness but from the refined feminine receiving of the moment.

Time contains within it all we might ever need for our healing at that moment. It is almost as if time were a magical nutrient that constantly adjusts itself so that it mystically gives us precisely what we need in each minute. There is only one proviso: You need to be present in the moment in order to receive its nurturing nutrients.

In a classic domestic scene, a wife says to her husband, "Why don't you tell me you love me anymore?" In a gross caricature of the male sensibilities, he responds, "I told you ten years ago. I'll let you know if anything changes." Or in the more moderate version, "Honey, I told you just yesterday. Do I need to tell you every day?" Well in this case, the answer is yes, because every day is a new reality of time. Contrary to the popular idiom, history never repeats itself— it rhymes. That is to say, although there are patterns in times, there are never repetitions.

For the biblical mystic, however, the rapture of the now is not at the expense of the past or future. The mystery of time is that in the moment of present eternity, all past and future moments are paradoxically gathered as well; you are able to connect the dots of your life and begin to make sense of your story, the sacred text of your days. The teacher of eternity, *Atik Yomin*, the ancient of days, is the elder who, according to mystical tradition, is the symbol of the Holy of Holies, seat of sacred eros, where the two cherubs lock in intimate embrace. Of course, Hebrew mystical tradition, much like the karate *dojo*, always insisted that being an elder was not dependent upon age. "Elder" is a state of mind. And yet the Talmud accords special honor to one who is old in days, even if that person has no other known claim to wisdom. There is something about the passing of the years that itself is an invitation to wisdom.

The Soul Print of Time

In both the old pagan and much of the contemporary New Age view, time is a cycle that repeats itself time and again. One of the most powerful revolutions in biblical myth was the rejection of precisely this view of time as a circle. Biblical myth originated the idea of originality in time. Every moment in time has its own soul print. It bears with it its own gift, its own challenge, and its own surprise. To receive the fullness of the present moment is to receive the soul print of time.

Exile, the ultimate dis-ease in biblical consciousness, exists if you believe that today is the same as yesterday and tomorrow is the same as today. Herein lies also the enormous sensitivity of Hebrew myth to the passage of time. The yogi seeks only to be liberated from time, while the Hebrew mystic has two relations to time—each one having its moment. In the first stage the mystic experiences great meaning in the flow of time. This is the first face of erotic time, where the mystic enters the fullness of the present moment. This is very different from the experience of a yogi. For the yogi, the past is no longer, the future is not yet, and the present is as the blink of an eye. For the Hebrew mystic, the past is present in the living reality of memory; the future is in the palpable presence of yearning; and the present is in the invitation and obligation of the moment.

In the second stage of time, the Hebrew mystic, like the yogi, permits herself to slip through the crevice in time and enter eternity. Yet the Hebrew mystic always returns to the present. Inspired—meaning "having breathed in eternity"—the mystic returns to the full presence of the present, ready again to participate in the full drama of life.

Like a Virgin

The power of the now is what lies behind the mystical secret of continuous creation. This is a doctrine that is incredibly important to both Hebrew and Islamic mystics. When I first came across this idea many years ago, I thought it was a clever piece of irrelevant theological sophistry. The question goes like this: Did God create the world in one act that took place in a specific moment of time, once upon a time? Or is creation a constant reality—the world being re-created anew every second?

The Hebrew mystics almost unilaterally express the second view. In their words, "God is the one who renews in goodness every day, constantly, the story of creation." It was only recently that I began to experience the deeper power of this idea.

What this mystical secret teaches is that every day truly is the first day of the rest of your life. That is a uniquely biblical idea. Said differently...God says "I love you" to the world every day anew. Or in the phrase of the mystics themselves, God makes love to the world anew each moment. Every moment in time is a new *ontos*, a new existence that never was and never will be again. Each time we make love with God in the moment, we are like virgins— touched for the very first time.

In one of the most famous of mystical dialogues in the Zohar, two sages meet a wagon driver. It turns out that this wagon driver, who is referred to as the *Saba*—Grandfather—is a great master. But a close reading reveals that he shared with them, not ancient traditions but wisdom he received from the moment. It is clear from the Zohar that a moment before he shares the secret, he himself did not know it! Similarly, the "hundred thousand songs of Milarepa," some of the most beautiful poetry known to man, composed by a Tibetan Buddhist master, was all done in the moment. There was no preparation. They were created completely spontaneously, in the depth of the moment.

One of the Hebrew words for *time* is *paam*. It also means "arousal." There is a unique arousal in every moment. Every moment has a new truth. Thus Buddhist masters could work for weeks creating an exquisite mandala in the sand and, a moment after it is done, destroy it. The mandala belonged only to the moment in which it came into being. For any other moment it was already passé.

This erotic understanding of constant creation is what moved the divine lovers of Hebrew mysticism to oppose so adamantly the idea of a one-shot creation. It would create a love-starved, de-eroticized world. How can we survive in a world where we don't hear the constant divine whisper of "I love you"? Is it possible to live without feeling the arching spasms of pleasure as we are entered by the divine?

What IS, as the mystical principle of constant creation teaches, changes every moment. To go against what *is* in any given moment is therefore to lose touch with the God force of love in the cosmos. All failures in love are rooted in losing touch with the love that is in the moment.

The mystery of love returns us to full presence. By doing so it reconnects us with the healing power of time. When we fully live in any moment we become powerful. We have complete presence and confidence. The infinity experienced in that time enriches us beyond measure. Indeed it is priceless.

Eating the Fruit Too Early

This is the underlying matrix of the Hebrew mystical notion of *ochlei paga*, which comes up in many critical passages in hassidic texts. Literally, the phrase refers to eating fruit that is presently prohibited, but after the passage of time (three years) will become permitted. This idea is employed by Hebrew mystics in a number of radical passages in regard to various prohibitions enumerated in biblical and Talmudic texts. Since, according to one Talmudic passage, all commandments will be nullified in the future world, then any violation of a prohibition is really just a case of bad timing. Sin, in this conception, is an inappropriate understanding of the quality of present time, an insensitivity to time. Mystic Isaac Luria applies this understanding to the archetypal sin of eating from the fruit tree in the Garden of Eden.

The sin is not that Adam and Eve ate the fruit. The sin is that they ate it too early. About three hours too early, suggests Luria. In three hours time the sun would have set and the first Sabbath day of creation would have begun. That fruit was to be their Sabbath day meal. If they had just had an intuitive connection to time they would have known to wait. Adam and Eve's disconnection from time is the essence of original sin. Every moment is new; to be awake is to be connected to the quality, potential, and invitation in every moment of time.

The Love Principle — Leaving Childhood Behind

All of this is not just a theoretical discussion. The core belief of biblical myth is that you cannot be a lover if you are unable to stay in the present moment. Intimacy is in the now. Alienation stems from getting lost in the past or future.

Let's now look at a love principle in biblical myth that will make this incredibly real in all of our lives: "Therefore shall man leave his father and his mother and be intimate with his wife and they shall be one flesh."

The text refers not just to the natural transition from parents' home to marriage. It talks of the necessity of leaving the original family circle of mother and father in order to create intimacy.

In the interpretation of a second-century scholar named Onkelos, this means you have to leave home in a deep way before you are able to have a free and intimate relationship with a partner. If you remain in your parents' home, you may well choose the wrong partner. Even if you choose the right partner, you will probably find it hard to create an intimate relationship. There are simply, in an adaptation of Onkelos's phrase, "too many people in bed."

That is an unbelievably powerful statement. You cannot create true intimacy without leaving behind, in a psychological sense, your parents. If you do not leave your parents behind, then you end up marrying them. You marry someone similar to, or the opposite of your parents, in order to finish your unfinished business with them. Through that person, who is similar to Dad, you seek to receive the love you didn't get from Dad. Or through that person who is the opposite of Mom you seek to run away from Mom. In either case you are in a relationship not with your partner, but with your parents.

The number one prerequisite for intimacy is leaving your father and mother.

No parent is perfect. No parent can fully meet all of their children's needs. Children, though, are formed in the cauldrons of their parents' love. As a result, children will often change themselves in all sorts of essential ways to please their parents. When our parents tell a part of you to get lost, it does! You are split off from a part of who you are. Your child self never grows up. This child is always looking to reclaim its lost self.

Now there are several different ways we can go about recovering our lost selves. The first two we do unconsciously. First, we look for a person who personifies our lost self. Let's say you had a wild side that got harshly tamed. If you have lost that side you will be attracted to someone who personifies in your unconscious that very wildness. Second, in a different scenario you might have a need for quiet introverted time. Your parents however needed you to perform. As a result you lost your ability to nurture that quiet place in you. Every time your yearning heart pulls you there you feel like you are disappointing your parents. So you marry someone extroverted and wild who cannot be with you in your quiet places, subconsciously seeking to finally win your parents' love.

Third, we will look to recover our lost self through the archetype of our parent. When you meet a person who is similar to your father or your mother image, you are often unconsciously attracted to them. You are not, at least overtly, trying to recover your lost self; rather you are seeking to complete unfinished business with your parents. That unfinished business has left you wounded. You seek wholeness and healing. You seek your lost healthy self.

Without a doubt, in all of the scenarios we just outlined, you are attracted to a person not because of who they are, but because they unconsciously meet a need created by your parents. In all of these scripts, you are not loving your partner. Perception is about experiencing your partners as *they* are and not as *you* are.

All of this is rooted in your inability to be in the now and leave your parents behind.

Now reread the biblical myth text and see just how in-sightful it is: "Therefore shall you leave your father and mother and be intimate with your lover." You think you are in the present, relating to your partner. Really you are in the past, arguing or pleading with a parent.

In this situation, the energy and wisdom that you need to be intimately present with your partner are not available. That energy is available in the present moment—which has in it everything you require for your healing. But you are not "present." You are stuck in a conversation from the past.

"Lost in the Past" Trance

Stephen Wolinsky wrote a wonderful work on what he calls Deep Trance phenomenon. Building on key ideas implicit in Milton Erickson, he suggests that the most important identifying characteristic of a trance is the distortion of time. Virtually every trance stage that is negative involves spontaneous age regression, what I call a "lost in the past" trance. All such trances are triggered by a narrowing of focus. In the middle of a conversation something is said that sends you back to a past moment of pain or trauma. You react in the present, subconsciously, from the place of old pain. Naturally the results are disastrous.

In Abraham Kook's language, "we forget our larger selves." We don't see options or resources that are right in front of us. We become virtually paralyzed and cannot change our course of action.

Since in the mystical understanding of time, the present moment contains everything you need for healing and health, by leaving it, you are bound to get sick and hurt. So the goal of spiritual therapeutic intervention should be to return the client to the name of God. Remember that God's name in Hebrew, YHVH, means "the God point in the present." So one could reframe the sentence and say that the goal of spiritual therapy is to return the person to the presence of the present moment.

To Walk in the Wide Places — Stories of Leaving Egypt

Hebrew mystics had another name for this loss of self in the trance state. Israel, Master of the Good Name, the Baal Shem Tov, called it *Galut Hadaat* in *Mitzrayim*—"the unconscious exile of Egypt." Remember, *Egypt* means "narrow," as in the narrow straits of passage in a sea lane. The trance that ejects us out of the present is caused by an automatic narrowing of focus.

Leaving Egypt, then, means moving from your narrow focus back to your natural, more expansive self, what William James called "your wider self." The Psalmist refers to this when he says, "My soul longs for the expanses, to walk in the wide places"—to show up in the wide expanse of the present... of the eternity that dwells in the moment.

Mind Trance and Meditation

Our minds spend an enormous amount of time avoiding the present. They think about everything that happened yesterday, usually dwelling on what did not go right, replaying it a thousand times. Or they dwell in the future, imagining all the things that might go wrong. It was Mark Twain who once said, "The worst things in my life never really happened." If you watch your mind for just a moment or two, you will see that there is a constant low level of mind chatter. Your mind darts like a monkey from thought to thought, moving in and out of the past and future, rarely settling anywhere for more than the shortest time. Unlike the "lost in the past" trance, the mind trance is not subconscious. It is, however, involuntary; that is, it seems to happen by itself. It is the default program of your mind.

The motive behind our monkey mind game is the a-void-dance of pain. We operate with a kind of dull throbbing pain that incessantly wears out our souls. Sometimes something happens to remind us of earlier trauma and the mind kicks into overdrive. Most of the time, though, there is a low hum of dis-ease that is always there, as in the invisible background noise of our lives. Usually you notice it only—like an air conditioner—when it is turned off. In order to avoid it, our minds take over and think about every-thing in the world except for the now.

One of the spiritual exercises that Hebrew mystics do that helps them notice the "monkey mind" is prayer. There is one section of the daily prayer— forty-two words in all—where all one must do is concentrate on the simple meaning of the words in order for the prayer obligation to be fulfilled. Devo-tees find it enormously difficult to get through this short passage before their mind wanders. When I began this prayer, it would sometimes take nine or ten tries until I was able to focus all the way through.

Our focus is disturbed when the mind wanders off in a thousand direc-tions; we will do anything not to stay in the present. Contemporary psychol-ogists have called this a "mindtrance." Hebrew mystics call this stuff that gets in the way of showing up in the now *machashavot zarot*, strange thoughts. The deep meaning of the phrase is *the patterns of the mind that make us strangers to our-selves because we are never home.* Here is the paradox: *The only way to turn off that low-level pain hum is to be home. By staying deeply in the now, you naturally plug into the healing energy of the Shechina.*

This radical presence in the now is modeled by the sexual. That's why the Hebrew wisdom master Akiva teaches that at the time of intercourse, *Shechina beinehem,* which means "the Shechina is between them." The Shechina fills the empty space in which man and woman meet. We human beings seek eros—Shechina—in all facets of our being. When we don't find it, our minds take control to insure that we are not conscious of the fact that we haven't found it. We worry about the future and we spend a lot of our time looking back. However, our access to joy and eros is only in the fullness of the now. We can never be too early or too late because it is always happening now. God is presence in the present. You have all the resources to deal with the now. The now may include planning for tomorrow; that is then part of the now. But anxiety over tomorrow is not an activity in the now.

Descent for the Sake of Ascent

The spiritual response to the Mind Trance is meditation. In meditation we do not leave Egypt; we rather intentionally enter Egypt in order to be able to leave afterward. This is called in mysticism *yerida tzorech aliyah*—"going down (to Egypt) for the sake of coming up (leaving Egypt)."

Going down to Egypt involves using the focus point or mantra of meditation. We narrow our focus (*Egypt* or *mitzrayim*, you remember, means "narrowing" in Hebrew) on a point or a sound and let that focus gradually quiet our racing minds. Once we have been freed from the monkey mind, we then gradually let the mind enlarge to its full natural expanse. In spiritual practice, this is called meditation, in clinical work it is called "therapeutic trance." The guide invokes a trance in order to break the superficial identity with monkey mind. This allows for a real merging with the infinite healing power of the universe, which is accessible to all who are in the now.

Spiritual Time Machines

We should not think of our past as definitely settled...my past changes every minute according to the meaning given it now, in this moment.

—CZESLAW MILOSZ

The most potent expression of the healing power of time circle consciousness is the mystical idea of *teshuva*, which is a word we have encountered before. Literally meaning "returning," it describes the process by which we make amends and try to fix the mistakes of the past. Mis-takes are the times when we misperceived reality or ourselves and were not at our best. As we saw early on, love and perception are virtually synonymous. So mis-takes are the times we weren't able to be lovers.

There is a provocative koan of the Hebrew wisdom masters where they say, "Great is *teshuvah*, for in it intentional sins become great merits." What is radical about "*teshuva*" is that not only are past sins erased, but they are also mysteriously transformed into great merits.

Three possible interpretations together animate this koan in our lives.

First, there is the great erotic principle of yearning. Sin in Hebrew mysticism is a force of separation and division. Sin separates the human being from her divine source. The further you pull away, the more powerfully the force to return builds. As Isaac Newton said, every action has an equal and opposite reaction. The greater the separation, the deeper and more powerful is the yearning to return. (Imagine a rubber band that is pulled taut and then released.) The energy of the fall is transformed into yearning, and the person winds up being a much better person than had they never fallen. In this way through the process of *teshuva*—implying recognition, regret, and future commitment—intentional sins are transformed into virtues.

Now let's go to the second stage and take it one level deeper. When we step back from our darkness, we don't want just to shut it up in a closet and slam the door. On the contrary: When we engage in real *teshuva*, we want to "turn" the energy of the darkness to good. Everybody knows that the energy of evil is, at least at first blush, more vital and committed than the energy of the good. Try to create a chain of calls to let people know about the human tragedy in East Timor. Although people have been murdered, tortured, and brutalized, it is not easy to mobilize support. Now, drop a rumor about some sexual dalliance of a public figure, a totally spurious rumor with no hard evidence to support it. Well, everyone knows you don't have to mobilize anyone. The rumor will be all over town in twenty-four hours. That's why the temptation for a journalist to cross the line from legitimate investigative reporting to yellow journalism that feeds on an alleged sexual scandal is so hard to resist. Everybody wants to hear about it. This is the vital energy of evil. It is pseudo-eros, which feeds the emptiness and requires great integrity to resist.

With all this in mind the concept of *teshuva* becomes more clear. The goal is not repentance but transformation. Of what? Transformation of the vital energy of evil into a powerful and potent force for the good. When this happens, then the intentional sins are not just erased, they also become merits. (How this precisely works I hope we will talk about in another book.)

Now, however, we come to the third and final understanding of the power of *teshuva*: the spiritual time machine. *Teshuva* literally means "to turn or return." To return to where?

It could mean to return to the scene of the crime and not do it again. If adultery with your best friend's wife is the sin, then it means that you have the same opportunity—sexy and willing woman, available apartment, alibi, and same level of attraction—but this time you set a sacred boundary.

Or it could mean something else entirely. It could mean that you return not only to the same situation and even the same place, but also that time itself warps and you return to the same moment. When the desire to make amends is driven by love, be it love of God, self, or other, then time warps and makes herself available. The mystery of love modeled in the sexual is that time is not absolute. It bends to the will of love and eros.

Now, you are correctly asking, did he really mean that? You can't go back in time. Everybody knows that. There is only past, present, and future, and it is a one-way ticket!!

Or is it? Everybody knows that time as a straight line is true for the broad public, educated as they are on Newtonian physics. But if the new physics has challenged anything, it is the old notion of time. Dr. Larry Dossey in an essay called "Time Displaced Prayer" correctly cites a biblical myth text from Isaiah which says something as strange as, "And it shall come to pass, before they will call, I will answer." I interpret that verse as talking not just about prayer but also as heralding a revolution in consciousness that will come to pass when the wellsprings of consciousness open and we realize that time is not linear and one-directional.

That evolution of the spirit will come, however, not from religion but from physics. In religion, it has *always* been clear that time was but another veil between man and divinity. From the Zohar to Luria, from Meister Eckhart to St. Augustine to the Zen masters to Rumi, it is clear that past, present, and future are only an illusion. Let Huang Po stand for all the masters when he says, "You have only to understand that time has no real existence."

Since that is not an easy idea to immediately wrap your head around, let's turn to physics. Listen to Paul Davies, world-acclaimed physicist: "Whatever we may experience mentally, Time does not pass, nor does there exist a past, present, and future. The notion of a moving time makes no sense...in spite of the fact that it dominates our language, thoughts, and actions."

Larry Dossey makes a very important contribution to this conversation. He gathered double-blind experimental data that indicates very clearly that our old notions of linear time are insufficient to account for the new information. He cites hard scientific data showing that a person's mental intentions can affect subatomic events that already happened. This conclusion is based in part on an essential principle of quantum physics that is demonstrated through the example of Schrödinger's cat. We know from past experiments that A will give off either particle B or C one minute after the experiment begins. B will kill the cat. C will not. We wait the requisite minute and then ask which particle was given off. Quantum physics teaches that the situation never resolves itself until we look inside the box. It is not that we don't know until we look in the box; it is that the cat is neither "alive nor dead" until we look in the box.

Emerging from this principle, a series of experiments was done to show that people could affect, through their intention, subatomic particles in a random events generator. However, Dossey's knockout punch is a set of experiments in which people are able to affect the outcome of experiments already completed in the past. If there are prerecorded results that have not been consciously observed, they can be retroactively changed by conscious intention. To cite the conclusion of the lead researcher, Helmut Schmidt, "Apparently present mental efforts were able to influence past events about which nature had not yet made up her mind."

Circles, Lines, and Time Machines

This is precisely the implicit notion of *teshuvah* in biblical mysticism. *Teshuvah*, "return," is literally a time machine where we are able to go back to the pivoting point where it all went wrong and change history. Of course it cannot be done with pro forma declarations of regret or insincere future commitments. Mystic Chaim Luzatto suggests that only a genuine shift within the will itself can rechart past history. Nonetheless, it is possible. Just as the perception of subatomic particles can affect their nature even in the past, so can a new perception of a reality and the willed commitment to act on the perception change the past. Nietzsche and Spinoza could not accept the biblical idea of *teshuvah* because they were rooted in the old Newtonian world. For them, time was only a linear process. There was no going back. But within the quantum reality, we understand that time can be both circle and line. Perception of an as yet undetermined reality can change its result and literally change the end of the story.

Time moves in a circle, which means that we also return to times passed. That is expressed in the ancient notion of a seven-day week. Despite having no cosmic parallel, the ancients nevertheless knew that time repeats itself. Yet within the cycle, there is a linear movement as well. Whenever we return again to the same point of time on the cycle, it is richer and more pregnant with possibility. Yet it partakes of the same quality as the time that came before it in the previous revolutions of the circle. Because of the participation mystique in time—that is to say, because time participates in all previous time—it can rework the past. The reason we keep trying even after a thousand failures is because we intuitively know that *if we get it right once, then the effects ripple back all the way through time.* The same is true in the subconscious "lost in the past" trance phenomenon. We are seductively drawn to revisit the past because until past time is healed it lives as malignant tissue in the present. Wondrously, however, if we regress to the past consciously and dance through the pain, breaking our pattern of a-void-dance, both time and our deep souls can and will be healed. This is the erotic invitation of time.

The idea that time is alive, that it is not the cold impersonal enemy we once thought it to be, is the essence of eros.

THIRTEEN

Union

We have walked many paths. In each one the sexual modeled, hinted at, and invited us to enter a deeper truth of eros. In our final path, the path of union, we seek not only wisdom but also enlightenment, in the realization of Union.

Again the sexual is our model. In biblical myth the first mention of an idea is always significant. The first appearance in biblical myth of *echad*, the Hebrew word meaning "unity" or "oneness," is found in regard to the sexual. "He shall cleave to his wife and they shall be as one flesh." The sexual in its highest expression is a moment of union. Similarly, the word *devekut*—meaning "cleaving," which is often the term for *unio mystica*, total absorption into the one—appears for the first time in the same verse, describing sexual union!

We are so overwhelmingly drawn to the sexual because at our core we are all seekers of unity. During loving sexual connection we realize that the ego walls that we have worked so hard to erect and protect are not real. In moments of bliss we experience union with another person, and through that person we catch a fleeting glimpse of the ultimate union, which underlies all reality.

We die to the world of separation and cry out "Oh God" as we are ushered for a moment into the reality of union.

Union does not mean that we disappear or dissolve, losing our core integrity as distinct individuals. It does mean, however, that we understand that our separateness is a limited, albeit important, perspective on our story. At a far deeper and more primal level we are like the cherubs atop the ark, intertwined with others. And not just with other people but also with all of being. Blake was right when he wrote, "Everything that lives, lives not alone, nor for itself." This is the deep truth of the erotic interconnectivity of all things.

Stages of Union

We are born into union. We make no distinction in the first few months of consciousness between ourselves and our environment. We feel part of the all. Even as we realize our own separate existence we understand that we are connected to our caretakers on the most primal ontic level. Our natural expectation is that the Shechina, mother earth incarnated in our biological mother, will meet our needs. That is stage one of our development.

We then grow into stage two. Psychology has taught us to call this next stage of separation individuation. We are treated to the rude surprise of our separateness. Not wanting to be sundered from our caretakers, we often recast the essential contours of our personality to win their love, for we understand that love is the currency of connection. At the same time we erect ego walls to protect ourselves. The older we get, the more vulnerable we realize we are and the higher the walls creep.

The walls are important, however: They create our individuality. They teach us that we are responsible for our actions. If we are lucky someone lets us know that we have a soul print, a unique story to live that no one else but us can unfold in the world.

Yet it is lonely behind these walls. We intuitively reach back to our primal memory of oneness, when belonging to something larger than our individual story was a felt experience.

In reaching for oneness we are warned against those who would prey on our sense of incompleteness, offering us pseudo-erotic salves that demand we give up our individual integrity as the price for belonging. There are many ways to buy belonging at the price of our integrity. These compromises often come wearing the guises of religion, propriety, economic necessity, or the demands of your professional peers. Sometimes they wear cruder guises—those of cults, racist causes, and false gurus. Hopefully we are able to avoid their seduction.

In stage two we incorporate the sense of individual integrity into the fabric of our being. That is good, even essential. But it is not enough, because it is only a part of the truth of our being. It is not enough because it will not satisfy us. It is not enough because if we do not move to level-three consciousness of union then the shadows of individuality may well destroy us all. In a world where twenty million people a year die of hunger, after a century in which a hundred million people were brutally murdered in war games of ego and power, on a planet that cannot sustain us for another century if she continues being so ecologically abused, this idea hardly needs elaboration.

The third stage to which Hebrew mysticism invites us—each in our own way—is the experience of unity consciousness as the guiding principle of our lives. This is the final stage on our journey. It is an invitation to *Aleph* consciousness. *Aleph* is the first letter of the Hebrew alphabet. In Hebrew each letter is also a number. So *Aleph* is *echad*, one. *Aleph* has no sound of its own.

Aleph is the ecstasy that is beyond. It is an invitation to the highest and deepest part of your soul, which is part of the oneness of God. Experience it, even for a moment, and your life will never be quite the same again.

You remember that way back in chapter 5 we showed that love is a perception. Now the mystery of love can be fully revealed. *Love is the perception of the essential oneness of all of reality.* The Hebrew mantra of the Shema—"Listen so that you know God is one"—is in biblical myth law the only prayer mantra that one recites every day. This Shema mantra is directly preceded by the word *love* and directly followed by the word *love*. A love sandwich.

Love in an ultimate sense cannot be commanded. Law can demand that a person act lovingly. Feeding the hungry and clothing the naked can be legislated by a government and executed by governmental bodies. Old school religion can demand that we behave charitably. Both government and religion are important in this regard and should be heeded and honored. But they are both woefully insufficient. In a world as traumatized as our own, it is painfully apparent that something is seriously lacking in our ethical motivation.

It is very clear that the ultimate motivation for loving must be self-interest. Self-interest does not mean selfishness. It means an expanded notion of self. When you fall in love what you are really doing is moving your boundary of self to include someone else. Before I met my wife, Cary, her moods, desires, and dreams had no impact on my life. When she became my lover, then all that changed. She became part of my identity. For that is what intimacy is— shared identity. All love is self-interest. If your circle of caring ends with your partner or immediate family, then what you feel is probably selfishness and not love. Expanding our notion of self in order to act lovingly in the world means we have to recognize the interconnectivity and union of all. We have to understand that *everyone* in the world is me, and not just my partner.

Seamless Coat of the Universe

Biblical wisdom invites us to become lovers. To do so all that is required is a shift of perception in which we realize that our identity is so much larger than we were taught in our limited stage-two thinking. To love is to realize that the boundaries aren't real. We are all intertwisted in what the scientist/ philosopher Alfred North Whitehead called "the seamless coat of the universe." Christians called this unity the body of Christ, Buddhists talked about the Buddhahood of all beings, while the Kabbalists called this underlying unity *Adam Kadmon*.

The Hebrew mystics teach that all souls come from different parts of the body of God. Being one body, there is therefore a natural affinity among all souls and a special affinity among souls who come from the same metaphysical neighborhood. The essence of things is that no one is ever really a stranger. We all share soul.

Given this it is not surprising that the Kabbalists insist that every action has a cosmic effect that ripples well beyond the obvious. Modern chaos theory calls this "the butterfly effect." For example, the gentle breeze from a butterfly's wing on one side of the world can, two months later, be the "cause" of a typhoon on the other side of the world. For the Kabbalists, this is a core principle of ethics and eros.

Let's say you stayed a few extra minutes at home to make a phone call. The purpose of your call was that you just had to share a piece of gossip. That caused you to leave for work late. Leaving late could set in motion infinite physical, physiological, and emotional variables that could eventually ripple into significant disaster for millions of people. To be a lover means to know that every action not born of love hurts the entire world, even as every action motivated by love heals the entire world.

Love is a radical redrawing of boundaries and complete revisioning of the whole notion of self-interest. A revisioning is, of course, a deepening of perception. The truth is, we all know that our narrow definition of the self—closed behind the walls of the ego—is not our highest truth.

The underlying metaphysics are really quite simple. We are made of divine substance. This is the *homo imago dei* that biblical myth speaks of, which teaches us that every life is sacred. "There is no place devoid of Him," writes the Zohar. "I am the light that illumines all things. I am all. Split a piece of wood and I am there; pick up a stone and you will find me there," teaches the Gospel of Thomas. *To love is to perceive the infinite divinity in everyone and everything.*

God's Disguise

All of us are called to live in the erotic awareness that we are interwoven with all of being. No human being is a stranger to us. We cannot eat if everyone cannot eat. If there is brutality in the world it affects us directly. We do not want to wait until the butterfly effect shows our children why our limited consciousness of living as separate monads destroyed our world. The planet will not go on forever with haves and have-nots. In our global villages, the intolerable proximity of massive starvation and obscene luxury will explode in our faces. When food is thrown out at a fancy uptown restaurant while a mother cannot feed her children in a downtown neighborhood, we can expect no real peace.

In the biblical myth of the Garden of Eden God asks Adam, "Who ate from the tree?" Adam quickly responds—my wife did it. She and not me. Disconnection. Shifting of blame. You and not me. Them and not us. That is original sin. The biblical project is to return to the Garden. That means nothing less than a return to eros—to the essential redrawing of boundaries to include all those we have placed on the other side of the tracks.

This kind of inclusiveness is what the Temple in Jerusalem with its lost ark is all about. It is a house of prayer for all the nations. Every form of spiritual service that was ethical and caring has a place in the Jerusalem Temple. This was the radical wisdom insight of Solomon—spiritual architect of the Temple. Solomon understood that the Temple needed to be a place of expanded consciousness in which the interconnectivity of all being was both experienced and showcased to the world. A place where the holiness of the feminine pagan Divine would find expression in the ethical matrix of the Hebrew Temple. In an ancient world in which every nation argued for the supremacy of its God, Solomon tried to redraw the boundary lines as lines of connection. (Solomon was ahead of the Hebrew consciousness of his day, which rejected much of Solomon's radically inclusive vision.)

Brother, Boundaries, and Cherubs

In Hebrew myth the reclaiming of eros always involves shifting boundaries.

An ancient tradition asks how it is that God chose this precise plot of land in Jerusalem as the place of the Temple. Does it have some special holiness built in from the beginning of time? At least one ancient tradition emphatically rejects such an understanding of Temple consciousness as the kind of thinking that just creates another boundary between those who control the land and those who don't. As we see all too clearly in Jerusalem today, every boundary line is also a potential conflict line. It separates "us" from "them" and eventually "them" will want to overrun the boundary.

The biblical myth tradition tells a very different kind of story—a mythic story of the Temple's origins, a tale of brotherhood, not boundaryhood.

There were two brothers who long ago lived in the field where the Temple would be built. These brothers were partners in the ownership of the field and farmed it together. One brother had a very large family. He said to his wife, "We have so much together—my brother has never married and raised a family. The produce from the field is all he has. Let me go and move the boundary marker between his portion of the field and mine so he will receive more." "It is good," said his wife, so every night after midnight, long after the day's harvesting was divided, he would go and move the boundary between his portion and his brother's. At the same time the following idea was going through his brother's head. "I have no family, no obligation, no one to support. My brother has so much on his shoulders. Surely he needs a larger portion of the field." So every night before midnight he would go and shift the boundary marker between his and his brother's portion.

Naturally both brothers were puzzled how it was that the other one was not receiving more. So one night the first brother went a little earlier than usual and the second brother a little later. They came to the field at precisely the same moment, each one to move the boundary in favor of the other. They realized what had been happening and fell weeping on each other's shoulders.

On the surface, it's just a sweet story about compassion and kindness. More deeply, however, this Temple myth suggests that all kindness and compassion must ultimately be rooted in the recognition of our radical interconnection. The boundaries of the field are the mythic expression both of ego boundaries and of all the other lines that artificially divide reality. Tradition has it that on the very spot where those tears fell—the tears that washed away the illusory boundaries—the Temple was built. It was in that place that Art with her embraced cherubs stood. For the essence of the Temple is the ability to expand your boundary to include your wider self. And your wider self is everything and everyone. Your wider self is the very width and breadth of God.

The Water and the Wave

The Zen Buddhists tell the story differently, but it is the same story.

Two waves in the ocean were having a conversation as they flowed toward shore. The larger wave was extremely depressed, and the small wave was peacefully flowing along. "If you could see what I see from up here," says the large wave to the small wave, "you would not be so happy." "Well, what is it?" "In not too long we will crash into the shore and that will be the end of us." "Oh that," says the small wave. "That's okay." "What, are you crazy!?" "No. I know a little secret that tells me it's all okay," says the small wave. "Would you like me to share it with you?"

At this point our large wave friend is both curious and suspicious. "Will I have to pay a lot of money to learn this secret?" "No, not at all." "Will I have to do zazen [sitting medita-tion] for thirty years in lotus position?" "No, not at all," says the small wave. "Really, the whole thing is only eight words." "Eight words!!! Well, tell me already!" So the small wave says ever so gently, "You are not a wave. You are water."

You're not a wave, you are water. This is why the symbol of love in Hebrew mysticism is water. For to love humanity is to get beyond the limited bound-ary of the wave that is bound to crash. To love is to fully experience yourself in the flow of what the Kabbalists called "the river of light that flows from Eden."

For this reason the prayer mantra prescribed by Hebrew myth to be recited the moment before death is the Shema—the meditation on the unity of all being. What we need to realize to face death is that we're not waves, we're water. When we hit the shore of the afterworld we don't disappear; we merely transform to the shape we need for the next part of the journey.

The Zen story understands that one of the primary symbols for eros is water. The Genesis story tells of the creation of all things yet never mentions the creation of water. Mystic Nachman of Bratzlav teaches that water is prior to the creation of the world.

Creation begins in the Genesis story with the letter *Beit*, which is the second letter of the Hebrew alphabet and stands for the number two. All of creation is about two, about separation and boundaries. All of our mistakes and all of our pain come from the illusion that we are separate. So water, the symbol of eros, cannot be part of the duality. It is before creation. Waterfalls and oceans enchant us because they summon up our primal memory of eros, that all being is interconnected and interdependent.

Water has no singular form in Hebrew. There is only the plural form because there is no such thing as water that is separate or disconnected. Whenever a new water molecule enters, all the other little water molecules make room to receive it, and they become one. This is the experience of the inside.

So to purify ourselves from the nonerotic world of sin and separation, the biblical myth invites us to immerse ourselves in a pool of water. Not in a swimming pool, not in a man-made still lake. According to the biblical myth law, ritual immersion must be in running water, a river or an ocean. For being dipped in water is our reimmersion in the erotic flow, in the systems of water that connect all life.

Defining Yourself

The fundamental question of your existence is always, "Who are you?" What that question is really asking is, "What are your boundaries?" "What is inside you and what is outside?" How you choose to answer that question will tell you more about yourself than virtually anything else. In the modern world, identity has become a decision. A *decision* is, in Latin, *de-cision*, a cutting or a limiting. We assume that we have a limited identity, and our concern is to precisely define that limitation.

When we decide on our identity we are drawing a boundary. Everything inside the boundary, I am claiming as myself. Everything outside the boundary is not me. An identity crisis occurs when you are not sure where to draw the line. Let's say I call myself religious. Then I have to explain—to myself—my impulses that seem less than religious. Or I could call myself a good person. I then have to disassociate from anything that does not support that identity.

The most important reality map of any age is quite naturally the map of personal identity. We moderns have been engaged in a radical narrowing of identity. The most powerful image you can use to internalize this idea is that of a castle. Imagine a gorgeous castle with winding staircases and hundreds of rooms. Each room holds its own magnificent treasure. The castle halls radiate with wonder, curiosity, and innocence. Each and every room is special. One day a visitor to your castle tells you that they didn't like one of the rooms. It was ugly, they said. Isn't it a shame because that room ruins the rest of the castle. Although you had never thought that room ugly, you certainly didn't want it to ruin what people thought of your castle. So you had that room carefully sealed away.

A few weeks later another visitor arrived. He told you that another room in the castle was just awful, ruining the image of the palace. So you hastily had that room locked as well. More and more people came, each one telling you about a different room that they found ugly. Room after room you swiftly shut down. Over time you forget about those sealed-off rooms. The castle becomes identified in your mind, and in everyone else's, as only that part which you inhabit. Years pass and you wake up one morning, finding yourself in a meager two-room flat. Hoping, still hoping, that people will like this place where you live.

And so it is with us. We are born with a magnificent interior castle, each room sparkling with gemstones of personality, aliveness, and creativity. Each time one of the rooms meets with disapproval your powerful need for love and acceptance moves you to shut it down. Little by little, you wall off more and more of the self from consciousness. You wind up living in one small room, too frightened to find out what treasures may lie behind all of the long-locked doors.

This narrowing is what the Kabbalists would call the exile of the Shechina or, in a different metaphor, Egypt consciousness. *Egypt*, you remember, means "narrowness." The Shechina is our essential erotic vitality. Modernity has exiled our eros to our psyche and then to a very limited part of the psyche.

Love the Stranger as Your Self

First we need to claim our body as part of our core identity. "Through my body I vision God," a verse from the biblical book of Job, is one of the most important mantras of the Kabbalists. Nineteenth-century master Elimelech of Lishensk teaches that only by trusting our body can we decipher the word of God.

The second step in the redemption of Shechina would be to reclaim all of my psyche. This includes the furthest reaches of consciousness, including the unconscious. You must embrace all of your light as well as all of your darkness. Any part of me that I split off and reject is in exile. By placing it on the outside, I am emptying my self. The more I place on the outside, the more empty I become. Using the Shechina language of our quest, I de-eroticize my self. My life becomes boring, vapid, and empty. The more of my psyche I include on the inside, the more erotic I become, and the "holier" I become. To be holy = to be erotic = to be on the inside.

Biblical myth expresses the same idea in the language of love. There are three love mantras in biblical myth: Love God; Love yourself; Love the stranger. Deeply understood, all three are of course the same thing. To love yourself is to love all of you—the God in you and the stranger in you.

The first step is to love the stranger in me. Which is why the commandment to embrace the stranger occurs thirty-six times in biblical text—far more mentions than any other topic.

The idea is very deep. Every boundary is a potential battleline. War is too often fought over where the boundary should be drawn. The parts of me that I find strange and inappropriate are my strangers. "Strangers are we, errants at the gates of our own psyche," wrote George Steiner. We very quickly turn the stranger into an enemy. This is true both spirituality and psychology on the level of Realpolitik. For in the end they are all one discipline.

If human history were to be the judge, the human being should be more aptly termed *homo hostilis* rather than *homo sapiens*. Since we cannot locate our own true inside we create a false eros by placing the other outside our boundary of self. If they are on the outside we subconsciously in-form ourselves—

then we must be on the inside. In order to fill up that primal hole of emptiness we are thus driven to violence and war. Since our erotic needs are so press-ing—we cannot live without feeling like we are on the inside—we need to create a constant stream of enemies to maintain the erotic illusion of being on the inside.

"Love the stranger" means to walk through your void and not try to fill it with false eros. "Love the stranger" means to love that part of you that has been split off and disowned. By loving the stranger you reinclude her in your persona. You redraw your boundary.

You escape the narrow walls of your ego's fortress behind, which you have hidden for so many lonely years. You realize that all of you is part of God. In loving the stranger in you, you are therefore loving God. It is specifically the strange places, the unique ways of your pathologies, that hold the key to your divinity. To love the stranger is therefore to love the God in you—which is all of you.

Finally it is loving the stranger inside of you that also opens your heart to love your neighbor. Remember that in Hebrew the word for "neighbor" (*Ra*) also means, amazingly, "evil." Love your evil—that is to say, integrate your shadow—and you will be able to avoid projecting it onto your neighbor. Only then will you be able to love your neighbor. By reintegrating the parts of you that have been split off you can begin to see your neighbor without the terrible blindness of projection. Biblical myth says it beautifully. "Do not oppress the stranger for you were strangers in the land of Egypt." The wisdom masters explain, "All who invalidate others always invalidate them with the very defect that they themselves possess." This is so often the case. All too often the moral crusaders who are especially vicious are themselves deeply tainted with the very vice that they so venomously accuse others of having.

If we cannot own the fact that there is a part of us that is a stranger in Egypt, if we deny our own narrowness and pathology, then surely we will project it onto others. If we do so we will never be able to love them. And of course we will never be able to love ourselves. "Love the stranger," "Love your neighbor," and "Love yourself" all really mean the same thing—love is indivisible. You can only be a lover when you have taken back the stranger inside of you. What self-love really means is to draw for your consciousness the widest possible map of self, knowing that all of it is God, all of it is lovable, and all of it is you.

You are now ready to reclaim your transpersonal self—that is, the parts of you that are beyond your psyche and body. This includes the awareness of your life as embedded in the great web of universal being.

Achieving Unity Consciousness

There are two primary paths to this awareness. The first, often favored by varieties of Eastern mysticism, is cosmic and totally impersonal. The goal is to directly embrace the erotic truth that we are all part of the impersonal living organism of God. In Zen stories, this is often characterized by startling and spontaneous moments of enlightenment.

The second path, often favored by biblical mystics, is to follow the ethical to the erotic. This is a more gradual path. Hebrew mystical stories are rarely about sudden moments of mystical satori or enlightenment. More typically they are about the famous master who disguises himself as a peasant in order to bring wood kindling to a poor woman living in a forest. In the ethical path to unity consciousness you expand your identity step by step. You understand that in order to be good, to avoid the evils of projection, you need a wider identity. To care for your body and the body of mother earth you need to include them as part of "you." Otherwise the displaced shadows and boundary lines foment great ethical tragedy.

Start with people you know. Expand your circle of caring and identity to include them in your core identity. Let them enter the inside of your boundary. You will see that your whole relationship to them will change. You might start with your partner, children, or perhaps more extended family or close friends.

At the next stage, you might want to move beyond your circle of individuals and include a community in your circle of identity and caring. If you are a

Baptist you may consider the Baptist fellowship part of your identity. If you are Jewish you might view the Jewish community as within your circle of identity.

Ultimately however you must move beyond these limited expansions. For if you arrest your growth at an early stage then you are left with dangerous boundaries. You may consider yourself as part of a superior chosen people, which excludes all other peoples. I emphasize of course the word *superior*. For *all* peoples should consider themselves chosen and special. It simply must not be at the expense of other peoples.

At this point you might want to expand your circle of identity and caring to include your environment—mother earth and all the sentient and nonsentient beings on the planet.

Each of these—shadow, body, environment, or Other—may have been strangers to you. As you redraw your reality map your world becomes more and more full. Slowly you expand. You learn to love the stranger.

All of these steps gradually bring you to the breakthrough of unity consciousness. This is the awareness that defined the biblical prophets, Kabbalists, Muslim, Christian, Hindu, and Buddhist mystics throughout the ages. This is the mystic's ultimate erotic awareness—when she experiences that she is inside the all and the all is inside of her.

The Perception of Love

For some passages in the Zohar, the mysteries of the cherubs are virtually a synonym for unity consciousness. The Zohar understands the union of the cherubs as symbolic of the union of all opposites. This is what mystic Abraham Kook means when he writes, "While all qualities have their opposite; good and evil, life and death, and even holy and profane—*there is no opposite to the Holy of Holies.*" The Holy of Holies is the place that overwhelms all distinctions. That which unites opposites, writes Kook, is love. It is love—the perception of the infinite Divine in all of reality—that allows us to embrace both pairs in the opposition as glimmerings of the one.

The Chinese master Lao-tzu saw this clearly when he said all opposites arise simultaneously and mutually:

Is there a difference between yes and no?
Is there a difference between good and evil?
Must I fear what others fear? What nonsense.
Having and not having arise together
Difficult and easy complement each other.

To suggest otherwise, writes Chuang Tzu, is not "to apprehend the great principles of the universe or the nature of creation."

What does all this mean? Ultimately reality is a unity of opposites. What that means is that there are no real boundaries. True wisdom is the sweetness of integration and union. Ultimately the world of two does not exist in the deepest reality. To love is to reach for the radical divine presence in all that is. To love is to know that ultimately there are no boundaries. And yet the road to the circle in which everything is on the inside is through the line. Ethics is the Hebrew mystic's path to eros.

The paradox of line and circle is captured wonderfully in the hidden teaching of an enigmatic Hassidic story.

The master of Rhizhin entered the study hall of his disciples unexpectedly. They were greatly embarrassed, for they were engrossed in watching a game of checkers between two students when they should have been studying. The master pretended not to notice their discomfort and went straight for the checkerboard. "There are three rules of the spirit," he said. "All of them are learned from checkers. You can only move forward one step at a time. For most of the match you can only move forward and not backward. When you have reached the highest rung you can move whichever way you want."

Mordechai Lainer of Ishbitz called this highest place *hitpashtut*, literally, "the spreading out beyond all boundaries." It is in this highest place that we are able to trust love. Love alone is what guides us. Even if we cannot live in this place all the time, the very awareness that this no-boundary territory exists pulls us toward it and transforms our lives.

No Boundary Symphony

CLAIMING THE LOST ARK

There is an extraordinary passage in the wisdom texts describing the ark in the Temple. The text does the math of measurements. The dimensions of the ark and the Holy of Holies are clearly described in the biblical text. Strangely, the sum of their measurements would not allow the ark to fit into the Holy of Holies. It was simply too big for the space. Yet that is where it stood. How could this be so?

The mystics suggest that according to the higher math of the Temple, the ark with its interlocked cherubs takes up no space. It has no measurement. While I offer no miraculous explanation, I nevertheless concur with the mystics. Of course. The Holy of Holies and her cherubs are the epicenter archetypes of eros and love. They are part of the great unity of being. The ark is mythically beyond all boundaries. It can have no limiting measurement, for the essence of measurement is limitation and boundary. This is the mystical secret hidden in the math and measurements of the biblical text.

POISON BISCUITS AND STOLEN WATERS

Now we begin to truly understand one of the first core principles of the mystery of love. A final Talmudic story of stolen waters:

A man comes home to his wife. His wife is in the bedroom. The man sits on the bed and reaches for a biscuit. A voice in the closet cries out, "No, don't eat that, it's poison!" The man opens the closet door and behold, the milkman is hidden behind his wife's clothes.

The question at stake is—Do we consider the man in the closet an adulterer or not? Jurists discussed this fifth-century text. On a simple level, they suggested that the person is not an adulterer. For if he had been, he would have wanted the woman. He could have had her if her husband had eaten the poison and died. Since he stopped the husband from eating the poison biscuit, he must not be an adulterer.

However, the text raises a completely different scenario. "Stolen waters are sweet," suggests the narrator, quoting the biblical verse. It could well be that he is an adulterer. Why then did he save the husband? Because he only wants the woman…if and when she is married. Concludes the Talmud, "From the day the Temple was destroyed the passion for sex was moved from licit to illicit sex!"

We asked at the very beginning of our study together: What does the Temple have to do with the sexual or even the erotic? What we have seen in a thousand different ways is that sex models eros and the Temple is the seat of eros.

Now we add one last level of depth. What happened on the mythic level when the Temple was destroyed? The Temple incarnates no boundary consciousness. As long as it stood it was the seat of love, eros, and ecstasy that shattered the bounds of the finite, reaching for the infinite. When the Temple fell and the rule of law/boundaries replaced it, then the erotic need for no-boundary consciousness had no place to go! It was displaced. Whenever essential human needs are displaced they reappear as shadow. When law becomes the order of the day then the core human need to break boundaries is suppressed. It needs expression. Its most natural outlet became boundary-breaking sexuality.

The rebuilding of the Temple is a deep internal process. It is all about filling up the hole, the emptiness, with true eros. When this happens the sexual becomes not an ominous threat but a loving guide and teacher.

THE BERDICHEVER PASSPORT

A story told by the kabbalists:

It happened in eastern Europe in the mid-nineteenth century. Wolfie had to travel to St. Petersburg and he was afraid. He knew it was a place that was not safe, and he did not have the papers he needed. But he needed to make the journey, for his very life depended on it. He went to his teacher, the great master Levi Isaac of Berdichev. "Please, please, help me master," and he poured out his woe.

The master listened intently and then left the room, bidding him to wait. Wolfie could hear that in the next room, the master was softly weeping. When Levi Isaac returned he gave

Wolfie a blank piece of paper still wet with tears. "This will be your passport. Take it with you and it will open all the doors."

Wolfie was not sure what to do, but he trusted his teacher. He took the paper and set out on his journey. When he arrived at the first border he was stopped by the guards. Shaking, knowing they could kill him on the spot, he took out the paper he had received from the Master of Berdichev. They looked down to examine it and then up at him again with the most intent of eyes. Wolfie was about to faint. One of the guards began to talk. "We had no idea it was you," he said. "We apologize for even stopping you at the border. What an honor it is to have you travel on our road. Please accept our apologies, sir."

Well, you can imagine how absolutely shocked Wolfie was. Mumbling his thanks, about to faint again—this time from disbelief and joy—he traveled on. He arrived at the next border, and remarkably, the same thing happened. Only this time the guards were so overwhelmed that Wolfie was traveling their road that they gave him an escort of four white stallions. And so it went—at each border crossing he would show the blank piece of paper with the tears of his master, his Berdichever passport. He arrived in St. Petersburg traveling like a prince, with a full escort and laden with gifts.

A story of mystery to be sure. Passports that open all the gates but not with words or letters. A magical sheet of white empty space. As we near the end of our journey, I want to gently remind you that there are many borders you need to cross when you go on a true quest. There are many guards—internal and external—who would block your way. Know that they cannot stop you. Have the courage to close your eyes and you will see clearly...they are but the illusions of your mind.

I pray that this book—although filled with words—has been a bit of a Berdichever passport for you. It too is soaked with tears. Tears of both sorrow and ecstasy. My great-great-grandfather was a Hassidic master in a small town in Europe. He taught that we should all bless one another. So I leave you with a blessing. May all the gates be open. May your life be filled with the erotic and the holy. For they are truly one.

Epilogue

Union is the ultimate erotic state. Interconnectivity, the fullness of presence, the inside of God's face, the yearning force of being, they all characterize our experience of Union. This is enlightenment. Yet for the Hebrew mystic if Union does not lead us to compassion and great love then we have missed the point. The medieval intellectual mystic Maimonides wrote a great book of mystical philosophy, *Guide for the Perplexed.* In the last sentences, after the book reaches its erotic crescendo (*Cheshek,* meaning "raw sensual passion" is the Hebrew translation of the Arabic term employed by Maimonides), he appends an implicit postscript. Paraphrasing: *If all this doesn't make you a better lover of people then you are no lover of God and certainly no lover of your self.* Eros must always lead to ethics.

The human being begins her journey as part of the circle of nature. In the creation story of Genesis 1, man and woman are created as part of the natural order. Ancient myth reflected this circle of being, in which mortals and immortals, humans and Gods, and all of nature participated together. This is the circle of eros.

Biblical consciousness injected the line of duality and ethics in the circle.

Compassion must always override eros. Mysticism—in every major system of thought—protested that this line view of reality was in itself distorted and called us back to the unity consciousness of circle. This return to eros how-ever is not at the expense of ethics; much to the contrary it becomes the most powerful motive and force for loving in the world.

Isaac Luria explains that rules and ethical obligation can never be suffi-cient motive for compassion. It is only when I realize that both my neighbor and I are part of the Shechina that true ethics begins. When a guilty person is punished the Shechina cries out, "My head aches, my arms are in pain." To slap another human being is to slap the Shechina. When you are kind to a fel-low human being you are befriending the Shechina. In Hebrew mysticism the Shechina is em-bodied in us.

This is the deep understanding of the most famous of all biblical maxims: Love your neighbor as yourself. The ultimate *source* of loving is knowing your neighbor *as* yourself. The ultimate source of loving is knowing that your neighbor is part of yourself. Both of you are woven in the seamless cloak of the universe.

When the Baal Shem Tov would engage in the spiritual practice of ascen-sions of the soul his wife would sometimes become very frightened. He would become totally inert, and she was sometimes unable to waken him from his trance. On one such day she had become quite desperate, not knowing how to return him to this world. As she paced to and fro his baby son pulled on his beard. Immediately he came to and gently asked his son, "What do you need, my son." To attend to a person in need, taught Master Israel, is deeper than even the deepest mystical communion. It is said that the Baal Shem Tov, while listening to the language of the birds and eavesdropping on the music of the spheres, could also hear the cries of all the tormented souls in the world. All of his work was for their healing.

The body leads to the soul, and the soul leads back to the body. "When I look at the I of my body I find the I of my soul. When I look at the I of my soul I find the I of God." The Sufis have a wonderful saying—"Say your praise to Allah and tie your camel to a post." What this really means is, touch the full-ness of God and let that inspire even the simplest service.

Dropping and Carrying Your Burden

My favorite Zen story is the one about the old Zen monk who has spent many years in meditation. He had attained deep levels of peace but had never achieved that moment of enlightenment when the I and the other collapse into one. So he asked his master, "Please grant me permission to leave the monastery and go practice on the great mountain by myself. There is nothing I want more than to realize the true nature of my non-dual self."

The master, sensing that his student's time has come, granted permission. Well, our old monk took his begging bowl and few meager possessions in hand and began the journey to the mountains. It took a while, but he finally left the last village behind and began his ascent of the great mountain. Just then he saw coming toward him, down the mountain, an old man with a very large bundle on his back. The old man of course was none other that Manjushri—who, according to some Buddhist traditions, appears to aspirants to give them their last nudge toward enlightenment.

So said the old man going down to the old man going up, "Friend, tell me where you are going." Well there was something about his voice that was kind, so the old monk told of his woe at being unable to cut through illusion and achieve illumination. "I've practiced for so many years…" His voice trailed away, and his eyes lowered. Suddenly however he raised his eyes and looked at the old man going down the great mountain. His face was shining and seemed so full of infinite compassion. "Tell me," he entreated, "might you know something of enlightenment?" At this point the old man with the shining face abruptly let go of his bundle. It crashed to the ground…and the old monk instantly achieved enlightenment.

It would seem to be all about dropping the bundle that we carry with us—past, future, needs, obligations, fears, and even hopes. At this point the newly enlightened monk looks at the wise old man and asks a bit sheepishly. "Now what?" The old man smiles, picks up the bundle, and walks down the mountain.

The difference is true compassion. It is not that one hand is good to the other hand because there is a moral obligation. How silly. They are of the same body. Unity consciousness. Eros. Ethics. Healing. *Tikkun.* So it is with us. We need to let our bundles fall. Only to then pick them up again and walk down the mountain.

p. 4 **"provocatively entwined cherubs"**—Babylonian Talmud, tractate Yoma
54a: "R. Katina said: When Israel would come for the holiday pilgrimage, they
would open the Veil [that concealed the Holy of Holies] and show them the
Cherubs, who were sexually entwined with each other, and they would say to
them: 'See how beloved you are to the Omnipresent One, like the love of man
and woman.'"

p. 6 **"the ark contained within it"**—BT, tractate Baba Batra, 14b: "'R. Huna
said: What is the meaning of the verse, "Which is called by the Name, the
Name of the Lord of Hosts Who sits upon the Cherubs"? [The fact that the
word *name* is repeated] teaches that both the tablets and the fragments of the
tables were deposited in the ark.'" The ark contained both the fragments of
the first tablets, which Moses broke, and the second tablets. Note the usage of
a biblical verse that emphasizes how the Name rests on the Cherubs. See
chapter 9, "Lishma," for a nuanced explanation of "Name" as a particular path
in the mystery of the cherubs.

p. 6 **"male and female"**—This is implicit from the passage quoted in the note to
page 4. In the *Additions to the Zohar*, vol. 2, p. 278a, the fact that the cherubs are
male and female is mentioned explicitly.

p. 6 **"face-to-face"**—Exodus 25:39.

p. 7 *"sod Hakeruvim"*—This expression is common to many different Kabbalistic
schools. It can be found as early as R. Joseph Gikitilya in *Sha'arei Orah*, the
Third and Fourth Gates, the Eighth and Seventh **sefirot.**

p. 7 **"spellbinding ancient text"**—This is my retelling of BT tractate Yoma 69b.

p. 7 *"all spiritual activity"*—The Maggid of Mezeritch reads *ba'u beiata*, which
should be translated as "they sought an egg," as deriving from the Aramaic *baei,*

which means "prayer," i.e., "spiritual endeavor." See *Perush Hachasssidut al HaShas*, tractate Yoma 69B.

p. 8 **"lion of fire, emerge from the Temple's Holy of Holies"**—The image of a lion in the Temple is not limited to the legend we just quoted and analyzed. Based on a similar image in BT tractate Yoma 21b, the Zohar says: "In former times, when that river's [the River of Kevar, already a symbol of eros] water would flow to the lower levels, Israel was whole, offering sacrifices to atone for their souls. At that time, the image of a lion would descend from above, *and it would be seen on the altar* crouching over its prey, devouring the sacrifices like a powerful man [emphasis added]" (*Introduction to the Zohar*, vol. 1, p. 6b, and in many other sources).

p. 8 **"Holy of Holies . . . as the marriage bed"**—See for example Zohar, vol. 3, p. 296a: When he [the high priest male image] enters the Holy of Holies, the female is intoxicated, and the Holy of Holies is blessed . . . and all the desire of the male for the female is here." All the imagery in this piece is radically sexual.

p. 8 **"the tablets and the ark"**—See for example Zohar, vol. 3, p. 296a. The tablets are phallic and the ark is vaginal.

CHAPTER TWO— EROS NOT SEX: THE FACES OF EROS

p. 11 **"Tibetan Story"**—This story is told in Jack Kornfield's book *Soul Food*.

p. 14 **"face-to-face"**—"The Cherubs, when Israel was with merit, they were face-to-face, entwined with each other, and when they lacked merit, they would turn their faces away from each other" *Zohar*, additional texts, vol. 2, 278a. See also BT tractate Baba Batra, p. 99a.

p. 14 **"face-to-face in biblical myth"**—See, for example, Exodus 33:11 and Deuteronomy 34:10, where the expression "face to face" is used to describe the intimate relationship between Moses and God. In Deuteronomy it says "that God *knows* him face to face." The Hebrew word *yada* ("know") has explicitly sexual overtones, as in Genesis 4:1. We will discuss this in chap. 5, p. 109.

p. 14 **"cherubs . . . being on the inside"** Interestingly enough, in the biblical verse that describes how the cherubs are to be positioned, the word *pnei,* meaning "face/inside," is used twice. Furthermore in BT Baba Batra 99a the essence of the cherub mystery quite literally pivots on the image of face. And let the hint be sufficient. See Exodus 25:20–22.

p. 19 **"priest and prophet"**—Indeed both the quest of prophet and the service of the priest are centered in the Holy of Holies. The prophet seeks to enter what mystics have called the *Shefa*, which means "the flow of reality." The archetypal source of the *Shefa* is naturally the place of eros: In biblical myth God speaks to the prophet from between the cherubs, the inside of the inside, the Holy of Holies in the Temple. The priest also seeks eros. Once a year, after immersing himself in water, he enters the Holy of Holies, where he lights incense, blesses the people with the ineffable divine name, and withdraws.

Both the prophet and priest seek interiority. To be present on the inside is to be in the Holy of Holies. The Kabbalist sees his/her role to continue the work of the prophet and the priest. This tendency is particularly pronounced in the school of the preeminent medieval Kabbalist Isaac the Blind. For a scholarly discussion see Haviva Pedaya, *The Spiritual vs. the Concrete Land of Israel in the Geronese School of Kabala*, pp. 225–264.

p. 19 **"inside…bayit."** The Hebrew word *bayit*, which means "home," also means "inside." See, for example, the description of how to insulate Noah's ark: "Seal it from inside (**mibayit**) and outside with tar" (Genesis 6:14).

p. 24 **"waiting for us to be present"**—The Torah, personified as a feminine Shechina figure, is pictured as waiting for a man to take notice of her: "[The Torah]…calls in a powerful voice (Proverbs 9:4): 'Whoever is simple, let him turn here. Whoever lacks understanding, she says to him: "Come, eat my bread and drink my wine," and no one listens'" (*Zohar* vol. 1, p. 227a).

p. 24 **"Emptiness and Addictions"**—The connection between these two states that I suggest in this chapter is in fact a recurring theme in *Tiqunei Zohar*, where the term *chilul Shabbat*, desecration of the Sabbath, is interpreted as "desecrating her emptiness" (*chilul*, "desecration," and *chalal*, "emptiness," derive from the same Hebrew root). The Sabbath is of course the Shechina, whom we have identified as eros. See, for example, the comment on the biblical verse "Keep [protect] My Sabbaths" (Lev. 19:3): "Concerning whoever introduces a foreign presence in her emptiness, [making her into] public property, wine used for forbidden libations, a prostitute, it is written (Numbers 19:13): "He has defiled the Sanctuary of the Lord, that soul shall be cut off from its people" (*Tiqunei Zohar*, p. 77b–78a).

p. 26 **"defining characteristics of the Zohar"**—The literary form of the Zohar is one of journey and sacred conversation. One of the Zohar's primary core texts is the *Idra Rabba*, the great Assembly, where R. Shimon bar Yohai reveals his most profound teachings, along with his disciples, each speaking in turn. Yehuda Libes has focused scholarly discussion on this Zoharic framework and argued—I think correctly—that in the context of the Zohar the medium is most certainly the message. Or to frame it in more Hassidic language—there is ultimately no distinction between the vessels and the lights.

p. 29 **"a word that dances *between*"**—See *Midrash Tanhuma* on Vayakhel, chap. 7, where it says that not only did God counteract (*tzimzem*) his Shechina to the tabernacle/Temple, but even to the ark. The author of *Avodat Hakodesh* (sec. 4, chap 24) interprets this as referring to the space between the two cherubs that were positioned on top of the ark. This is the intensification of Presence. Note that the *Tanhuma* uses the word *tzimzem* for "limiting," the same word used in Lurianic Kabbalah to describe God's "withdrawal" of his infinity so as to create the emptiness where creation unfolds.

p. 30 **"the pit was empty"**—Genesis 37:24.

p. 32 **"Temple in biblical myth is called the Garden of God"**—See endnote to chap. 8, page 191.

p. 33 **"access the internal witness"**—See note to chap. 9, p. 238.

p. 35 **"a fifth-century Hebrew wisdom text"**—BT tractate Berahot, p. 32b.

p. 35 ***"near dusk"***—"On the Sabbath day, when the time of the afternoon prayer approaches [toward sunset], the Desire of all Desire is present, and the Ancient of Days reveals his will." This is the only time of the week when this particular divine revelation is fully accessible.

p. 37 **"Male and female he created them"**—Genesis 1:27.

p. 37 **"biblical myth recorded in the Zohar"**—"The desire of the woman for the man creates a soul, and the desire of the man for the woman creates a soul... and Lower Desire is integrated with Higher Desire, and one integrated will is created... and both their desires unite as one, and then everything is unified with everything else. When souls emerge, they emerge male and female as one. After they descend [into this world] they separate, this one to this side, this one to that side. Then the Holy One, blessed be He, brings them together" (*Zohar*, vol. 1, p. 85b).

p. 38 **"held itself apart"**—This idea is expressed in the Zohar and later developed more extensively in Lurianic Kabbalah. It is associated with the legend of the Death of the Kings, based on Genesis 36. The story of how each king reigned and died is mystically interpreted as referring to those primordial lights whose vessels could not contain them, therefore causing their demise. When the biblical verse speaks of the last king, it suddenly mentions his wife "Maheitavel the daughter of Matred the daughter of Mei Zahav" (ib. 36:39).

According to the Zohar, the mention of this king's wife is very significant—
unity rather than separateness has now been introduced into creation, and
when male and female unite, creation is sustainable: "They [this king and his
wife] did not dis-integrate like the others, for they were male and female, like
the date palm, which is also androgynous" (*Zohar* vol. 3, p. 135b).

CHAPTER THREE—SEX SYMBOLS

p. 45 **"Isaac of Acco"**—R. Isaac of Acco is quoted by Elijah De Vidas at the end
of the Fourth Gate of *Shaar HaAhava* in his master work *Reishit Chochmah*:
"Whoever has not desired a woman is like an ass and less than an ass; the
reason being that it is from the *Murgash*—the sexual—that one understands
divine service."

p. 50 **"the exile of the Shechina"**—The original idea of the exile of the Shechina
emerges when the people are exiled from Israel to Babylon. In its original
formulation it indicates that the divine presence moved with the people
wherever they were exiled (see for example *Midrash Rabba* on Lamentations,
chap. 34). The home, the study hall, and the communal worship center all
became places where the Shechina—eros—dwelled. At the same time, the
exile of the Shechina indicates a fallen state. The Shechina is not in its natural
home. The people are not in their place—in their story.

This is both a geographic and an existential reality—the former and the
latter are emphasized in different ways in various strains of rabbinic and
Kabbalistic thought. I am of course not claiming that this reading exhausts
the idea of the exile of the Shechina; I am rather—in the tradition of all
creative thought—weaving together a number of different Kabbalistic strains
of thought into the fabric of a larger vision.

p. 52 **"mythic Talmudic discussion"**—The passage I have used here is from the
Babylonian Talmud, tractate Sanhedrin 75a. The other passage can be found in
BT tractate Nedarim 91b. It involves a possible adulterer hiding in the closet
because the husband entered at a bad time. There is poison cake on the table,
and he sees the husband is about to eat it. He calls forth from his hiding place,
saving the husband's life. Although prima facie one would think this proves
that he is not an adulterer—after all, if he were, then the husband's death
would be to his advantage, as it would make his lover available—the Talmud
reasons that nevertheless, we should consider him an adulterer. Why? Since
he is only attracted to her while she is a married woman. If she were to become

available, he would soon lose all interest in her, as it says, "Stolen waters are sweet and hidden bread gives pleasure."

p. 52 **"Stolen waters are sweet"**—Proverbs 9:17.

p. 54 **"Song of Songs ... Holy of Holies"**—*Midrash Tanhuma* on T'tzave, chap. 5.

p. 55 **"nineteenth-century mystical masters"**—R. Simha Bunim of Pshischa in *Kol Simha*, quoted in *Kol Mevaser* on I Kings 11:6: "King Solomon desired to heal evil, that is, that evil be integrated in good. This is why he married foreign women—in order to rectify them and to introduce everything into holiness, just as it will be in the future, at the time of the Messiah. Since it was not yet the time of the Great Fixing, Solomon was incapable of completing this work. R. Mordechai Lainer, *Mei Shiloah*, on I Kings 11:1: "For all the strength of the nations of the world can be found in their women, especially in their princesses. For this reason he married princesses, in order to subjugate their energies to the sacred." These are not isolated passages but part of a broader strain of thought that runs through Pshischa and Isbitz. I expand significantly on this strain of thought in my doctoral thesis. This school picks up on earlier strains in exoteric and esoteric Hebrew literature, which read Solomon's wives as part of a broader proto-feminist mystical project initiated by Solomon and opposed by the prophets. In this reading, which I expand somewhat in chapter 8 of this book, the prophetic opposition is tactical, not essential; they argue that Solomon was before his time. There were not yet vessels to hold the full erotic power of Shechina consciousness.

This reading is in partial response to modern writers who accuse the prophets of slaying the goddess. I significantly expand on this topic in chapter 8 and in *The Dialectics of Acosmic Humanism in the Thought of Mordechai Lainer of Ishbitz* (forthcoming).

p. 62 **"Akiva—Mystic and Lover"**—BT tractate Nedarim, 50a.

p. 65 **"Zohar ... seemingly innocent passage"**—*Zohar* vol. 1, p. 49a.

p. 66 **"Israel, Master of the Name"**—"Prayer is coupling with the Shechina. Just as at the beginning of coupling there is rhythmic swaying, so, too, he should rock himself at the beginning of prayer" *Tzva'at HaRibash*, Right Conduct, no. 68.

p. 66 **"become the feminine waters of the Shechina"**—"The passion of the woman for the man is only when his spirit enters her, and she flows with water to meet the higher male waters. So, too, the passion of the community of Israel [the Zohar's code word for the Shechina] is awakened for the Holy one, blessed be He [the divine masculine] only through the spirit of the *tzaddikim* that enter Her. Then water flows within her to meet the male water, and all become one passion, one tie, one connection, and this is the desire of all" (*Zohar* vol. 1, p. 60b).

p. 67 **"Elijah of Vilna—*ever chai*"**—See his commentary on the Zohar, *Or Yahel*, p. 18b.

p. 68 **"described in the Zohar"**—Vol. 2, p. 99a.

p. 75 **Dionysus"**—The Dionysian wine theme and its relationship to eros is explored extensively in a chapter in my forthcoming work on Mei Hashiloch, "Acosmic Humanism and Mordechai Lainer of Ishbitz."

CHAPTER FOUR — IMAGINATION

p. 83 **"Imagination, that gorgeous erotic quality"**—One of the classic phrases that captures the notion of imagination in Hebrew wisdom is **Medameh Milta LeMilta**—the Talmudic discipline of association. This faculty is often associated with the *sfira* of *Binah,* one of the primary archetypes of eros in Hebrew mysticism. *Binah* is called the higher Shechina, as compared to *Malhut,* the lower Shechina. Although imagination is often associated with *Malhut,* the lower Shechina (a recurrent theme in *Tiqunei Zohar,* which holds that *Binah* is beyond even imagination), the higher erotic imagination we are presently discussing may in fact originate in *Binah.* One example of this may be found in the *Raya Mehimna,* which says the following: "How many visions she has! How many [forms of] imagination and appearances! And all of them become known through the Heart's Eye of Intelligence, concerning which it is written, 'The heart knows, the heart understands.' As to that which is written "And through the hands of the prophets I will be imagined"—[true] imagination can only be found in the Intelligence of the Heart, which is not the imagination of the eyes. As it says, 'To Whom can I be compared,' 'To Whom can God be compared.'" (*Raya Mehimna* Ki Tetze—*Zohar,* vol. 3, p. 280b).

The "imagination of the eyes" refers to superficial illusion, unlike that of the heart, which is the erotic imagination we are discussing. The heart is *Binah* ("*Binah* is the Heart—through it the heart understands") (*Tiqunei Zohar,* p. 17a). It seems that the intention of the *Raya Mehimna* in quoting the two biblical verses that refer to "Who" in the context of imagination is to point to *Binah,* since the Hebrew word for *Who* is *Mi,* which is identified with *Binah* (*Zohar,* vol. 1, p. 1b). In other words, the verses should be read as follows: I can be imagined as (compared to) Who—the *sfira* of *Binah,* where imagination is the portal to the Higher Shechina Goddess. In fact, the *Tiqunei Zohar* (which scholars such as Gottlieb hold to be of the same authorship as the *Raya Mehimna*—a premise I would question, although they are clearly of the same school) explicitly attributes this verse to the *sfira* of *Binah* (*Tiqunei Zohar* 28a).

One of the primary qualities of Binah is found in the Hebrew wisdom epigram *Davar Mitoch Davar*—to derive one idea from the inside of another idea. The erotic allusion is *Mitoch*—a word that bespeaks the interiority that is the essence of Eros.

p. 83 **"The Shechina ... imagination ... exiled into the sexual"**—This is implied from the *Zohar*, vol. 1, p. 103a–b. To quote some of this passage (the bracketed explanations are mine):

"Her husband is known in the gates" (Proverbs 31:23). "Her husband" refers to the Holy One, blessed be He [the masculine Divine], Who is known and experienced intimately [clung to] according to the imagination of the heart [the Hebrew word for *gates*, *she'arim*, can also be read as *le'sha'er*, a verb that means "to imagine"]. Each and every person according to their heart's ability to imagine [see previous endnote], each and every person according to their ability to cling to [become intimate with] the spirit of wisdom...

Now, this gate is not known, because Israel is in exile, and as all gates have become distant, they are not able to know and achieve intimacy [clinging]. But at the time when Israel will be liberated from Exile, all these higher levels [gates of imagination] will dwell within them, and then all the children of the world will know the higher, precious wisdom."

For an explicit identification of the Shechina with imagination in the main body of the Zohar, see Zohar 1; 91a. There the Shechina is identified as the *Hezu*, in which all supernal images are seen.

p. 84 **"the women found ... mirrors"**—See Rashi on Exodus 38:8.

p. 85 **"makkif"**—See *Liqutei MoHaran*, vol. 2, discourse 7. When R. Nahman presents this interpretation of **pnimi** and *makkif*, he suggests not only using it in regard to oneself, but also as a tool that allows the higher self of the other to unfold. For a discussion of *makkif* and *pnimi* see chapter 11 in my Hebrew book *Safek: On Reclaiming Uncertainty As a Spiritual Value*.

p. 85 **"Go forth from your land ..."**—Genesis 12:1 and *Zohar*, vol. 1, p. 77b.

p. 88 **Nun, a Hebrew slave**—*Pirke d'R. Eliezer*, chap. 47: "R. Eliezer said: All those years that Israel was in Egypt they were secure, peaceful, and comfortable. Until one day Nun, one of the grandsons of Ephraim, came and said to them,

'The Holy One, blessed be He, appeared to me, [revealing] that you must leave Egypt.'"

p. 89 **"said to incarnate the throat"**—See, for example, R. Isaac Luria's long discourse on the spiritual symbolism of the exile in Egypt, which is found in *Sha'ar HaPesuqim* on parshat Shmot. For details on Egypt as the throat, see ibid., 22c specifically.

p. 89 **"I will be what I will be"**—Exodus 3:14.

p. 89 **"the freezing of God"**—An amazing passage equating inflexibility toward God's law with idolatry can be found in *Mei HaShiloach* vol. 1, p. 25c. Indeed, the biblical verse "You shall not make for yourself molten Gods" elegantly supports this reading. The Hebrew phrase for "molten Gods" is *elokei masecha.* *Masecha* could also be translated as "mask." An alternative reading would then be "You shall not make Gods of your masks." The freezing of the unfolding dynamic God consciousness is idolatry.

p. 90 **"Nachman of Bratzlav"**—For further discussion on this matter, see Tzvi Mark's doctoral dissertation on R. Nachman, Hebrew University, Jerusalem, 2001 (unpublished).

p. 90 **"a fantasy-aroused existence"**—See Joseph Soloveitchik's *Family Redeemed,* p. 50, from which I have borrowed this nomenclature.

p. 90 **"man ... created in the divine image"**—Hebrew uses two words: *tzelem,* which is usually translated as "image," and *dmut,* which is "likeness." A careful rereading of these words is highly suggestive. *Tzelem* means "image" in the sense of graven image or idol. The word *tzelem* itself is used in other biblical texts referring to idols. Indeed, in the Midrashic image God is described as fashioning man from the clay of the earth much in the manner of the artisan idol maker. The word *dmut* derives from the Hebrew root meaning "imagination." Thus our humanity is defined by the tension between image and imagination. It is the dialectic swing between the limitation of the image and the expansiveness of the imagination, between the finite and infinity. To get lost in either our *tzelem* or *dmut* qualities is to betray our humanity.

p. 91 **"has a color that incarnates it"**—see for example R. Moshe Cordevero's chapter on colors (*Sha'ar HaGevanim*) in his epic work *Pardes Rimonim.*

p. 91 **"man creating God in his image"**—See chapter 5, note to page 125. See also *Tiqunei Zohar,* p. 86b, where, during a discussion on man's ability to affect the divine, R. Elazar asks his father, R. Shimon: "Father, is man actually capable of returning the Holy One, blessed be He, to His place?" And

R. Shimon immediately answers him with an emphatic "Yes!" Man can defi-nitely re-create the Divine through his imagination. While God may be an expression of our imagination, our imagination is an expression of God.

The formulation "imagination is a figment of God" I heard from Professor Arthur Green in an oral conversation. His works and personal example are both a model and an inspiration.

p. 93 **"imagination chambers"**—For an important discussion of the Temple and its relationship to contemplative and visionary mystical experience, see Joseph Dan's work *Early Hebrew Mysticism*, p. 56. See also Joseph Dan *Hadrei Merkava*, Tarbitz 47.

p. 93 **"taught by God"**—In the Midrash (*Yalkut Shimoni* on parshat Ki Tisa, comment 389) it says that although Moses did not tell Bezalel exactly what God had told him, Bezalel understood it intuitively. When Moses discovered this, he exclaimed "You must dwell in God's shadow and *know!*" The Midrash goes on to say that Bezalel knew the secret of the combinations of sacred letters used to create the world.

p. 94 **"a tabernacle of flames"**—*Midrash Rabba* 15:10 on Numbers.

p. 94 **"the golden calf"**—On the golden calf as a symbol of the refusal by the people to hold uncertainty see chapter 4 of my book *Safek: Reclaiming Uncertainty as a Spiritual Value.*

p. 94 **"Moses is late"**—The Hebrew verse reads, *"boshesh moshe larededet min hahar,"* literally, "Moses tarried in coming down the mountain." This is read by the Midrash as *"bashesh"*—six o'clock came and Moses did not show up (*Midrash Rabba* on Exodus, 41:10).

p. 96 **"Whatever you imagine, exists"**—*Orot Hakodesh.*

p. 96 **"but waiting for Messiah"**—In Maimonides's classical formulation: "I believe with a perfect belief in the coming of the Messiah. Even though he tarries, still I wait for him to come every day."

p. 97 **" 'children' and 'builders' "**—On the verse "And all your children [banayich] are proficient in Godliness, and there shall be great peace on your children," R. Elazar says in the name of R. Hanina: "Do not read *banayich* [your children], but rather *bonayich*—your builders" (BT, tractate Berahot 64a).

CHAPTER FIVE—PERCEPTION

p. 102 **"Maggid of Mezritch"**—This story is recorded in *Or HaMeir* in the first entry on parshat Hayye Sarah, column 1.

p. 103 **"he laughed with joy"**—based on Talmudic story. See BT, tractate Avodah Zara 20a.

p. 103 **"the feminine Divine"**—*Or Hameir*, first teaching on parshat Chaye Sarah, columns 1 and 2.

p. 104 **"in the marketplaces"**—See Professor Moshe Idel's discussion in his excellent monograph *The Beauty of Woman in Jewish Mysticism.*

p. 104 **"sexual seeing to the soul's perception"**—The relationship between sight, perception, and sexuality is expressed very succinctly in a passage found in *Midrash HaNe'elam* on the Song of Songs, page 62a. Referring to the desire of the Lower Radiance (in the original, *zohar,* which we have previously identified with eros) to merge with the Higher Radiances, the *Midrash HaNe'elam* says: "The desire of the Lower Radiance is to sing praises, to *gaze inside* those (higher) radiances (zohars), to unite with them, to rise, to see the Highest Pleasantness. Concerning this, King David said (in Psalms 27:4): "I have asked one thing of the Lord: That I sit in the house of the Lord all the days of my life, that I *see* the pleasantness of the Lord and visit His Sanctuary." The erotic overtones of this passage are clear. The *Midrash HaNe'elam* goes on to point out that this secret was transmitted by King David to his son Solomon, the builder of the Temple, as the biblical verse quoted from Psalms indicates that that "sexual seeing" is one of the Temple mysteries. This is also echoed in the words of the prophet Ezekiel when he calls the sanctuary (Ezekiel 24:21): "the pride of your strength, the delight of your eyes." Commenting on this verse, R. Nachman of Brazlav equates the Temple with the eyes (*Liqutei Moharan*, vol. 2:67).

Another powerful example of "sexual seeing" is found in *Tiqunei Zohar* (29b). After the Shechina, who is captive of Evil [eros in exile], is liberated, he whose source is the Tree of Life [as opposed to the Tree of Duality Consciousness, i.e., the Tree of Knowledge of Good and Evil] "shoots seed like a [Zen archery] arrow towards the bride...who is the pupil of the eye, the receiver of the seed...the Sacred Moon...the pupil is the small inner point, the 'target'...It is toward her that he sends arrows *with the love of the eyes*—[his] target is clearly the Shechina."

p. 104 **"receiving...guests"**—*Yalqut Shimoni*, Genesis chap. 18, comment 82.

p. 105 **"Celebratory Seeing"**—This sacred sexual seeing is explicitly mentioned by R. Isaac Luria in *Sha'ar Hapesukin* on *parshat Vaye'tze*, where he explains that Jacob models Adam. Just as Adam had two wives, Lilith and Eve, so did

Jacob—Leah and Rachel. Lilith is identified with the unredeemed part of Leah's psyche, in which a holy soul lay dormant—that of Mrs. Turnus Rufus. As Luria goes on to say: "Akiva *saw with the Holy Spirit* that she [Mrs. Turnus Rufus] would convert in the future, and he would marry her. When she did so, the soul of Leah, Jacob's wife, clothed herself in her." This is the force of Luria's identification of Mrs. Turnus Rufus with Lilith! For a full unpacking of this Lurianic identification in the story of Akiva, see: *Lilith and Sacred Feminism*, Gafni and Ezrahi; (Heb) Modan Publishing, 2002.

p. 105 **"The Babylonian wisdom masters"**—BT, tractate Berahot 43b: "If he sees pleasant creations and good trees, he should make the blessing: 'Blessed is He... Who thus is His world.'"

p. 109 **"carnal erotic knowledge"**—See Genesis 4:1.

p. 110 **"Abraham Kook"**—"*Orot Hakodesh.*"

p. 112 **"The bride and groom are revealers of the Divine"**—*Zohar* vol. 3, p. 44b.

p. 112 **"the bride perceives"**—Just as in Judaism the bride is the feminine aspect of God and the groom the masculine aspect, in the Hindu tradition Rama and Sita are the prototype of love and marriage. Thus, every bride is called "Sita," and in the wedding ceremony she dresses up as this goddess and reenacts the scenes from the great myth of these two coupling gods.

p. 114 **"only with eyes closed"**—As R. Nachman of Brazlav puts it in his beautiful discourse on the "The Master of the Field" (*Liqutei Moharan* vol. 1—65:3): "When one wants to see Ultimate Reality, where all is good, where all is One, it is necessary to close the eyes... to shut them tightly, to close the Vision of This World and its illusions."

p. 114 **"the Lover's Prayer"**—I have termed Shma the Lover's Prayer both because it is bracketed by two love prayers and because it is understood by Kabbalists as being the most radical expression of love of God. In it we declare a love so passionate that we want to give up all for our beloved.

    Tiqunei Zohar (26a) also relates to the Shma as a lover's prayer: "Behold, the bride is adorned with her jewelry—it is now necessary to call her groom. This is the meaning of the biblical verse "Hear O Israel"—they are now at the *huppah!*" The bride is the Shechina, while the groom in this case is Israel in its supernal or spiritual sense. "Hear O Israel" is therefore a call to the cosmic bridegroom to take notice of his beautifully adorned bride and to come join her under the bridal canopy of unity.

p. 114 **"erotic union with Being"**—See Mopsik, "Union and Unity in Kabbalah," where he cites a long list of Kabbalists who so interpret the Shma prayer.

p. 118 **"Love your neighbor as yourself"**—Leviticus 19:18.

p. 119 **"Three partners . . . in creation"**—*Midrash Job*, comment 33.

p. 123 **"Abraham Kook"**—See R. Abraham Kook, *His Rooms*, p. 27.

p. 125 **"entire biblical project"**—*Midrash Rabba*, Genesis 22:7.

p. 125 **"I am part of God"**—This became a very basic idea in all the different schools of the Hassidic movement. To quote one example from R. Levi Yitzhak of Berdechiv: "Each and every person is a part of God above. This is why everyone is capable of perceiving God's greatness. It is like a son free to search his father's treasures" (*Kedushat HaLevi*, Collected Sayings).

p. 125 **"Lookers or Seers"**—For example, R. Abraham Abulafia, the renowned twelfth-century Kabbalist and founder of the School of Prophetic Kabbalah, referred to himself as "Avraham HaRoeh"—Abraham the Seer.

p. 126 **"even 'creates' God"**—When speaking of Abraham, the Zohar in vol. 1, p. 4a, says: " 'These are the generations of heaven and earth when they are created' " (Genesis 2:4)—[In Hebrew, *b'hibaram*, which means "when they are created," is composed of the same letters as *Abraham*]—all were waiting for the name of Abraham. Only when this name was complete could the Sacred Name be complete." In other words, the totality of the divine name is dependent on the archetypal Hebrew (Abraham the Hebrew). As He and his name are one, the implication is that man in fact creates the divine.

p. 126 **"the biblical verse tells us"**—See Exodus 34: 23–24.

p. 127 **"If I am here, all is here"**—Babylonian Talmud, Tractate Sukkah 67a: "They said of Hillel the Elder: When he was joyous at the Water Drawing Ceremony, he would say, 'If I am here, all is here. And if I am not here, who is here?' "

p. 127 **"The Zohar explains"**—See *Omissions from the Zohar*, vol. 1, 261a: "Come and see: When Hillel the Elder rejoiced at that festival . . . he would hint and say: If the Shechina Who is called I rests here, then All is here—the place called All [the divine masculine procreative *sfira* of *Yesod*] comes to mate with Her."

p. 127 **"Maimonides"**—In a beautiful *halachic* passage that comments on the joy one should experience in the Laws of Resting on Holidays, Maimonides says: "When one eats and drinks, he is obligated to feed the stranger, the orphan, and the widow, together with all the unfortunate poor people. If someone locks the doors of their courtyard while he and his wife and children are eating and drinking, and does not give food and drink to the poor and embittered of soul, it is considered the joy of the belly rather than the joy of fulfilling a commandment."

p. 127 **"adorned the curtains, walls, and vessels of most of the Temple."**—See Exodus 25, 26; I Kings 6–8, and Ezekiel 41.

p. 128 **"they feasted on the vision of the Shechina"**—*Midrash Rabba* Leviticus 20:10.

p. 128 **"the sexual gaze . . . is but the model"**—My interpretation of the Tantric nature of seeing and its transmutation into loving derives from three primary sources in my study. First, a reading of primary sources—both biblical and mystical—in which the sexual sense of vision seems to hold out a more expansive vista of the spirit. Second, a spiritual psychological survey of the contemporary situation in which erotic gazing has been exiled into pornography; this is the exile of the Shechina in our day. Third, through a combination of speculation and meditation. Late in this process a friend referred me to Eliot Wolfson's work *Through a Speculum That Shines: Vision and Imagination in Medieval Jewish Mysticism.* Wolfson's work was for me a wonderful validation of my core readings and intuitions. It also introduced me to a host of other texts, both printed and manuscript, to which I either had not access or had not seen. Wolfson documents extensively the praxis of sexual erotic gazing at the Divine—in the form of meditation or visualization—as a major practice that may lie at the heart of several different Jewish mystical schools. For the interested reader see in Wolfson pp. 43, 44, 101–104, 286–87, 336–37. What is critical to note at this juncture is that there are clearly different schools in regard to visionary praxis. There are those that view it as important and possible, there are those that forbid it on the grounds of its being too dangerous, and there are those that deem it impossible other than in very narrow circumstance such as the moment of death. Wolfson does not deal with Vision as an essential part of the secret of the cherubs in the way we suggest in this study. Our essential suggestion is that sexual seeing is a door to a more expanded love and eros, which is purely nonsexual. In this context, it is also interesting to note that the motif of vision begins and concludes the biblical narrative, which begins with "and God saw" as a recurrent refrain of the creation story, and concludes with "In the eyes of all Israel" as the finale.

CHAPTER SIX — GIVING: SELF-TRANSCENDENCE

p. 132 **"a divine love expressed in an infinite desire to give"**—This is the basic Lurianic world-creation model, which may be found in the various descriptions of the process interspersed throughout his writings. As he phrases it in the first "gate" of *Otzrot Haim:* "It arose in His simple reason, which is to be called Merciful [rahum may also be translated as "a Lover"] and Gracious—for if there is no one in the world to receive His love, how can He be called a Lover?"

p. 133 **"in the heat of the day"**—Genesis 18:1–2, and see *Yalqut Shimoni* on those verses, comment 82.

p. 134 **"is called by the text a 'lover'"**—Isaiah 41:8: "And you Israel My servant, Jacob whom I have chosen, the seed of Abraham My lover."

p. 135 **"tzedaka"**—It is interesting to note that throughout the Zohar, *tzedaka* is also one of the "code names" for Shechina. Since the Shechina is also known as *Knesset Yisrael,* the interconnected community of Israel, we see how the form of justice called *tzedaka* is actually an expression of the interdependence of the human community.

p. 135 **"the Tosafists"**—See *Tosafot* on BT Baba Batra, p. 8b.

p. 135 **"essential metaphysical truth of reality"**—The Babylonian Talmud in tractate Kiddushin, p. 31a, says that "someone who is commanded to fulfill a commandment and does so is greater than someone who is not commanded to fulfill a commandment and does so." The reason for this is not because one is obligated to fulfill the commandments because of legislation, but because the commandments constitute a fiber that links all of humanity. The Hebrew word for commandment, *mitzvah,* also means "connected," Tzavtah—a common equation in Hassidic and earlier mystical literatures.

p. 136 **"for the giver as it is for the receiver"**—This is why many Hassidic sources suggest that Abraham's great story of Giving—the feeding of the angels when he was sick after his circumcision—is set up as the paradigm of giving. The point is that the receivers in the story—namely the angels—were not in actual need, as angels need neither food nor drink. The essence of giving is the act and obligation of the giver.

p. 137 **"expansion of consciousness"**—*Liqutei Moharan,* 60:18.

p. 146 **"very act of giving, he has received"**—In the introduction to his monumental commentary on the Zohar, *HaSulam,* the modern-day Kabbalist R. Yehuda Ashlag describes the historical healing process as comprising three stages. The first is precreation, when all is undifferentiated undeveloped One; the second is creation itself, which is characterized by a marked dichotomy between giving and receiving. In the third stage, in which creation is ultimately healed (receives its *tikkun*), "receiving itself...will be transformed into a pure form of giving, and then [the receiver] will be able to truly receive all the goodness, pleasure, and delightfulness that creation contains." (*Introduction to the Zohar*, p. 6).

p. 149 **"Daat is only found in the mouth"**—See *Zohar*, vol. 2, p. 123a. In Kabbalistic literature, *daat* (literally "knowing") is generally considered the power of union and communication. When Man knew (*Yada*) his wife Eve in the biblical text, it refers to sexual intimacy. "*Daat* in the mouth" refers to the intimacy of conversation. The oral Torah is thus said to be rooted in the *sefira* of *Malhut*, which is also identified with the mouth. It is through the sacred conversation of study that the Oral Torah is revealed and created. Only by means of erotic merging with the text can we unfold the new layers of divinity that we term Oral Torah.

p. 149 **"gap between subject and object"**—In a long discourse on the Secret of Kissing, the *Midrash HaNe'elam* says: "The kiss of love is only with the mouth, as spirit [breath] and spirit combine, and intertwine, and each kiss therefore has two spirits—his/her own spirit, and that of her/his partner. Ultimately they are both creating four spirits. Certainly this is also the case when male and female unite—there, too, are four spirits. The child born to them is therefore a spirit born of four spirits [directions], as it says, 'From four directions the wind will come.' And this is a complete spirit."

Each partner has "two spirits," since each lover is both giving a kiss and receiving a kiss, and therefore it is as if each kiss is actually composed of two kisses. Kissing is also intimately identified with breath (spirit) and life, and is therefore part of the birthing process. (*Midrash HaNe'elam on the Song of Songs*, 60c.)

p. 149 **"Kiss me"**—Song of Songs 1:2.

p. 150 **"Amnon and his half-sister Tamar"**—II Samuel 13.

p. 151 **"You shall eat, be satisfied, and give blessing"**—Deut. 8:10. See also the *Zohar*, vol. 2, p. 153a, where this verse is discussed. The Zohar says, "The fulfillment that comes with satisfaction is then his. This is why the biblical verse says: 'Open Your hands and satisfy all living beings with fulfillment'—'fulfillment,' not food. Therefore you must certainly bless."

p. 152 **"Babylonian wisdom texts"**—BT, tractate Berahot 20b.

CHAPTER SEVEN—GIVING UP CONTROL

p. 160 **"invite their lovers to witness"**—In this context it is interesting to look at how the Shma, which we have previously called "the Lover's Prayer," is written in the Bible. The last letter of the first word (*Shma*) is an irregularly large Hebrew *'Ayin,* and the last letter of the last word is an irregularly large *Dalet.* Together they form the Hebrew word *'ed,* which means "witness" (see Deut. 6:4).

p. 163 **"creation is not a one-time event"**—In Lurianic theurgy, the world must be re-created every Rosh Hashana (see *Pri Etz Haim* 111c). Indeed, a careful reading of the Lurrianic daily meditations (*kavanot*) reveals that this is really a daily process. It is reflected in the words of the liturgy "who renews creation every day through His goodness."

p. 163 **"we give up lower self-control"**—See *Ethics of the Fathers*—"Make His will like your will, so that He will make your will like His will." (chap. 2:4).

p. 168 **"You shall not return home"**—I Samuel 18.

p. 168 **"as soon as the desire to control entered the story"**—Midrashic image: Genesis Rabbah on ch. 35. Jacob places Dina in a box to protect her from his brother Esau. He is afraid Esau will want to marry her. Was he protecting her out of love or was it an attempt to control who she would marry? Control often uses love as its cover.

p. 171 **"S-mothering"**—This aspect of the Great Mother is depicted in the *Zohar,* Vol. 1, 221a–b: "A thousand mountains grow before her, and she blew them away with one puff. A thousand rivers surround her, and she swallows them up in one gulp. Her nails reach out in twenty-four thousand directions. No one can escape her in either direction."

p. 171 **"mother's job is to become more and more absent"**—Commenting on the biblical injunction to "send away the mother, and take the nestlings for yourself" (Deut. 22:7) in the case of a person who hunts birds, the Kabbalists say that even the supernal mother must sometimes be sent away in order to allow her children to develop.

p. 172 **"loving and giving up control"**—1 Kings 3:16–28.

p. 172 **"Rebecca loves Jacob"**—Genesis 25:28.

p. 174 **"reintegrate them with their divine source"**—To get a sense of what this might mean, let's look for a second at anger. Hidden inside rage may well be some sparks of light. You are furious at your wife for saying that you need to spend more time connecting to your body and a tad less on your work. What does she know about your work? She doesn't understand how important it is. You cannot waste time exercising. But a part of you actually identifies with her critique and feels the need to revisit the amount of time you devote to your work. But you cannot own to that consciously, at least not at this point in your development, so it is expressed in anger. When you can redeem the light of your deeper knowledge from the anger and integrate it into your self-understanding, then you have engaged in the Kabbalistic process of gathering the sparks.

p. 174 **"the centrality of failure"**—"A person does not attain the teachings of the Torah unless he fails at them" (Babylonian Talmud, tractate Gittin 43a). This surprising Talmudic statement became one of the pillars of the radical Ishbetz school of Hassidism, which I will examine in a forthcoming book.

p. 175 **"who creates worlds and destroys them"**—*Midrash Rabba* on Kohelet, 3:14.

p. 176 **"We cannot force the universe's hand"**—This is true in reference to New Age philosophies as well. Many of the New Age philosophies suggest that if we would only engage in this or that practice, get clean or clear in this or that way, all would be well. If it is not well, then it must be that we have inflicted the hurt on ourselves by virtue of some spiritual psychological failing. The result is a "found guilty" verdict on the sick or distressed person. Such an attitude derives from a lethal cocktail of cruelty and hubris. Now many of the practices may be important and even beneficial, but there are no fail-safe guarantees in the universe. No one can control or predict patterns of illness and health.

p. 179 **"The Sage and the Courtesan"**—Babylonian Talmud, tractate Avoda Zara 17a.

CHAPTER EIGHT—CIRCLE AND LINE:
THE DANCE OF MALE AND FEMALE

p. 183 **"two essential forces of the universe"**—This is perhaps the major premise of the entire Zohar. The *Sifra Detziniyuta*, which is possibly the most abstruse passage in the entire Zohar, begins its mythical cosmology with: "Until the Scale existed, there was no possibility of gazing face to face. The ancient kings died, their coupling did not exist, and the earth was eradicated, until the Head [beginning], the Yearning of all Yearnings, developed and transferred the Clothes of Glory." The first shift toward the creation of reality as we know it was the introduction of the scale, whose function was to divide the highest root of the Godhead into the basic binary division of male and female. In the Primordial Unity, there was no possibility of "gazing face to face," so there could be no coupling, and earth could not subsist. Only when the (God)Head allowed for the single one cell to begin dividing and developing into the basic male/female paradigm could creation take place.

p. 184 **"balancing of these two forces"**—See the *Ohev Yisrael* on Vaethanan in Deuteronomy: "For everything in the world must have the aspects of male and female. A person committed to spiritual work [literally servant of God] must be especially certain to contain both male and female." It is important to note that each person contains and must realize both aspects.

p. 184 **"recite a blessing before sexual relations"**—*Ta'amei HaMinhagim* on marriage.

p. 184–85 **"Cordevero"**—See *Tfilla LeMoshe*, R. Moshe Cordevero's prayer book.

p. 185 **"to mend the cosmic rent"**—To again quote a startling passage from the *Ohev Yisrael* that expresses this very idea within the cherubs context: "Everything must be male and female, therefore the cherubs were entwined in sexual embrace. So too…is the reality of this lower lowly world. Like a baby whose limbs are very small, and then grows up, the Divine [grows] through the creation of all worlds. Through the Torah, right behavior, and the Arousal from Below, strength is added to the Higher Power, and all the worlds expand. Understand this well" (*Ohev Yisrael* on Ki Tisa in Exodus).

p. 187 **"Men are lines and women are circles"**—In Lurianic Kabbalah, the world was first created in circles, then in lines. In fact, the Sefirotic tree and the Divine Human Image only appear in the "lines." This extremely complex and detailed theory is described in length at the beginning of *Etz Hayim* in the first gate, and later on in the eighth gate, as circles and lines emerge at the root of every stage of emanated creation. Although Luria says (Gate 8, chap. 1) that "the form of man as male and female is only in the lines," we can still say that the lines are the root source of the masculine and the circles are the root source of the feminine. The basis for this would be that circle reality is identified with the *nefesh* level of soul, which corresponds to the feminine *Malehut*, while the circles are identified with the *ruach* level of soul, which corresponds to *Tiferet*. In addition, the circles are identified with the permutation of the divine Name known as "52," which derives from the last feminine *he* of God's name, while the lines derive from the "45" Name, which emerges from the masculine *vav* of God's name. See also *Sha'ar Hahakdamot*, 8a.

p. 188 **"Luria writes"**—See previous note. See also R. Abraham Kook in *Orot Hakodesh* for an excellent mystical treatment of circles and lines and their modern implications. For a cursory intellectual history of circles and lines from Luria to Luzatto to R. Isaac Chaver, a student of the Vilna Gaon, see *Iggulim VeYosher*, Mordechai Pachter, Daat, 1987. I thank Tamar Ross for bringing this article to my attention many years ago.

p. 190 **"distinctly linear and masculine"**—As has been pointed out by countless writers in the ecofeminist movement.

p. 191 **"serve the earth and guard it"**—Genesis 2:15.

p. 191 **"Temple as the Garden of Eden"**—Commenting on the biblical verse from Song of Songs, the *Midrash Tanhuma* on Naso, chapter 20, says: "When the Tabernacle [the portable desert sanctuary] was erected, Israel would say: 'Let my Beloved come into His Garden.'" This Midrashic comment identifies the Temple with a garden, and, in some takes, with the Garden of Eden, emphasizing the overtly erotic overtones.

p. 191 **"the Gardner"**—Commenting on the state of purity and forgiveness achieved on Yom Kippur, R. Isaac Halevi Hurvitz says in his masterpiece the *Shla*: "We are then pure, without sin, as was the original intention of creation. Then the high priest enters the inside of the inside [the Holy of Holies], just as Adam, when he was alive, entered the garden." Actually a close read of the biblical text itself identifies the Temple with the Garden, particularly the Garden of Eden. The Temple is seen as the portal through which one can consciously reaccess the eros of Eden. This is the healing (*tikkun*) after the shattering (*shevira*).

p. 192 **God is the place of the world"**—*Midrash Rabba* on Genesis 68:9.

p. 192 **"inside of God's face"**—See chapter 2, p. 26.

p. 192 **"Luria's graphic and daring vision"**—See the first note on this chapter. See also the beginning of *Etz Hayim*, where the first move toward creation is described as a withdrawal of infinite divinity to all directions simultaneously in the form of a circle. This allowed the Empty Void, where creation of the finite occurred, to come into being.

p .192 **"every ... blade of grass"**—During a stroll through a field, R. Nachman said to one of his disciples: "If only you would merit to hear the sound of the songs and praises of the plants, how each and every blade of grass sings to the Lord without ulterior motive, with full concentration, without any expectation of receiving something in return. How beautiful and pleasant it is to hear their song! Being among them inspires one to serve the Lord with awe" (*Sihot MoHaran*, 163).

p. 193 **"suggests Kook"**—See *Iggrot HaReiya*, vol. 2, letter 43, Mossad HaRav Kook, Jerusalem, 1948.

p. 194 **"Book of Kings"**—I Kings 18:19.

p. 194 **"radical passage in the Zohar"**—Rennaisance Kabbalist Moses Cordevero says explicitly, "Malchut [a Kabbalistic appellation for Shechina] is called Ashera." Cordevero bases his reading on the following radical passage in the Zohar, for which he cites the pagination (vol. 1, p. 49a) without a citation or explanation. Here is the passage: "It is written: 'You shall not plant an Ashera tree near the altar of God which [asher] you make for yourself' [Deut. 16]. 'Near the altar' (you cannot plant an Ashera)—does that mean that you can plant one above it or behind it?! We rather interpret the word *asher* as referring to Her husband; and She [the Shechina] is called Ashera, like her husband Asher. In the same sense it is written 'for Baal and Ashera' (II Kings 23). This is also the meaning of 'You shall not plant for yourself an ashera near the altar of God'—in the place of the altar of God, for the 'altar of God' is already there [mizbeah, altar, is often a Shechina image in the Zohar] and therefore, facing it, do not plant another Ashera [the implication is that the Altar of God—a Shechina image—is like an Ashera—you can therefore not have another one in the same place. It would be spiritual architectural redundancy!].

"Come and see"—everywhere, those who worship the sun are called worshippers of the Baal, and those that serve the moon are called servers of Ashera. This is what the biblical verse means by 'for Baal and Ashera'—Ashera is called by the name of her husband *Asher.*

"If so, why did this name (Ashera) fall out of usage? Ashera derives from 'For I have been fertile (*ishruni*) with children' (Gen. 30:13, concerning the birth of Asher). The name Asher, however, was not approved by other nations, as they have put another one in her place. It is also written 'All who honored her held her in disgrace' Her name was changed in order not to embolden those nations that worship idols; we have called her (Ashera) an altar, which is of the earth, as it says, 'Make me an altar of earth' (Exodus 20:21)."

p. 195 **"The two cherubs are"**—The scholar Jules Morgenstern made this point in an obscure essay some sixty years ago, *Amos Studies III*, Hebrew Union College, vol. 15, 1940, p. 121, note 98. See also "The Ark and the Ephod and the Tent of Meeting," Cincinnati, 1945, p. 95, notes 96, 107, 111, 159. The relationship between Ashera, cherubs, and later Kabbalistic manifestations of the feminine Divine in the form of Shechina constitutes the major implicitly and explicitly stated thesis in R. Patai's *Hebrew Goddesses.* The book's key motifs are summarized in tersely worded conclusions at the end of each chapter.

p. 195 **"wisdom masters of Babylon"**—The Babylonian Talmud in tractate Yoma 54b relates that when the Temple was conquered and Nebuchadrezzar's army saw the cherubs, the Jewish religion was immediately cheapened in their eyes. "Said Reish Lakish, When the foreigners entered the Temple and saw the cherubs sexually intertwined they took them out to the market place, saying 'Israel, whose blessing is a blessing and whose curse is a curse—is this what they were engaged in?'" A parallel text in the Midrash (*Midrash Rabba* on Lamentations, sec. 9) is more explicit in relating the cherubs to paganism. "Ammonites and Moabites entered the Holy of Holies and found the two cherubs. They paraded them around the streets of Jerusalem [saying] ... did you not say that this nation does not worship idols? See what we have found, what they have been worshipping."

p. 198 **"no slave had ever succeeded"**—*Yalqut Shimoni* on Exodus, chap. 2, comment 269.

p. 200 **"human and divine"**—In Lurianic Kabbalah, the Fall is an essential part of creation, necessary to create a finite world in which there are human beings with free choice, with whom God can "dialogue." Adam's original purpose was to redeem the fallen sparks of divinity. However, as a result of eating from the tree, the Fall was harder than originally intended. One of the basic questions in Lurianic cosmology is to what extent the Godhead Itself was affected by the Fall. Although it is generally stated that the two lower divine *partzufim* (countenances) of *Za'ir Anpin* and *Nukva* were primarily affected, there are comments that imply that the "flaw" *(pgam)* went as high as *Abba* and *Ema*, and even *Keter*, the highest divine countenance (see for example *Etz Hayim* Gate 9, chap. 2). Although the higher countenances are said to heal themselves, ultimately, since creation is one, until the lower levels are healed, the *tikkun* is not complete. According to Luria, the real significance of creation is that this healing of the Divine and human is dependent on the actions of man.

p. 200 **"Kabbalists who introduced the idea"**—One of the foremost propagators of early Spanish Kabbalah, R. Meir Ibn Gabai, writes: "The Upper Levels are dependent for their revelation and healing on the healing of the lower levels.... And just as the healing of the Higher [worlds] was dependent on the healing of the lower worlds at the beginning of creation, that original *tikkun* did not suffice, for all the higher chariots are [still] dependent on Man's [reaching a state of] completion for their existence ... and by his actions ... he adds strength and valor, flow, light and blessing to the Higher Man [the Divine] in Whose image he was created" (*Avodat Haqodesh*, section 3, chap. 45).

p. 200 **"above the sun"**—*Zohar*, vol. 1, p. 91b: "Does the biblical verse not say 'There is nothing new under the sun'? R. Yehudah said: 'It says *under* the sun—*above* the sun is different.'"

p. 200 **"outside the circle"**—BT tractate Shabbat 156a.

p. 201 **"Go forth" story**—See Genesis 12:1 and 22:2.

p. 203 **"Aron of Barcelona"**—*Sefer HaChinuch* on the sixteenth commandment. **"Peor idol itself"**—BT tractate Sanhedrin 106a.

p. 206 **Jung"**—See *"The Aryan Christ,"* Richard Wolin.

p. 208 **"with the Ashera tree ... under every tree"**—See Isaiah 44 and I Chronicles 1:16.

p. 208 **"mamash"**—This principle was made famous by R. Schneur Zalman of Liadi, who claimed that the human being was *helek eloka memaal mamash,* an actual part of God above (*Tanya,* chap. 2). *Mamash* here means that God is not only the creator of the human being, but that human beings are also actually divine—literally participating in divinity. The source of the phrase is to be found in the writing of Luzatto.

p. 208 **"Schneur Zalman of Liadi writes"**—*Tanya,* chapter 38.

p. 208 **"Nachman of Bratzlav"**—See note to page 192.

p. 209 **"for its ethics truly to thrive"**—This idea is beautifully expressed by Maimonides in a *halachic* context (*Yad HaHazaka,* Laws of the Temple, chap. 5): "the Room of Hewn Stone, in which the Sanhedrin [High Court] sat. Half [of the chamber] was sacred, and half was not. It had two doors—one led to the sacred [part of the Temple], one led to that which was not sacred. The Sanhedrin sat in the half that was not sacred."

p. 209 **"basks in His perfect Presence"**—See Gerona's great Kabbalist and exegete Moses Ben Nachman's interpretation of Genesis 18:1.

p. 209 **"Greater is the feeding of guests"**—*Yalqut Shimoni* on Genesis, chap. 16, comment 82.

p. 210 **"When prophet and pagan meet, the Temple"**—On the relationship between the Temple and paganism, see R. Tzadok Hacohen, *reisisei Layla,* discourse 43. Also see BT tractate Sanhedrin 102b, the classic story of how Menashe appears in a dream to R. Ashi, with special attention to Rashi ad loc s.v. "You would have to raise the hem of your skirt." On hugging and kissing idols, see BT tractate Shabbat 83b, and tractate Sanhedrin 63b–64a. See also *Yalqut Shimoni* on Judges, section 64, and on Hosea, section 529. See also the Kuzari, 423, the Maharal in *Netivot Olam,* Netiv Hashalom, chap. 6. See also the

Vilna Gaon in *Haghot HaGra to Seder Olam Rabba*, chap. 3. See also *Michtav MeEliyahu*, part 4, p. 175, and part 3, p. 226. For additional discussions of R. Tzaddok on this subject, see *Dover Tzedek*, s.v. "ve'kol hakolot," pp. 145–146, *Resisei Layla*, chapters 13, 23, 35, and *Mahshevet Harutz*, chap. 9.

p. 211 **"Abraham Kook, the greatest modern Hebrew mystic"**—Abraham Kook, *Orot Hakodesh*, vol. 3, sec. 1.

p. 213 **"Zohar is replete with imagery"**—The following passage is quite startling in its radical reading of the biblical verse: "And the righteous shall inherit the earth": "Come and see: The awakening of the love of the Community of Israel [one of the Zohar's code names for the Shechina, i.e., the group soul] for *Kudsha Brich Hu* [the Divine Masculine] is awakened through the souls of the righteous.... Similarly, the desire of woman to let her feminine waters flow toward the upper [masculine] waters is only through the souls of the righteous...the secret of it all is that the *tzaddik* [righteous one] is (the sefira of) *Yesod* above, and also *yesod* below [the earthly *tzaddik*]. The Community of Israel [Shechina] unifies with the *tzaddik* above and the *tzaddik* below—a *tzaddik* from this side, and a *tzaddik* from that side, inherit her. As it says [Psalm 37] "*Tzaddikim* [plural for righteous] will inherit the earth" (Zohar, vol. 1, p. 245b). The implication is that the supernal sefira of *Yesod*, which is called *tzaddik*, and the righteous ones on earth, are the two lovers (inheritors) of the earth (the Shechina).

p. 214 **"Luria, the world itself is re-created every moment"**—*Etz Hayim*, Gate 1, Branch 5: "See what is written in *Tiqunei Zohar* (p. 65): 'The clothes He wears in the morning are not the clothes He wears in the evening, the clothes that He wears today are not the clothes He wears tomorrow.' Through this [quote] understand how the status and the situation of the worlds, which are the clothes of the Infinite, experience myriad changes at all times and at every moment."

CHAPTER NINE—LISHMAH, FOR THE SAKE OF THE NAME

p. 218 **"The taste of the tree is as the taste of the fruit"**—See Rashi's commentary on Genesis 1:11.

p. 218 **"the source of the vessels is higher than the source of the light"**—In the Lurianic myth this is rooted in the "order of emanation," during which vessels are formed. Vessels are essentially ossified light that derives from a higher source than the light that fills the vessels.

p. 220 **"this is a positive commandment"**—*Mechilta De R. Yishmael*.

p. 223 **"Moses' Hebrew name spelled backward"**—See note to page 229.

p. 224 **"nicknames"**—The names of God and their relative status in the divine
hierarchy is a subject that many Kabbalists devoted a great amount of
attention to. One major issue was to identify the *shem ha-etzem* (essential name
of God—usually held to be the Tetagammeron—YHVH) and define how it is
distinct from other names. One very comprehensive example of this type of
discourse can be found in R. Moshe Cordevero's *Pardes Rimonim*, Gates 19–21.

p. 225 **"typological slavery"**—See the classic article by R. Joseph Soloveitchik,
Reflections of the Rav, vol. 1, the last three articles.

p. 229 **"become almost interchangeable"**—Pinchas of Koretz teaches that
when a *tzaddik* (righteous person) enters the future world he is transformed
into a divine name. Similarly, Reb Tzvi son of the Baal Shem Tov tells us that
his father told him that he (his father) was the divine name *Ana Bacoah*. See
M. Idel: *Hassidim Reappraised*.

The biblical text itself already alludes to this blurring between the human
and divine name—"And he called his name Enosh; then he began to call with
the name of God" (Genesis 9:26). It could be understood that through the very
receiving and living of his name—Enosh—he called in the name of God.

Later Kabbalists point out that just as *Moshe* (Moses) in Hebrew is "the
Name" (*Hashem*) spelled backward, so too the numerical value of the name
Moses is 345, while the numerical valuation of the divine name linked with
Moses is the reverse—543. When Moses asks God "What is your name?" God
replies, "I will be what I will be." "I will be what I will be" is regarded by the
Talmud as one of the names of God. Its numerical value is 543.

R. Joseph Karo, better known as the author of the epic code of law known as
Shulhan Aruch, was also a Kabbalist who wrote a unique diary called *Maggid
Meisharim*, in which he records the teachings he received from his "*maggid*," a
nonearthly female spiritual teacher. Commenting on the biblical verse "any place
where I mention My name, I will come to you and bless you" (Ex. 20:21), he says
(p. 64b): "Meaning to say—when *you* mention My name, it will be as if I am
speaking, for you will have become the Shechina, and the Shechina will speak
through your mouth, and I will therefore come to you full, loaded with blessings,
and I will bless you." The identity of the lover and the beloved have merged, so
although Man is calling on the Divine, it is as if the Shechina is calling her own
name through him. See also the *Shl"a* (on parshat Yitro), where he quotes the
Tzror HaMor, and explains that this merging of identity was the psychical state of
the high priest when he called out the Divine Name in the Temple, our next topic.

p. 229 "incarnation of the flow of love in the universe"—"Any priest that does not love the people, or that the people do not love him, should not lift up his hands to bless them" (*Zohar*, vol. 3, p. 147b). In this reading, to bless Israel with love means to incarnate and channel the love of the universe (God) to the people.

p. 230 "The priest is described in the Zohar"—See *Zohar*, vol. 3, p. 296a: "Therefore only the High Priest can enter that place [the Holy of Holies], since he stems from the side of *hesed* [male love], for only he who is called *hesed* may enter that place. He enters the Holy of Holies [the female], and the Female is intoxicated [with love], and blessed.... And all the passion of man for woman is encountered here, and they [man and woman] are called blessed, for from this place blessing flows to all worlds, and all are blessed."

"cried out the name"—See Babylonian Talmud, tractate Yoma, p. 66a.

p. 233 "we participate in the name of God"—This is echoed by the fact that many biblical Hebraic names contain names of God—the *El* or *Yah* suffix (e.g., Samuel or Uriyah), the *Yo* or *Yehu* prefix (Joel or Judah), etc.

p. 233 "Nahum of Chernobyl"—*Me'or Ainayim* on Numbers 1:1.

p. 236 "in the language of the Zohar"—*Zohar*, vol. 3., p. 296a.

p. 237 "The source for the decree"—Not surprisingly, the context for this edict in the wisdom texts is a discussion of the Holy of Holies at the place where the lover/priest called out the Name in ecstasy (see Mishna 5 in chap. 9 of tractate Berahot).

p. 238 "The exile of the Shechina is the exile of the Name"—Concerning the Messianic era, when the Shechina is redeemed, the biblical verse says (Zechariah 14:9): "On that day God will be One and His name will be One." The name will be redeemed from Exile and once again be one with Divinity.

CHAPTER TEN—STORY, VOICE, CREATIVITY, AND PLEASURE

p. 239 "a prostitute"—Of course in a literal reading of the Zoharic literature the Shechina and the harlot are separate figures. A deeper reading, however, collapses them into one complex persona. See, for example, *Tiqunei Zohar* 24b: "The maidservant enters the place of her mistress. She is unclean, a servant, a heathen, a harlot, and she defiles the place where the Shechina would rest."

p. 241 "Abraham Kook"—*Orot Hateshuva* 15:10.

p. 242 the "more" is your soul story—The biblical verse immediately after the

Calling of the *Shma* can be translated as: "And you shall love the Lord your God with all your heart, and with all your soul, and with all your *more*." [emphasis added] "The Hebrew word *me'od* used here literally means "very," implying additional, i.e., *more*.

p. 243 **"intimate whisper of divinity"**—See, for example, *Zohar*, vol. 2, p. 128b, which is referring to the state of unity attained when the *tzaddik*, i.e., the *sefira* of *Yesod*, is fulfilling its function of erotically uniting all the limbs of the divine masculine so as to become one with the feminine Shechina out of complete fullness: "to connect everything in one unity. Then everything, above and below, whispers with the kisses of passion."

p. 243 **"remezie deorayta"**—In *Liqutei Etzot*, in the section on Money and Living, R. Nachman says: "then he merits to hear the hints and calls of the Torah, which are the good thoughts that constantly arise in his heart, calling him to return to the Blessed Name, until he eventually is so fortunate as to become truly intimate with the divine."

p. 245 *"the merging of spirit in spirit"*—*Zohar*, vol. 2, p. 124b: "R. Yitzhak opened by saying [Song of Songs 1:2]: 'Let him kiss me with the kisses of his mouth'— Why does it say 'let him kiss me'? It should say 'let him love me'!... But this is what we learned: What are kisses? The merging of spirit in spirit. This is why kissing is with the mouth, for the mouth is the source and the outlet of spirit [breath]. Therefore, kisses are with the mouth with love, with the merging of spirit in spirit, which do not separate from each other."

p. 245 **"it is called kissing"**—According to the Zohar, this union takes place during the *Amida* prayer. Since this is the time when Shechina Goddess and male God are in the blissful union of kissing, it is a time to ask for one's needs, but in a whisper, so as to respect this intimacy. See *Zohar*, vol. 2, p. 200b.

p. 246 **"disallowed the Temple prostitute"**—Deut. 23:18.

p. 247 **"failing to get involved in making the world a place"**—This may be the intention of the biblical verse in Leviticus: "And you shall surely rebuke your fellow man, and not bear sin because of him." The implication is that if one fails to get involved, he is guilty of "sin"—ethical violation.

p. 248 **"violators of the path"**—The formal Hebrew term is *Ovrei Averah*, which is usually translated as "sinners." These words, however, are far more subtle in the original Hebrew. Indeed, in Hebrew, the word *Hebrew* itself is *Ivri*. *Ivri* derives from the same root as *Ovrei*, and *Averah* means "the one who went to the other side." Abraham is called the *Ivri*—the Hebrew—because he left the old path and went to the other side (of the river), forging a new path. In Hebrew, *averah* means "sin"—or a violation, as it is often translated, in the sense that it is a violation of the path. Similarly the other Hebrew word for *sin* is *het*. Using an image drawn from the world of archery, it means to miss the mark. That is to say the arrow strayed from the trajectory of its path. Indeed, the word *Torah* itself derives in part from the Hebrew word *yoreh*—"to shoot." That is to say Torah is about intending, aiming in the right direction, being on the right path—returning to our point of origin. The words *Ovrei Averah* mean not merely "sinners," but more significantly "violators of the path." Their own path!

p. 250 **"briefly reconstruct the narrative"**—I fully unpack this reading with a careful literary analysis of the relevant biblical and Midrashic sources in my more footnoted Hebrew works "*A Certain Spirit, Vadai—Toward the Redefinition of Certainty,*" chapters 1 and 9, and "*Lillith and Sacred Feminism,*" O. Ezrahi and M. Gafni, section 2, "*Lillith Is Leah.*" Both "*Lillith*" and "*A Certain Spirit*" will soon be available in English, so I will not cite all the sources here. I only recapitulate the material briefly in light of the new discussion of the erotic and the sexual in this chapter, particularly with reference to Leah as a Talmudic archetype of the prostitute and a Kabbalistic archetype of the Shechina.

p. 250 **"Jacob's older brother Esau"**—See Rashi on Genesis 29:17.

p. 250 **"gives Rachel signs"**—Babylonian Talmud, tractate Baba Batra, p. 127a.

p. 251 **"Her fifth son"**—Her fourth son, Judah, is a temporary breakthrough moment, the source of which I have called the "Judah Moment" typology. See my Hebrew book, *A Certain Spirit, Vadai—Toward the Redefinition of Certainty.*

p. 252 **"Leah our Matriarch was a whore that night"**—Midrash Rabba on Genesis, 80:1.

p. 253 **"sex as a form of speech"**—In tractate Ketubot (p. 13a) of the Babylonian Talmud there is a discussion as to what the Mishna means when it says "she was seen speaking with someone." Zei'ri says that it means she secluded herself with someone, while R. Assi says that it means she had intercourse with someone.

p. 254 **"Mouth" is one of the erotic mystical names"**—*Tiqunei Zohar,* 17a: "*Malhut* [the *sefira* which symbolizes the Shechina] is called the mouth." Some Kabbalists view the mouth as the sexual organ of the face, hence kissing is a form of copulation, as we discussed in the previous chapter.

p. 254 **"Birrur"**—The process of "separating the wheat from the chaff," i.e., that which is authentic and my own from that which is not.

p. 255 *"chashmal"*—This interpretation can actually be traced to the Midrash: "R. Yehuda said: What is *chashmal*? . . . In the Mishna it was learnt. Sometimes they are silent, sometimes they speak. When Word comes from the mouth of the Most Powerful they are silent; when no Words emit from the mouth of the Most Powerful they speak" (*Yalqut Shimoni*, Ezikiel, chap. 8).

p. 256 **"the Black Fire"**—*Zohar*, vol. 3, p. 154b.

p. 256 **"A great voice which did not continue"**—See Rashi's commentary on Deut. 5:19.

p. 257 **"I am not a man of words"**—Exodus 4:10.

p. 257 **"we are able . . . to speak the word of God"**—"Come and see: As long as Word was in Exile, Voice had left it, and the words were sealed, with no voice. When Moses came, Voice came. For Moses was voice without words, for word was in exile . . . and Moses had a voice without words. This is how he lived until they came close to Mount Sinai, where the Torah was given" (*Zohar*, vol. 2, p. 25b). We often sense that we forgo some degree of authenticity the moment we speak as a way of communicating with others—as if we have "lost our voice." When the Torah was given through Moses as an intermediary, he found the way to bridge the gap between his own unique voice and the words he spoke.

p. 257 **"Moses . . . Shechina speaks from his throat"**—The source of this well-known quote appears to be *Tiqunei Zohar*, 79a. See also *Raya Mehimna, Zohar*, vol. 3, pp. 232a, 265a. All are based on BT tractate Berahot 45a.

p. 257 **"Egypt . . . the throat"**—See note to p. 89.

p. 258 *"Ish HaElohim"*—This idea is found in the Zohar in numerous passages. See, for example, vol. 1, p. 6b, or p. 236b. An even more radical interpretation of *Ish HaElohim* is found in *Midrash Rabba* 11:4 on Deuteronomy 33:1: "What is meant by 'a man of God?' R. Avin said: His [Moses] upper half was divine, his lower half human"—a very strange notion indeed! R. Isaac Luria, in *Etz Hayim* (Gate 38, chap. 9), combines these two interpretations. He says that Moses, the biblical inheritor of Jacob's legacy, had two "spiritual wives," just as Jacob had two wives, Leah and Rachel. His "upper half" merged with the Higher Feminine Shechina, symbolized by Leah, and is therefore seen as divine. His lower half was wedded to Rachel, the Earthly Shechina, and therefore human.

p. 258 **"When Moses comes"**—See note to p. 257.

p. 259 **"There is a Moses in every generation"**—*Tiqunei Zohar*, 114a.

CHAPTER ELEVEN — THE HARLOT BY THE SEA

p. 269 **"The Harlot by the Sea"** — See Babylonian Talmud, tractate Menahot, p. 44a.

p. 271 **"Four hundred"** — Abraham, in the book of Genesis (23:17), buys the burial plot for his wife with four hundred coins. Esau comes to greet Jacob armed to the teeth and accompanied by four hundred men (Genesis 33:1).

p. 273 **"between the cherubs"** — Numbers 7:89. See also page 29 and the note thereto.

p. 275 **"He writes and puts it in her hand"** — Deut. 24:1–3.

p. 275 **"the essential self is given over"** — See tractate Shabbat p. 105a in the Babylonian Talmud, where it says that *Anochi*, the Hebrew word for *I*, is an acronym for *Ana Nafshei Kativt Yahivt* — "I give my soul through my writing."

p. 276 **"conversion ... for the name's sake"** — Indeed in later legal literature this story is cited as a source for reinterpreting more liberally the requirement of *lishmah* in conversion.

p. 277 **"the Shechina becomes a prostitute"** — See note to p. 239.

CHAPTER TWELVE — TIME

p. 283 **"simultaneously past, present, and future"** — As the *Raya Mehimna* puts it: "All being is dependent on YHVH, and It and Its Manifested Beings [literally *Havayan* — Beings, YHVHs], give testimony concerning the Master of the World, Who was before all Being, and is within all Being, and is after all Being, and this is the secret that Being testifies to: Was, Is, Will Be" (*Raya Mehimna*, Zohar, vol. 3, p. 257b).

p. 284 **"passage written in 1944"** — C. G. Jung, *Memories, Dreams, Reflections*, Fontana Press 1995, pp. 320–329.

p. 285 **"peer between the lattice works"** — Commenting on this verse from the Song of Songs, the *Raya Mehimna* says: "The Temple must have windows, as it says in Daniel (6:11) [concerning his private prayer chamber] 'and open windows' — just as it is above [just as there is a Temple on earth, so there is a spiritual Temple on high, and both must have windows]. [The biblical verse] therefore says: 'Watching from the windows, peering between the lattice work'... so that the lower home can be like the higher home, so that the higher dwelling can descend to the Lower dwelling." (*Zohar* vol. 2, p. 59b). Both the physical and the inner sanctuaries must have openings so that man can fix his gaze on the eternal and the eternal can yearn for man.

p. 285 **"longevity has become our goal"**—R. Nachman of Bratzlav interprets the desire for long life (the Hebrew literally translates as "long days") in the following manner: "A man should seek to lengthen his days, which means that he should strive to make each and every additional hour and day longer, greater, and more expansive than those that preceded them, as they become more sacred...this is the real meaning of 'longer days'...and so for each successive day of his life" (*Liqutei Etzot* on Awe and Spiritual Work).

p. 286 **"foreplay"**—In prayer there is also a first stage—"fore-pray" (a term coined by my friend and mentor Reb Zalman Schachter-Shalomi). This is identified with the first stage of prayer, the introductory psalms (*Psukei d'zimra*): "When Israel on earth prays the introductory psalms, She [the Shechina] adorns Herself and prepares Herself in all Her manners of preparation, like a woman who prepares herself for her man" (*Zohar*, vol. 3, p. 200b).

p. 287 **"obscure passage by ... Mordechai Lainer"**—*Mei Shiloah*, vol. 1, comment on Genesis, 49:33.

p. 288 **"Rahav"**—BT, tractate Megilla 15a.

p. 291 *"Atik Yomin"*—In the system of Sefirot, *Atik Yomin* is Keter. Keter is often a symbol for Kadesh Kadoshim. See Arthur Green, *Keter: The Crown of God in Early Jewish Mysticism*. Princeton University Press, 1957.

p. 291 **"two relations to time"**—Two time cycles that coexist simultaneously are hinted at in the *Idra Rabba* (Great Assembly) section of the Zohar. They are termed *Yemai Kedem* (Days of Old) and *Yemai Olam* (Days of the World). The *Yemai Kedem* time cycle originates in *Atik Yomin*, the Godhead before, beyond, and after this and all other potential or realized realities. *Yemai Olam* is time as it is expressed in *Za'ir Anpin*, the Godhead as It is revealed and disclosed in this world of human consciousness. In his/her spiritual endeavor, the Hebrew mystic strives for participation in both time cycles—the eternal as expressed in *Yemai Kedem*, the present as expressed in *Yemai Olam*. (It is interesting to note that the term for the "eternal and beyond" is *Yemai Kedem*—Days of Old. There is an implicit implication that Eternity is the Given, the Old. Human beings' everyday reality represents the "newness" and singularity of creation.) (See *Zohar* vol. 3, pp. 134b and 138b.)

p. 291 **"the present is in the invitation"**—In Hebrew, *zman* is "time," *zimum* is "invitation," and *mezuman* is "readiness"—the openness to receive.

p. 292 **"touched for the very first time"**—BT tractates Eruvin 54b and Baba Batra 16b.

p. 292 **"a close reading"**—See Yehuda Liebes, *Zohar and Eros*, pp. 89–90.

p. 294 **"all commandments will be nullified in the future"**—BT tractate Niddah 61b.

p. 294 **"Sin ... an insensitivity to time"**—This line is explicitly unpacked in Jacob Lainer of Ishbitz in *Beit Yaacov* on Genesis, Torah 36: "All commandments will be nullified in the future—The fact that [certain things] are presently forbidden is because they are before their time. If Adam had waited, it would have been permissible for him to eat [from the Tree of Knowledge].... The prohibition is because [if one eats before its time] it closes the heart of man and imprisons his consciousness and thoughts... if he would only wait, God would grace him with expansive consciousness so that he could receive this thing rather than it causing him forgetfulness."

p. 294 **"eating from the fruit tree in the Garden of Eden"**—In fact, Luria's understanding goes even further. Commenting on a passage from the Babylonian Talmud (tractate Sanhedrin 46a) that tells of a man who had intercourse with his wife under a fig tree, Luria says that this man is actually Adam: When Adam had intercourse with his wife under the fig tree, *it was as if he ate something unripe* [emphasis added] [the Hebrew word used for *unripe* is *paga*, similar to *fig*]. He should have waited until Friday night, which is the time for scholars to have intercourse with their wives. Adam's sin was exactly like that of King David (with Bathsheba—Luria writes in *Sha'ar HaPesuqim* on Judges that Bathsheba was David's soul mate, the problem being that he took her before their time) (see *Liqutei Shas* on Sanhedrin). All a question of erotic timing!

p. 294 **"and be intimate"**—The Hebrew word is *davak*, which literally means "cleaving" but is better translated as the more evocative English word "intimacy." See Genesis 2:24.

p. 296 **"we forget our larger selves"**—*Orot HaTeshuva* 15:10.

p. 297 **"the God point in the present"**—A popular Kabbalistic meditation suitable for everyday life is to imagine YHVH, the four letters of the divine name, in the place of the third eye as one carries on daily affairs. This is based on the biblical verse "I will place YHVH before me always" (Psalms 17:8). See for example *Hanhagot Tovot*, suggestion 73.

p. 297 **"the unconscious exile of Egypt"**—*Toldot Yaakov Yosef*, toward the end of parshat Vayishlah.

p. 297 **"My soul longs"**—A conflation of two biblical verses—Psalms 84:3 and 119:45.

p. 298 **"one section of the daily prayer"**—The first blessing of the silent meditation in Hebrew liturgy.

p. 298 **"the Shechina is between them"**—*Yalqut Shimoni* on the second chapter of Genesis, comment 24.

p. 300 **"Great is *teshuvah*"**—*Yalqut Shimoni* on the fourteenth chapter of Hosea, comment 530.

p. 303 **"Mystic Chaim Luzatto"**—*Mesilat Yesharim*, chapter 4.

p. 303 **"literally change the end of the story"**—This is the notion of God being *Erech Apayim*, "long suffering." It is the divine look that creates reality—"God saw and it was good." In the case of human misdeeds, God suspends the potentially vengeful divine gaze in order to allow human perception to reframe and heal the past.

CHAPTER THIRTEEN—UNION

p. 305 **"He shall cleave to his wife"**—Genesis 2:24.

p. 306 **"Shechina, mother"**—All through Zoharic literature, the first Hebrew letter *He* of God's four-letter name YHVH is the mother who nourishes her children, the son, symbolized by the letter *Vav*, and her daughter, symbolized by the second letter *He*.

p. 308 **"all souls ... different parts of the body of God"**—This is how R. Haim Vital understands the relevant passage in *Tiqunei Zohar* (32a, which, although it begins with a discussion on how different forms and types of prophets and prophecy [erotic imagination] stem from different parts of the divine body, can certainly be interpreted as referring to souls in general): "All prophets and all people, each one ascends to the limb [part of the body] that their soul emanated from. Some are from the head of the King, some are from the hair, the eyes, the ears, the nose, the mouth, the neck, the hands, the torso, the hips, the thighs, the legs, the genitals, the mind, the heart. And all these limbs correspond to a given *sefira* of the ten *sefirot*. And all these limbs are in the image of the body of the King. And there are those whose souls come from the King's garments" (*Sha'arei Kedusha*, sec. 2, Gate 3).

p. 309 **"there is no place devoid of Him"**—God's presence in all reality is compared to the soul of man, which is in all of his limbs. This principle, which became one of the pillars of Hassidism (especially Habad Hassidism), can be found in *Tiqunei Zohar*, p. 122b.

p. 310 **"Who ate from the tree?"**—Genesis 3:9–13. Eve, too, when confronted by

God, passes the buck to the snake. President Harry Truman had a paperweight on his desk inscribed with the words "The buck stops here."

p. 310 **"as lines of connection"**—See M. Gafni and A. Leader, *"Men and Women, Lines and Circles,"* chapter 8 in the *Erotic and the Holy* (forthcoming), for a more complete unpacking of the spiritual worldview of Solomon's Temple.

p. 312 **"the river of light that flows from Eden"**—This phrase, oft repeated in the Zohar, takes advantage of an Aramaic play on words: *nehora* is "light," *nehar* is "river." The text intuits that light is a ray, a river of particles.

p. 315 **Through my body I vision God"**—(Job 19:26). R. Shneur Zalman of Liadi reads this verse in this manner: "The intention is to partially understand Godliness by means of the life-force invested in the body" (*Tanya, Iggret Hakodesh*, chap. 15).

p. 316 **"strangers in the land of Egypt"**—Exodus 22:20.

"All who invalidate others"—BT tractate Baba Metzia, p. 59b.

p. 318 **"writes Kook, is love"**—*Orot Hakodesh.*

p. 319 **"the spreading out beyond all boundaries"**—*Mei Hashiloah*, commenting on Deut. 12:20, "When God expands your boundaries": "It is not written that they will violate their boundaries—rather that God will expand their boundaries. From God's side...there are no boundaries. One can expand in all of the realms of Good. For it is divinity seen from human understanding, through the limit of human consciousness, which is the source of all boundaries." The notion of boundaries and no boundary consciousness is a major theme in *Mei Hashiloah* that I expand on in *The Dialectic of Mystical Humanism in the Radical Theology of Mordechai Lainer of Ishbitz* (forthcoming).

*H*ebrew *tantra* is a term coined by a cluster of people in the last thirty years. The anthropologist and Hebrew scholar Raphael Pattai, the Kabbalah scholar Moshe Idel, myself and others have all used the term independently. Each person is referring, in a different way, to the sexual symbolism that lies at the core of the Holy of Holies—the Secret of the Cherubs.

What I mean by *Hebrew tantra* is ancient Hebrew wisdom rooted in the esoteric mysteries of Solomon's Temple. These teachings understood implicitly that the sexual models the erotic. They viewed the sexual act itself as a great sacred mystery that reflects the deepest truths of the spirit. Most of these teachings are hidden, for two reasons: first, they are scattered among vast amounts of ancient material, with no obvious way of tracing the ideas; and second, the mysteries are embedded in the internal symbolism of the Kabbalah, a code virtually inaccessible to the unversed.

Yet in all quests after the mysteries, the first source is never textual; it is, rather, the soul itself. In the words of Job, which take on dual meaning in this context, "Through my flesh I vision God." At an early age I was convinced that religion had lost what I believed must have been its original erotic vitality. I knew that the sexual, if liberated and ethically expressed, must somehow hold the mystery of return to this much-larger-than-sexual eros. Moreover, I was convinced that the vitality of paganism and the goddess cults, stripped of their non-ethical practice, had much to offer us in the renewal of the old religion for our post-modern souls. And yet a prima facie reading of the sources did not seem to support my intuitions.

The first hint at another more profound if esoteric reading of the sources—one that alludes, however vaguely, to sexuality as an erotic model—came when I was twenty-two years old and studying a text of Tzadok the Priest cited in a work by Gedalia Schor. It enigmatically alluded to the secret of the cherubs, and cited the key talmudic texts that I adduce in the second and third chapters of this work. In his *Michtav MeEliyahu*, Eliyahu Dessler makes scattered veiled references in the same direction. In the academic world, Raphael Pattai's 1947 book, *Man and the Temple*, also contained important hints. Helpful too was an excellent short monograph by Saul Liberman on the esoteric mystery of the Song of Songs, to which I was referred by Daniel Abrams. Similarly helpful was Pattai's later work *Hebrew Goddesses*, as well as the work that greatly influenced Pattai, *The White Goddess*, by Robert Graves. Two recent monographs—Ohad Ezrahi's "Shnei Keruvim" Heb. 1997, and Moshe Eisen's "Ye Shall Be as Gods: Conceptions of the Yetzer Hara," 1992—draw on this material and more in referring to the eros as the central mystery of the temple. The same is true of a number of articles by Moshe Idel, most important among them being "Sexual Praxis in Kabbalah." Although I have not seen it, Idel's forthcoming work *Eros and Kabbala* will undoubtedly open up new and important vistas. What is true of virtually all the works cited here is that while they note that there is a mystery and that it is connected to sex, eros, and the Temple, they do not examine the nature of eros, using it for the most part as a kind of evocative catchphrase and often not distinguishing between it and sexual vitality. Similarly, they do not suggest sex as a model for eros, nor do they make our essential suggestion that the term *Shechina* in many passages is virtually identical to eros or that the exile of the Shechina is the exile of the erotic into the sexual. Most important, however, they do not unpack distinct and specific paths of eros that are modeled by the sexual. And yet eros in one of its important expressions is interconnectivity, and I happily acknowledge my debt to all the important work that informed my thinking in this book.

To the best of my knowledge, this work is the first modern attempt not only to establish the existence of such an esoteric body of knowledge but also actually to gather and interpret the essence of Hebrew tantra.

The ten paths discussed here are unpacked in a more scholarly manner in a significantly longer forthcoming work on the subject, *The Erotic and the Holy*. In this work we approach the material not in an academic scholarly sense but as part of the chain of tradition, receiving, interpreting, and adding to the ancient wisdom.

ACKNOWLEDGMENTS

This is my favorite page of the book.

It takes a community to write a book.

I want to thank and send great love to all the wonderful students, friends, and teachers (and usually all three appellations apply to the same person) in the Bayit Chadash spiritual community and social movement. First, to my holy co-creators and partners in vision, Jacob Ner David and Avraham Leader. A person could not have better friends. Many of the footnotes to this text emerged from our chevruta, which is pure pleasure and keeps us both grounded in what is real. To wonderful Dafna and all of the holy *hevre* who do so much to make Bayit Chadash a reality. To my friend Gabriel Mayer, with whom I have shared many extraordinary moments of grace over these last two years. To Lilach and Ori from Segol, who shared the dream from the beginning. To Roni Tabachnik—*Ish Berishit*—the highest of the high. To the friendship and chevruta of Ohad Ezrahi, of Project Hamakom. To Zivit Davidovitch, my holy sister and TV producer, and to my wonderful friends Chava Rimon, Illi Bar, and Avri Raviv from *Chayim Acherim*—many, many blessings.

To the truly beautiful Bayit Chadash board—each one of you means so much to us; without your friendship and support our world would be far emptier: Suzy Rogovin, Jennifer Laszlo Mizrahi, Sam Fried, David Friedman, Erica Fox, Mel Brown, Marcia Wexberg, Neil Markowitz, David Kunin, Peter Pitzele, Bruce Arbit, Shoshanna Cardin, Gary and Cheryl Kaplan, Daniel Abrams, Devin Sper, and Micah Greenstein. To the wonderful advisory board of Bayit Chadash: Rabbis Bill Berke, Arthur Waskow, Tirzah Firestone, Daniel Siegel, Michael Lerner, Leonid Feldman, Arthur Kurzweil, Jeff Roth, Joe and Rolinda Schonwald—each person has taught me something special and I thank them all. To Boaz Jorabin, a true friend. To the wonderful teaching community of Jewish Renewal, such special souls who enrich my life in so many ways. And finally *achronim chavivim*—Reb Zalman Schachter—Shalomi and Reb Arthur Green. I am so glad you are in the world!

Much thanks to two people who have been gracious and supportive in every way: my thesis advisors, Prof. Moshe Idel of Hebrew University and Prof. Norman Solomon of Oxford University. Norman's guidance and patience and Moshe's magisterial scholarship and clarity have given me much. To my esteemed colleagues, to whom I have often turned for advice and guidance: Rabbis Saul Berman, Daniel Landes, Daniel Tropper, Joseph Telushkin, Tzvi Blanchard, Donniel Hartman, Hillel Goldberg, Daniel Gordis, Phyllis Berman, and Noam Zion. To Avraham Infeld in love. To Irwin Kula and Brad Hirschfield for the future dream. To Amy Fox, for trust and commitment.

To my adopted sister, Patricia Niehoff, and her wonderful husband, Buck. Patti copyedited the manuscript in its first draft and has become a beloved part of our family. To Donna Zerner, who began as a brilliant editor and ended as a new friend—for all the hours, the proficiency, and the caring, thank you. To Emily Bestler at Atria Books—once again you have guided the process with grace and with wisdom. To Sarah Branham, who gently kept us all on time and on track. To Mitchell Waters, for all his work and good humor—thank you!

To Mum and Dad and all the wonderful Winiarz/Subar *mishpacha*. Thanks again to Gary and Cheryl and the fabulous Kaplan clan. Most important of all—to Eitan and Yair, my unbelievable sons. Abba loves you! To Lisa, their terrific mom, and David, their wonderful stepfather. To Rachel, with hope for the future. And finally to Erica Fox, student, friend, teacher, wise woman.

ABOUT THE AUTHOR

Marc (Mordechai) Gafni is a spiritual teacher and scholar. He is the head of Bayit Chadash, an international spiritual community based in Israel, and also writes and teaches at Oxford University, England. He writes and hosts a regular television program on spirituality and ethics on Israel's leading station. He is a visiting scholar at the Hartman Institute and the New Theology contributing editor for *Tikkun* magazine. He also lectures extensively throughout Israel, Europe, and the United States.

In addition to *The Mystery of Love*, he is the author of *Soul Prints: Your Path to Fulfillment; Reclaiming Uncertainty as a Spiritual Value; Redefining Certainty;* and coauthor with Ohad Ezrahi of *Lillith, Luria and Sacred Feminism*. He is married to Cary (Chaya) and has three children.

Among his forthcoming books are: *The Erotic and the Holy* (with Avraham Leader), a two-volume scholarly work that expands on the material in *Mystery of Love*, and an extensively footnoted scholarly version of *Soul Prints*.

Reb Gafni can be reached for teaching at synagogues, federations, churches, and other spiritual fellowships at rmgafni@netvision.net.il.

For information about the Bayit Chadash Spiritual Community, please visit www.bayitchadash.com.

For custom-designed corporate and organizational seminars, consultation, and training, please contact Erica Fox at Third Eye Partners Inc. at 1-877-456-8400 (inside the U.S.) or 1-617-868-844 (internationally). E-mail: thirdeyepartners.com. Website: www.thirdeyepartners.com.
